HERE I'M ALIVE

HERE I'M ALIVE

THE SPIRIT OF MUSIC IN PSYCHOANALYSIS

ADAM BLUM
PETER GOLDBERG
MICHAEL LEVIN

Columbia University Press
New York

Columbia University Press
Publishers Since 1893
New York   Chichester, West Sussex
cup.columbia.edu
Copyright © 2023 Columbia University Press
All rights reserved

Epigraph for chapter 4: Gregory Orr, "To be alive: not just the carcass," from *Concerning the Book That Is the Body of the Beloved.* Copyright © 2005 by Gregory Orr. Reprinted with the permission of the Permissions Company, LLC, on behalf of Copper Canyon Press, coppercanyonpress.org.

Library of Congress Cataloging-in-Publication Data
Names: Blum, Adam (PsyD) author. | Goldberg, Peter (Psychologist) author. | Levin, Michael (PsyD) author.
Title: Here I'm alive : the spirit of music in psychoanalysis / Adam Blum, Peter Goldberg, and Michael Levin.
Description: New York : Columbia University Press, 2023. | Includes bibliographical references and index.
Identifiers: LCCN 2022040876 (print) | LCCN 2022040877 (ebook) | ISBN 9780231209441 (hardback) | ISBN 9780231209458 (trade paperback) | ISBN 9780231557948 (ebook)
Subjects: LCSH: Psychoanalysis and music. | Music—Psychological aspects.
Classification: LCC ML3838 .B607 2023 (print) | LCC ML3838 (ebook) | DDC 781.1/1—dc23/eng/20220826
LC record available at https://lccn.loc.gov/2022040876
LC ebook record available at https://lccn.loc.gov/2022040877

Cover image: Photo credit: © The Baron Alan Wolman Collection, Rock & Roll Hall of Fame

Dedicated to the muses of this record:

John Adams, Beyoncé, Björk, Kate Bush, Johnny Clegg, Joe Cocker, Disclosure, Peter Gabriel, Beck Hansen, Jimi Hendrix, Michael Jackson, Györgi Ligeti, Paul McCartney, Tom Misch, Joni Mitchell, Radiohead, Steve Reich, Fred Rogers, Robert Schumann, Shabaka and the Ancestors, Paul Simon, Stephen Sondheim, Talking Heads, and Yes.

My frame was not hidden from you

when I was made in the secret place,

when I was woven together in the depths of the earth

—Psalm 139

With music, I am almost incapable of obtaining any pleasure.
Some rationalistic, or perhaps analytic, turn of mind in me
rebels against being moved by a thing without knowing why
I am thus affected, and what it is that affects me.

—Freud, "The Moses of Michelangelo"

Every illness is a musical problem—its healing a musical solution.

—Novalis, *Notes for a Romantic Encyclopaedia*

CONTENTS

Preface: Liner Notes   xi

SIDE A

1. THE BODY'S WAY OF DREAMING
—
3

2. THE RHYTHM OF THE HEAT
—
27

3. MIND WAVES
—
55

4. LEARNING TO LIVE TOGETHER
—
88

5. THE LIVING FRAME

117

SIDE B

6. RE-MEMBERING, RE-BEATING, AND WORLDING-THROUGH

143

7. STRANGE LOOP

172

8. THIS IS HOW WE DO IT

198

9. THE ART TEACHER

217

10. OLD FOUNDATIONS IN PSYCHOANALYSIS

251

Acknowledgments 271
Notes 273
Index 291

PREFACE: LINER NOTES

As he tells his friends in prison, there often came to him one and the same dream apparition, which always said the same thing: "Socrates, practice music."

—NIETZSCHE, THE BIRTH OF TRAGEDY OUT OF THE SPIRIT OF MUSIC

This book was born out of the spirit of music, in the spirit of recording an album. It was played like music, through a musical practice—three players practicing music together. *Music* here extends beyond the everyday definition; recalling Boethius's ancient concept of *musica humana*, it plays neither on instruments nor through speakers but instead resounds through psychical life, both as a shared grammar of embodiment and as the perceptual fabric in which human beings live. This understanding of music grounds the key argument advanced over the course of this book, which can be summarized in the following way.

Before we can become fully functioning emotional, rational, linguistic, cultural, social, or political animals, human beings first become musical animals. The process of human musicalization begins in utero and undergirds many aspects of human psycho-somatic-social life to a degree that has been largely underappreciated in the modern era. This hypothesis has significant foundational implications for the theory and practice of psychoanalysis and, perhaps, for other disciplines in the humanities and human sciences.

The following chapters flesh out these points and explore their ramifications in detail. Written in a spiraling musical mode that layers and elaborates recurring motifs, they yield an integrated whole that will provide the reader with an experience of what the book describes. By way of introduction, we begin with a brief overview of some of our key assumptions, along with a bit of their historical context, to orient the reader embarking upon our musical voyage together.

Our view begins with the premise that *Homo sapiens* are not born fully human. To fulfill our potential as psychical, embodied, and social beings, we must acquire a kind of operating system from those who raise us.

In the process of acquiring this system, we are also acquired *by* or induced into it and thus become recognizable members of a cultural collectivity that both includes the nuclear family and extends beyond it in social scope and history. Many observers and theorists have made versions of this claim, most often identifying this acquired system as language or cultural practices and norms. Where we depart from the majority of these other observers is in our view that this human operating system is essentially *musical*. We call this socio-cultural-individual musical system *the weave*.

In locating music at the center of human existence we are aligning ourselves with some of the more radical thinkers of modern history from the worlds of the arts and humanities as well as with an increasingly rich and compelling body of contemporary research in developmental psychology and neuroscience. Even more so, however, we align with a view that was common throughout the West until the modern era. A detailed exploration of why this perspective has moved to the periphery of learned discourse in our time is beyond the scope of this book, but a brief overview of this history here will help the reader contextualize and grasp some of the deeper import of many of the issues we discuss in the following chapters. Perhaps the most significant of these is not only how deep cultural assumptions and norms can affect approaches to the treatment of psychological suffering (like psychoanalysis) but also how, on a deeper level, they can influence actual psychological development and functioning. In other words, another aim of this book is to show how powerfully our shared and often unquestioned picture of the kinds of creatures we are influences the kinds of people we become.

Until roughly three hundred years ago, the various belief systems that shaped Western culture shared the view that the human soul was an integrated part of a wider meaningful world in which music played a natural and influential role. Accordingly, and in contrast to our now deeply established assumptions, our ancestors looked mainly *outward*, not inward, for identity and meaning. To be human meant being open and receptive to forces and signs originating far beyond the self, and often these signs came in musical forms. This basic view was so common that it was not until the late sixteenth century that anything like our modern conceptualization of a private, inner, discursive self began to emerge and take hold in the way it has ever since.

The ancient Greeks, for example, placed special emphasis on exquisite sensory *perception*, the channel through which the gods could orchestrate the universe and express their will in earthly form, enchanting the physical world with metaphysical resonance. Only if we listened and looked sensitively to particular phenomena in the world around us could the messages of the gods be perceived. Most of our forebears' understanding of their place and role in the world was accessed through what could be called *aesthetic* channels—"aesthetic" in terms of its original definition, which was not simply "beautiful" but *having to do with the senses*. And as often as not, what was there to be sensed was divine music, the "art of the muses," a gift from the gods who directly expressed themselves in *mousike* through human composers, performers, and their audiences, who were their instruments and vessels.

Accordingly, the Greeks believed that *mousike* deeply influenced the soul's formation and functioning and thus played an ethical role in society. The profound intimacy of this connection can be seen in the definition of their word *ethos*, which referred to both human character and also to the manner in which a particular piece of music attuned the listener's soul and movement through the world. Ethical music was sanctified and transmitted to fellow humans through the rites and rituals of culture, never more vividly than when sung in unison by a congregation of members. The unifying and transportive effects of these musical forms are undeniable to anyone who has experienced them, and these effects have undoubtedly been crucial to the enduring power of these communities over thousands of years. Our Greek ancestors implicitly understood that the deepest and most definitive sources of what the world was, what it meant, and how we should live in it were *outside* of us, in the metaphysical dimension from which the gods *presented* the ordering of the physical and human world.

The tectonic shift that occurred in Western thought in the period of the Enlightenment produced a new perspective and *ethos* regarding what both the universe and human beings are. This perspective displaced music from the role and meaning it held for our ancestors, along with the aesthetic sensibility at the center of their way of being. Inspired by the spectacular achievements of the Scientific Revolution in the sixteenth and seventeenth centuries, Enlightenment thinkers like Descartes and Locke sought to apply the sensibility and methods of science recently established by Bacon, Galileo, and Newton to establish a fresh understanding of the human being, free of what they regarded as outmoded superstitions. In doing so, they also quickly came to assert that the scientific sensibility and method were the natural mode through which the human mind apprehended the world. In other words, they believed not only that a scientific approach could give us a more accurate picture of what human beings are but also that the natural basic functioning of our minds is remarkably similar to the methods and spirit of a typical scientist of the sixteenth century. This meant human beings were no longer understood as divine instruments integral to a meaningful world but instead as disengaged intellects, that is, *subjects* set against *objects* in a universe of meaningless, mechanistic processes.

The same perspective that boils down the universe to these mechanistic processes regards our very bodies as objects and regards our sensory perception with suspicion. Our perceptions and experiences were no longer expressions of divine desire but of atomistic impressions and representations of an external world upon which we had no inherent purchase—a world of discontinuous phenomena of which we need to "make" sense. The only way for us to understand the world in this way was to ascribe meaning to it rationally. This was done by painstakingly breaking down and then linking our impressions and thoughts as carefully and rationally as possible in order to slowly build up an intelligible picture of external reality and grasp its mechanistic operations. The mental, representational picture thus formed then needed to be vigilantly scrutinized and tested for validity on a perpetual basis, lest we err and descend into unenlightened madness. To be mad was to be irrational; to be sane was to be empirical.

This change in the basic view of human nature that characterized Enlightenment thought marked a great turning inward: away from trust in the community in favor of the isolated self as the locus of understanding and meaning. It displaced holistically integrated, aesthetically informed *being* with disengaged, disembodied *thinking* at the foundation of human existence, as epitomized in Descartes's most famous statement: "I think, therefore I am." In the new world framed by these principles, music, language, and all other cultural media moved from a central role in the determination of meaning to a marginal or trivial position as a derivative form of expression.

In this new world, the sources of identity and meaning are not outside of us and communicated to us by the gods through natural or cultural forms; they are *inside* our own intellects and selves, and cultural forms are simply instruments to communicate them to one another. Easily instrumentalized, symbolic modes like verbal discourse and scientific notation are held as manifestly superior to murkier ones like art or gesture, which are seen as more primitive or derivative. A contemporary example of this view comes from the popular cognitive psychologist Steven Pinker, author of the recent bestseller *Enlightenment Now* (as in *the* Enlightenment), who writes that, just like the other arts, music is an incidental spinoff of language, as evolutionarily and thus existentially meaningless as our interest in pornography or taste for megadoses of sugar: "auditory cheesecake."

E pur si muove.

"And yet it moves"—as Galileo whispered after being forced to recant his claims that the Earth revolved around the Sun. The new Enlightenment way of thinking about ourselves did little if anything, in fact, to make us different kinds of creatures. Despite the shift away from acknowledging the communal nature of psychical life, the Enlightenment lurch toward thinking over being did not mean that the weave of collective embodiment had somehow evaporated or been made redundant—it had simply been invalidated by our discourse. Our view of ourselves had changed. As in the psychoanalytic renunciation of its ancestral, intricately interwoven practice of hypnosis (a shift that we contemplate in chapter 3), the weave of shared sensation and communal *habitus* became the *dibbuk* of the Enlightenment, eclipsing the fundamental nature of human being with a fantasy of scientific mastery and self-sufficiency.

Our project explores ways that this Enlightenment paradigm has permeated the history of psychoanalytic theory and practice as we endeavor to unearth an older substratum of experience that has remained present but obscured. In doing so, we are aligned in some ways with what came to be known as the Romantic movement, a collection of countervailing sensibilities and ideas that emerged roughly one hundred years after the Enlightenment kicked into high gear. The Romantic critique of the Enlightenment was introduced most forcefully in philosophy in the eighteenth century and has evolved through the work of twentieth-century philosophers like Martin Heidegger, Maurice Merleau-Ponty, Peter Sloterdijk, Byung-Chul Han, and Robert Harrison; anthropologists like Clifford Geertz; sociologists like Pierre Bourdieu and Charles Taylor; and psychoanalytic theorists like Donald Winnicott, Marion Milner, Jean Laplanche, Thomas Ogden, and Adam Phillips. With different emphases, all of these thinkers and artists have worked out accounts of how it is that culture shapes human perception, thought, and comportment on the deepest levels of embodiment. We extend this account by proposing that the interface of psyche and culture is fundamentally musical.

In the effort to expunge what they saw as a discredited ancient metaphysics and get down to indubitable truths, the Enlightenment thinkers (and much of psychoanalysis too) lost sight of and failed to account for the fact that human beings are still what we might call metaphysical creatures. We don't perceive or think about ourselves, nature, or any experience in a purely, directly unmediated physical way but in ways that are always aesthetically and interpretively mediated by culture. We think and feel only through and with cultural forms; to try to do so without them is to be thrown out of the humanized world and into a devitalized, disenchanted universe and an essentially nonhuman mode of existence that can take on inhuman dimensions. It is not simply that the gods used music to sing to or through us but that music and the gods are in fact the same thing. Music is God.

A number of Romantic artists cautioned against the potential consequence of this tragic flaw in Enlightenment thinking. One novel, published in 1818 (when its ingenious author was only eighteen years old), describes a brilliant, isolated, and arrogant scientist, a "modern Prometheus," who seizes from God and nature the power to create a human life according to scientific principles—that is, a pure creature of the Enlightenment, created by man, not God or nature, strictly according to the principles of physics, instead of metaphysics. The scientist's name was Victor Frankenstein, and his creation was, of course, a monster. The heartbreaking condition of being alive and humanoid but unable to live a recognizably human life in a recognizably human body resonates uncannily with the difficulties faced by increasing numbers of patients who find their way to our offices today. The practicing psychoanalyst must now work out the place of this musical dimension in clinical work as the foundation of a "living frame" (chapter 5) and formulate the pathological consequences of being compromised or disengaged in our contact and facility with these sources. If hysteria was the sexual illness that called forth the cultural response that became psychoanalysis, then dissociation in turn demands a remusicalizing of the psychoanalytic situation, beginning with the analyst. There is, more than ever, a dire risk of transmission, of reenacting failed musicality, transmitting trauma. There are forms of care that deny, defile, or destroy rhythm and melody and thus abort or explode *musica humana*. Many of us, for example, took instrument lessons as children, but very few of us still play instruments as adults. What happened? (A good question psychoanalysis may be uniquely suited to ask about music, as it asks about sex, is how a site of such pleasure, of such aliveness, can become the site of such rupture, lifelessness, hypochondriacal misuse—can make us so sick.)

Our effort is to retrofit the infrastructure of psychoanalysis with help from this pre- and post-Enlightenment line of musical thought and to reexamine assumptions that have made it unusual for psychoanalysts to think in the terms that we are presenting—to help bring psychoanalysis back into the weave. The dominant account of Freud in contemporary discourse is that of an Enlightenment man par excellence, who fiercely rejected the existence of God and declared on several occasions that he could not find any feeling for music—right on cue—*inside* himself. (One of the projects of this book will be to recover, as Laplanche once did, aspects of Freud's monumental oeuvre that suggest an alternate, perhaps more musical Freud—indeed, as Phillips once put it, a "post-Freudian" Freud, a Romantic Freud.) The psychoanalytic emphasis is almost always on the ego's responsibility for saddling the wildness of the body—less often on the pleasure of the ride, the pleasure of the body's musical expression through the harnessing potential of shared forms of movement, for conducting the electrical current of live energy along a communal, psychesomatic network, what Laplanche once described as "work that does not require the overcoming of resistances,"[1] what Phillips has called our unforbidden pleasures. We suggest that the primordial source shaping our most fundamental perceptions, emotions, thoughts, and comportment rests not merely upon the forbidden pleasures of repressed sexuality but more importantly upon a publicly accessed, shared, metaphysical weave of communal practices in which we are embedded, into which we are inducted as members by our early caregivers, and without which it is impossible to have a human life (let alone an unconscious) in the first place.

The weave provides our original equipment for binding to one another through what Laplanche, in his revolutionary reading and translation of Freud, called the "language" of attachment, which subtends the "mythosymbolic order" of all subsequent cultural forms of expression. (How much myth remains in our world and how to find it is one of the ongoing interests of this book.) This weave underlies the various metapsychologies that psychoanalysis has described thus far and, indeed, constitutes their necessary foundation and nourishment in normal functioning. Even the most prominent advocates of attachment theory have recently come to recognize a more historically and culturally conditioned phenomenon than originally imagined. This opens a hollow where the body, instinct, music, and dance are *equiprimordial* in the original binding and syncretics of what Winnicott called the psyche-soma.

In order to engage patients at this level of experience, the contemporary analyst needs to be both a good conductor, a maestro (which might be one way to talk about what a good parent is)—*and*, in order to inspire or crack up or, indeed, analyze one's patient, the analyst needs to be able to jam. A musical *ethos* of psychoanalysis calls upon each of its members to continue in the psychoanalytic tradition of finding and elaborating new aspects of psychical life, the tradition of becoming an artist of one's life—an ethic to help one's patients become not necessarily fellow analysts but fellow artists, moved in kind by the *ethos* of the weave. The course of this shared movement, like the physics of musical sound, evolves through a series of increasingly nuanced tones and forms. (We propose a model of this evolving series in the second half of the book.)

Psychoanalysis has traditionally occupied a particular station on this course, making conscious meaning out of unconsciousness, representations out of the presentational, analyzing. We're not going to be analyzing here, at least not primarily. Instead we'll be doing something closer to *synthesizing*: stitching together samples from the weave (we will explore "sampling" in chapter 7), syncretizing our attention with the musical dimension of experience and investing our interest in the human processes that precede and subtend any form of meaning making and reverberate in their own right throughout all subsequent and concurrent life processes. These include the *inductive* process by which the world is beaten into rhythms and harmonies by fellow humans; the *seduction* through which we are traumatized, for better and for worse (as Laplanche discovered), by the enigma of sexuality; and the weave work that enables us to *conduct* ourselves, to live together, to find a livable groove that folds the disruptions of our excesses into syncopations of what Winnicott called going-on-being. The work of psychoanalysis, in this view, is to facilitate fuller and freer vibration at each node of this series, cultivating and amplifying the idiomatic freedom of each instrument to sing through the chorus of *musica humana*, to resound the psyche-somatic energies of being human, to surf the waves of the weave.

HERE I'M ALIVE

SIDE A

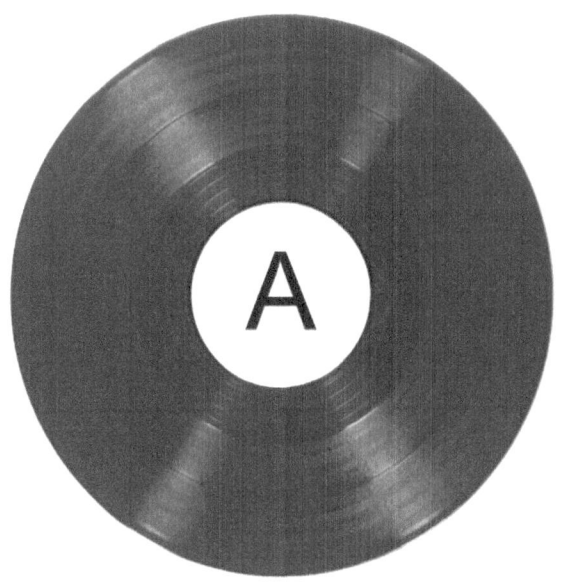

1

THE BODY'S WAY OF DREAMING

I

The idea of a "musical" dimension of lived experience has recently found its way into psychoanalytic discussions. In referring to the "music of what happens" in the clinical encounter, contemporary analytic theorists have marked a shift in interest from *what* is being communicated between analyst and patient to *how* it is communicated.[1] Yet the implications concerning clinical method have only tentatively been recognized—a shift, for example, from an emphasis on interpretation to one of engagement at the level of shared perception. Perhaps a fuller account of the musical dimension of what goes on in therapeutic work would shift the focus from the *representational* to the *presentational* dimension of the analyst's contribution—a shift in emphasis from the reverie-based, waking-dream-thought of the mind (that gives a central place to symbolization and figuration) to nonrepresented (or simply *presented*) types of experience and communication that are centered on the vicissitudes of attention, sensory perception, and psychophysical phenomena. The use of the term "unrepresented states," increasingly used in psychoanalysis, tends to imply an immature state of mental functioning that will eventually be superseded in normal development or a shortfall in mental organization or structuration that can only be overcome by the therapeutic strengthening of representational capacities. Here we would like to alter the vertex to focus on another meaning of the term "unrepresented," to focus on the *presentational* aspect, the way things present themselves within their own mode of organization and with their own functional transformations, ones that are never superseded—a domain of embodiment.

There is inherently a gulf, a confusion of tongues, between how the living body presents itself and how it is represented in the mind. This gulf has often led psychoanalysts to view the body as lacking organized qualities of its own or as possessing only primitive, anarchic, protomental energies: the drives. The body does not communicate in words but, from the traditional psychoanalytic view, "speaks" (or is spoken) through symptoms that are manifestations of repression and psychical conflict. But does this mean that the body is psychically mute, always awaiting the civilizing influence of the thinking mind? Is it just a primitive, id-like realm, its crude impulses barely able to cross over from the terra incognita of biology to the meaning-filled world? Or is it possible that the body does "speak" (and is spoken to) in a language of its own, in a register involving the patterning of sensation rather than pictorial or symbolic thought? Can we entertain the possibility that the body is given psychical organization only secondarily by phantasy or thought or language, all the while organizing itself primarily according to a shared pattern of sensory, somatic organization?

The question could be posed in terms of Bion's nomenclature, whereby raw sense impressions denoted as "beta-elements" must be digested by the mind and transformed into "alpha-elements" if they are to be psychically usable. But can we conceive of a mechanism by which beta elements can be organized in their own right—comprising something like a *beta function*? A function whose distinct purpose is to effect transformations at the level of sensory and somatic experience—a psychosensory patterning of experience that depends not at all on the work of mental representation but rather is a psyche-somatological domain that directly engages the physiology, motility, and affectivity of the actual body? We have lacked adequate language to describe the elaborate and evolved ways in which this sentient body is organized, the ways in which the semiotics of movement and patterning of sensation shape the nonrepresentational domain of lived experience. Perhaps music can help us imagine this.

Can we bring music more fully and integrally into our psychoanalytic model making? How are we to think psychoanalytically about something as essential as music—something that is so fundamental to our sense of meaning and being in the world yet so independent of words for the way it orders our experience? This question is not primarily meant as a challenge to the centrality of verbal-symbolic thought in the talking cure but as a further inquiry into what we are really doing when we are talking. Are we mainly singing? If we recognize the importance of the "music of what happens," as a wide range of clinical theorists now seem to,[2] is musicality nevertheless seen as merely the support—the soundtrack—for the true meaning-making work of analyzing phantasies, thoughts, enactments, projections, and so on? Or might the "singing" itself serve a vital therapeutic activity in its own right—not an aid or a prelude to the talking cure but an essential type of syncretic meaning making that embeds us in the world and thus creates the conditions of possibility for embodiment, meaning, communication, and shared understanding?

If music is the way the individual body "speaks"—organizing and vitalizing all body language, from the primitive olfactory domain to the patterns of visual experience and the haptic pressures of touch—it is nevertheless always a shared psychosensory language. Music is never the creation of an individual in isolation. To paraphrase both Wittgenstein and Winnicott, there is no such thing as private music. As we speak and move, sound and energy reverberate within a sensory matrix—or fail to. When the language of the body is inaccessible, blocked, or dissociated, it cannot be recovered through the meaning making of the mind but can be restored only in the context of a shared sensoriality. Sensory isolation—the inability to access the domain of shared musicality—is a malady that cannot be remedied by understanding or talking about it but only by experimenting with new ways to sing. ("Singing" refers here not only to the cadences and musical elements of speech in the analytic setting but also to actual singing, which can occur unexpectedly and is often very moving.)

How far can we venture into conceptualizing the formative role of the music in itself—the way it wordlessly gives shape to our psychical lives? To utter the truism that we cannot really separate the words from the music is not enough. Music's impact, its physical feelingfulness, emits directly from the sound shape and rhythm formation of the notes themselves, rather than from anything the mind does to represent it or give it symbolic meaning, and the sound-pattern semiotics of music are uniquely tied to the way the body is "heard" or felt in psychic life. The body expresses itself in musical sound patterns, affording an avenue through which we may discern something about the makeup and the modus operandi of a *presentational* dimension of psychical life—a domain in which the experience of living in a body (perceiving the world as an embodied being) is expressed directly in a kind of somato-psychic "language" of its own, without having recourse to symbolic thought. In contrast to Freud's notion of music having a fundamentally sublimatory or *de*materializing function, and in contrast to the more recent interest in the musical qualities of speech or conversation within analytic work, the view being expressed here is that music plays an irreducible, distinctive, elemental, *psychical* function, *tapping directly into and reconfiguring the presentational domain of the body in a way analogous to how dreams tap into and reconfigure the representational domain of the mind.*

Colloquially, the term *music* is most often used to refer to a discrete piece of music, or perhaps a type of music, in a genre that is recognizable to our ears. Inevitably what we recognize as a "piece" of music depends upon the acculturation and group affiliation of the listener or music maker and the symbolic meanings it has accrued. All of us have developed a mental idea of what music is, so that we know it when we hear it. But knowing a certain collection of sounds as a "piece of music" tells us nothing about what it *does*, what psychical effect it has. Identifying a piece of music and experiencing it as music are not the same thing. One may instantly recognize the sound of orchestral music and even have a mental picture of the way it sounds—its thematic compositional structure, the typical instrumentation of strings, brass, woodwinds, and percussion—yet be unable to "hear" or experience this music in one's mind. Just as hearing a hundred "pieces" of music in any of its many habitats may fail to move us musically, the most incidental and accidental collection of sounds within a functional timeframe may prove capable of producing a musical experience. To put it another way, we can be affected musically by a collection of sounds that we do not formally recognize as "music," just as most of the music pieces we hear are musically inert or redundant (or may even serve to obstruct the psychical function of music).

Musical experience, or what we could define as *musicality*, is a mode of sensory patterning, occurring within spatiotemporal frames, that directly affects what it fundamentally feels like to be in the world. Our inherent tendency toward this musicality always evolves in a shared aesthetic environment, drawing us beyond the singularity of our individual personalities and structuring the conditions of our musicalization. While the particular pieces of music through which we apprehend this musicality, or which make it memorable, will always depend upon our sense of sociocultural identity (particularly evident in teenagers, for example), which might affect how we *relate* to a piece of music, the *actual* musical experience takes place in a psyche-somatic register that does not depend at all on memory, knowledge, or thought.[3] In fact, what we recognize and know as a piece of music may, for a number of reasons, actually stifle the function of musical experience and rob it of its transformative potential. Musicality is felt when the sounds are *actually* heard and physically registered, as when humming a tune, or playing it on an instrument, or hearing it being played. This means that actually "recalling" a piece of music entails a direct contemporaneous reliving of the sounds in our ears, presented to the psyche-soma for fresh sensation, activating a psychosensory event. Here we can invoke Bion's injunction that we strive to put aside memory and desire in order to make us available to psyche-somatic experience as it presents itself to us in real time; to the degree that we can relinquish what we *know* about pieces of music, the actual musical experience will be enhanced.

The psychic function of music is easier to see in action in those instances where we really attend to it—through concentrated listening or participating in music making by means of voice or instrument. When we really listen to it or enter into it, something different happens: The music affects us more distinctly, and we find ourselves more or less transported to a different place, an altered state of one sort or another, invariably involving an increase in feeling and heightened sensation. But how do we understand the changes in our subjective state wrought by music? A more traditional psychoanalytic answer might assume that music evokes dormant or repressed mental representations or elicits fresh associations that affect our feeling state and way of thinking, at least momentarily. But these *associational* effects, such as they do occur, are secondary. The evocation of memories—the associations to other places and other times—is the work of the mind; it is what our minds produce in response to musical experience. Immersion in music affects changes in our subjective state not because of its evocation of associations and memories but because of its power to awaken the psyche-soma and *configure the somatic language of the body*, which revives the body's role in the life of the mind. Music shifts our consciousness closer toward the presentational domain, the soul-logic of the body, and in so doing broadens the sources of perception to include the distinctive patterning and organization of sensorial being-in-the-world. Musical immersion activates and gives voice to what Winnicott referred to as the psyche-soma, affecting a shift in consciousness that is as real as it is hard to describe. The emphasis here is on the way music *expresses* and meaningfully organizes bodily experience. We are not able to find an embodied way of being in the world without it.

Just as entering a dream state allows for a temporary rearrangement of associative and symbolic links in the mind, the shift in consciousness that accompanies music listening effects a transient reconfiguration, a rearranging of psychic life in bodily terms. Between the psychology of the body and the mind there inherently exists a kind of confusion of tongues. Consider for a moment how much constant motion and organismic activity goes on at the level of our corporeal reality, the multiple networks of neuronal and hormonal and physiological activation and concatenation. How on earth does all of this corporeal activity present itself and get represented psychically? It might be said that psychoanalysis was born in this confusion of tongues between the presentational and the representational, between wordless (*infans*) and worded, between body and mind. The musical patterning of beat, tone, and silence forms a kind of body consciousness, a psychosensory patterning that approximates how a body's physiological processes function as we move around in the world. If it is true that music helps give communal shape and expression to the nonrepresented, psyche-somatic sphere of psychical life, then this "language" of embodiment remains largely indecipherable to—or out of sync with—the thought processes of the mind. Indeed, the way we represent our bodily experience in our minds is notoriously unreliable and subject to misconception. The mind pictures and comprehends bodily experience in the most oblique ways, as we learn every day in clinical practice. Body phenomena are often semitranslated into the most generic, partial, oversimplified categories (to say nothing of the more pathological distortions, manipulations, and misrepresentations that the mind is notoriously prone to in its dealings with the body). A piece of music is potentially powerful, then, not only because it brings the sentience of the body closer in to the life of the mind and revives our communion with the embodied existence of others but because it restores the immediacy of psyche-somatic aliveness; the vitality of being-in-the-world, as a phenomenologist might put it; or, using the South American psychoanalyst Jose Bleger's terminology, because it taps into the basic psychical *syncretism* of nondifferentiated experience of the world.[4] If we do not come into the world or discover it independently but learn to perceive things through shared sensory experience, then the most essential basic working arrangement of analyst and patient may be characterized by a kind of musicosensory *symbiosis*. Here the work of the beta function makes available, for mental apprehension, what it is like to live in one's body among other bodies, the rhythms of being alive.

II

Music, then, could be described psychoanalytically as a formation of sounds:

- that gives shape to the patterns of bodily-based psychical experience;
- that is expressed entirely in a nonsymbolic register of tempo, rhythm, tone, harmony;
- that occurs within a functional temporal framework; and
- that effects an extension of consciousness by shifting the locus of attention to the presubjective, nonrepresentational domain of shared perception (the psychosensory commons).

According to this description, music is something that is going on all the time, a foundation of human existence that is the body's way of presenting itself as the necessary matrix for the emergence of the mind, of being present in the world. This conceptualization jettisons entirely the symbolic function of music, which is of course a crucial aspect of how music is regarded in everyday life. When a piece of music is created and becomes recognizable as such (named and represented in memory), it enters the domain of symbolic exchange, but in doing so it is no longer simply music but becomes something else—it enters the fields of language, of remembrance, of nostalgia, of economic exchange, identity formation, social affiliation, and ideological relations. The symbolic uses and appropriation of music may be for good or for bad, but they are more or less inevitable; it is part of the fate of music that it be used for something else. Any part of music can become part of a chain of symbolic meaning. The roll of drums and the blast of horns in a symphony might well denote a wordless reference or theme because it is historically associated with social rituals in which music would be used to accompany the ceremonial entrance of an important figure. And in Western music, switching to a minor key accompanied by a certain instrumental coloration denotes something in the range of sorrowful emotions or loss. But these are merely examples of how music has been captured and deployed for non-music purposes. There is nothing intrinsic about musical forms that carry any particular meaning or emotional resonance. The beating of drums in an African communal ceremony may mean something quite different than what they denote in a Western symphony or may carry little or no narrative meaning at all. (Indeed, in such ceremonies, the beating of drums may have much more to do with the trancelike induction of an altered state, more like the function of dance music in a club setting, than with any kind of symbolic gesture.) The point is that the qualities of attunement—the shape, form, patterning, movement, and coherence of experience at the level of the body—so vital for a sense of embodiment are provided by the rhythmic and tonal sequences rather than by the imposition of symbolic meanings.

Yet musicality—*music*—is constantly being exploited for the induction of particular emotional states or to activate a sense of group affiliation or identification or communal memorialization, which can lead to the reification of musical experience. The trumpet playing reveille at a funeral may hardly be working as music at all; it is using musical forms to do the work of personal and communal memory. Jimi Hendrix's deconstruction of the "Star-Spangled Banner" at Woodstock, on the other hand, subverts the way music is employed to garner nationalistic feeling. But the intrinsic nature of music is not defined by any of these uses, even if it naturally lends itself to all of these. The associations evoked by the flourish of drums and horns in a symphony is not *the music*; it is the effect of the appropriation of music by a symbolic and narrative structure, an appending of historical meaning onto the shape of sounds that our bodies need.

The relevant question, then, concerns the degree to which a particular musical experience has the potential to affect a useful psychophysical transformation, a revitalization of the link between the thinking and feeling aspects of self. This depends on certain individual factors, such as the capacity of the individual to access and enter into transitory states— states in which attention moves toward a kind of psychosensory consummation, what Marion Milner called the "concentration of the body," an alteration in consciousness that shifts the psychical center of gravity back along the psyche-somatic spectrum toward physical sensation. Music functions like the score of embodied experience; it dreams the experience of the body in the psyche.

But if the power of music lies in its capacity to conduct the idiomatic rhythms and patterns of the individual body, it is nevertheless something that exists beyond the singularity of our individual personalities. A piece of music is not something we create entirely for ourselves; it is inevitably a phenomenon of shared perception. We borrow sound shapes from others, from the cultural milieu, and in this way music binds us to the psychosensory experiences of others and gives a social and cultural shape to the intimate experience of the embodied self. Music, then, is never something simply of our own making. Pieces of music circulating in the environment are woven into our ongoing personal music making, providing sound shapes that we could never produce alone. In this sense, the cultures of music provide a variety of colloquial body languages through which one's individual musicality might be expressed. Viewed from this perspective, music appeals to us because it offers the possibility, through rhythmic and tonal variation, of a fresh take, as it were, on what it feels like to be alive in one's own body. In other words, music gives us a way to live in our bodies through the presence of other bodies.

But for the very reason of its privileged role as a portal to the psychesomatology of lived experience, music always comes to occupy an ambiguous status: By conducting the experience of the body in sound patterns, music makes it possible for the lived body to participate in psychical life and to intermingle with the verbal-symbolic thought patterns of the mind. But by the same token, music becomes a point of access through which the patterns of personal, embodied experience are shaped by the culture, and thus music may be colonized, be brought under the control of symbolic systems, of social and economic forces. It is always a two-way street. Because it is fundamentally a shared language that is always culturally mediated, music will therefore always be received both as a gift and an imposition. Ill-fitting music will always be a source of discomfort and self-alienation. The question of whether the psyche-soma is given adequate voice and sway in the life of the mind is never truly settled. We need music in order to access our own idiomatic musicality, we depend upon this shared cultural creation to provide us psychical access to our own body-aliveness, and it has tremendous power to alter our states of consciousness. So we will always hate music as well as love it. For all of these reasons, music can easily take on pathological features, becoming implicated in strategies of pseudoenlivenment, fetishization, and addictive entrapment and in the maintenance and the enforcement of trancelike states of distraction and dislocation.

The contest over the ownership of the musical imagination has real consequences for the individual, who in striving to discover a personal musical idiom is engaged in nothing less than a struggle for a viable way of being embodied in the world. The struggle over whether the psychology of the body can find expression in psychical life is played out above all in the control of perception and shifts in states of consciousness. Insofar as there is a musical dimension—a signature of tempo, rhythm, tone, and melody—to all communications within ourselves and with others, we can see how music and musicality play a part in the everyday regulation of self-states and interactions within the self. But musicality, by its very nature, also exists and evolves in a shared aesthetic environment. We learn body language through proximity to and communion with other bodies. Here we can distinguish resonant musical experience—which is born of communal perception and returns us to a nondifferentiated domain of shared being-in-the-world—from a very different use of sound patterns, observable in the mute sound prisons of obsessional, autistic, and compulsive mental states, where access to the sensory commons has been replaced by addictive and repetitive use of sound patterns within the echo chamber of a sensory cocoon. When familiar pieces of music become fixtures in how we self-regulate and self-soothe and in the way we induce certain affective states or alterations in consciousness, then we can see how the activity of listening to music may also become implicated in pathological formations—in addictive states of mind, in the maintenance of dissociated states, and in the pathological autistic use of the sound envelope. Under these circumstances, the function of music is perverted, used exclusively to regulate and control emotional life rather than give expression to it. Here, music is no longer available for the kind of intrapsychic rejuvenation (the ongoing interpenetration of the psychology of the body with the mind) that is so vital to the possibility of embodied living. In these circumstances, music has become detached from the collective and is deployed instead as a means of distraction in the service of sensory isolation.

During long periods of history, the mode of human sense perception changes with humanity's entire mode of existence. As Walter Benjamin elaborated, "the manner in which human sense perception is organized, the medium in which it is accomplished, is determined not only by nature but by historical circumstances."[5] Our ways of seeing, hearing, sensing, and being—literally the way we carry ourselves and speak and move in the world—are affected not only by the music dimension of our childhood conversational milieu but equally by the prevalent cultures of music in our current lived environment. This can readily be seen in the way adolescents, for example, shape the movements of their body to accordance with musically conveyed cultural motifs (posture, rhythm of speech, communicative and perceptual style). We seek out and identify certain pieces of music that implicitly *do* something for us, that produce a shift in our psychophysical state in order to soothe, to elicit an affective state, to awaken the connection to one's own body or the body of another, but also to help the mind recall what something in the past felt like or imagine what the future might feel like. When we seek out musical sounds that play so intimately in the psyche, connecting us to ourselves and others, the patterns of sound we hear are inevitably woven out of pieces of other people's music as they are refracted through cultural production. This borrowing of sound shapes from others always takes place in a particular social-historical milieu. The sound communities we live in, which shape our bodily sense of self, are inescapably also ideological communities embedded in specific economic and social relations, and so our entry into the shared sensoriality of music is also the way that our embodied subjectivity is shaped culturally. At the broadest level, the way music is heard, felt, and embodied has utterly changed since the advent of recording devices, leading inexorably to ever-increasing availability and omnipresence of bits of music in every part of our lives and along with this the overwhelming prevalence of music consumption over music participation. If the prevailing forms of music in the culture affect and shape the way we experience ourselves and live in our bodies, this also means that our relation to music is intrinsically contentious; there exists an inherent tension between the personal experience of music and its social and public character. If a piece of music has the power to express our body-aliveness, it also has the power to rearrange our sense of embodiment, to impose a shape on our embodiment that constrains us. Hence the love/hate relationship to music. An implicit struggle is perpetually waged over the way the music we hear in the sound environment affects our embodied musicality. While we are usually aware simply of whether we are drawn to certain kinds of music—whether or not we "like" it—unconsciously there is an ongoing struggle over what music is doing to us—whether it "fits" the personal idiom of our embodiment, whether it disrupts or too-readily smoothes over or stifles our bodily-based patterns of experience. A soothing, slow-tempo, harmonically pleasing piece can readily become stultifying, while the stimulating discordant atonalities of New Music or free jazz can soon make one long for the familiar grooves of pop or indie rock. Beneath the conventions of taste and preference, we are unsettled about what we want from all the music that is available to us, perhaps because we have a deeply ambivalent relationship to what music can do to us, the ways in which our bodily longing for music leads to disturbance, disappointment, dissatisfaction, and alienation whenever we actually listen to it. There was a time, after all, when a new symphony or opera production could elicit public outrage and even violence in the music hall, and the widespread creeping revolt against Muzak, which led to its demise and disappearance from elevators everywhere, may be an example of how an uninvited musical form can have a deadening and soul-destroying effect on the way people feel; its replacement in supermarkets and elevators by 1970s "light rock" has begun to taint the latter in a similar way. Adorno captured this effect succinctly: "The reactions to isolated charms are ambivalent. A sensory pleasure turns into disgust as soon as it is seen how it only still serves to betray the consumer. The betrayal here consists in always offering the same thing."⁶ So there is always a political dimension to our individual encounter with the culture of music, an unconscious struggle over how much the imaginative potential of the body can find expression through music and how much the culture of music will subject the embodied self to an enforced soundscape alien to its own way of being. Just as music has the transformative potential to give expression to the personal experience of embodiment and help us perceive the world in a most personal way, so too can it impose upon our perception and sensibilities. In our hunger for music, we are liable to consume things that do little to express our personal reality but foist upon us an alienating pattern of psychosensuality. Junk food is something avoidable, with enough will, but junk *sounds* enter at will, uninvited and indiscriminate.

What does it mean, then, to be surrounded by a highly commoditized representation in our minds of what constitutes music, which these days is exacerbated by the ubiquitous presence of highly produced, mass-marketed, and electronically compressed music in the lived environment? Of all the sensory envelopes that constitute what Anzieu called the "skin ego"—the composite of sensorial registers that forms our fundamental sense of ourselves as corporeally intact and distinct from our surroundings—is the aural surround perhaps the one that is most encroached upon by manmade and socially shaped stimuli? One might contend that the visual environment is the most affected, but most of us are fortunate enough to see trees and the earth and clouds and even birds every day, and we still usually notice daytime turning to night. But what do we hear in our everyday environment? What happens when we are buffeted by an ocean of uninvited, prerecorded, digital sounds—sounds that are usually utterly unattuned to the idiomatic perceptions of the listener and impervious to the intimate dance of feeling and body movement that marks the distinctive musical signature of the individual? Sounds travel, and ears are not designed to easily shut them out. ("In the field of the unconscious," Lacan once wrote, "the ears are the only orifice that cannot be closed." Nietzsche called the ear "the organ of fear.")⁷ The possibility of developing a satisfactory personal musical idiom is severely challenged by an implacable soundscape that impinges its impersonal tones and beats on the individual's musical sensibility. Subjection to self-alienating music is nothing other than a form of overstimulation and may be seen as a constituent of a type of social trauma that could be contributing to the current epidemic of dissociation that is sweeping through the population of patients seen in psychotherapy.

Perhaps it is a search for the liberation of the ear from enslavement to increasingly impersonal hegemonic musical forms that drives compositional music to every kind of deconstruction and innovation in musical form. The frenzy of new invention over the last century has increasingly led to the alienation of the work of serious composers from mainstream music consumption, their listening audience being limited to academic and art-house settings—though popular genres have always benefited from the innovations of the avant-garde. For its part, popular music has gone through a parallel struggle of its own, with regular eruptions of new musical forms (most recently hip-hop and electronic music) that have the power of enlivening the connection to musical experience but then quickly become reified and commercialized. Witnessing how rapidly fresh attempts at music making in recent times are appropriated and turned into forms of control over the musical imagination is like watching a struggle for our collective musical soul played in fast forward.

The place where the everyday sound environment retains some truly musical potential—the potential of bringing body-based perception to life and thus revive the links between mind and psyche-soma—is in live interaction with other embodied beings. If the prototype for musical life is to be found in the prosody of sound exchanges between infant and caretakers (as developmental researchers are finding to be the case with increasing complexity and depth), then it is no surprise that the vocal exchanges we have with other people over the course of the day carry the potential, in the music of conversation and embodied interaction, of a renewed connection between our embodied existence and our being in the world. There is, after all, a musical signature that inheres in all truly embodied exchanges, whether vocal or physical. (Everything said here about music likely applies equally to dance.)

Engagement with others, however, will inevitably bring with it the burden and the demands of *difference*: to the degree that we converse, we will of course be confronted with the otherness of the interlocutor, the conflicted demands of intersubjective relating, and the rigors of being a speaking subject. But the struggle to remain in a live exchange with others is crucial, since the human voice in conversation naturally possesses musical potential, the prosody and tone *inducing* us into the possibility of a shared body psychology and participation in the sensory commons. From this perspective, the clinical situation must be capable not only of engendering differentiation and a viable separateness but of reviving the nondifferentiated domain of shared sensoriality where meaning is born.

III

Conceiving of a domain of psychical phenomena that functions parallel to representation and close to the phenomenology of the body inevitably affects our clinical approach and modifies the way we think about mental incapacity and disorder. The clinical task, in these cases, turns to the activation of transformations at the level of beta function, which entails bringing the psychology of the body back into the clinical field; it centers clinical technique on revitalization of the mind-body link in the context of shared psychosensoriality. Clinical psychoanalysis, confronted with the subjective dislocation and disruption afflicting so many modern-day patients—disorientation and alienation in the sense of self, of identity, of *being*—has tended to focus on failures in *representational* capacities (impairment in symbolization, mentalization, thinking, and reflective ability), as well as impairments in *relational* or interpersonal capacity. But these emphases underestimate the significance of failures in the *presentational* domain—ruptures in the sense of an embodied continuity of being-in-the-world, which result in disorders of self-regulation, of sensation and sensuality, and of embodiment as much as disorders in thought, often resulting in a dissociative or adhesive picture in which mental life is removed from the life of the psyche-soma, leaving the psyche unmoored from lived experience and at the mercy of the tyranny of a dissociated body.

What does this imply for our understanding of the music of what goes on in the clinical situation? Surely the sensation of the mother's voice is recalled or repeated in the transference or, perhaps—through the auspices of projective identification—can be heard in the voice of the analyst. Are these not representations of the mother-child relation being revisited in the present? Alternatively, we might consider that what is repeated from the past, what is enacted and re-presented in the transference-countertransference context, is not the music per se but its *record*—transcribed through the media of symbolization, memory, phantasy—in the mind. This record typically includes aspects of the intersubjective context in which the musical experience was transformed into mental representations but also the notation of some version of the sounds themselves—whether literally the sound record of a piece of music or of the conversational "music," like the sound of a parent's voice. What is repeated (and perhaps, ultimately, remembered) is the picture in the mind of a musical experience, a picture that might cause some version of the piece of music to actually "play" in the sensorium. In other words, the record in our minds might cause the music to play in our ears.

One may choose to analyze and interpret the "recordings" in the mind of past, nonverbal, "musical" experiences, whether these are stored in memories or revived in the associative networks of dreams and phantasies or in the transference, but if the aim is to *facilitate* contact with the psychology of the body (which is the first order of business with dissociated patients, for example), then it is better to relinquish the urge to interpret—to postpone any attempt to translate or explicate the patient's material in terms of something *else* (like an unconscious wish or something from the past) and especially to forswear transference interpretation, in favor of providing an animated framework for the linking of sensation and thought, body and mind in the present. (Trying to locate the source of somatosensory experience in the past or in the "unconscious" may actually rob the patient of the opportunity to find a personal mind-body link, and it can be particularly misleading and counterproductive to attribute an experience of the "musical" dimension in analysis to transference or treat it as a tune from the past.) Music in the analytic situation involves *hearing and feeling the sounds being heard and felt in actual time*—in the actuality of mind-body communion and communication. The clinical implication of this is that the music happening in the analytic session can only come alive—be "heard" or felt—if one is able to relinquish the mental activity of interpreting. Crucial to analytic work in this subsymbolic area is the analyst's capacity to enter into a state of psychosensory participation that invokes something like a sensory symbiosis with the patient, what Henry Markman has evocatively described in terms of the psychosensory communication that inheres in the ensemble improvisation that is the hallmark of certain kinds of jazz.[8]

The music of what happens in the clinical situation, in other words, does not lie in the repetition of unconscious object relationships; instead, the music is the psychology of the body expressing itself in the moment, nothing more and nothing less. Whatever else is involved in the analyst's choice of words or interpretive intent, the music lies in the patterning of the analyst/patient embodied experience. This is not a matter of biological rhythms; it is, rather, the psychology of the living body, the psyche-soma, with its own nonsymbolic language of rhythm and tone and movement and tempo, alive in real time in the clinical encounter. This entirely contextual and concrete pattern language is never fully translated into the representational language of the mind and is not dependent for its relevance and existence upon being translated into the verbal register. (Lacan referred to this physical, acoustic aspect of language as the "materiality of the signifier," the strictly musical dimension of the human voice.)

From this point of view, the somatosensory dimension of psychical life is not less "developed" than symbolic thinking and relational capacity, nor does it belong to a "primitive" part of the mind. It is therefore misleading to refer to phenomena in the presentational domain as "proto-" phenomena, since this would imply that it is only by means of transformation by the more sophisticated processes of representation that the psychic life of the body can be more fully realized. "Primitive" mental states refer to types of *psychopathological* development in which mental processes have become unable to process subjective emotional experience, resulting in phantasy structures taking over perception, what the post-Kleinians refer to as a pathological organization. But pathological formations of the personality cannot simply be accounted for in terms of underdevelopment of mentalizing or representational capacities; indeed, the problem of impairment in the nonrepresentational domain itself—and hence damage to the musical function—is invariably a part of the problem.

The implication of these ideas for our clinical theory is twofold. First, the musical dimension of therapeutic communication should be given greater credibility and theoretical attention. And second, the temporal dimension of the analytic frame should be viewed as part of a dynamic configuration, a living or animated framework that can and should be maintained or adjusted, where possible, in response to the needs of the patient.

The musical dimension in clinical work is ever present, though usually implicit and not the focus of clinical attention. Its main instrument, of course, is the voice, though physical gestures may also play a prominent role, as does breathing and audible body movements. We are biased toward the value of interpretation and the referential power of language in the clinical encounter, but the performative and prosodic dimensions of speech may be of far greater importance in establishing and maintaining communication. In our use of language, the more concrete, experience-near quality of words plays a particularly important role, as contrasted with the more representational, denotational, and conceptual uses of language. Metaphor connects language directly to lived experience, but where a shared psychosensory framework for expression is absent or damaged, our clinical approach necessarily turns to the task of reframing or rebuilding the very matrix of communication.

The pattern of interaction within the session cannot be reduced to a standard technical approach. Many patients cannot access the embodied dimension of their psychical experience and hence are unable to speak in an associative way. In these clinical situations, the analyst will necessarily find him- or herself in the position of a "conductor," someone who sets the tempo and regulates the intensity of the exchange in order to facilitate the participation of body-psyche rhythms. This *inductive* function of the analyst, which is distinct from interpretive and receptive functions, is present in every clinical encounter but usually remains implicit and unnoticed because patient and analyst naturally form a shared psychosensory network; their rhythms of movement and speech are attuned to each other unconsciously. But especially in those cases where personality development or current anxieties cause the individual to remain divorced or dissociated from embodied experience (and hence, by definition, isolated from the sensory commons that only body language can afford), the inductive function of the analyst comes to the forefront. This does not involve the application of a certain technique or approach but entails the analyst's experimental approach to finding some shared perceptual elements in the clinical encounter, some way of facilitating the patient's discovery of their embodied experience. (Winnicott in his later work provided examples of how he adapted the temporal and interactional framework to facilitate psyche-soma participation—in one case eschewing interpretation while providing a long-enough meeting [three hours] that the patient could begin gradually to speak from a more embodied location, an evolution within a single meeting that depended upon the analyst's acute presence while refraining from any demand upon the patient for thought or interpretive meaning.)

Insofar as the analyst is able to relinquish the state of mind in which the tendency toward interpretive processes predominate, there opens up the potential for a different kind of psychical motility, where the movement of sensation and feeling is less hindered, can flow or spill over into thought without being hindered or obstructed by thought. The task of the analyst in this area is to facilitate the movement of the psychology of the body in the life of the mind, to *let the music play*, which may require that the analyst set it in motion, for example by initiating a certain kind of conversation or by setting a tone. This induction involves a different kind of psychical and analytic "work" in analyst and patient founded less upon the "demand upon the mind for work" (for representation, symbolization, thought, or sublimation) that Freud ascribed to the pressure exerted by the drives in the absence of satisfying objects. Instead, what is demanded here is another kind of work, the work of expanding contact and communication at the level of what Freud called *Darstellung* (presentation), the work of *sensing together* the very pulses and energies coursing through the psyche-soma in the first place. This sensory activity does not depend upon interpretation or reverie (the alpha function of the analyst) but on engagement as an embodied presence, the beta function of the analyst, which builds upon Winnicott's insight into the non-interpretive function of the analyst toward engendering a live connection to the patterns of embodied experience in a shared psychosensory field, the area of perceptual identification, and experiential unity between patient and analyst. Activation of this "inductive" or beta-function activity, concretized in the analyst's live presence and activity, is an essential precondition for any meaningful work of interpretation of mental contents or analysis of the representational workings of the mind through analysis of dreams, associations, or unconscious wishes and motivations. *The psychology of the body must be joined (psychosyncretics) in order for the psychology of the mind to be differentiated and interpreted (psychoanalysis).*

The experience of music effects a transformation of consciousness, certainly a shift in the direction of the psychology of the body. These shifts in consciousness, these altered states, constitute a dimension of psychical functioning—namely, the dimension of dissociative functioning—that has not received much airtime over the years in mainstream psychoanalytic theory. The work of dissociation, which takes place by way of shifts in consciousness, is distinct from that of repression and splitting, which operate in the domain of unconscious processes, phantasy structures, and agencies. Dissociation takes place on the terrain of states of consciousness, and it works by means of hypnoid alterations of attention. It makes no use at all of mental representations in the way that repression and splitting do; dissociation acts simply by shifting a pattern of attention, not by manipulating the content of a thought or the affective meaning of an action. It leaves no mark in the unconscious, no signification that can be retrieved by the lifting of repression or the taking back of a projected phantasm. Dissociation is also the mental mechanism that operates by divorcing the mind from the body (or the psychology of mind from the psychology of body), and in so doing it usually robs the psychology of the body of its influence on perception and on consciousness. When we dissociate, which we all do all the time, we abandon the multiple perspectives of perception in favor of a narrower angle of perception; we stop sensing the world through body psychology and see things in a limited way, reducing the polymorphic potential of perception into an amorphic reification we know as the mind. All this is normal and understandable; we must be able to titrate the distance from our body psychology for many good reasons, most of which help us respond to the demands of the social milieu. Dissociative detachment, which is a part of everyday life, only becomes a serious problem when it becomes fixed, rigid, permanent, even perverse, when the stabilizing function of pauses and privacies becomes an end in its own right, a way of preventing things from happening, rather than a necessary stability for enhancing our capacity to affect and be affected by the world. And here we must reckon with psychosocial complexities of real significance; not only personal trauma but also *impersonal* trauma arising from the social milieu can activate dissociative responses and make it harder to find those places, those time periods that afford the possibility of integrating mind and body.

There exists such widespread and pervasive alienation from the libidinal body and such hegemony over the life of the unconscious that the center of gravity of what ails us has moved, to some degree, from neurosis to dissociation. Generally speaking, today's patient in analysis is as much (if not more) in need of an opportunity to experience one's passions as one's own—as opposed to the noise of overstimulation—as in need of an adjustment in one's way of defending against them. And for this, a therapeutic experience of dedifferentiation is vital, so that the detached, overbusy, overstimulating, hyper-regulating processes of the mind can dissolve a little and a rediscovery of the psychology of the body and the revitalizing of the unconscious can take place. For those patients who use their precocious ego capacities to build discrete alter worlds in which they live in trancelike states of consciousness, where the desiring body and wishful unconscious are kept under vigilant control, the quality of the analytic encounter that is most vital is the space and the *quality of time* that it offers for a therapeutic broadening of consciousness, one that will induce the body into a shared temporality in which the vitality of the primary processes can reinvigorate the detached and overcontrolled type of consciousness that will otherwise colonize our psychical existence.

In situations that are not pathological, we modulate the mind-body relation constantly, which allows us to shift our perceptions as they are refracted through the various sensory, phantasmatic, and conceptual lenses. There is no fixed state of consciousness but constant alterations. Variations in sensory perception, including transitory visitation to altered states, help us stay alive to ourselves and to the world while staying safe. We move between association and dissociation constantly. It is no surprise, then, that we *like* our altered states, seek them out, and cultivate them. Rituals and activities that facilitate the elective entry into altered states may be among the most highly valued in cultural life—few more than the experience of music. Music helps shift our consciousness toward actually being in the world, in the sense of an immediate and palpable concrete vitality that is both embodied and imaginative. That is, it lets us feel real. It helps ground us in psychosensory reality. It makes us sane. (This is the foundation of what Winnicott would eventually call "creative living.") Transient alterations in consciousness help us find a space and place where we can live, fresh modes of perception, new ways to "imaginatively elaborate" our bodily and unconscious experience; they allow us to move beyond ourselves while remaining tethered to our embodiment *without becoming too dislocated*, thus averting the threat of depersonalization that haunts those who become too detached.

If listening to music in an attentive way is capable of affecting a shift in perception and consciousness, it is worth bearing in mind that the analytic method itself depends on a comparable setup—a specialized framework for the shifting of attention from everyday consciousness to something closer to dream consciousness. Free association, regression, and transference occur solely under the auspices of the peculiar altered states of consciousness induced by the workings of the analytic frame, affording access to fleeting preconscious imagery, to associations that are otherwise usually suppressed, and to the return of the repressed. The analytic setting and temporal framework bring the oneiric function, the dream-work capacities of the psyche, into the forefront, so that we can see waking-dreaming (Bion's "dream-work-alpha") at work in the clinical field. Indeed, some of the most influential contemporary analytic theorists have given the oneiric function a central place in their clinical models, highlighting the role of dream-work and reverie in the analytic encounter, the importance in clinical psychoanalysis of the moment of insight or of a fresh association arising from a dream or parapraxis. The quality of experience of time is strikingly nonlinear at these moments—ideas, images, and affects, memories and perceptions interweave and rapidly dart meaning backward, forward, and sideways all at once or suddenly condense in an affective image. In these instances, the timelessness of the unconscious makes a special appearance as a kind of disruption in our accustomed state of consciousness. This guest appearance from the unconscious is sometimes disturbing, often funny or anachronistic, and always surprising. For many, these are the quintessential psychoanalytic events in a treatment. But these events only become possible under the temporal conditions of a vastly different timeframe, the time *of the frame*—the long haul of psychoanalytic consistency, the steady unfolding of the transference neurosis, and the oft-repeated cycles of working through material. The particular temporal framework of the analytic session, the number of minutes in clock time, may not be the important time measure per se; what is important is that it is a time period in which one may enter into an altered state of consciousness *for a duration sufficient to register a significant alteration of the self.* Another way of putting this is that it offers a temporal framework in which the psychology of the body (the work of beta function) can be brought together with the mind and the work of alpha function. Without this psychosensory syncretics, no psychoanalysis can take place; the essential dimension of the psychoanalytic process—perhaps the most important—rests on this entry into an altered state in which the mind and body can rediscover and reestablish their communion, which depends upon this particular temporal signature.

But the analytic situation, its frame, is designed not only for a kind of expanded dreaming but also—and fundamentally—for the *enhancement and facilitation of musicality.* The analytic frame not only delineates a specialized space within which a clinical process may unfold but also facilitates a particular kind of temporality that gives a central place to the experience of being embodied. In our everyday life, the experience of time is dominated by the regime of the Big Clock, a superstructure beneath which persists what André Green called a *heterochrony*, an always heterogeneous lived reality of many contrasting and contradictory kinds of time.[9] One of the remarkable things about the invention of the frame is how it marks off a temporal area that allows many different kinds of time to be woven together into a heterogeneous metatime, a kind of "experiential time," a discrete, framed time period within which we live in many time registers at once—a mixing, weaving, and warping of different modalities including linear-sequential time, biological time, historical time, timelessness of the unconscious, instantaneousness of association, suspended time of daydreaming, the time travel of memory and of dreaming, the reversed time of deferred action and *après-coup*, and the compulsive repetition of the drives and of trauma relived. This particular form of experiencing oneself in many time registers at once is made possible by the particular function of the analytic frame, which is not merely the delineation of a space but always—and perhaps more importantly—the creation of a temporal framework.

But of all the different time modalities that the framework of analysis allows us to access, the most important for the purposes of this discussion is *body time*, the way that time is experienced in corporeal reality and in the play of senses. The argument of this book is that music is the great mixer of body time with the other kinds of time that we live in. It keeps the body alive to the mind, so we don't drift away from ourselves in our mind travels and get lost in the many time universes far removed from our lived embodied experience. And music allows us to find in communal experience a version of embodied living that may help us attune to ourselves. Listening to a piece of music does not happen in a flash, like a sudden association, nor does it go on over days or months or sit inert in one's memory for decades. It is something that can be experienced within a certain temporal framework (like the analytic session), long enough to have the tempo and rhythm and harmonic shapes of the psyche-soma be felt in a live and actual way—long enough for an experience of feeling and embodiment in connection to the thoughts, memories, and phantasies that occupy the mind. An effective experience of music requires that it go on for just long enough, and in a concentrated enough setting, to bring the psychic qualities of the body into the mix. The particular temporal framework of experiential time that we potentially find in a piece of music or an analytic session activates a transitional state of consciousness, expanding the boundaries of conventional perception. It is a broadening of consciousness to include a range of temporal modalities but in particular the sense of *being alive in real time*. Being alive in real time is the characteristic of body time, and it is the most important and inevitably the most difficult to bring into the mix, because it is where we actually live. And we only live in this body time when we are woven into the repetitions of common time, pulsing our humanity through shared rhythms, the *beats* of beta function.

2

THE RHYTHM OF THE HEAT

repetition
beta function
rhythmizing

We repeated ourselves into this culture. We may be able to repeat ourselves out.

—ROBERT FINK, *REPEATING OURSELVES*

I

One of the great tensions in Freud (and, as Freud showed us, in everyone else) is between that which he feared, or didn't care for—like music, for example, or riding trains, each of which Freud famously avoided—and that which he found himself doing, which was, much more famously, psychoanalysis. So it is noteworthy that the way he communicated what he called the "fundamental rule" of psychoanalysis to his patients was to invite them to "free associate," to say whatever comes to mind as if they were, of all things, riding a train: "Act as though, for instance, you were a traveler sitting next to the window of a railway carriage and describing to someone inside the carriage the changing views which you see outside."[1] This proved to be (like actual train riding, at least for Freud) harder than it sounds. Upon attempting to "free associate" in this way, as Freud and his patients soon discovered, one often begins at something like a dead end. No sooner does one attempt to describe these "changing views" than one finds oneself speechless—as, perhaps, at the beginning of a piece of music, or at the ocean's shore—paralyzed by the vast unspoken and unspeakable: a haltedness, tongue-tied, a struggle. Yet somehow the fundamental rule has not fundamentally changed since Freud's time, perhaps because this struggle itself proves to be extraordinarily interesting, one of what Adam Phillips has called the "side effects" of psychoanalysis, which are neither accidental nor marginal to the analytic process but rather form its very core, its most recurrent and promising repercussions.[2] So why might the suggestion to simulate riding in a train carriage have proven a lasting, useful strategy for inducing the mode of consciousness required for the work of free association? Or to approach the situation another way, we could ask: What might riding trains have to do with the deep communion between human beings, which also characterizes musical experience—and why the ambivalence about trains or music, let alone both?

While the fundamental rule explicitly invites free association from the patient, it implicitly relies upon the analyst to interrupt this association periodically, at the end of each psychoanalytic hour, producing a pattern that we now acknowledge by referring to the *frame*. As one practices this ritual regularity, the starting and stopping of sessions becomes inextricable from the analytic work itself, as well as a precondition for that work; no analytic work, in fact, can proceed without it. As the French deconstructionist Jacques Derrida wrote: "One must learn the necessity of a scansion that comes to fold and unfold a thought. This is nothing other than the necessity of a rhythm—rhythm itself."[3] Without these scansions, these stations, implicit at the outset, no one would ever board the train in the first place. But while everyone involved in the work of psychoanalysis knows this to be the case, we are often at a loss to describe *how* exactly these pauses operate, at what level they are working, and why they are so crucially necessary. And in order to investigate this question, it may be helpful to occupy precisely the kind of space Freud would have rather not, one of the only spaces that our generally unflinching founder was not inclined to ever find himself. "Seated in the compartment of a train," the Hungarian philosopher and psychoanalyst Nicolas Abraham writes in his meditative collection, *Rhythms*:

> I distractedly contemplate the receding landscape. Without paying any particular attention to it, I feel myself surrounded by a whole world of presences: my fellow passengers, the windowpane, the rumbling of the wheels, the continually changing panorama. But now here I am, for the past moment or so, nodding my head, tapping my foot, and my whole body is vibrating to the beat of a rhythm that seems unending. What has happened? A radical change of attitude must have taken place within me. Just a minute ago, the monotonous rumbling of the wheels striking the joints of the rails was simply there, like my neighbors in the compartment or the landscape I was contemplating. But from the moment my body embraced the cadencing of the wheels, the surrounding objects appeared to lose their solidity and they took on the flavor of an almost dreamlike unreality.[4]

Abraham is broadcasting live from the frontier of *repetition* and *rhythm*. The subrelevant noise of just a moment ago now gives way to an altered state of consciousness, a "dreamlike unreality." This is the original zone of psychoanalytic inquiry, the inner (un)reality of the dream. Dream-work, as Bion elaborated, is actually—in health, when it "works"—happening all the time (Bion called this sublime working of the mind "dream-work-alpha": we dream our experience all the time), but the dreams that interested Freud, like the sessions in which he studied them, happened nightly, at regular intervals—though perhaps it would be more accurate to say that they happened *through* regular intervals, only once the dreaming apparatus, the psyche, had internalized the intervalic patterns themselves. (Infants, as any sleep-deprived, new parent will attest, must be acculturated to the difference between awake time and sleep time, day and night.) Freud occasionally contemplated the repeated patterns that he believed constituted "rhythms" when he wrote about young children. One example included rocking infants to sleep, a kind of "beat-function," rhythmizing the infant into dreaming, as well as the muscular activity of young boys in the *Three Essays on the Theory of Sexuality*; he later contemplated rhythm in the religious repetitions of obsessive rituals (and the obsessive rituals of religion); the tick-tock of *fort-da*; and the on-off pattern of sensory perception and pleasure-unpleasure, gatekept by the stimulus barrier, to name a few.[5] But he did not locate rhythm at any specific level of his original psychical topography (another point Bion would eventually elaborate in his own quasi-mathematical system for classifying psychoanalytic material, which he called the Grid), perhaps because rhythm cannot comfortably be referred to as a perceptual object. This left future scholars to reconcile the repetitions Freud called rhythm with the system he called "perception." "Instead of saying 'perception of rhythm,'" Abraham explains,

> it would be better to speak of a "rhythmization of perception." For rhythmizing consciousness does not apprehend its object in the same way as unembellished perception does. To return to our example, the rumbling-of-the-wheels-on-the-rails is transformed into the rhythm-rumbled-by-the-wheels-on-the-rails, which means that in the rhythmizing attitude, the object does not appear for its own sake, but only as the substratum of a detachable element, the rhythm.[6]

Freud could never write comprehensively about the role of rhythm in perception because rhythm is not perceived. Rhythm is itself a mode of perception, what may be best understood as a *quality of perception* induced by an organization of events that embodies time, that makes time feel real in a bodily way. We cannot actually perceive rhythm from some spatial, specular remove. To perceive in the mode of rhythm is to feel a sense of *becoming* time itself, to identify and synchronize with the temporal patterns that give the sense of continuity of self, what Winnicott famously called "going-on-being." The relation of body to rhythm is one of mimesis, of identification, vanishing the distance between subject and object, erasing the categories altogether. A human being must be *rhythmized*; it is through rhythms that one becomes human, and it is in these rhythms that embodiment takes place.

But why does the psyche-soma take to repetition in this way—identifying with patterns, becoming rhythmized? Being immersed in sensory excess is the psyche's most familiar state of affairs; the train, the world, is always leaving the station. We are always, at best, along for the ride—and often struggling to catch up. But this excess is not wholly undifferentiated; some of this excess is somehow different from the rest.

The world may be always coming at us, imposing itself upon us; so the psyche, in its resourcefulness, must find a way to mitigate this onslaught, a proprioceptive *hexis* that allows one to begin to make use of the stimuli. And the first order of business may be to simplify the situation by identifying (and identifying *with*) patterns, wrangling the chaos of undifferentiated sensation into a more mastered, predictable sequence of events. Back on the train:

> In the compartment of a train . . . I feel myself surrounded by a whole world of presences. . . . A moment ago, too, I was perceiving the monotonous sound of the wheels, and my body was receiving the same periodic jolts; but in the interval between the sounds, I was taken hold of by a tension, an expectation, which the next shock would either fulfill or disappoint. And so the jolts, which were merely endured before, are now expected; my whole body prepares to receive them. My passivity of a moment ago has changed into an active spontaneity: I am no longer at the mercy of external forces; on the contrary it is now they who obey me. At just the right time, I tap my foot—and instantly I trigger the event. My expectations have no other meaning: in reality, they are desires, demands, incantations. When the event occurs, I experience the satisfaction of my efficacy. Thus, rhythmizing consciousness is apprehended as activity, as spontaneity.[7]

What Abraham notices here is the way in which the psyche-soma manages sensory experience first and foremost by organizing it according to its predictability, a kind of musical world building (through *beta function*), in which the homogenesis of repetition helps the body anticipate the next iteration of the pattern. Once we find the rhythmic beat, it is as if we can *make* the next one happen *as it happens to us*. We can find-create it. (Adorno once observed: "Music represents at once the immediate manifestation of impulse and the locus of its taming.")[8] Rhythmizing consciousness is, accordingly, for Abraham "a variety of expressive consciousness," a musical being-in-the-world in which the distinction between perceiving the world and expressing the world is transcended through rhythmizing consciousness, through a musicopoetic style of being-in-the-world.[9] (What Freud metaphorized as a "contact-barrier" is in fact nothing but this temporal organization of perception, a rhythmic patterning that both conducts and periodically insulates, or "represses," the dynamic resonance between the body and the world.) As Virginia Woolf once wrote to her beloved,

> Style is a very simple matter: it is all *rhythm*. Once you get that, you can't use the wrong words. But on the other hand here am I sitting after half the morning, crammed with ideas, and visions, and so on, and can't dislodge them, for lack of the right rhythm. Now this is very profound, what rhythm is, and goes far deeper than words. A sight, an emotion, creates this wave in the mind, long before it makes words to fit it; and in writing (such is my present belief) one has to recapture this, and set this working (which has nothing apparently to do with words) and then, as it breaks and tumbles in the mind, it makes words to fit it.[10]

Rhythm is a way for the mind to work, an orientation to thinking itself. (The term for rhythm in flamenco music is *compás*.) Perception may be rhythmized with relative ease when immersed in the metronomic sonority of train riding, but the music of the world is seldom so easily apprehendable as rhythm. When Winnicott wrote that "there is no trauma that is outside the individual's omnipotence," he was implicitly referring to the psychical need for rhythms that wrangle experience within the parameters and pentameters of the mind's patterning.[11] Winnicott believed (as he elaborated through the end of his life) that any impingement that exceeds the capacity to register its imposition (what he called "breakdown") does not really occur psychically in the first place; one simply is "not there" to experience it. (The Botellas distinguish this lacuna as "the negative of trauma," what they call a "non-representation.")[12] What distinguishes that which is capable of psychic registration and what is not, what is within and not within one's omnipotence, is, however, hardly a simple matter of excitation quantity, as in the original Freudian schema, or, to put it another way, the determination of this quantity has relatively little to do with objective stimulus and almost everything to do with the *way* it is perceived, which perceptual styles or attitudes have been available and incorporated, through a primary form of mimetic identification, into rhythmized consciousness—in other words, it has to do with the shared sensoriality that forms the fabric of where we live, with other people. (Even Freud mentioned there are "other passengers" in the carriage.) When infants encounter the strange, uncharted territory at the liminal boundaries of their ever-expanding world, they look not toward the void but toward the parent who is (hopefully) looking with them, to figure out what to do, how to perceive what they are sensing, to figure the world. Without this perceptual apprenticeship, the nonhuman environment registers only as an arrhythmic, erratic onslaught of bodily stimulation from which the psyche must insulate itself through a kind of zombie consciousness. When consciousness fails to become rhythmized, it can get no help from shared beats and becomes a slave of quantity, without quality; when things are dysfunctional in the rhythm section, there is only noise, nausea, the disintegration products of a quantified, reified world.[13]

When viable strategies for world perception are successfully transmitted, we get a different picture. Getting the hang of rhythm, vibrating in sympathy with the world, seldom if ever announces itself to the mind; it need not be "counted" explicitly but rather takes hold without fanfare as a kind of found creation; to paraphrase Winnicott, the question of whether the rhythm should be located in the parent or the child, in the self or the world, need not, ideally, be asked. (Having to count a rhythm aloud, to spell it out, is only ever necessary to get it started, or when the train is veering off the tracks.) Consider the great refrain of latency: "Stop copying me"—"I'm not copying you." The mimetic core around which perception forms is not to be interpreted, not to be symbolized, because it is not to be noticed as such; its participants are not meant to be looking at one another, as in what Harold Boris calls a "couple," but looking together toward the world, Magritte-like, in the mode of what Boris calls a "pair."[14] In the beginning is the world; rhythmized perception precedes subjectivity, organizing the otherwise traumatic unpredictability of the world into the shared anticipation of reliable patterning through the power of a groove.

"Changes come in an analysis," Winnicott continues, "when the traumatic factors enter the psycho-analytic material in the patient's own way, and within the patient's omnipotence." We know something has changed in an analysis when the changing views, the viewing itself, has been transformed through the emergence of one's own way of perceiving the world, which is simultaneously a "style" for expressing one's views. And the trick that Woolf reveals to her writing companion is that style is all a matter of rhythm, and the words just follow suit. Didier Anzieu's seminal collection *Psychic Envelopes* provides a vivid example of this fundamentally psychoanalytic process of developing the beta function of rhythm through the rhythmizing of shared perception. In an essay titled "The Musical Envelope," an analyst uses a tape recorder to document work with her four-year-old patient. The recording device itself quickly becomes the focus of the treatment (along with the piano in her consulting room), with which, the author believes, the patient "used *repetition* to attempt precisely to 'grasp' something"—a grasp, we might understand, underwritten by an essential, periodic interruption, a repetition made rhythm:

> David asked me to repeat an action: pushing the "stop" button of the tape recorder. This lasted for a moment (because each time he made it go again), and I understood nothing of this, especially since he knew perfectly well how to do it himself. After a few minutes I heard him say "Top" and then realized that I had very often associated "Stop"—or, by abbreviation, "Top"—with the action he requested. Was David's quest not to appropriate the word (specifically a word of mastery) by means of differentiation within global excitation?[15]

So far, this is a charming if familiar story about language as mastery, the potency of the Word in the terra incognita of "global excitation." The treatment continues:

> On this day, when David wanted to take the tape recorder, which was on the piano, I intervened—in view of the roughness of his gesture (he was still in omnipotence)—by snatching the machine, while commenting on this action by saying something like "you have to hold the tape recorder properly to put it on the table." Since David was still very impatient, he could not wait for the tape to be rewound, and we have therefore never had the chance to hear a beginning of a session—it is always the last minutes (of the recording, not the session) that are replayed. This time, therefore, my injunction was among them. It was repeated five or six times in a row, to suit David's manipulations.
>   In the next session, after a moment, David stopped his piano playing, looked around, and found that the corner was filled up with the piano

cover, put on a pile of chairs. I wondered what he was looking for, when I saw him go into the room and return with a chair that he brought me so that I could put the tape recorder on it. The usual table was not, in fact, there. It was the first time that David had taken such an initiative.

The tape recorder offered David the possibility of finding the sonorous situation again and repeating it as many times as necessary to master its degree of excitation and to differentiate its elements.[16]

For young David, the meaning of his analyst's injunction—"you have to hold the tape recorder properly to put it on the table"—was not usable as a symbolic communication, as a suggestion, but it turned out to be usable as a repeated figure, a *sample*, a piece of music. And this sampling phenomenon—which can be found in such diverse musical corners as the nineteenth-century Romantic fragment, the experimental tape pieces of twentieth-century composers like Steve Reich and John Adams, and the now-ubiquitous genre of hip-hop—is precisely, Freud tells us, how perception itself functions, "as though the unconscious stretches out feelers, through the medium of the system *Pcpt.-Cs.*, towards the external world and hastily withdraws them as soon as they have sampled the excitations coming from it."[17] We perceive the world by sampling it, via beta function, in a different register than we make meaning of it, through alpha function. The world must be *con*-figured, dreamed together, before it can be figured; only once David configures the world, musically, with a sample of his therapist's voice (an analog of her reliable recurrence through the frame of their meetings) can he figure out what happens to him in the last minutes of his session. There is no meaning to be made of the world until we can grasp it, "in omnipotence," via our own found-created rhythmized consciousness, looping our samples of the world as the fabric of our dream-work.

There is no rhythm in a vacuum, nothing to sample. Samples must always sample *something*; the world must present itself, or perhaps be presented, in order to be sampled. And the most fundamental determinant of sampleability inheres not in the thing itself, nor in the amount or the quality, but the *frequency*, the rate, of opportunity in which it is presented. Whatever else she does, David's analyst keeps the beat going, session to session, sufficiently for David to make use of the rhythmic aspect; Freud called this "working-through," keeping the beat going despite resistances.

Resistances are never worked through in isolation, not only because we lack sufficient awareness or understanding of their overdetermination, their meaning, but because in isolation we would lack the sense of temporality required in order to continue psychical work, to go on being. We cannot make time on our own, as "individual subjects" (a term that is anyway a contradiction); we can only be *subjected by* something else, something other (including, ultimately, the otherness within the self). We can only be subjects in time once we are induced into time, and the primary channel for this vital induction is rhythm, which only ever comes through the beta function of mutually induced beats. Mere repetition, on the train and elsewhere (including the consulting room), is not yet rhythm; the experience of repetition as rhythm is potentiated by the bits of sensory experience that are, for better or worse, imposed upon the psyche-soma within a psyche-somatic *community*. Our perception of the world is only ever routed through this shared network of cultural practice and habit. (This is how we do it.) Human beings must become *subject*, thrown under a larger, communal experience, before we can have a *project*, or project ourselves, into anything meaningfully. (Some patients turn themselves into projects when no one has turned them into subjects.) The train goes nowhere unless there are tracks along which to travel—and, above all, a *conductor* that orchestrates the coming and going, starting and stopping, authorizing and personalizing the otherwise mechanical venture. We are only ever directed toward that which is of value to perceive, induced into perception itself, by our fellow passengers. And we have sexuality to show for it.

II

"At this point," Freud writes in the *Three Essays*,

> we must also mention the production of sexual excitation by rhythmic mechanical agitation of the body . . .
>
> The existence of these pleasurable sensations—and it is worth emphasizing the fact that in this connection the concepts of "sexual excitation" and "satisfaction" can to a great extent be used without distinction, a

circumstance which we must later endeavour to explain—the existence, then, of these pleasurable sensations, caused by forms of mechanical agitation of the body, is confirmed by the fact that children are so fond of games of passive movement, such as swinging and being thrown up into the air, and insist on such games being incessantly repeated. It is well known that rocking is habitually used to induce sleep in restless children. The shaking produced by driving in carriages and later by railway-travel exercises such a fascinating effect upon older children that every boy, at any rate, has at one time or other in his life wanted to be an engine driver or a coachman. It is a puzzling fact that boys take such an extraordinarily intense interest in things connected with railways, and, at the age at which the production of phantasies is most active (shortly before puberty), use those things as the nucleus of a symbolism that is peculiarly sexual. A compulsive link of this kind between railway-travel and sexuality is clearly derived from the pleasurable character of the sensations of movement. In the event of repression, which turns so many childish preferences into their opposite, these same individuals, when they are adolescents or adults, will react to rocking or swinging with a feeling of nausea, will be terribly exhausted by a railway journey, or will be subject to attacks of anxiety on the journey and will protect themselves against a repetition of the painful experience by a dread of railway-travel.[18]

The world arouses our senses before it means anything in our minds; then, our senses awakened, the world proceeds arouse our interest in meaning, our wish to know and to not know. As Laplanche formulated, what we eventually come to regard as the sexual drive is originally (and forever) a drive to translate. But this curiosity is never a risk-free enterprise. We not only pursue but avoid our sources of satisfaction because they may be too stimulating, too exciting, to have more than a sample of them, which would threaten interruption to the continuity of the self, the ego swamped by too much energy. So we need a rhythmic pattern to alternate between our need for relaxation and our need for tension, to know and to not know what things mean. The same "nucleus"—around which symbols, like electrons, will later orbit from a great, irreducible distance—can induce polar-opposite effects. We need rhythmic encounters to induce sleep and arouse fascination, but rhythm can also overstimulate if the psyche-soma is not protected—not only, as Freud imagines, from unrepressed sexuality but also perhaps from the incongruity of living in a world (and in a body) in which things pop up unexpectedly, and don't already fit, and which cannot be mastered in our mind, a world of avant-garde music. Protection, in other words, from what things mean (which Freud calls "repression") is only one form of psychical guardianship; before one can have thoughts to repress, one needs, as it were, something to think with, a mode of psychical experience, a "wave of the mind," in order to give thinking shape. And the biggest wave that the mind must find a way to surf is inevitably the ebb and flow of "sexual excitation," the frustrations and satisfactions that become possible living in one's body among other humans, who stimulate us into thinking with the different parts of our bodies, precipitating new ways of thinking. In order to find a way for the mind to sort the stuff of desire and interest in the world, and to do so usefully, without becoming epically defended, a rhythm of perception must be found. We turn to the very humans who stimulate us to teach us how to conduct our newly stimulated bodies, borrowing from the public library of human being the repetitions and patterns which rhythmize sexual excitations into new pieces of psychic equipment, new instruments in the music of shared living.

Rhythm, in other words, *leans on* repetition just as sexuality leans on the sexual instincts; it avails itself of processes that are occurring at the bodily level—the repeated patterns generated by physiological and neuronal activity and by coming together with and apart from other people—and makes these phenomena "usable" to the psyche-soma. This on-leaning may be much more than an analogy; rhythmizing may in fact be identical to, *nothing but*, the very *Anlehnung* (on-leaning) described by Freud and elaborated by Laplanche with respect to sexuality. Laplanche's revision of Freudian sexuality, which he called his "general theory of seduction," supposes that the sexual unconscious of the adult is expressed through messages, enigmatic signifiers, activating the hermeneutic instinct of the infant—the lunar gravity that gets the infant's psychosexual life going, the infant's first surfing lessons, an original wave of the infant's mind. (He called this entire setup the "fundamental anthropological situation.") These messages are physically conducted through erotogenic contact that is for the adult always already sexual—perhaps never so much as in their rhythmicity. (In the wake of adult sexuality, rhythm can never be not sexual.) Rhythm may in fact be the most reliable indicator of a *sexual* incoming signal, the beat that announces the arrival of something libidinally attention worthy, the mode of perception in which fascination can reliably find purchase. (In this sense, the "rhythm" of heartbeats or walking is not natural or primary but rather subsequent to the establishment of rhythmized consciousness through contact-induced forms of perception.) Psychoanalysis invariably reopens this fundamental situation (*seduction*) through its fundamental rule, its frame (*induction*), toward its own interminable continuousness, its going-on-being (*conduction*).

Rhythm, we have seen, is the most rudimentary organization of perceptual experience (the "changing views" that are being organized and reorganized all the time), rendering perception usable through a regular, anticipatory structure that naturally becomes internalized and relegated to the background, what Bleger called "non-process." The frame of psychoanalysis hides this foundational phenomenon in plain sight; it organizes the psychoanalytic experience on this day, at this time, repeatedly—further fractalized, at another level of rhythmicity, by the wave styles within the sessions themselves, made possible by the primordial rhythms of shared time. This repetition is necessary but not sufficient for the establishment of rhythmized consciousness. The constancy of the frame produces its own intramural patterns of experience that infuse the overall frame structure with the humanity and sensory vitality that make it tolerable to be alive and thinking in a body, effecting what Bion once called a "consummated" mind and body, thought and muscle.[19] The primary function of the analytic frame, in this sense, might be the way it embodies space and time, the domain of shared psychosensoriality, the way it sets up and taps into the rhythmic weave in unison.

But just like the original consummation of infant and parent, the psychosensory communion of patient and analyst comes with significant risk of overstimulation, a guarantee of sexual excitation. (The ego may be first and foremost a bodily ego, but even a bodily ego is first and foremost a fundamental anthropological situation.) In a sense, we wouldn't have it any other way; as in a marriage contract, sexual intercourse confers a sense of profound legitimacy, unparalleled synchrony. And the psychoanalytic frame, even as it explicitly prohibits this form of consummation, nevertheless presents a demand on its participants to do something with sexual energy—to *conduct* it, if not through physical contact, then perhaps in some new way. The challenge of negotiating sexual energy in the primary relationship between parent and child reverberates throughout the history of psychoanalysis, as indicated in the psychoanalytic ethic to mitigate the potential for exploitation and traumatic repetition by prohibiting sex between patient and analyst. This prohibition, in fact, is not just one element or aspect of psychoanalysis; it may be, as Adam Phillips has formulated, its defining principle, its basic counterassumption, its even more fundamental rule. Psychoanalysis is precisely, for Phillips, whatever happens when two people sit in a room and agree not to have sex, to insulate the potential for sexual overstimulation. This restraint, in other words, is not simply a legal consideration or a technical formality but a constitutive, indispensable psychoanalytic invention, a veritable technology for the induction, opening up, sustaining, and going-on-being of sexual desire, what Freud originally called "transference-love." The violation of the sexual boundary, like the trauma of incest, is not just an exploitation of the patient, a catastrophic betrayal of trust, but also the collapse of this vital suspension of the space where a self can develop, the letter arriving prematurely at its destination, a pyrrhic victory, the end of a world.

Psychoanalysis, Boris suggests, could be conceived as the Pair studying the Couple.[20] The Couple is studied rather than consummated. But in order to study the Couple, to perceive it in the first place, the Pair must be paired, and in order for there to be a Pair to pair up, there must be an unconsummated Couple. But what if the capacity for shared experience that would otherwise occur at the Pair-level has been damaged or missed—*im*-paired? Then there must be consummation at the level of the Pair, *in the mode of the Pair*, in its own dimensionality: in other words, a *conductive* experience of singularity rather than complementarity, shared rather than exchanged. This happens first and foremost, in analysis, at the level of the frame, *as the rhythm of the frame*, insofar as it involves shared sensoriality. The site at which contact is prohibited is precisely what forms the necessary gap that motivates the need to pair, clearing the way to induce and practice perceptual pairing, to heal impairment at the level of shared perception. The potential for liking each other, as members of a couple, rests upon *being like* each other, as members of a pair. So the frame first brings us together, rhythmizes us, in a paired way, so that we can encounter each other as familiars, eligible for transference- love.

The frame in this sense may function for the treatment as the *contact-barrier* functions for the psyche-soma, creating sufficient separation that things can come together in new ways. In its uniquely German ambiguity, Freud's invaluable term connotes both barrier-*of*-contact, a prohibition, and barrier-*plus*-contact, a hybrid, a paradox. If psychoanalysis is always necessarily constituted by a barrier of sexual contact, it also provides a practice, a habitus, for habituating oneself to the irreducible barrier in even the fullest possible forms of contact, the gap that can never be closed, as the solid nuclei of our bodies are always separated by a counterforce of opposition, the asymptote of touch. Without this gap we would simply merge, dissolve, and have no use for identification, no opportunity to cultivate it. By staging and sustaining this crucial separation, mitigated by the unifying power of mimesis and identification, the frame potentiates its contact-barrier as a psyche-somatic conduit of shared perception (an echo of what the Greeks called "primordial union"), approximating the "dreamlike unreality" of unconscious life and providing a refuge in which to rediscover a world being formed in real time, a fullness of shared experience materializing between the twin horizons of our primordial histories and our potential futures.

For some, the analytic frame may be usable as rhythm from the get-go; the analyst drops the beat, and the dance begins. But for many among us it is hard to join in, to pick up the cue, which arrives unprecedented and alien. The schedule of analytic work is not already usable as rhythm, a threshold that can often only be determined when the beat stops. There is a difference between a "pause," a weekend or a vacation or a missed session, in which there is a felt sense of continuity of the frame—in which the work of analysis can continue, in which its constituents can miss or hate or dream of each other—and a "stop" in which the treatment simply ceases to exist, after which the treatment does not resume so much as assemble itself for the first time, which for some patients happens each time anew at each session. One is only really *in* analysis, in other words, when one is rhythmized by it; there can be no analysis until this rhythmic substructure is joined in a psyche-somatic link, which is then internalized and essentially forgotten by its participants.

This notion of rhythm may influence our picture of the analyst's responsibility to manage the frame not merely as protective of the patient but *provisional* of a musical mode of being together, what Frances Tustin once called a rhythm of safety.[21] Winnicott's insight about ending the hour as an expression of hate in the countertransference notwithstanding, we can see the analyst's responsibility as closer to the function of the rhythm section, the drummer's setting of the beat. But the beat-provision of drumming is hardly automatic, by no means mechanical. The analyst is not a metronome, and rhythm is not the same for the drummer as it is for fellow players. There is a contrast between the consciousness involved in the responsibility for the external structure of the frame—setting the tempo and articulating meter, the attentiveness of watching the clock and managing the calendar—and in the *rhythmized* consciousness of surrender to free association and play within the treatment. "Each of the consciousnesses is," Abraham explains,

> in its own way, tension, expectation, activity. But what radically distinguishes them is the very structure of this activity, the nature of this tension, the intentionality of this expectation. Cognitive consciousness, having *observed* the phenomenon, turns toward the future in order to *establish* the coincidence of the expected and the real events. Thus knowledge, stemming from an experience of the past, is grasped as something distinct from future experience, by which it may be either refuted or confirmed.[22]

The analyst manages this thought-based, cognitive aspect of time—tracking patterns, recording history, considering the future, anticipating breaks. These constitute the "holding environment" (Winnicott's term for the reliable, often rhythmic pattern of activities that form conditions of care over time) in which the psychical life of the patient can incubate and become elaborated.

> There is nothing like this in rhythmizing consciousness. For it, the future is not defined by the categories of the known and the unknown. It neither observes nor predicts. What *happens* happens by virtue of rhythmizing consciousness itself. Its future results from its own

decisive act of will. Rhythmizing consciousness creates itself in creating the world. Yet, if ever its demiurgic activity is hindered by the world's refusal to obey its commands, it rapidly modifies these arrangements.[23]

In a founding creation myth of demiurgic activity, God finds-creates the days of the week; reserving one of them, as a time of rest, transforms the days from an ever-changing succession of physical, planetary flux into the rhythm of a meaningful world-beat, transforming nature into second nature. Religion—from the Latin *ligare*, to join or link—aims to rejoin our animal nature, with its human excesses, with human nature, into world creation. Our shared beta wave, religious or otherwise, rebinds, through embodied sensation, the overwhelming buzz of the world into the music of rhythmized perception. When conditions are sufficient to be converted into rhythmizing consciousness, subsumed within one's "omnipotence," the sense of time-rhythm itself becomes increasingly resilient to disruptions—a late start, vacations, illness, loss—which, securely in the mode of rhythmized consciousness, are experienced not as collapses of time or rhythm but as *syncopations* of an ongoing groove. When the drummer drops out, everyone still knows where the beat is. The rhythm itself can be suspended, as in a soloist's cadenza or a vocalist's fermata, as long as everyone knows that it will be brought back in—and whose job it is to bring it—which often yields ecstatic, celebratory relief. (Entire genres of dance music—namely, trance and, more recently, progressive house and dubstep—are essentially built around pushing this *fort-da* envelope of removing the beat for stretches of time to build tension for the moment of ecstatic return, when it drops back in. Even Freud's grandson's pleasure in his wooden-reel game-invention, frequently interpreted as the pleasure of symbolization, may have been equally if not more pleasurable as a triumph of rhythmization, the *eros* of rhythm.) The successful percussionist creates the conditions for the music to keep going, even when the beat stops; perhaps our sense of this continuity can only be appreciated during this kind of pause, during these rests.

But even at its most internalized, its absolute grooviest, the analyst must not take this continuity for granted. Things happen. And if they are too numerous, too arrhythmic, too impinging, there could be no groove that would be, in and of itself, immune to falling apart.

Integrating the accident into the whole, rhythmizing consciousness becomes the expectation of what has just been constituted. And the appearance of the now-expected recurrence becomes a brilliant confirmation of its initially endangered power. Thus, as long as it is active, rhythmizing consciousness always has the last word. But when it is faced with obstacles that are too numerous, too capricious, too difficult, it purely and simply abdicates: No longer creative, it abolishes itself; the spell is broken.[24]

The point of the frame, in this model, is to reserve time, to manage time so that the patient doesn't have to. But this is not always sufficient. (In this sense-mode it is not possible to "miss" a session; the rhythm continues, the session happens, but as absence instead of presence, silence rather than sound.) But when the beat is too much, or too little, failure to maintain rhythmic continuity, this rhythmized consciousness, throughout the vicissitudes of lived experience will tend to lead to a rupture, constituting a kind of negligent stewardship, leading to dissociative phenomena, what Winnicott called a "mind object," an "overgrowth of the mental function reactive to erratic mothering" that precipitates "an opposition between the mind and the psyche-soma, since in reaction to this abnormal environmental state the thinking of the individual begins to take over and organize the caring for the psyche-soma, whereas in health it is the function of the environment to do this."[25] But there is an equal danger to lifeless execution of the framing, a perversion of the beta function, if the analyst has lost sight of the rhythmizing aim, losing the connection between the frame and the sensorium, dissociated from its own beta functionality. One must be a drummer and not a drum machine, lest we become slaves to the rhythm, despite our best intentions. "Unadorned rhythm," Abraham continues,

> appears in *succession*. But it is a succession that *does not advance*: the same cycle is constantly repeated, and duration—the very environment of consciousness—marches in place. For this duration has split off itself, become alien to itself, in the service of an objective, measurable time. It may take a momentary pleasure in this activity, of course, but the tick-tock of the pendulum soon becomes monotonous. If a consciousness were to remain within time continuously, it would ultimately annihilate itself—sinking into sleep or catalepsy.[26]

The potentially annihilating monotony of the beat raises important ethical questions about how the music ever stops, whether or not we ever wake up. As a field, we may be more articulate about the need to end sessions that about the need to end analyses. We may be more resolved about the need to interrupt the fascination of analytic process, to give it texture and form, than about the question of when and how to break the spell. Freud's primary goal in shifting away from hypnosis, after all, was the fear of it becoming too necessary, working too well: "If circumstances demand a persistent use of hypnotism, the patient falls into a habit of hypnosis and dependence on the physician which cannot be among the purposes of the therapeutic procedure."[27] He felt it had to end, more than he knew how to end it. So he changed the name and tried to make it pull less for dependence and be more like a therapeutic procedure. Freud's invention of psychoanalysis was his attempt to improve upon hypnosis by eliminating (or at least marginalizing) the role of *suggestion*, but the "procedure" has never been without this soporific, cataleptic catalyst, this hypnotic "tick-tock," which is its material structure in space-time. "We are experiences," wrote Merleau-Ponty,

> that is, thoughts that feel behind themselves the weight of the space, the time, the very being they think, and which therefore do not hold under their gaze a serial space and time nor the pure idea of series, but have about themselves a time and a space that exist by piling up, by proliferation, by encroachment, by promiscuity—a perpetual pregnancy, perpetual parturition, generativity and generality, brute essence and brute existence, which are the nodes and antinodes of the same ontological vibration.[28]

"This 'ontological vibration,'" Jessica Wiskus asks, "this movement of depth: what is it but rhythm? The 'double formula'—the 'double movement'—of the flesh of time: what is it but rhythm? For rhythm expresses the cohesion and the encroachment of past, present, and future."[29]

There is nothing inherent about a rhythm, or the kind of rhythm that is a psychoanalysis, that tells it when to stop. Years pass. Categories of time emerge from the rhythmic practice of dismantling time, of approaching timelessness. Nothing happens so that everything can. (Almost everything.) But this assumes, of course, that someone is keeping an eye on the clock. Abraham warns:

A deliberate act of will may be required for consciousness to break free from rhythm's grasp. Rhythmizing consciousness is thus to some degree a prisoner of the rhythm that comes implacably to fill the protention of "what comes next." Rhythmizing consciousness thus emerges as a *fascinated* consciousness, subject to a fatal, horizonless future. This fascination admits of degrees, ranging from the normal to the pathological. Although duration usually refuses to let itself be carried away by the game to the point of total self-alienation and ends by relegating the haunting rhythm to the "background noises" of the universe of presences, certain recognized cases of pathological stereotypy are habitually characterized by the annihilation of lived duration, and in them a nearly absolute servility is manifested toward an initial and self-perpetuating rhythmizing attitude.[30]

So the very need for rhythm as the beat of life is subject to its own dangers. Adaptive, life-enhancing rhythmizing can also induce mesmerizing, tick-tock, dead states. Rhythm always needs to be limited by an agentic drummer consciousness that is itself not (only) in the thrall of the consciousness it produces. It is always incumbent upon the analyst to navigate the tension between dangers at either pole of this powerful procedure, of not enough and of too much rhythm, the prison of isolated nowness and the trance of timeless forever, the poverty of dissociation and the tyranny of mind-control. Rhythm can effectively lose its *rhythm*; like anything else, rhythm can become reified into an enclosed pseudo-music unrelated to the rest of life and not allowing anything or anyone to fuck with it.

The danger here is that the frame acts like a dead institution. And the best safeguard against this temptation is the analyst's *living of the frame* through one's own inspired, creative communion, through expressed musicality, through one's own behavior as musical being, through flow, inducing the patient into rhythm, seducing the patient into parallel communion with the mysterious otherness within oneself, subjected by one's own unconscious life. In rhythmized consciousness, the analyst's task becomes first and foremost to infuse the periodicity of the frame with the rhythmicity of groove, the mimicry of repetition with the choreography of expression, the relief of hypnotic fascination with the enigma of rhythmic variation and the evolution of musical forms.

III

Repetition only becomes a substratum for psychical life once consciousness has become fascinated, hypnotized, by rhythm—*as* rhythm. And with this hypnotic power comes an ethical responsibility, a musical *ethos*, framed through the rhythm itself. "How is it that I come to possess the rhythm-object?" Abraham asks: "By making myself a rhythmic object. And so I *have* it because I *am* it. Perceptive apprehension of the rhythm-object as such becomes possession in the double sense of having and being."[31] If having a rhythm, getting into a groove, always involves becoming perceptually organized toward a lower level of differentiation, then one should never forget, in the rhythmizing practice of psychoanalytic work, that this state of fascinated rhythmicity is maximally vulnerable to colonization and exploitation, which is why what happens in this subjected state—who and what *subjects* the subject (lit. "throws under")—is a matter of such consequence. The responsibility of the analyst in this situation is not simply to behave oneself (though this is of course paramount) but to have and to be—to *be-have*—the rhythmic object, to *become* oneself in a reliable way that is presented to the patient through none other than the analyst's musicality. ("Behaving" in this sense is one's best form of behavior, conduction one's best form of conduct.) The hypnotized subject, as the French scholar Mikkel Borch-Jacobsen writes in *The Freudian Subject*, "does not submit himself *to* the other, he *becomes the other*, comes to be like the other—who is thus no longer an other, but himself."[32] In this sense, training in analytic work may be nothing so much as the finding of the notes and chords that communicate one's music, one's *ethos*, which constitutes the mode of induction whereby the patient is brought into the free-associative mode of the analytic process.

But rhythm, like any aspect of music, can take on a life of its own and become a runaway train—may be, in fact, the means by which the train ultimately runs off the tracks. The precious quality of perception that is rhythm can never be taken for granted. Even once established, it is never guaranteed to continue. The pulse of a rhythmic groove can at any point be stripped of its libidinal potential and reduced to thanatic repetition in ways that may present themselves as utterly "normal," and the difference may be difficult to discern or evaluate. "Any activities whatever may become obsessive actions in the wider sense of the term if they are elaborated by small additions or given a rhythmic character by means of pauses and repetitions," Freud writes in "Obsessive Actions and Religious Practices."

> While the ceremonial is first being constructed, the patient is still conscious that he must do this or that lest some ill should befall. ... But what is already hidden from him is the connection—which is always demonstrable—between the occasion on which this expectant anxiety arises and the danger which it conjures up. Thus a ceremonial starts as an action for *defence* or *insurance*, a *protective measure*.[33]

The fixity of repetition, of what Freud calls a "ceremonial," is easily exploited in the service of obsessive (and dissociative) strategies and the creation of alter worlds that may be difficult to distinguish in appearance and performance from genuine forms of aliveness (or "sublimation" in the Freudian system)—perhaps more difficult to distinguish now than in Freud's time as technological and cultural support for these strategies have proliferated and accelerated through virtual realities mediated by digital screens. Freud was of course working within a very different psychoeconomic landscape, one in which the fundamental problem with energy was that there was too much of it; "it" (or *Es*, "id") was too much. Hysterics suffered from an abundance, not a deficit, of tragedy; obsessives from a surplus of sexuality. Illness—*psychoneurosis*—was what one did to manage it, which inevitably diminished the capacity to contribute, to offer oneself, as a participant in the social bond; therapy worked through the taking apart, the *analysis*, of an otherwise crushing density of superimposed, overdetermined meaning. But the illness of our day is much closer to what Freud would have considered an *actual* neurosis. There is no mystery to it, nothing behind the scenes. Overstimulation simply fries the physical circuitry of perception. (Perhaps the inflection point occurred toward the middle of the century, when the problem shifted from "suffering from reminiscences" to what Bion, working at that time, described as "being able to suffer.") *It* (the id), as Freud said, must be ridden like a horse, but this assumed the unity of horse and rider, so its gallop (like Abraham's train on the tracks) could make rhythm, its animal physicality could be woven into our human musicality. Today, when the rider is disembodied from the horse and no longer guided by the tempo of the gallop, psychoanalytic practitioners find themselves in the position of having to seek out new ways to refresh vitality at the psyche-somatic level, to reconnect rider and horse, to the world of sensation transmitted through the beat of its hooves; without this embodiment, psychoanalytic technique has no leg to stand on; the domain of the drives, of the body, of emotions, finds no ready organization and can only seek discharge or submit to the floods of overstimulation. Where there was meaning to repress in Freud's time, there is now often sheer anarchy to suppress, compact, and quarantine. The foremost (though of course not exclusive) contribution of psychoanalysis at the moment may be its safeguarding of a reliable interruption of the intromissive onslaught of sense-ablating stimulation in contemporary life that is amplified exponentially by the mechanically generated and constantly proliferating channels for repeating itself.

In an effort to relieve his patients of the protective measures that had become problems in their own right, Freud developed his own ceremonial, his private practice, in which he imagined his patients to be caught between conjuring up and protecting against the anxieties of sexuality, and invited them to relinquish the repetitive forms of self-holding they had constructed themselves in favor of the rhythmic form of patient-holding that Freud had constructed for them. There may be no more constant element of psychoanalytic practice across decades, theories, or geographical locations than the discipline of doing it rhythmically, and experiments with altering this element have largely fallen by the wayside or forfeited their designation of being psychoanalytic. And the staying power of the rhythmic character of the psychoanalytic ritual may be attributable in part to the rhythmic character of sexuality itself, which, as Laplanche elaborated, arrives originally as a series of untranslated "messages" with the full force of adult maturity but none of the mutability of adult understanding. Before we have sexuality, we have only the pressures and counterpressures of physical contact, the percussive regularity of care giving that is either scrambled or syncopated by the errata of being an adult, the stray strains of sexuality, which the nascent psyche suspends in repetition, in reminiscences, in phantasies, preserving them in the most fundamental dimensions of psyche-somatic experience for the work of translation, constituting the drive. But this drive has no rhythm; it is only insistent movement (*Bewegungstrieb*), anarchically present, pure pressure, *presión*. (Contemporary patients present something closer to an essential or "pure culture" of primordial sexuality than Freud's presumably did.) Repression could thus be understood as *re-pression*, pressure against pressure, a repressurization, a pushing-back-against (which can manifest powerfully within the psychoanalytic session, either through the transference or with physical objects in the actual room). This pressure and repression, force and counterforce, can develop into a dance of adult and infant, message and translation, a coordinated being-together-in-time through rhythm. When Laplanche formulated that the magnetism of sexuality is always underwritten by the vulnerability of *Hilflosigkeit*, conducted through the bonds of attachment, he implicitly acknowledged that the people who seduce us with the enigmas of adulthood are the same people we depend upon to show us how to handle them, how to conduct ourselves among and through one another. One's sexuality, ultimately, is temporalized in the ways one has learned to rhythmize the sexual drive through the groove of shared forms of movement, how to go on being through the erotics of identification.

Rhythmized consciousness—which might be considered a musical correlate of "evenly-suspended attention" (a term to which we shall return)—is a form of perception that goes-on-being, back and forth, between sameness and difference, each both drawing consciousness toward itself while always sending it back toward the other, surfing a wave of Merleau-Ponty's ontological vibration. Here the function (or in Lacan's nomenclature, the desire) of the analyst is, at its best, an *ethos* consisting in a provisional framing of time in order to invest psychically in the rhythmic dimension of experience. (To appreciate the amount of work required for this framing function, consider how few activities with another person, even in the context of genuine and sustained interest, are coordinated as rhythmically and consistently as psychotherapy.) We would go crazy without this shared rhythmic perception-activity to find-create, to generate and fall into, and would be left to manage the onslaught of experience through idiosyncratic strategies of self-management, isolated music, which would leave us highly susceptible to archaic forms of organization, authoritarian forms of how to live a life. Shared rhythms, on the other hand, "unburden the individual's temporal economy," as the philosopher Byung-Chul Han puts it, providing a system that allows one to make variation.[34] The framing tempo, in other words, is just the beginning—the beginning, in some cases, of livable time. What the framing function generates, what becomes discernible when contextualized by this pulse, is the polyrhythmic perversity of humanized sexuality, which could never be as regularly rhythmic as frame. ("The sexual instinct," Freud writes in "'Civilized' Sexual Morality," "is probably more strongly developed in man than in most of the higher animals; it is certainly more constant, since it has almost entirely overcome the periodicity to which it is tied in animals.")[35] The sexual is constant but not periodic; it is ever present but never rhythmic; it is present nowhere so much, in fact, as in its interruption of rhythm, its disruption of attempts to control it, even through sublimation: "It seems to us that it is the innate constitution of each individual which decides in the first instance how large a part of his sexual instinct it will be possible to sublimate. . . . To extend this process of displacement indefinitely is, however, certainly not possible, any more than is the case with the transformation of heat into mechanical energy in our machines."[36]

Conduction always generates surplus heat; the rhythms we use to regulate the sexual drive produce, in turn, more untamed energy to disrupt these rhythms, more need for new music. ("Transference" in this model would be better understood in its thermodynamic sense, the "transfer" of heat.) In the afterwardsness of psychoanalytic experience, the conditions of excess which generate *pulsión*, the sexual drive, become evermore manageable, evermore translated, within the context of fixed temporality, and by the same token, temporality itself depends upon the erratic, chaotic presence of the drive in order to generate and fuel new rhythm. Without the trains passing, the double movement, of *nachträglichkeit*, the libidinal potential of each moment becomes flattened into a kind of bodily discharge, while the potential resonance of these moments, with their psychical, bodily histories, collapses into the prison of a permanent now. "The sexual behaviour of a human being," Freud continues, "often *lays down the pattern* for all his other modes of reacting to life."[37] The patterns of sexuality, which rhythmize the drive, crystallize the inchoate enigmas of unconscious messaging into the images and music of sexual fantasy according to the material available for use, the sounds that can be sampled and looped to create beats. (Freud's own pattern appears to have been the chugging of his near-constant authorship, the train he never got off.)

The oscillating pattern formed by the forces of drive pressure and repression, which is the true achievement of sexuality, is never a perfect rhythm. We need sexuality to buck the reins, to rattle the rhythm, as much as we need it to obey. We rely on sexuality to shake things up, to imbue the continuity of experience with the skips and jumps that remind us the continuity is there, to drive and animate the discovery of the syncopations and polyrhythms that are present (or tragically absent) in every potential expression of sexuality, every genre of psychical-bodily conduction. The strict rhythmizing of entropic sexual stimulation is necessary but not sufficient for sustaining one's sense of libidinal aliveness throughout the waxing and waning pulls of seduction, the ebbing and flowing of hydraulic, bodily pressures in response to the world. The disruptive, destructive, or deconstructive—indeed, *analytic*—power of the sexual, even as it becomes increasingly harnessed by imagination, at the same time dissolves our reliable attachments to one another through new encounters with the never fully assimilable source objects of psychosexual fascination, new scenes to imagine with a fresh supply of available sounds and images, perpetuating our coming together and coming apart over the course of a life, *into* a life.

The rhythm of sexuality, in other words, and the rhythmized consciousness it both requires and generates, engenders our experience of what Laplanche refers to as *time*. And what psychoanalysis has in one sense always implicitly acknowledged and may now be discovering anew is that the impoverishment of rhythmic experience, which erodes the possibility of temporal continuity, has become the most common cause of psychical difficulties. The illness of nontime is the illness of our time. Perhaps only against the backdrop of a frame, through the double movement of deep musical accompaniment (which the Botellas have called "working as a double" and what the psychoanalyst Stephen Purcell has called "duetting"), a new experience of being in time can occur, a *first time*, a living-in-the-body-in-the-world in which psyche-somatic experience can become resonant in the present, with the past, toward the future, what Heidegger called the *ekstases*. (Laplanche's notion of "psychoanalytic time," in which the future is born in the *après-coup* of the past, reverses the *avant-coup* vector of Heidegger's being-toward-death.) Living through these accompanied rhythms, altered and renewed by the vicissitudes of being alive, begins to accumulate into a continuity of going-on-being, a music, what Pichon-Rivière once called a *spiral*, in which different modes of time can begin to gather and reverberate through one another.[38] In his essay "Psychoanalysis and Music," Richard Sterba suggests that music recapitulates "primitive infancy in which the discovery of the limbs and their movements is followed by a gradually acquired domination over the entire body."[39] He continues:

> The factor *movement* in music, therefore, not only causes a regression to a kinesthetic pleasure of early infancy, but also the intense pleasure of experiencing the dissolution of the boundaries between the ego and the external world. This dissolution—through motor activity—identifies the domination over one's own body with the ideal domination over the cosmos and, in this manner, provides the possibility of experiencing the unity between the ego and the cosmos.[40]

In its heterochronous mixing of times, in its regularities and synchronies and freedom, music plunges us into the richness of heterotemporal experience, the embodied patterns in which we become attuned to the rhythms of the world—such that the arrhythmic errata, the fruitful failures, of psychical continuity can be elaborated as the syncopation of an embodied groove. The antiphonic call and response of *après-coup* (which Laplanche describes in terms of enigma) is as much of a rhythm as could (or should) ever be made of sexuality. To attempt to hyper-regulate its tempo, to become preoccupied with the management of its calendar, to pervert the groove of human nature through the tyranny of dehumanizing mechanization, is to drastically diminish its animating potential, to fabricate regularity at the cost of spontaneity. To turn the asynchrony of sexuality into something like a horse under submission perverts the ever-unbridable, untranslatable nature of the beast, as if one can know this beast, as opposed to true sexuality, which is always more of a rodeo, a spiral, a musical negotiation between opposing forces that need one another.

The beta function of the frame structures a kind of psychical garden for these emergent, idiomatic possibilities, and whatever else the analyst does, cultivating this structure, catalyzing this movement, is always of the essence. And this happens not because we want to help people but because what we want to do helps them. Whatever may be the point of living one's life—which contemporary psychoanalysis most often tells us is *to be alive*—it inevitably turns out to have a great deal to do with being *alike*, like other living people, through mimesis. And the culture seems to place at least an implicit value on this function by continuing to employ psychoanalysts—and musicians, at their most hypnotic (*Sometimes your words just hypnotize me . . .*)—as *conductors* of this music, which in turn patterns and shapes the psyche-soma, conducts the voltage of experience continuously, lest it become dammed up to the point of neurosis, until dissociation simply pulls the plug and we abandon the body as domicile. These perversions of body time are the sequelae of neglecting to nourish temporalized ways of being, the communal movement that is always trying to happen, trying to bend us toward a more perfect union with one another and the sources of our inspiration—union with what Freud called our ego ideal, what Lacan called the asymptote of identification—through iterations of what de M'Uzan called repetition of the same (as opposed to the identical), repetition made rhythm.[41] Untended by conductive concern, our bodies are simply left at the mercy of the greediest bidder, the latest death-driven madman to usurp the podium, who fucks with time in order to disorient psyche-somatic continuity, of whom no sense can be made and who leaves only a trail of bodies for posterity, collapsed under untranslatable meaninglessness, convulsed by electrical excesses, and compelled by repetition through the remainder of their timeless days. A living psychoanalysis dismantles compulsive repetitions by offering its own, musicalized repetition, its own rhythm, which renders the repetition of the death drive obsolete, by providing its own habitus, its own inspired spiral along which the inevitable throes and throws of being alive may play out, the back and forth of elaborating and translating, of dreaming and dissociating, playing and pausing. In this way, psychoanalysis tunes its participants to the music of a shared and personal idiom, a library of source drives, a record collection of identifications, an archive of hypnotic fascinations.

3

MIND WAVES

hypnosis
enchantment
mourning

I

Resuming analytic work always involves a change of rhythm, a shift toward the temporality of the frame. Through the reliability of the frame's beat we are given an opportunity to feel what Milan Kundera once called "slowness," to sense what the philosopher Han calls the "scent of time." To work psychoanalytically is to become practiced at this slowness, this *adagio* movement, to eddy the torrential stream of stimulation in a harbor of temporal restoration, of slow, steady beat, which also serves as a bulwark against what Han calls "the violence of non-time." Heading into a session, the world's atmospheric frequencies lengthen toward the pulse of analytic time, embodied by the particular analyst-companion who, in days and weeks and years of practice, has become a living expression of the analytic frame, inducing the patient into analytic consciousness. To flip the light and invite the patient into what is still evocatively referred to as the consulting room, the spatial dimension of the frame, is to induce a potentially jarring shift of gears, a slackening of tension, an elongating of time's amplitude that may provoke a fleeting yet palpable reticence: What happens to us when the rhythm changes? What tempo plays within the frame, intoxicating us with the scent of time?

To become rhythmized through the *ritardando* of the analytic frame is to decelerate a particular form of selfhood, a whizzing succession of nows, in exchange for the possibility of feeling quite differently—in some cases, of feeling anything at all. One paradox of this enterprise is that it requires a form of abandon, a relinquishing of control to a total stranger; an act of faith, if not exactly trust, which would only ever emerge naturally from the process that is about to unfold. (To paraphrase what Ferenczi once said of the capacity to free associate: Trust would be not the precondition of psychoanalysis but an indicator of its ultimate success.) Without this trust fall, this initiating risk, this suspension of disbelief in a gesture toward a kind of openness, the process of analysis cannot begin. Here one's very existence feels far too tentative, and no faith can be found, leaving the psyche-soma isolated, forced to rely on itself for holding. The inability to enter and partake in psychoanalysis reflects a problem of our time—the loss of access to communion with others, resulting in sensory isolation, cocooning-in-the-world, an anticulture of sensory imprisonment and personal isolation. In the face of forces of atomization that make embodied relating scarce, how does something like psychoanalysis—something that asks us to forgo isolation—stand a chance? What *induces* our participation, carrying us across the intimidating threshold of the rhythm change, into new territory, a new time signature?

This conception of *induction*—does it not ring a bell? In psychoanalysis, the idea that we *induce* states may seem out of place in psychoanalytic thinking. But this idea is not new. Psychoanalysis has not usually spoken of the need to induce certain modes of experience in order to facilitate the clinical process. We might wonder whether it has remained unremarked because it has indeed been absent from clinical practice or, rather, has been *absented*. Induction, in other words, may have been exiled from the clinical theory of psychoanalysis when it was negated at its very inception as its prehistory—perhaps by calling it, as Freud did, "hypnosis." In hypnosis, induction was always front and center, first and foremost, hidden in plain sight. Any attempt to theorize the role of induction will be aided by the work of the historian of psychoanalysis

Mikkel Borch-Jacobsen, who comprehensively traces the putative shift from hypnosis to psychoanalysis (to which he has devoted staggering scholarship) with respect not only to those aspects of hypnosis that were rejected at the birth of psychoanalysis but to those aspects that may have been unwittingly preserved. In this account, psychoanalysis is less, as Freud asserted, a replacement of hypnosis than it is a kind of compromise formation, a deal struck between old and new—the need for which, as in all such formations, is motivated at the level of the unformed, by anxiety about the shapes and boundaries of feelings. The prehistory of psychoanalysis, like the prehistory of the subject, is always for Freud that morass of undifferentiation, what Borch-Jacobsen calls the "primordial crowd," from which the ego is supposedly struggling to emerge and heroically separate itself. This crowd, as Borch-Jacobsen defines it in his *The Freudian Subject*, shares more than a few characteristics with what Freud, having rejected hypnosis, would recreate and reformulate, in terms of his notion of the unconscious. Here is Borch-Jacobsen: "The crowd is impervious to contradiction, to logical argumentation; credulous, it knows neither doubt nor degrees of conviction; it cannot be restrained, for it tolerates no lapse between desire and its realization, to the point of being careless about its own preservation; the only reality it recognizes is psychic reality (image, illusion, the 'magic word')."[1]

What Freud considered the law of the unconscious—namely, the absence of differentiation that would be necessary for distinguishing moments in time or for contradiction—is also a defining quality of what Bion called the basic assumption of the group, the way that groups operate unconsciously without regard for external reality. In Borch-Jacobsen's reading, Freud's modification of hypnosis, which is his invention of psychoanalysis, was his attempt to wrangle the problematics of being social creatures within the parameters of having internal conflicts; his strategy, ironically, for breaking from his own crowd (the hypnotism of Charcot and Janet) was to create a sovereign refuge from crowds altogether and to designate it with his most magical word: *das Unbewusste*, literally "the unbeknownst," the none-the-wiser-ed, the Unconscious. Freud's description of the mode of psychical life that is undifferentiated is always a description of that which exceeds the individual's capacity for representation—not simply unknown, but post-known, known-and-then-un-known, unbeknownst. But this presumes that the individual is primary, that our individuality is threatened by the prospect of dissolution into group experience.

Freud was skeptical of a domain of psychical life marked by credulity over logic, by what we know implicitly over what we can prove empirically, for that which already immediately *is* over whatever theoretically could be, transcending the limits of individual doubt through immersion in communal conviction. Accordingly, his "new" psychoanalytic setup posited an allegedly sovereign subject, an (Enlightened) analyst, who could apprehend, under the required conditions, the dynamic forces at play within the (un-Enlightened) unconscious of the equally separate patient, illuminating darkness (or the "black mud of the occult," as he once described this dimension to Jung). But perhaps no one knew better than Freud precisely what was being given up, at least nominally, in this redescription of the therapeutic enterprise. His paper "On Psychical (or Mental) Treatment," which is his earliest recorded attempt at providing a history of the nascent technical invention that would become psychoanalysis, reads like an elegy to hypnosis. In this early paper, Freud's interest lies not primarily in what psychoanalysis was becoming (which is only briefly mentioned at the end) but in what it used to be. The "most significant indication of hypnosis, and the most important one from our point of view," Freud explains,

> lies in the hypnotic subject's attitude to his hypnotist. While the subject behaves to the rest of the external world as though he were asleep, that is, as though all his senses were diverted from it, he is *awake* in his relation to the person who hypnotized him; he hears and sees him alone, and him he understands and answers. This phenomenon, which is described as *rapport* in the case of hypnosis, finds a parallel in the way in which some people sleep—for instance, a mother who is nursing her baby.[2]

This particular form of hearing and seeing, understanding and answering, is not a matter of communication in the usual sense. Like sleep, *rapport* involves relinquishing a barrier, opening up a channel, an "attitude," a capacity to surrender (in Emmanuel Ghent's crucial understanding of that word), on a promise that a certain environment can be counted on. The guardians of the gate, the contact-barrier between known and unbeknownst, can only ever relax, break for rest, and tolerate more vulnerability if there exists a sense of some company, some other agency beyond one's sleeping self: someone to watch over me (at first an actual person and eventually just the continuity and community that an actual person helped one feel). But at this point the distinction between self and other has already been significantly muted; the other is now acting as an extension of the self (as the nursing mother once did, once the infant had become separate enough to nurse, and umbilically before that), which means that it no longer makes sense to speak of "communication" in the mode of *rapport*, the communicative mode that involves not sending and receiving, cause and effect, but rather the communion (or, in the key of Winnicott, "not communicating") of synchrony, simultaneity, and sharing, more in the mode of alreadyness, of the digital cloud, the primordial crowd. "Taken to the extreme," Borch-Jacobsen writes, "it is thought transmission, telepathy.* The transfusion or merging of subjects is such, here, that one can no longer speak of communication (feelings, opinions, but also 'communication between unconsciousnesses') because there are simply no more subjects communicating among themselves: the members of the crowd are merely *mediums* controlled (entranced, possessed) by suggestion."[3] The asterisk points to the following passage from Freud's *New Introductory Lectures* (1933):

> If only one accustoms oneself to the idea of telepathy, one can accomplish a great deal with it—for the time being, it is true, only in imagination. It is a familiar fact that we do not know how the common purpose comes about in the great insect communities: possibly it is done by means of a direct psychical transference of this kind. One is led to a suspicion that this is the original, archaic method of communication between individuals and that in the course of phylogenetic evolution it has been replaced by the better method of giving information with the help of signals which are picked up by the sense organs.[4]

"Thus the mass bond," Borch-Jacobsen appends, "may have to be thought of as a telepathic umbilical cord." If Freud stopped short of securing a place for telepathy in his psychoanalytic metapsychology (without ever quite losing interest in the possibility), the notion of a "telepathic umbilical cord" as a dimension of "psychical transference" has been ever present, most prominently among the Río de la Plata analysts in their use of

Pichon-Rivière's concept of the *vínculo* (which is the Spanish name for the umbilicus) as a complex process that forms the structural foundation of all interpersonal communication (while stopping short of a living, transpersonal organism constituted through shared musicality). Even when not being put to symbolic or associative uses, the psyche-soma is always in need of this umbilical, telepathic connectivity in order to sustain a basic sense of sensory aliveness in the world. The primary role of a link, a direct line, lies not only in its capacity for in-forming the mind but also for *forming* the subject through this identificatory "mass bond," the conduction of lived vitality through the *rapport* of group orientation toward the world.

But the spell of hypnosis, for Freud, is never cast by *rapport* alone, because *rapport* is not (or is no longer) the natural state in which strangers find themselves; it must, as even the most mechanized treatment manuals acknowledge, be "established"—in other words, *induced*. But in conjunction with the horizontal, symmetrical, egalitarian, inductive quality of *rapport*, Freud tells us there is another relation, a more asymmetrical differentiating that seduces the patient into another relation he called *gefügig*, literally "fugued" (*fucked?*) or "gapped," in which one becomes "docile," as Strachey translated it (what Laplanche will later conceive as *passivity*)—an admittedly less settling proposition, a perfect storm for exploitation, though no less necessary than *rapport* for Freud's project. When we lose ourselves in the fugue of docility toward another person, a gap is created—perhaps a correlate of what Laplanche described as the *translational* lapse caused by generational difference—which precipitates dependence, and hence conditions for psychical movement, for leaning on another person, for *attachment*. (Peter Fonagy, whose name has become as synonymous as John Bowlby's with that term, has recently concluded that attachment is little more than an excuse for establishing the conditions of this matrix of dependence and translation, what he calls "epistemic trust.")[5] As in a musical fugue, the fugue of hypnosis expands the interval through which layers of resonances can form new wave patterns, forcing the psyche-soma past the constrictions of making sense of every line at every moment into a realm of musical surrender, what Michael Eigen has described as the "area of faith," a state in which to relinquish what one thinks one is, to relinquish ordinary thinking altogether, and be remade by the music of the world.

From this perspective, becoming a hypnotist involved developing the benevolent authority to induce this surrender while conducting oneself in a manner that establishes *rapport*—which sounds an awful lot like becoming an analyst. If *rapport* and docility are, for Freud, the constitutive elements of hypnosis—indeed, the *frame* of hypnosis—one might wonder what it is that actually distinguishes psychoanalysis from its hypnotic ancestor. If upon inspection the framing functions required for each phenomenon prove to have more in common than their distinct discourses might otherwise suggest, it nevertheless remains clear that Freud wanted psychoanalysis, as a way of affirming itself as a new or different discipline, to be purged of any residue of that key ingredient of hypnosis known as "suggestion." As Freud insists decades later, Borch-Jacobsen notes, "It is not only in the saving of labour that the method of free association has an advantage over the earlier method. It exposes the patient to the least possible amount of compulsion [*Zwang*], it guarantees to a great extent that no factor in the structure of the neurosis will be overlooked and that nothing will be introduced into it by the expectations of the analyst."[6]

Freud wanted psychoanalysis to resolve the problem of dependence fostered by the hypnotist's expectations by replacing the element of compulsion, the *Zwang*—whatever one was meant to do upon waking, which always included forgetting that one had been instructed to do something—with indications and observations, "interpretations," to be mutually contemplated in a state of shared attention and thoughtfulness. But the fundamental rule, to say what is on one's mind, is of course nothing other than a very strong suggestion, and a challenging one at that. In fact, the components of the traditional analytic frame—schedule, payment, abstinence, neutrality—are precisely a collection of suggestions bordering on compulsory demands. But the psychoanalytic idea seems to be that the suggestions end there, that the remaining work, the work of analysis, is of course to analyze, to break down, to ex-form, such that psychical material, as Laplanche has formulated, can eventually be assembled and synthesized by the patient, whom he regards as the only true "therapist" in the dyad. (Only the patient, Winnicott said, has the answers; Bion said that the patient is the analyst's best colleague.)

Borch-Jacobsen, however, as the reader may be starting to anticipate, is not convinced by even this account. (Like Freud himself, Borch-Jacobsen is a rhetorically hypnotic writer, raising one objection at a time to his own claims only to dismantle them, inducing in the reader a sense that all possible counterarguments have been addressed.) Through the lens of his thorough scrutiny, the supposed change in technique away from suggestion becomes questionable.

> Hypnotic suggestion had undoubtedly been relegated to the obscurity that bordered and preceded psychoanalysis. But precisely *as obscurity*: it had been rejected with no one the wiser as to exactly *what* had been rejected.... Hypnosis was abandoned, in other words, not because suggestion theory had been incorporated within a more powerful theory; rather, it was abandoned by virtue of a denial, a rejection, a suppressed hostility that was obscure, so to speak, to itself. Freud simply wished to hear nothing further on the subject of hypnosis.[7]

What happens when words are made obscure, when speech is silenced, is obviously a subject of great psychoanalytic interest, not to mention sociopolitical relevance. (Whatever else it may have been, a vote for Trump was a vote for saying whatever comes to mind, for the untwisted tongue, for catastrophically free association.) And Borch-Jacobsen picks up on this very point, suggesting that a certain repression of language is itself at the genesis. At the ontological level at which psychoanalysis formed itself, as in the content to which it attends, the wish never to hear a word again, the repudiation of a specific influence—which, psychoanalysis tells us, is always a form of repression, a sexual matter—begets a particular symptom, a particular return. "For it must be understood," Borch-Jacobsen writes, "that hypnotic suggestion had returned *into* psychoanalysis, *as* psychoanalysis.... The dependence of the hypnotized subject on the hypnotists; the establishment of an elective, exclusive, somnambulic bond; suggestibility, even thought transmission—all this had come back up, at the very core of analytic treatment, in the form of transference."[8]

If the original mode of human relatedness, what Laplanche named the fundamental anthropological situation, is a situation of helplessness and extreme dependence, then it is naturally also a state of hypnotic fascination, of hanging on every word, reading every gesture, every swell of energy, for News of the World. And if psychoanalysis emerged as a kind of technological form that this fundamental situation takes—following hypnosis—in order to reopen itself for reworking and rearrangement of what had not gone very well in the first place, so too does it reduplicate the excess of that original situation in the form that substitute arrangements always do: creating a new symptom. The suggestions, the spooky actions, the magic words, having been supposedly exorcised, psychoanalysis unconsciously mutates these like a side effect through the idea originally called "transference-love" and eventually simply "transference." But characterizing transference as the symptomatic remainder, the return of the hypnotic repressed, that resulted from the anxious rebranding that produced psychoanalysis is little more than an admission of the resilience of the ethological need to depend on one another. "What else is hypnotic suggestion," Borch-Jacobsen writes, "if not a 'bond' that inextricably mingles the 'self' with the 'other'—a bond that transcends all (op)position of identity or identities and that must therefore be characterized as a non-bond? Hypothesis: Is it not this undifferentiated, indeterminate (undialectizable) sameness that Freud rejects when he repudiates hypnosis?"[9]

The bond that is not a bond (having, at this level, insufficient separateness for a bond to bond) manifests at the beta level of psychical life, the specifically clinical version of which is the living frame, the *vínculo*, of psychoanalysis, the way it weaves us together. And perhaps more than the dependence it fosters, an aspect of hypnosis that is more or less retained in psychoanalysis (and that dogged Freud until the end of his life), it is the very muddiness of this dimension of experience that compelled Freud to reject this foundation, as he did repeatedly, out of what reads insistently as a kind of anxiety about insufficient separateness (what Michael Balint would later redeem as a "harmonious mix-up"),[10] which predominates as an anxiety in Kleinian theory. But even if this sameness in undialectizable in its own mode (in which there can be no dialectic), it nevertheless represents, at a wider zoom, one pole of the dialectic between sameness and difference, between bringing together and breaking down—in other words, between hypnosis and analysis. The most crucial dimension of the model of the living frame—bypassing the activity of the mind to establish shared, embodied engagement closer to the level of the body—may in some sense be a return to theorizing the hypnotic dimension of clinical experience (which after all has never been absent in clinical practice) from which psychoanalysis emerged in the first place. What is induced, and must be induced in the treatment situation, is the peculiar state of hypnosis-in-body-time, Abraham's rhythmized "fascinated consciousness," which can be contrasted with the zombie trance of a traumatized, dissociated, colonized body produced by modern life. Induction is an alternative (or original) therapeutic that reestablishes the sensory conditions in which the psyche-somatically intact thinking of psychoanalysis could never otherwise take place.

Indeed, an absence of the somnambulistic bond can leave the treatment devoid of the vital, shared connection, so that it starts to sound and feel, as Bion famously formulated, more like talking about something rather than doing or *living* it (and thereby retaining only a distant or ambiguous relevance to real life). The somnambulistic bond of hypnosis enhances therapeutic action by relieving the participants of the onerous burden of excessively boundaried subjectivity as one starts to become lived through by an other, an actor through whom a character comes to life, a dancer through whom the voltage of experience courses itself as movement, a musician through whom a melody can begin to sing itself, the form of going-on-being that Ogden once described as "all verb, devoid of a subject" (to interrupt going-on-being is to become a subject),[11] the very process of *subjection*—or, in Borch-Jacobsen's coinage, "suggection"—itself. "Once we are dealing with neither a question of recollection (as Freud thought) nor one of narrative speech (as Lacan would have it)," he writes in his most clinically relevant formulation of this history, "Hypnosis in Psychoanalysis,"

> should we not attribute the healing process, if not to hypnosis proper, at least to the mimesis that characterized it? Wasn't it this trance, this forceful invasion of the "subject" by another identity, that was decisive? If so, this would mean that from the outset Freud led analytical therapy down the wrong path by basing it on recollection and narration. This idea is actually not so surprising if we bear in mind that the "psychotherapies" (or, better yet, the "sociotherapies") that preceded psychoanalysis—from shamanistic techniques to "animal magnetism," not to mention exorcism of the possessed—have always included, in one form or another, an element of trance or disappearance of self.[12]

Borch-Jacobsen is perhaps less than fair when implying that Freud, whatever path he led his therapy down, forgot that the decisive mechanism of the healing process is not simply recalling or narrating the events of one's life but the conduction of experience that occurs during this accompanied narration. Certainly by the time he wrote "Observations on Transference-Love" in 1915, Freud had rediscovered the therapeutics of the trance, which he now named "erotic transference," a crucial course correction that is diminished in Borch-Jacobsen's emphasis on Freud's metapsychology over his clinical work, to say nothing (literally) of the work of Freud's followers. There is little if any mention in the whole of Borch-Jacobsen's scholarship of how psychoanalysis evolved and of how new models took into account, implicitly if not systematically, the non-narrative dimension of the process, for example, anything like working *in* the transference, in the mode of what John Steiner called "analyst-centered interpretation" or what intersubjectivists have conceptualized as co-creation and enactment, let alone what field theorists have called transformations in hallucinosis. As perhaps there well should not be. But Borch-Jacobsen is on solid ground in critiquing Freud's fantasy that by moving away from the discipline of hypnosis in which he was originally trained, he would bring the collaborative, dyadic division of labor between hypnotized and hypnotist, self and other, within the auspices of the patient's own intrapsychic world, from living through the hypnotist-other to living one's history in the presence of an other, as Freud believed hysterics were unconsciously wont to do. As the analyst and historian George Makari has noted, clinical hypnosis was itself a drawing out of hysterical "auto-hypnosis" into a dyadic configuration;[13] in turn, the Freudian development could be considered an attempt to "transfer" this collaboration into an intrapsychic, autohypnotic fascination within the patient, a fascination with the otherness within the self.

But by focusing so much on the intrapsychic, Freud in fact turned away from the fundamental nature of our primordial inwovenness with one another, leaving what he theorized as "the Unconscious" stranded on an island of self-enclosure. By burying alive the transpersonal dimension of hypnotic mimesis, Freud condemned a now isolated, permanently discontented ego to a life sentence of civilizing sociality (much in the tradition of Rousseau's social contract) in order to achieve what he famously called "ordinary unhappiness." In a partial correction of this error, Laplanche reminded psychoanalysis that there is no state of nature, no noble savage, outside the group, that one's inner world was always irreducibly an other, outer, *social* world, a repository of archived, backlogged, enigmatic messages to be sifted through and translated through communal and consensual forms of understanding. This archive, in Laplanche's account, far from being an isolated silo or bunker of forbidden wishes, is always (in health) an in-progress conversation with other human beings in which the subject is forever trying to get more of the gist. If transference, in the final analysis, is essentially a return of hypnosis in psychoanalytic form, it also potentiates, in contrast to hypnosis, the transference *of* hypnosis—transferred from the commanding injunction of the analyst to an inspired fascination with the enigmatic message of the other, now refound, in residence, within the psyche, as the message in need of translation. As Laplanche points out in *Freud and the Sexual*, Freud wrote that "in order to remove one stimulus, it seems necessary to adduce a second one at the same spot."[14] At its most inductive (and least colonizing), psychoanalysis is *adductive* in exactly this way, infusing enigmatic fascination in the same spot—through the same portal, the same "mass bond"—where hypnosis once required pure docility, pure submission. The well-known analytic practice of abstaining from direct suggestions could be reconsidered in this light as the analyst's fostering a kind of therapeutic hesitation, a pause, a breather, an inspired thoughtfulness through which to catch up on the backlog of received transmissions to which one has been meaning to get around (let alone those one has been meaning to avoid), providing a sufficient slowing down of the endless influx of tantalizing mystery enough to literally make sense of it. Psychoanalysis transforms the hypnotist's suggestion—to do or not to do something—by gesturing toward the infinite possibilities of experiencing the world, of that in which it may be worthwhile to be interested, toward what the world might mean. These modified suggestions, better known as interpretations, are therefore always suggestions to interpret oneself, to read one's dreams as a form of life (and one's life as a form of dreaming), to feel one's life more as if it were a digestive process than a diegesis, more music than story, by simply saying (and hearing) what happens to be on one's mind.

But even a purely free-associative practice does not elude Borch-Jacobsen's skepticism of its being less suggestive or artificial than hypnosis—"Nothing," that is, "*except the hypothesis of the unconscious.*"[15]

There is apparently no metapsychological way—at least not one that can withstand Borch-Jacobsen's critique—to distinguish having an unconscious from following a suggestion. Borch-Jacobsen is never dissuaded from the idea that there is always a hypnotic remainder, a reminder of hypnosis; that whether you call it faith, trance, hypnosis, psychoanalysis, transference, or the unconscious, there is always a buy-in, a premise to accept, a legal fiction; that there is always a gap for the uninducted to jump, a node of Ranvier, in order for the trance to take hold and therefore always a question about how to jump it, how we get to the other side. So in order to think psychoanalysis beyond its anxiously hypnotic history toward its next dialectical (r)evolution, toward and away from its past and future, we may need theoretical models that do more than rebrand the problem, reduplicating the symptom in the theory, under the guise of a new magic word. We may need forms of experience that get us even closer to the terrain in which these gaps have never existed, in which "self" and "other" have never been meaningful terms. We may need models that inflect at the limit of difference and spiral back toward its opposite pole, toward syncretics, of *Bildung* and undifferentiation, of vibration, unison, resonance—music.

II

How many times has the word "hypnotic" been used to describe a groove? One of the most immediately organizing responses one has to a piece of music has to do with whether it *moves* the body, not just literally causing sensations—for example, vibrating the eardrums—but whether it resonates with what Gilles Deleuze once called an "secret vibration," a way of being musical in time.[16] Some pieces of music, in other words, make us move, animating the psyche-soma by reorganizing its relation to time. As the musicologist Robert Fink explains in *Repeating Ourselves*, his book-length history of minimalism, disco, and the advertising industry in the 1970s, pieces of music that are based on repetitive figures potentiate the occupation of time in a way that a Beethoven symphony never could; by atomizing the interplay of tension and release into repeated, miniature cells of musical material, these contemporary styles and genres assemble repeated iterations of frustration and satisfaction into a nonteleological continuity—"multiple orgasms," as Fink suggests in his analysis of "Love to Love You" (1975), Donna Summer's totemic disco classic.[17] To be carried along and through this ecstatic, collective continuousness is to be plugged into, possessed, and *enchanted* by the pure suggestion of musical experience. Which we always need to be—the question is never *whether* but simply *to which* musical suggestions we will be induced, by which music we will find ourselves moved. (If Nietzsche was floating in the airwaves of Freud's formative years, psychoanalysis may be precisely the tragedy that was born of the spirit of Nietzsche's music.) The need for enchantment, in other words, is inherent and natural, but which "chants" move us to dance (or leave us cold, unmoved) is always historically and culturally determined, never universal or given. "Enchantment" (or "en-song-ment") is the state of living in music, being lived through by music, identification through vibration, musical hypnosis. "Music captivates the listener," Erik Wallrup writes in *Being Musically Attuned*,

> And when the listener is captured by music, there seems to be nothing else in the world—the music is world. This musical moment is ecstatic but may take place under ordinary circumstances, not to say prosaic conditions. A melody in the background music on the radio can tune us in unexpectedly when we are busy tidying the house: it can be intimate music like a *moment musical* by Schubert, a bittersweet *cazone napolitana* from the 1950s or just something unknown. Everything is changed in a moment. We are being attuned.[18]

For Wallrup, attunement is, for better and worse, a form of psychical captivity. Music not only moves but *tunes* us, calibrating the psyche-soma to an entire world of rhythmic and harmonic properties, the atmosphere we require to live and breathe as humans. (The Greeks called the gods the "attuning ones.") Music therefore has a double-edged potential: Being captivated by music—our deep susceptibility to being "attuned," our need for attunement—is something that does not always enhance the project of finding our own embodied idiom, but it may also colonize our relation to ourselves. We hardly need rely on Colwyn Trevarthen's tender footage of mothers and infants making music together to remind us of the foundational role of an originary musicalizing enchantment that occurs between parents and children in the earliest and (hopefully) subsequent stages of life. But the obverse is equally apparent and affecting; without this hypnotic form of engagement, human bodies are left perilously disconnected from the musical register, from the vibrations of living together. Viewed from the perspective of social history, may we suppose that one of the reasons psychoanalysis came into being, and perhaps its main claim for continuing clinical relevance, is the challenge of what Weber called the disenchantment of the world? The individual disrupted by trauma is torn away from the embodied domain of shared music. The psyche-soma flinches at trauma, losing the beat. To be dissociated, dismembered, is to be disenchanted. And when the society that otherwise keeps the music going *loses* its music, it leaves each member dislocated, deworlded. Disenchantment in the world leaves the individual dissociated, devitalized, demoralized, and desperate for the music to resume.

So our need for music makes us vulnerable, and we often end up being taken over by an other's music, which we may have to protest by refusing to hear new sounds or by taking refuge in our own echo chambers of reified, repetitive music. How has psychoanalysis viewed this powerful phenomenon of ongoing attunement at the musical level? While disavowing the enormous power of music in the ontological reality of human being, psychoanalysis has also implicitly recognized something like the need for enchantment in psychical life, though often simultaneously pathologizing its manifestations. We can find some reference to the presubjective, mimetic domain in every psychoanalytic school of thought without having to look too hard, going back at least to Freud's unusually mystified (and perhaps horrified) reference to the prehistory of the maternal and his conspicuous dismissal of the "oceanic feeling" as a regression to primary narcissism, if not back even further to Breuer's account of "hypnoid states," which he considered pathological. For Klein, the yearning for fusion through projective identification, which may be a need to return to attunement, is also rendered pathological; on a less pathologizing note, there are phenomena like the transitional in Winnicott and his idea of necessary "omnipotence," Bion's "O," Ogden's notion of the autistic-contiguous, and the contemporary Italian notion of the field. So it seems that psychoanalysis has always known about the need for enchantment because of the ways in which it has been conflicted about it and determined to delimit and contain it in a developmental framework. And it comes by this conflict (and its various strategies and scrambles for containing it) honestly. There is a good reason why psychoanalysis has been ambivalent about, if not terrified, of enchantment, which is that it's overwhelmingly powerful and potentially extremely hazardous. Why? Because at bottom the human being *seeks and needs* induction. We are thus radically suggestible and susceptible to influence and in-form-ation (and possibly ex-form-ation) by the environment, a "dethroning of the ego" that Freud could never accept. Our need for enchantment renders us essentially and permanently vulnerable to being taken over, and the crucial distinction between whether we are malevolently exploited or benevolently induced into culture is harrowingly historical, a matter of what world into which one is born.

Emphasizing the inductive dimension of the clinical situation allows us to see how psychoanalysis works like other hypnotic, enchanting, attuning, rhythmizing forms of life that tap into and depend upon the primordial power of the mimetic—group and social formations that underpin and shape the sense of being and belonging (which can be perverted and exploited in ways too numerous to name here). As one of many practices of inductive enchantment, the actual work of psychoanalysis lies not in its discursive, rational, and object-relational dimensions alone but depends upon the effectiveness with which it weaves the individual into the collective, depends, in other words, on work that takes place beyond the individual transferences. We have something like an instinctive need to interpellated; being dissociated is to be dis-sociated from the *socii*, the tribe, that is uniquely capable of meeting this need. This means that the analyst has a special responsibility to conduct analysis with *a very strong ethical and moral position on what a human being is*—an *ethos*-dependent creature, a creature in need of an *ethos*.

While this need for interpellation may have a phylogenetic foundation, the specific content of its fulfillment is always grounded in the particular, historical content provided by our place and time and our unique cultural and personal experience. And while the practice of psychoanalysis is inevitably that of conducting an *ethos*, psychoanalysis has shied away from or has had difficulty in articulating this crucial aspect of clinical work and has avoided it in part by claiming scientific objectivity and neutrality. We are not doctors practicing psycho-orthopedics; we are more like missionaries, artists, and soldiers in an ethical-cultural-existential slugfest. At our best we are liberators in tactical formation, holding ground against the colonizers, but we are always promoting our *ethos*, one way of being in the world among others, and we are saying ours is better than many others.

Promoting any particular formation, leading any dance, is always a transmission of a way of being, to suggest a way of behaving not only by delimiting a set of rules (to be internalized as what Freud will refer to as the superego) but also by constructing what Freud referred to as the "ego ideal," a term that, as Borch-Jacobsen writes in "Ecce Ego," connotes in the original German not only "the ideal agency constituted within the ego (the ideal formation, as one would speak of a 'cloud formation'), but also the way in which this instance is constituted (the formation of the ideal, the *Bildung des Ideals* . . .)."[19] By constituting and demonstrating ways of being that nourish and express our psyche-somatic potential in a shared world of fellow humans, the musical *ethos* of any given culture not only makes these forms available for purposes of mimesis but also induces each new member into the practice of model building, ideal forming, identification. (*Bildung* is also at the center of Gadamer's argument in his classic text *Truth and Method*, anchoring his key ontological claim that we are not born but *formed* into humans.)[20]

This inductive function of the ego ideal sets it apart from its lookalike, the superego. While the superego judges and commands at a symbolic remove, the ego ideal infuses the ego, inspiring formation through mimesis, learning how to learn. Where the superego prohibits and possibly also threatens pain and punishment, the ego ideal guides and eggs on, is affirmative and aspirational; it is a "positive injunction," as Janine Chasseguet-Smirgel puts it in her *The Ego Ideal*.[21] The superego tells you what to do; the ego ideal helps you find-create a repertoire of thinkability, letting you think the ideas are yours. The ego ideal forms a bridge between shared and individual movement, a guidance system for exploring what moves each of us, an affirmative feeling of grip or rightness that potentiates each individual perspective. And while the superegoic cloud formations bound by morality and guilt may have the coherent borders, the sculptural definition, of a cumulonimbus, the formations of the ego ideal are always more iterative, stratocumulative, bending toward a more perfect union that is achieved only virtually, in the very patterns of its repetition.

Both the superego and the ego ideal are vulnerable to tyranny, though in different ways. We have long since been living in an age in which the ego ideal has been co-opted and exploited by the forces of commodification and mechanization, disguised as the virtues of a good life. (Psychotherapies, chillingly agglomerated and referred to nowadays as "the mental health industry," are no exception; Winnicott wrote presciently that "those who have spent their lives doing psychoanalysis must scream out for sanity against the insane belief in surface phenomena that characterizes computerized investigations of human beings.")[22] But it is only in recent decades that this mechanical coup has become exponentially more pervasive through the digitization of almost every aspect of daily living. By confusing the process of education with the content of what it aims to teach, our opportunities for apprenticeship and cultural learning have been reduced and impoverished by forms of automation that, whatever they achieve in reliability and efficiency in the transmission of information, lack the sensual texture of being *presented* by one human to another. ("Information," Han writes, "has no scent.")[23] The nuance of *how* we do things becomes neutralized by the averaging reductivity of so-called best practices, while the array of *why* we do things is reduced to its most primitive and greedy justifications for achieving a fragile sense of health and fleeting vitality. The erotic qualities that keep our psychophysical molecules charged are tragically missing in action.

How much humanity is lost in this devolution of cultural practice? While so much information is being collected on human beings, are we in fact losing a deeper understanding of how learning happens, of how human beings are built? In Fonagy's formulation of "emulative learning," humans (and their primate ancestors) reproduce the behavior of their elders not because they understand the intention behind it but because behavior is perceived as a kind of demonstration of how to act upon the world. These demonstrations, which Fonagy calls "ostensive cues," create an additional byproduct of the learning situation, "epistemic trust." He suggests that we are wired for this trust, endowed biologically with an "epistemic highway"—though he offers no model of a post-Cartesian, *ontological* substrate for this highway, how the highway gets constructed—along which this trustful learning can conduct itself, but so too are we wired to barricade ourselves from the excitation of these transmissions, to protect ourselves from overstimulation. Fonagy's diagram of learning inverts our more common notion of what trust is; we don't simply learn from our trusted sources, but in fact we learn *because* we have already been induced into this trust, trust that is simply one word to describe being moved by music—enchanted, hypnotized.

If you look at psychoanalysis from the vantage point of this model, it changes many things, beginning with the implications of the mimetic basis of learning and trust for our notion of lifespan development. The mimetic model of emulative learning engenders a temporal mode that differs from a traditional notion of a lifespan trajectory, which privileges a process of individuation as the ego gradually opposes itself to the group; in the mode of enchantment, the emphasis is less on accomplishment of self-definition, the edifying journey (like a symphony or a pop song) to the higher plane, and more on the reduction of difference, on nonteleological continuity (like the *ostinati* of a Steve Reich piece or a Nile Rodgers set). Clinically, this shift in perspective away from the task of getting or keeping a patient on the track of a normative realization of progress (for example, a notion of achieving the "depressive position") redirects the therapeutic task toward inducing habits for nourishing and sustaining capacities for dreaming and going-on-being. The psychoanalyst (not unlike the musician) may be in an unusually good position to present this mode of being, devoted as the analyst is to attentively, exclusively, and reliably drawing out these nascent capacities in one's fellow human. If in learning the music of going-on-being in the world the first piece the patient learns to play (once the beat is set), the "Heart and Soul" of psychoanalysis, is how to behave as if one took seriously the notion of having an unconscious, to speak as if being spoken to (or through), to play, or at least to try to play, one's free associations at the tempo of the frame, then the analyst's musicality is the at the heart and soul of the procedure.

The steep learning curve of incorporating the unconscious, through the body, into one's idea of oneself can, in more extreme cases of trauma and dissociation, become a sheer cliff. It is not uncommon, upon beginning one's psychoanalysis, in other words, to be bad at it, and one can hardly begrudge the uninitiated for not being fluent at solving such an ancient riddle. "How to obey the demand to be unconscious without being conscious of it?" Borch-Jacobsen asks:

> We find here, in another form, the objection Sartre (1943) once raised to the Freudian idea of repression: how to repress an idea or a desire without knowing what one is repressing? For that, Sartre said, one needs a lot of "bad faith." One needs, in other words, to pretend one doesn't know, to simulate unconsciousness, to split oneself into an actor who knows and a role which doesn't.[24]

To be consciously in communication with one's unconscious, to be musical in the context of psychoanalysis, is to be good at the particular kind of faith that simulates having an unconscious, faith that the notes will come, that the muse will sing, if one is faithful enough to listen. In this sense "bad faith"—like "bad dancing" or being "bad in bed"—is not an indictment of an entire discipline but rather a designation for its *being done* badly, inadequately conducted, or simply done before one has the hang of it. (Or perhaps after one has lost an innate capacity; Winnicott was the great philosopher of the difference between being a child and "being a child.") What Trevarthen interprets as infants "conducting" their mothers' lullabies in perfect time (aside from being consistently ahead of the beat, an errant detail he rationalizes away too quickly) may be better understood as what conducting looks like when you're still learning how to do it, when you're struggling to get into time. (A great conductor does not simply preempt the beat but rather potentiates, paradoxically, its precise articulation with an implicit anticipation of the music to come.)

But even this bad faith can go a long way. There are two reasons, in this model of learning, for being bad at something: having a bad teacher or insufficient practice. The difference between good faith and bad faith, in other words, is almost entirely a question of apprenticeship, of learning, which means it is a question of helping someone tolerate being bad at something (which everyone is at everything, of course, before they're good at it). A model of development that values giving it up for the groove, losing oneself on the dance floor, implicitly downplays and interrogates the bias in psychoanalytic theory toward mastery, knowledge, and expert individuation, and the formalization that produces it, across all aspects of psychoanalytic theory and technique. Emphasizing the role of faith in psychoanalysis (as Bion did), the importance of encouraging the patient to listen for something that will speak back, for the music that will carry you, that is actually there, calls into question many post-Freudian notions of psychical development, psychical structures, and contents, including the roles and behavior of analyst and patient and the trajectory of treatment (especially termination). Viewed as a musical process of enchantment and faith, many of the formalizations made popular during the era of ego psychology are revealed as dubious and reified forms—even if formalization itself remains indispensable. (Formalization, too, must go on being.) As Bion elucidated in the container/contained theory, all forms of formalization tend toward reification, the deadening of what they were bringing to life, robbing actual experience of its truth and vitality, and therefore the satisfied understanding must be exploded in favor of new forms, new music. This ongoing formalization process is the true imperative; adhering to a given form for too long privileges the certainty and limiting function of what Levinas once termed "totality" over what he called the "infinity" of the spiritual, reducing the novelty of musical development to the humdrum of the same old song and dance.[25]

In this sense repression, alongside its Laplanchean definition as a "failure of translation," could be considered a *failure to give form*, a seizing up of formalization. What is rather good even about bad faith is its persistent pursuit of the new, the next, its ongoing approximation of the ever-present limit of conscious thought, the asymptote of translation, the horizon of what is always yet to come, already on its way. As it obstructs translation and formalization, repression is nevertheless at the cutting edge, the threshold, of bad faith getting better; if anything, in fact, repression lets us hang on unconsciously to material that, thanks to its enchanting and enlivening (as in, its sexual) nature, may someday be transformed for psychical use, for the elaboration of the self, to bring lived experience into psychical life.

In fact, what is truly bad about bad faith is always the gap it can't quite close between self and other sufficiently to erase enough difference, to engender enough sameness, that the genuinely new and different can begin to emerge and affirm itself. As Deleuze posits in his early work *Difference and Repetition*, sameness (which often takes the form of repetition) is always the fundamental precondition of difference:

The world is neither finite nor infinite as representation would have it.... *Re*-petition opposes *re*-presentation: the prefix changes its meaning, since in the one case difference is said only in relation the identical, while in the other it is the univocal which is said of the different.... The ultimate element of repetition is the disparate [*dispars*], which stands opposed to the identity of representation.[26]

True difference only ever emerges not, as one may expect, in simple opposition to the same (which merely "*re*-presents" the identical, invoking it in order to oppose it) but rather as a "univocal" expression of itself, grounded directly in the traditions and rituals of a wider chorus conducting vibrations that precede any individual variation and enchant each member-voice to sing out something genuinely new: "In the theatre of repetition, we experience pure forces, dynamic lines in space which act without intermediary upon the spirit, and link it directly with nature and history, with a language which speaks before words, with gestures which develop before organised bodies, with masks before faces, with spectres and phantoms before characters."[27]

In the theater of repetition that is the analytic frame, the dream-work of the unconscious is rendered as the art of becoming oneself, the work of drawing out one's creative expression by finding out what one finds oneself repeating (what the philosopher Peter Sloterdijk calls our convictions). The mimetic mask that Sartre regards as "bad faith" is in fact the repetition at the foundation of all difference, the precondition of differentiation itself. For Deleuze (as for Winnicott) there is no originary "true self" prior to or outside these conditions.[28] Repetition in "bad faith" is the only condition from which the rhythm or habit of living ever forms itself, the beta-level ground of thingness from which one's own idiomatic possibilities could only ever eventually emerge. In this sense, all cultural practice begins in "bad faith"—we listen to music or go to the theater or start a book or enter psychoanalysis first and foremost *badly*—which is to say, in an aspirational yet unintegrated mimetic impression of someone else. For Sartre, "bad faith" is a conflict, a refusal to choose one's role or fate freely and fully, born out of resistance to existential freedom, resulting in the "fake"—as opposed to an unavoidable deficit, the beginning stage of acquiring a skill through immersion, through doing as others do, through learning *from* experience (as Bion put it, rather than learning *about* experience), resulting in the faking-it-'til-you-make-it or perhaps simply 'til it makes (or remakes) you. "We learn nothing from those who say: 'Do as I do,'" Deleuze writes. "Our only teachers are those who tell us to 'do with me.' . . . In other words, there is no ideo-motivity, only sensory-motivity."[29] We do with our teachers, over and over, repeating (lit. "seeking again"), until the repetition of identity yields the dis-parity of the new.

We can, of course, only take so much of repetition before we lose our minds, which we—periodically, regularly, rhythmically—desperately need to do. But this need to be unburdened of the demands of the always-busy mind cannot be accomplished alone: If, as Winnicott has shown, "mind" is fundamentally a kind of allergic response and adaptation to environmental impingement on psyche-somatic continuity, then it would require an environmental version of continuity, a world beat, to relieve the mind of its protective function, of its otherwise unceasing labor. To be induced into hypnotic fascination is to be subjected to the madness of repetition to the point of mental-muscular failure, to the point of letting oneself go, such that the elements that constitute that former self can be revitalized by shared sensation and refreshed into a configuration that molds itself around the present of what is actually happening. The projector becomes a camera, the record an instrument, the citadel a city.

The clinical question, then, becomes whether the sensory-motivic, mimetic ritual provided through the auspices of the frame echoes sufficiently with one's inner vibration to effect, recalling Woolf's evocative phrase, "this wave in the mind," along which one's own style can catch the surf. For Borch-Jacobsen, this effecting of selfness is nothing other than "the birth of the subject,"

> perhaps not a repetition of the birth event, but birth as repetition, or as primal identification: in it the subject comes into being (always anew: this birth is constantly repeated) as an echo or duplicate of the other, in a sort of lag with respect to its own origin and its own identity. An insurmountable lag, then, since it is a constitutive one, and one that without any doubt constitutes the entire "unconscious" of the subject, prior to any memory and any repression.[30]

Despite the almost complete absence of references to Laplanche's work in Borch-Jacobsen's comprehensive critique of psychoanalysis, there exist points of close intersection and resonance at several points in their writings. Laplanche's theory of the enigma at the heart of subjectivity, which he attributed to the encounter between the speechless infant and the speaking adult, is evoked at every turn in Borch-Jacobsen's work, and Laplanche's account of sexuality accords with and elaborates Borch-Jacobsen's description of the birth of the subject: It is precisely when one is lagging optimally, *legato* (as opposed to left behind), translating the enigma well enough, that the lag functions as a driver of the fascinated persistence, the slow-but-steady, the trance state, of being born as a subject. Through the repetition of primal identification, we become mimetic echoes of hypnotic rhythms, variations on shared themes, reverberating as individual subjects to the vibrations of communal music.

The absence of Laplanchean sexuality in this account may in fact indicate a meaningful elision, a significant navel at the center of the psychoanalytic attempt to repress and redream hypnosis in terms of the "somnambulistic passion" of transference. Sexuality, in other words, is the passion that the enchanted subject must never thoroughly think, no matter how diligently or generatively one tries to think it, because it is born beyond the frontier of necessary difference, beyond the temporal structure of generationality, beyond the limit of thinkability—in the domain, in other words, of incest. We pay an unthinkable price, suffer the irreducible lag of intergenerational (sexual) trauma, even as we are born and reborn through its crucial partition, its irreducible gap. Of course, even Freud, our great philosopher of loss, who as a physician and cultural figure filled in so much of the blank left by repressed sexuality, dreaming psychoanalysis into being, was perhaps too mercifully repressed, too appropriately afraid of losing his mind, to actually *think* the object of his own sexuality—though he did produce the near-psychotic vision, a nightmarishly primordial crowd (which he called the "primal horde"), as a fevered image at the heart of his sexual theory. Freud's reworking of phylogenetic history as his own book of genesis in *Totem and Taboo* leaves to his future students that strangest of Freudian assertions: to endlessly contemplate, to finish dreaming.[31] The story of a horde of sons murdering and quite literally devouring their father viscerally evokes, of course, the indigestion, the insufficient metabolism, the inadequate dream-work, of another subject on which Freud simply wanted to hear nothing further, the topic of exactly what he knew would happen when his life came to an end, when he would no longer be able continue holding himself such that he would never have to surrender to anyone else to do the work potentiated by the true book of genesis of the psychoanalytic revolution, the work that he only ever trusted himself to do—

Interpret his dreams.

III

It was there, inside the song, that you had permission to lose yourself and not be wrong.
—OCEAN VUONG, ON EARTH WE'RE BRIEFLY GORGEOUS

We discover in the hypnotic rhythms of the beta world a recurring triumvirate, each of which we have mentioned—in-duction, se-duction, con-duction—but can now recognize for their common element, their *-duction*, a leading, shaping, forming function. Each of the three elements works as a unique conduit along which libidinal energy travels, wanting, as a law of physics, to stay in motion. Each *-duction* occurs before and after the other; each is required, but none is given. As we saw earlier, Freud understood *rapport* as essential to myelinating any psychomusical network; one rarely starts to like a song, let alone an artist (or an analyst), that one has already decided to hate or been too injured to risk giving a chance, to be open to, to let in, to channel. When *rapport*, that most fundamental of umbilical links, has (as Bion famously elaborated) been attacked, pushed to capacity, or unplugged altogether, a sufficient counterforce, a pull, may be required to induce enough (bad) faith to give it a try. And even in the most faithless, hopeless of circumstances, the best practice for getting something going is always a form of seduction—despite the best efforts of his detractors and, consequently, Freud himself to suggest otherwise. If the suggestion of widespread, incestuous abuse made the seduction theory too scandalous to sustain, it nevertheless may have captured something crucial about the far-reaching power of seduction, in evidence nowhere more than in Freud's most seductive suggestion, his magic words: "*das Unbewusste*," the unconscious. To believe that one is moved and spoken by the un-be-wiser-ed forces of psychical life—that we are always responding to more than we understand, that we are always living more life beyond the frontier of consciousness—is to simulate an endlessly interesting world. Surrendering to that which happens through oneself yet outside one's control—enduring the *petit mort* of the self one thinks one is in order to transcend one's previously established form—is what Breuer and Freud (Borch-Jacobsen reminds us), way back in the days of hypnosis, originally called *catharsis*, a term Freud returns to in *An Autobiographical Study* in 1925. Freud characterizes catharsis, Borch-Jacobsen notes, not as a form of remembering the past but as a current experience, "*in statu nascendi*, in the state of being born," a form of radical and original presence, of presentation. Catharsis "is neither telling a story nor representing a past event as past":

> It is, as Freud and Breuer also write, reliving (*wiederdurchleben*) the event, with all the intensity of the first time, by repeating it in the present. If we add that the events thus enacted ("tragedized," says Breuer) were highly doubtful (as Freud realized later), and if we go on to say that these reexperienced events and their corresponding emotions occurred under hypnosis (that is, in a state of absence from self), then we can understand that Freud's and Breuer's hysterics remembered nothing, had nothing to tell; they were playing, living, and acting roles, not so much by means of fantasy representation (*Vorstellung*) as by "acting out" (*Agieren*).[33]

To repeat is not to remember but to relive; to fall ill, in this model, to suffer from one's reminiscences, from inadequate repression, from formal failure, is to suffer from insufficient presence, from re-presentation that does not do justice to the original. The great discovery of hypnosis, preserved in psychoanalysis, was the curative effect of fuller being, bearing together what could not originally be borne alone, now born for the first time.

Freud, by his own admission, could not bear music, at least not as a form of pleasure. "I may say at once that I am no connoisseur in art, but simply a layman," he wrote in "The Moses of Michelangelo":

> Nevertheless, works of art do exercise a powerful effect on me, especially those of literature and sculpture, less often of painting. This has

occasioned me, when I have been contemplating such things, to spend a long time before them trying to apprehend them in my own way, i.e. to explain to myself what their effect is due to. Wherever I cannot do this, as for instance with music, I am almost incapable of obtaining any pleasure. Some rationalistic, or perhaps analytic, turn of mind in me rebels against being moved by a thing without knowing why I am thus affected and what it is that affects me.[34]

Freud says he could feel himself rebelling against music because his mind could not accommodate how affected he felt by it. Music made him feel too much. One of the ironies of the story of Freud, the man who gave us psychoanalysis, is that he never had an analyst, at least not one that could help him feel more feeling than his own "rationalistic, and perhaps analytic, turn of mind" would permit, someone to help him surrender to music. When Nietzsche suggested that tragedy was born out of the spirit of music, he may have been alluding to the catalytic effect that the presentation of music has (as opposed to the representation of fantasy) in making things feel-able, in tragedizing one's history, in making oneself a *conductor*, as opposed to exclusively an insulator, of the world's energy. And in order to let that energy do what it wants to, to jointly go-on-being, electrifying the psyche-soma in concert with the rest of the human world, one must periodically relinquish one's previously held form, release oneself sufficiently to be reorganized by new music, new concentrations of the body, as Marion Milner once put it, and the new mind waves they effect.[35] "The loss of consciousness, the '*absence*', in a hysterical attack," Freud wrote,

> is derived from the fleeting but unmistakable lapse of consciousness which is observable at the climax of every intense sexual satisfaction, including auto-erotic ones. . . . The so-called "hypnoid states"—*absences during day-dreaming*—, which are so common in hysterical subjects, show the same origin. The mechanism of these *absences* is comparatively simple. All the subject's attention is concentrated to begin with on the course of the process of satisfaction; with the occurrence of the satisfaction, the whole of this cathexis of attention is suddenly removed, so that there ensues a momentary void in her consciousness.[36]

What is revealed as healing or curative in this quote is the ability to lose oneself when one is sufficiently satisfied. Might we say, then, that psychoanalysis, at its most transformative, induces the hypnoid state that constitutes an essentially needed experience of satisfaction—one that involves the meeting of a most fundamental, erotic need, the relief from subjectivity, the moment of zero gravity, the hang time, the *absence*—through which going-on-being, previously stuck, can then proceed? Perhaps in such states, the isolation of too-well-formed subjectivity, running under one's own power, can be surrendered for a seat on the train, guided by a conductor. Bion called this process learning from experience (and later, transformations in O); Freud called it unbinding (and, later, mourning). In both cases, the self is reorganized to accommodate a fresh experience of the world ushered in by what Bion called catastrophic change, the kind of experience or psychical adjustment that changes the world as one knows it. (All transformative psychic change is catastrophic.) And navigating one's journey through these world transitions is never a solo act but is on the contrary always an interval of maximum reliance and sinking in with the available forms of companioning, borrowing from charts and chords laid out by others, charting the course of going on living.

If, as Adam Phillips frequently reminds us, Winnicott defined madness as the need to be believed, perhaps sanity is the need to be *relieved* of the strain of individuality, re*lived* through festivals of repetition, through mimetic identification. We need to have faith (however badly at first) that there is a way out of the torture, the sheer electrocution of unwovenness, of what Freud called "helplessness" (*Hilflosigkeit*), faith that someone knows how to work this thing, can show us how to go on being in a body. If hypnosis provided one strategy for compelling patients, who found themselves at the mercy of the demands and refusals of their bodies, to transfer the inner conflict of their predicament to a more collaborative endeavor—now at the mercy of the demands and refusals of the hypnotist: "Listen to my voice . . . Do as I say . . . You will not remember . . ."—Freud's new technology was meant to provide a lighter touch, suggesting not *what* to do but *how* to do it, not to do what one's hypnotist says but to listen to oneself like an analyst does. (Of course, Freud's new technology actually, and crucially, *abandoned* touch, jettisoning physical contact so as to mitigate the very sort of seduction that Freud invented psychoanalysis to cure.) There was limited value, Freud believed, in exploiting people's need for one another in order to literally *make* them feel better (or to feel more like their doctor believed they should feel); it worked better, Freud discovered, to induce patients, rhythmically, into a listening practice, a sustainable form of curiosity, that could forever replenish itself.[37] And through this kind of attentive listening, one would be released from the tyranny of unconducted electricity, relieved of the angular energies of the disruptive drives, and free to conduct what Adam Phillips (sampling John Stuart Mill) calls experiments in living, to come up with your own stuff. (The true gift of mimetic identification, inspired in the mode of *rapport*, is freedom.) When Laplanche said that infantile sexuality was surely present in whatever people told you as a child to stop doing (what is "condemned by the adult"), he was implicitly saying that infantile sexuality is what people couldn't stop watching you do, what was always being kept at a specular remove, unable to fit into culture, in need of more apprenticeship, more practice, to weave into a personal idiom. (What will become adult sexuality, in this model, is nothing but this fascination with the as yet untranslated, driving the project of one's life.) And at every developmental node on the trajectory of one's life, those fellow humans who present a way for libidinal energy to be grooved through the psyche-soma, who demonstrate a sense of how to do the right thing, the thing that fits, the thing that works, at the right time (what Freud called "tact")—become fascinating to the point of hypnotic.

If hypnosis and seduction are the explicitly disavowed (if never fully disentangled) antecedents of what Freud asserted as psychoanalysis, music may be the unacknowledged ancestor, the *medium*, the immediacy of presence and feeling, out of which all tragedy, especially psychoanalysis, could only have ever been born and only through which any loss could ever be mourned. It is not the music per se that provides the satisfaction; it's the embeddedness in musical patterning, the weave, that allows one occasionally to disappear from one's life for a while, to *dwell* in the music itself. As the philosopher Philippe Lacoue-Labarthe wrote, "Music in general laments.... What it laments is always my own death (unrepresentable as such, said Freud: its very inevitability is refused by the unconscious, and the Ego must learn of it through the intermediaries of figure and scene). What touches or moves me in music, then, is my own mourning."[38]

Music always presents a paradox of presence and absence; it is no sooner played than it has faded away. Unlike the plastic arts, music is always in a state of decay. It is always dying; as the Barangers once claimed of bad faith, it is a constantly fading contingency.[39] Its continuity in time and its disappearing through time are the same thing. Like hypnosis, it reconciles self-possession and loss of self, the impressions left by the vanished force; the beat goes on, even when the music stops. And the fact that the musical beat continues is what makes it possible to *experience* loss, to *tragedize* it. Tragedy can only be experienced as such within the context of a larger framework; as Bion formulated it, "catastrophe" is an embedded form of breakdown (as in "catastrophic change"), as opposed to what Laplanche called "dis-aster," a star knocked out of orbit, led astray.

When one can use the accompaniment of music to bear loss, which is always a matter of communal reinforcement, "through the intermediaries of figure and scene"—only then can one begin to bear to lose the world. One of Freud's most famous formulations—"In mourning it is the world which has become poor and empty; in melancholia it is the I itself"—suggests that if I can mourn, I can bear to lose the world I felt I was living in because I can actually be there for the loss (as opposed to being traumatized by it, in which case, as Winnicott formulated, I'm not really there to lose anything). But the inversion of this formula is equally striking: In the work of mourning, which is the work of analysis, one can perhaps surrender to a self-forgetting, a relinquishment of oneself, a bereavement, such that the elements of one's history can be reconfigured and refound within the reliably constant world, rich and full in its woven texture—paraphrasing Jean-Luc Nancy, a world that is "absolutely other," within which the self can always be resynthesized, re-tuned (or re-toned) to its resonances, and inhabited anew.[40] (The "earworm" phenomenon, hanging onto a melody, may be an instance of the psyche in mourning training, binding the self through repetition as its tonality stretches to accommodate new tones.)

Music is present at the birth of psychoanalysis only as an absence, an erasure, a symptom—in the person of Freud, as an absence of feeling (or a refusal of too much feeling). Perhaps if music had been more thinkable to Freud—or for that matter, to his translator, Strachey—we might have ended up with "enchantment," as opposed to "cathexis," as the currency of psychical exchange in our theoretical parlance. To cathect the object is to be enchanted by it, each new instance of fascination and investment in the irreducible alterity of the world recalling our original, primordial experience of being sung-in to the world, the original excesses and disruptions transmitted through ordinary care giving that stimulate the capacity for interest, the deviations and goings astray that turn sounds into music of what it's actually like to be alive, into the enchanted world that sings us into being. Enchantment is, in fact, closer to the word Freud used for "cathexis," *Besetzung*, which literally means "occupation" (we "occupy" that in which our libido is invested—we *live through* it, identificatorily, mimetically), but that word, *Besetzung*, implicitly includes the sense of being induced or seduced (like "beset") in a way that "cathected" fails to capture—the ways we are occupied *by* the world or the object. (Might Strachey have selected the Latinate term "cathexis" for its consonant similarity to "catharsis," the hysteric's attempt to release energy through the mimetic choreography of unspeakable tragedy?) In order to occupy the object, we must already be an object of concern, a *preoccupation*, to an existing member of the weave. (If not, we are left preoccupied by our own alienation.) Our parents are our designated weave ambassadors; it is conducting the currents of the weave that is the primary parental function. (Everything else is simply the excess of the adult's sexual unconscious, which awakens the sexual drive of the infant.) Like a film soundtrack, the weave establishes the *resonance* that enables us to follow, identify with, feel, and understand the otherwise enigmatic characters that populate the foreground of the action.[41]

Both "occupation" and "cathexis" point toward the same conclusion: When I am lost, when I am in the music—or, in the case of cathexis, in the "object"—I can bear the tragedy of constant change, the ceaseless losing of form. In this sense, what is arguably Freud's most famous formulation—*Wo Es war, so will Ich werden*—can spiral back from "Where Id was, there Ego shall be" (or, more colloquially, "Where it was, I will become") to something more like: Where I was, *there it becomes me*—"it" (or "id") being, through the Laplanche lens, the impression left by an other that has now become occupant in the realm of body, remaining in the form of the message-in-need-of-translation, the sexual drive, and, through the Winnicott lens, "it" or "id" being the world *it*-self, potentiated through psychesomatic collusion and realized in a transitional space of shared perception.

This continuity of aliveness does not belong to us as individuals but to the highly attuned communion within a realm of meaningful—that is, human—life to be taken for granted, which we move away from but return to. (The transitional world highlights the weave in its transcendence of capsular individuality, throwing light on the fundamentally postmodern quality of Winnicott's theory, its recognition that we live beyond ourselves.) And even as this quality of enchanted thing-ness, of animated it-ness, brings the world to life, so too does it disrupt the integrity of self and world, shattering the assembled structures into elements. (If we're not in our bodies, we're lost; if we are in our bodies, we're disrupted. Take your pick.) At these disruptive inflection points, we rely on enduring cultural forms, none more than music, to sustain the translations and transformations of going-on-being.

Returning to the topic of mourning, we can see that mourning requires us to come together socially, closing one separation in order to bear another, transforming the disaster of unaccompanied loss into the tragedy of communal grieving. It returns us to the site of both injury and healing, suspension and resolution, painfully renewing through shared movement the poignancy of exclusion from what Nietzsche called primordial union. (The so-called Oedipal situation may be nothing so much as a mythologically important instance of where the issue comes home, as it were, but the problem of how to proceed along the continuum between coming together and saying goodbye is always there.) Clinically, mourning shows up regularly as a matter of how to frame through the joint compact of patient and therapist, the impact of patterned interruptions of continuity (and their working-through), right up to (and including) the final mourning unfortunately known as termination, as opposed to "commencement," or "delivery," or "readiness." (Or as Laplanche calls it, in different ways: "escape velocity" and "transference of the transference.") We are only ever ready for the music to end when we feel it is not the end, when we know in our bones that the music continues.

Freud showed he was alert to the significance of shared embodiment and musicality as a marker of psychological health in *Studies on Hysteria*, a five-track demo with Breuer, which was a forerunner of what became Freud's first solo album, *The Interpretation of Dreams*. In the case of Fraulein Elisabeth von R., Freud concludes the presentation of clinical material with what he implies to be prima facie evidence that his patient was cured: "In spring of 1894 I heard that she would be attending a private ball, to which I could also obtain an invitation, and I did not let the opportunity escape me of seeing my erstwhile patient fly past in a lively dance."[42] The cultural processes that are best at freeing up the blockages of overly constrained or protective forms of self are those that invite its participants into the trance of shared movement, processes that sanction the release of self-possession in favor of being claimed through the weave, lifted into flight through the lively dance of identificatory commemoration. (As Borch-Jacobsen writes in "Mimetic Efficacity," the implicit social message is: "Truly you are no longer yourself, *but that's normal*, so be yourself, that is, another.")[43]

The vectors of induction in psychoanalysis travel both ways between patient and analyst within the analytic frame through the effects of mutual sensorial prompts and attunement, which evolve into the complementarity of free association and evenly suspended attention, a mutuality in contrast with the autoinduction, autohypnosis, and autosuggestion that we find in everyday dissociative states, "alter worlds" where mutual induction has been eclipsed. This mutuality—this cueing through gesture, tempo of exchange, and breathing—may be nothing other than "framing" itself, a mutuality that, if not symmetrical with respect to the functions of the participants within the psychoanalytic structure, nevertheless seeks and establishes a symmetry of perceptual experience, a shared orientation engendered by the most basic configuration of bodies with respect to one another, our fundamental ontological situation. Analyst and patient may only be working at optimal capacity when both are functionally hypnotized, fascinated by the world in the slowness of a moment, the attunement of being together in the frame of shared music.

4

LEARNING TO LIVE TOGETHER

attunement
going-on-being
disclosure

As in strings equally wound up, the motion of one communicates itself to the rest.
—DAVID HUME, *A TREATISE OF HUMAN NATURE* (1739)

To be alive: not just the carcass
But the spark
That's crudely put, but ...
If we're not supposed to dance
Why all this music?
—GREGORY ORR

I

We are born not yet human. More than any other living creature, we emerge in a state of utter insufficiency, what Freud called *Hilflosigkeit*, helplessness, total dependence on an adult other to meet our physical needs, which are experienced at first as alien attacks; instinctual urges are felt to be, as Winnicott once put it, "as much external as can a clap of thunder."[1] It is only once the electricity of this lightning and thunder becomes tempered by the forecasting of temporal continuity, organized into the weather of play, that the routine meeting of our instinctual needs by the environment transmutates into a sense of self, an induction into the human race. Our small bodies must be brought into the fabric of this humanity, stitched in time through the music of habitual, mimetic movement; the ever-repeating trauma of psychosexual aliveness must be humanized through an induction into the shared habitus of music.

Over the span of its history, psychoanalysis has gradually had to reckon with what it means when this induction into the psyche-soma fabric cannot be taken for granted, when isolation from social embodiment becomes the predominant malady over the internal conflicts of the embedded subject. This embeddedness—which would have been a matter of course, a kind of obvious provision—has devolved from its assumed background into the foreground, and we are now faced with an alarming insufficiency with respect to this crucial communion, one that increasingly approaches scarcity. What Winnicott regarded as ordinary care giving is not quite as ordinary anymore. While it may have been natural in Freud's day to regard neurotic troubles as an individual concern—with little or no need to worry about the ontological status of his patients, the question of their embeddedness in the fabric of humanity—the travails and conflicts of those patients could, in our current moment, be considered a kind of achievement in their own right, a kind of luxury, even privilege, because the neurotic, for all the serious suffering entailed in neurosis, had the privilege of being born into a world of functional relatedness, constituted by points of shared contact. But as cultural institutions become increasingly imperiled and fragmented, this universal basic income seems to find fewer and fewer channels, less of a public broadcasting system, by which to distribute itself, leaving the reservoirs of communal being exposed to the bankruptcy of special interests. If, previously, the psychoanalyst could assume the invitation to the dance of humanity always arrived at its destination, the clinician today confronts the question of what happens when the invitation is never sent and the problem that one therefore might never make it to the dance. To work and think psychoanalytically becomes a fundamentally ontological matter of getting the music going, a question of theorizing how to find one's way into the rhythms and chords of the world, an enterprise that, as it does for every musician, begins with tuning one's instrument.

If the concept of "tuning" resonates in its English form between musical and psychoanalytic discourses—playing in tune, attuning oneself to one's child or one's patient—its resonances in German are even richer, harmonically denser. In his book-length study of attunement, *Being Musically Attuned*, the Swedish musicologist Erik Wallrup grounds the concept in the German word *Stimmung*, a term usually translated as "mood" but that in fact ranges widely enough to be variously translated as:

- "to do something with the voice,"
- "to harmonize with,"
- "to give something a musical or verbal expression,"
- "the act of giving voice to somebody,"
- "the determination (*Bestimmung*) of something" (its destiny),
- "voting,"

and, in its most explicitly musical form, "the tuning of an instrument."[2] Like the very term it defines, the word *Stimmung* seems to support and generate variations on a theme, stemming from a common element. (The contemporary philosopher Hans Ulrich Gumbrecht, a *Stimmung* specialist, beautifully emphasizes the objective, actual effect of *Stimmung* on the entire body, the "lightest possible physical impression" that unifies inner vibration with the climate of the surrounding environment, citing Toni Morrison's description of "being touched as if from the inside.")

Keats once wrote: "Every point of thought is the centre of an intellectual world."[3] In the form of temporal worlding that we call music—that is, the musical induction into temporal existence in the world—the centering function of *Stimmung* (or attunement) pivots on the effect of a harmonic "key" in which some notes sound like they belong while others don't. Musically speaking, the contours of this harmonic worlding are often articulated in the bass (or "left hand"), at times as a repeated figure (*ostinato*), an element that does not vary with melodic or improvisational variations but rather holds them together, relating them; to paraphrase the psychoanalyst Jose Bleger, it is a "non-process" (which he identified as the primary function of the *frame*) valued not for musical development in its own right but for providing what it takes for the rest of the music to stay alive.[4] Wallrup traces the evolution of accompaniment over a repeated figure from the era of Bach, whose *Goldberg Variations* are attuned to one another through a bass theme, to Schubert's "play figure" (*Spielfigur*), "a repeated accompaniment figuration used from the first to last bar which enables the composer to be emotionally penetrating in a new way."[5] Imagined at a piano keyboard, the constancy of a repeated figure in the left hand frees the right hand up to melodize, harmonize, and improvise in real-time response to the unfolding interplay between registers and musical dynamics—volume, attack, counterpoint, syncopation, blend. The effect of this kind of left-right collaboration, between process and nonprocess, creates a whole that is greater than the sum of its parts, a thickening of emotional vibrancy, an atmospheric effect not accounted for by a simple inventory of constitutive elements, a musical *Gestalt*. Through this synergy of constancy and variation, the world itself takes on new qualities. Wallrup discovers this kind of change when music enters the Romantic era, in which composers like Robert Schumann develop a musical language that imbues their work with a quality of undifferentiation; as Wallrup writes, "the dichotomy of inside and outside is eliminated; the time-consciousness is changed; and the gentleness of the landscape has become the gentleness of the soul."[6] In the harmonic worlds generated by the great compositional masters of attunement, the laws of nature begin to more closely approximate something like Freud's laws of the unconscious, the logic of undifferentiation, the keys in which our dreams play. (Or perhaps the qualities shared by Schumann's music and Freud's metapsychology were simply culled from the same source, drawing upon the shared weave of nineteenth-century Romanticism.) Psychoanalysis relies precisely on this quality of undifferentiation in order to render in statu nascendi the conditions from which the psyche originally formed, presented anew in the clinical setting for novel presentation, disassembly, and rearrangement. And the scene of this psychomusical orchestration, Wallrup tells us, is what he calls "the lived body" (*Leib*). Though he credits Heidegger—whose silence on music, as Wallrup reports it, rivaled Freud's—for developing Nietzsche's notion that "feeling is not just something emotional standing free from the body" but also "feeling oneself where the body is included in that self," it is Wallrup who connects this qualitative claim about the nature of feeling and emotion to *Stimmung* and, transitively, to music, focusing on the lived body as the scene of musical attunement.[7] (In this sense, Wallrup reinfuses Heidegger's reading of Nietzsche with music, making it even more Nietzschean.) Once activated at the level of the lived body, attunement produces characteristics of experience that surface in Nietzsche's later writings: "The feeling of potency is stressed, the perception of time and space widened. Indeed, time seems to reach a standstill; sensibility is more acute, as is understanding; the perception of reality is changed."[8] What is at stake in the question of attunement, in other words, is not primarily a matter of symbolic value, of art as sublimation, but a matter of how we perceive, the conditions of possibility for meaningful perception, that which is rendered perceptible in a musicalized state of consciousness, an expansion and enrichment, an organization and focus, at the level of perception. And the shift in state induced by attunement provides a background and framework for the expressive variation that is elaborated in the foreground in both music and psychoanalysis, so that something can get going. The rhythmic bass lines of Bach's *Goldberg Variations* and Schubert's *Spielfigur*—not to mention Queen's "Another One Bites the Dust" or Radiohead's "The National Anthem"—ground and frame musical variation just as the psychoanalytic frame syncretizes and rhythmizes the work of association and interpretation, which in turn form their own themes and repeated figures. Through the repeated figure of the frame, the psychoanalytic situation recapitulates this progression from unison to variation, the repeated framing of the session in length and frequency (as well as the analyst's conduct in terms of greeting, prosody, accentuation, and closure) forming the basis of repeated figures in content and form.

But if the shared embodiment of attunement functions like a garden bed, working to frame and ground the subsequent psychical activity, then what varietal of psychical experience grows under these conditions? What does the frame frame? In the key of Laplanche, the psychoanalytic setup is always conceived as a reopening, a reliving, of the original situation of *Hilflosigkeit*, of being at the mercy of something we don't understand. From the beginning, the infant centers on the adult, and unlike many traditional psychoanalytic accounts, which depict the infant as being born into some kind of narcissistic carapace or omnipotent solipsism, Laplanche believes that the infant begins life in active communication with the adult other—which means that, like the Earth in its orbit around the Sun, the child's universe and attention are centered asymmetrically upon another person. In this sense, the infant perceives the adult "objectively," as the actual objective other, not as a projection, a subjective object, or a part object. The infant is born maximally open and prepared to begin communicating with the real other.

Winnicott's view may seem precisely the opposite. The object, centered upon the infant, is first a *subjective* phenomenon experienced as an undifferentiated aspect of emotional life, little more than the rhythm of going-on-being in tune alternating with the beginnings of a sense of proto-otherness, which he calls "object-relating." This oscillation eventually evolves into a perception of the adult's actual otherness ("objectively perceived"), coming and going, tuning up and falling out of tune, and ushering in the developmental era of what he calls "using" an object. But as Dominique Scarfone traces in his brilliant essay "Laplanche and Winnicott Meet . . . and Survive," the two perspectives are mutually enlivening. If object relating, like attunement, can be understood as occurring in the terrain of the shared, lived body, then the infant's "subjective" experience is precisely nothing other than an "objective" registration of the attuned presence of the caregiver. "It is really an experience where—looking back on it theoretically—one can only detect the intention to stop experiencing some unpleasant emotional state and to recreate the blissful non-separateness . . . the intention of keeping a pleasurable experience going on. 'To put inside' (introject), at this juncture, means: 'Let the good experience go on.'"[9] By the time one can recognize the separateness of the care-giving other—which presumes that object relating has become sufficiently tolerable, or perhaps sufficiently rhythmized, to tolerate a more complex psychorelational configuration—the child can start to experience other people not exclusively as a binding agent of one's experience of oneself (a "bundle of projections," as Winnicott famously put it) but as a transitional conduit to the irreducible otherness of the world, something one didn't see coming, a sexual object for the first time.

The opposition between subjective and objective qualities of the object posed by Winnicott and Laplanche respectively is thus easier to reconcile than may appear at first glance, as a clearer contrast emerges between Winnicott's notions of relating to and using the object. The phase of life characterized by object relating may be organized, not unlike music, with respect to temporal continuity (and interruption), while spatial presence (and separation) may be qualified more by the availability and use of an object. Winnicott further suggested that the way that individuals in this latter phase, now separate individuals, "communicate" with one another may correspond to a kind of opposite form of communion, a "noncommunication" in the mode of object relating. In his magnificent late-career essay "Communicating and Not Communicating Leading to a Study of Certain Opposites" (which features Keats's "world" claim as its epigraph), Winnicott develops the notion of explicit communication, communicating through symbols, as the consequence of the parent's (specifically the mother's) unavoidable alterity, an essentially though irreducibly symptomatic form of connection that emerges in response to environmental insufficiency; conversely, "when her *reliability* dominates the scene the infant could be said to communicate simply by going-on-being, and by going on developing according to personal processes of maturation," the ordinary business of growing up and becoming oneself—"but this scarcely deserves the epithet communication."[10] In order to deserve the epithet "communication," presumably, the parties in question must be sufficiently separate to allow for a space that a communication would traverse. But in one opposite of communication, a terrain of noncommunication, the substrate of the mother-infant communion, there is, to use Winnicott's famous turn of phrase, no such thing. The musical transmission of psyche-somatic energy at the level of object relating has less to do with signals or ideas being passed back and forth (as implied by a term like "communicative musicality") and more to do with the shaping and contouring of bodily experience, the nonsymbolic transubstantiation of the intensities and slackenings that emerge simply from being alive in a body into the force of an *ethos* that forms the "common ground" that Winnicott would later identify as the foundation of creative life and cultural experience, the capacity to transcend what will later come to be regarded as the "self" in an everyday way, a transformation of perception that lies at the heart of both psychoanalytic and musical experience, whether they know it or not.

Winnicott here is expanding what Keats called an "intellectual world" from a point of thought about not communicating, thinking his way through the forms of communion that may sponsor and potentiate the use of what other people actually have to offer one another, rather than relating to the world exclusively as the contents of one's own mind; he is curious about which rhythmizations and schedules of time keep the players tuned to one another, in which playing is more than sufficient "communication" in its own right, as opposed to the *amusia* of being out of tune, which stops the music altogether. "There are two opposites of communication," he continues, "simple non-communication, and active non-communication. Put the other way round, communication may simply arise out of not-communication, as a natural transition, or communication may be a negation of silence, or a negation of an active or reactive not-communicating."[11]

For Winnicott, as for a musician (which Winnicott certainly was—banging out a few chords on the piano, his wife, Clare, reports, at the end of each day's work),[12] this "simple non-communication," the profound communion underpinning the possibility of all communications between people, exists for Winnicott in the going-on-together continuously through time, moving from one moment to the next in such a way that little or no attention is called to the passage of time itself. This shared continuity constitutes the holding dimension of psychical life, the vital presence of a live psychical environment within which the self can be realized. We are most in time when we need not say or think about time, when time is already accounted for in the musicality of our not-communicated, shared ways of being. The health of the infant registers most clearly and deeply in the parent by simply continuing to be—by not, thanks to the parent, having to think too much about it.

Transposed to the analytic setup, the frame serves the function of embodying and carrying forward this shared way of being, this largely unspoken continuity. (The spoken disruption at the end of a session, "We have to stop," rhythmically reminds the participants how little needs to be said about the rest of frame-time.) The frame's architecture in space-time allows, when functioning properly, for the shared sensory communion from which the life of the psyche-soma can proceed more or less uninterrupted. This in turn provides the environment for Freud's signature mind-body state, a verbal form of going-on-being engendered by the frame, which he thought best served the task of analyzing the unconscious, which Freud termed *freier Einfall*, translated as "free association," though the German *-fall* perhaps connotes a greater sense of gravity, surrender, freefall. (The British emphasis on regression to dependence may mistake the ostensibly historical return of becoming infantile again—which analysis is never as suited to handle as, say, a hospital, or the care of one's family—with the psychoproprioceptive sensation of falling, the downhill coast of going-on-being itself, the *progress* of heading back into the weave.) And if there is a flourish of potential meaningfulness when imagining the patient's activity within the frame as the freefall of *freier Einfall*, the rabbit hole of free association, the analyst's corresponding activity—translated variously as "even-hovering," "evenly-suspended," and "free-floating" attention—is equally if not more expansive in its semiotic reach. "The rule of 'evenly suspended attention,'" Laplanche notes, "whose very wording refers us to the 'well-tempered' (*gleichschwebende*), i.e. 'balanced' musical scale," connotes the tuning of an instrument (lit. "same-" (*gleich*) and "-weavened" (*schwebende*)—the tuning, in other words, of the analyst.[13] And in a musical context, the term for that which is well tempered in balanced tuning is precisely *Stimmung*—making Freud's "evenly woven" quality of attention all but synonymous in German with, for example, the "well-tempered" tuning of Bach's clavier. That is to say, in its mother tongue, the psychoanalytic notion of attunement approximates the attunement of musical instruments to the point of etymological identity. Patient and analyst, associating and attending, are instruments on the same wavelength, playing in tune.

Whether accessed through a form of psychoanalytic attention or a form of musical experience—or, for that matter, through any of the many other eligible cultural forms, like dance, or conversation—attunement is the medium by which one embeds oneself in the fabric of human experience, weaving one's perceptual understanding of the world with threads of communal sensation. And the frequencies to which one refers in tuning one's instrument to play with a separate other, to become less separate—not to mention setting one's clock, or speaking dreams to one's analysts—always draws upon the tuning of other instruments, a chorus of collective calibration, an orchestra of the shared convictions we find expressed through our consensual ways of being. Only through this attunement, as well as the particular forms attuned within it, including psychoanalysis, could Freud's original mission to relieve patients of their "reminiscences" be truly accomplished, not just by turning reminiscences into memories to forget but by dissolving the problem and demand of having to be re-membered. Through attunement, which is effectuated by the shared psychosensory framing, one is "membered," and being successfully membered relieves one of having to remember one's life.

The natural patterning of this weave function is inherently musical, dialectical, and continuous, its alternating activities guaranteeing its going-on-being. Freud's opus one, his prescription for analyzing that great night-fabric known as the dream, was a deliberate rebuttal of the dime-store decoding that was the extant form of so-called dream interpretation at the time of writing, proffering alternatively a form of analysis in which the elements of a dream did not correspond archetypally with associations or meaning in a 1:1 ratio but led instead to a multiplicity of associations ($1{:}n$), every one of which could potentially link back to any other element of the dream ($n{:}1$), yielding a network of cross-referencing, interpenetrating descriptions, a fabric of potential meaningfulness—$n{:}n$ (or simply n), a functional identity between dream weaving and *freier Einfall*, work and dream, dream-work. In Freud's genre of translation known as the interpretation of dreams, the weave of psychoanalytic attention begets the weave of dream association, the frame its constant dreamcatcher. The superstructure of extant meaning can fall away only when the actual fabric of the communal domain is felt psychically, without which one cannot fall (because one would never be caught). And the attunement of the analytic space becomes, in turn, a portal of entry into the collective quilt into which patients present themselves to be woven, entering the shared realm of being human.

Embeddedness in this weave becomes crucial not only as a basic precondition for aliveness but for sustaining continuity precisely at moments of disorienting change, of suffering loss. "Come on over a minute," invites Fred Rogers, America's great seamster of ritual and feeling, our stateside Winnicott, at the beginning of the radiant documentary *Won't You Be My Neighbor?* Mister Rogers is seated at the piano, playing through what is known as a circle of fifths, the chord progression that trolleys through a land of make-believe called tonal harmony, with the option to disembark in any key:

> I just had some ideas that I've been thinking about for quite a while, about—modulation. It seems to me that there are different things in life, and one of my main jobs it seems to me is to help, through the mass media, for children, to help children through some of the difficult modulations

of life. Because it's easy for instance to go from C [*plays the chords C–C7–F*] to F. But there are some modulations that aren't so easy. For instance, to go from F to F# you've got to weave through all sorts of things. And it seems to me if you've got somebody to help you as you weave—maybe this is just too philosophical, maybe I'm trying to combine things that, that can't be combined, but it makes sense to me.[14]

Those to whom the idea of combining music, "the difficult modulations of life," and "somebody to help you as you weave" makes sense—anyone who uses music and other people to navigate difficult transition, to sustain dissonance—may have come to appreciate the value of being accompanied when forms of suffering have made the world excessively alien, when the hermeneutic capacity to generate vitalizing meaningfulness has become too elusive. And because, as Laplanche has formulated, the contents of the human unconscious are irreducibly unintelligible, the frustration of insufficient meaning is always terribly familiar. Artists may seduce us sufficiently, through their work and company, to help us with the experience of not knowing; they offer a kind of aid or apprenticeship in these periods of suspension, of not knowing when one will land in the home key, when one has forgotten the sound of it. If, on the other hand, one has suffered too much uncertainty, having been excessively suspended without the anchor of the repeated phrase or home key or rhythm, and hence being always compelled toward the certainty of the resolved chord, these periods of coming apart become terrifying. Fleeing the weave of human feeling and relatedness, the prosthetic refuge of an auto-tuned life becomes an attractive proposition. But in between these extremes of good- and nowhere-near-good-enough accompaniment there is a considerable span of emotional territory where one might be capable of appreciating the significance of loss and grief, but we also, in an utterly human way, have moments of wishing it were otherwise, that the chords could all resolve. In this situation, alongside all other artforms of relating—friendship, education, work, play, service, music making—the kind of art practiced in psychoanalysis may become useful as a kind of holder of memory, of history, of the conviction that there is no way to establish what the enigmatic messages, the unharmonized vibrations of the world, "mean" once and for all. For Laplanche—and no less for Bion (not to mention, in an essential way, for Freud)—unconscious contents are essentially, permanently unknowable, and thus they are more like things—mysterious things—than symbols or representations; they don't refer to anything but themselves, not unlike things in the outside world. A moment in which meaning collapses, in which the world becomes mysteriously thinglike, always recapitulates the disorientation of earlier experiences, all the way back to an original moment or era, when one's original psychical orientation—Copernican, focused on the external other—shifted to a "Ptolemaic" (self-orbiting) focus on the internal other, an alien *message*, for the first time. Instinctively, Laplanche formulated, children do their best to translate (or, if not fully translate, at least bind) this message, at first using the materials of the semiotic field, which are bodily, such that these early translations tend to be scenes of bodies or body parts interacting, usually with one body doing something very stimulating to the other. (The Kleinians describe "phantasy" structures as the products of this process.) These "bodily components of our sense-experience," Wallrup writes, "are a starting point for a meeting with that which is alien."[15] In Laplanche's view, this is what Freud discovered in what he called infantile sexuality. But no matter how successful each translation is on the baby's, child's, and eventually the adult's part, they can never exhaust the meaning of the enigmatic message, because there isn't one down there to exhaust; it has no final signification, just the continued work of ongoing translation. Translation thus always fails at some point. ("A failure of translation" is Freud's original definition of repression, which Laplanche unearths and uses.) We translate all we can, but at some point we fail, and then we're left with a highly stimulating, enigmatic remainder of the original message, which is more like a chunk of memory, a mnemic trace, that has no meaning, a thing more than an image or idea. We then must quarantine this remainder by other means, lest it overwhelm the other functions of the mind necessary for survival.

But while the repressed, dynamic unconscious is forever backlogged with untranslated and untranslatable messages, the so-called unrepressed unconscious—or perhaps, we might say, the *not* repressed unconscious—is accessible for those woven into the social level of communal being, available for public access. In its concern for the robustness and usability of other people (and of cultural objects), as demonstrated by what Winnicott called their "survival" and their usability, their unanxious response in the face of the flood of unchanneled impulse and urgent need, psychoanalysis has historically underemphasized the broad accessibility, the public library, of culturally embedded, usable objects who know how to keep the beat and help us stay in time, how to go on being. The depth of one's embeddedness in the ontological fabric, in the song of being, is conveyed nowhere as clearly as in one's not-communicated unshakenness, one's enduring, inner calm—Wallrup offers the term "reservedness" (*verhaltenheit*), which Winnicott values as an important quality of the ordinary mother's capacity when engaging with emotional storms, what Bion described as the turbulence of emotional experience—in full contact with what Bion called an emotional storm, enough to be affected by it without being destroyed. Attunement would be the surround of this contact, the very weather. "It is all about attunement to something unknown which is in conflict with the established order of self," Wallrup writes, "but at the same time brings about resonance in that same self. The alien is never simply alien."[16] For Laplanche, following Freud, this resonance is sexuality, an echo between the impression that strikes us at present, like a mallet hitting a piano string, and its echo in some other part of the psyche, the way another object across the room may vibrate in sympathy, except that the "concurrence" of *après-coup* transcends the temporal as well as spatial dimension, attuning adult and infantile sexuality.

No such attunement can occur within the psyche without a quality of *Stimmung* in the environment; just as the ego, as Freud formulated, takes its formal and developmental cues from the body, so too does the psyche internalize the attuning function from its surroundings. The form this attunement takes in the clinical situation—dependent upon the establishment of *rapport*, the ability to look at things together—follows the analyst's adjustment in listening and speaking to that which is alien within the patient, modeling how the two shall grow to evenly regard the free associations of the unconscious. As Ogden writes in his seminal paper on the initial analytic hour, this experience can be daunting to patient and analyst alike and elicit impulses in either party to skip to the next track. But "when something alien appears that has no given meaning," Wallrup assures us, "the reaction does not necessarily have to be one of dismissal; we may also be struck (*getroffen*) by it, a reaction followed by a response where meaning is produced.... The contrast between these two worlds is conceived of in terms of a lack of *Einstimmigkeit*, a lack which I shall call distunement."[17]

The analyst's capacity to establish conditions of attunement, to address the lack of *Einstimmigkeit* through a tuning of one's perceptual apparatus to the field created within the frame of each treatment, to respond to the initial blow of otherness with the afterblow of meaning making, becomes the opening riff of what will become a repeated figure, an even-weaving of attention between the strike of distunement and the concert pitch of unison harmony, such that a process can form through oscillating rhythm, the continual weave, of attunement and distunement, going-on-tuning. If the mechanism of this weaving is inherently musical, the driver of psychoanalytic efficacy becomes directly contingent on the analyst's attention *to the attunement* between the patient and the world, which, for the master analyst (like the master musician), becomes unconscious, effortless; the weave weaves one's movements, just like the groove to those firmly in its gripping continuity. An analyst at work is tuned in to both genuine and fraudulent embodiment of gesture and being—what Laplanche once called being an art critic. If one cannot harness the anarchy of the sexual drive in what Wallrup called reservedness (*verhaltenheit*), if one cannot allow the shaping of the drive through the regular pulses and rests of natural and cultural rhythms, one cannot find purchase in the vitalizing field generated by living together, cannot evenly weave oneself into the fabric of shared musicality, of sexual being. Planted firmly in this fabric, absorbing the dissonant clash of moments of disassembly, of registering the beat enough to keep listening, becomes a collaborative task, our dreamwork, a job the unconscious gives us to do, a job that becomes our life.

II

Freud had two jobs, or at least did the job that became his life in two ways: doctor by day, author by night. And while he never authored any essays about music, he did occasionally write about sculpture and fiction, once at the same time. Freud's original foray into his own brand of psychoanalytic art criticism, "Delusion and Dream in Jensen's *Gradiva*," is an essay about a short story, a love story, about a piece of art. And while love is certainly less scarce a topic than music in his writing, it never quite secured as definitive a position as "sexuality" in Freud's metapsychology, where an emphasis on instinct, drive, frustration, and satisfaction predominate. But in this early meditation on a work of art, love is front and center in Freud's thinking about the psychoanalytic cure. Nowhere does Freud write more freely (and more passionately) about the relevance of love to the psychoanalytic project, in other words, than when he is turning his attention to the topic of art, though he finds love, so to speak, in clinical psychoanalysis precisely as it comes to an end.

> The process of cure is accomplished in a relapse into love, if we combine all the many components of the sexual instinct under the term "love"; and such a relapse is indispensable, for the symptoms on account of which the treatment has been undertaken are nothing other than precipitates of earlier struggles connected with repression or the return of the repressed, and they can only be resolved and washed away by a fresh high tide of the same passions. Every psycho-analytic treatment is an attempt at liberating repressed love which has found a meagre outlet in the compromise of a symptom.[18]

In his reflections about Jensen's *Gradiva*—whose title character, Zoe Bertgang, reminds the story's narrator of the eponymous sculpture, a bas-relief of the Roman god Mars Gradivus—Freud freely declares the centrality of a "fresh high tide of the same passions" that give rise to the sexual conflict ("the compromise of a symptom") if the psychoanalytic participants are to find their own form of relief, their own better deal, a new compromise known as a cure. And this clarity about the function of love in psychoanalytic cure affords Freud a particular angle on the work of the analyst—disguised, as Freud might say, as the work of the author. The doctor, he tells us, induces a relapse into love, reopening the amorous negotiations in which symptoms are formed.

> The author no doubt proceeds differently. He directs his attention to the unconscious in his own mind, he listens to its possible developments and lends them artistic expression instead of suppressing them by conscious criticism. Thus he experiences from himself what we learn from others—the laws which the activities of this unconscious must obey. But he need not state these laws, nor even be clearly aware of them; as a

result of the tolerance of his intelligence, they are incorporated within his creations.[19]

Distinguishing the doctor's approach from the author's approach to the unconscious is in some sense a symptom itself, a denial of the potential identity between the two. We can imagine that Freud's efforts to identify himself to his public as a doctor at the expense of being identified as an author is understandable given the stakes involved—the invention of psychoanalysis, its legitimacy as a healing art, its protection from antisemitism. But there may also have been an unanticipated cost to insisting upon a medical approach to the unconscious, a detour from the direct access cultivated by the inspired author. Perhaps inspired himself by the creative freedom of the author of fiction—he later purchased a cast of the *Gradiva*, which he hung near his analytic couch—Freud discerned an important capacity in the fiction writer, a directing of attention toward one's own unconscious, a communion with one's own animating otherness, which in turn infuse his creations with genuine properties of psychical life. First and foremost an attentive listener, the creative author, in Freud's vision, essentially transcribes into words whatever of the unconscious can be allowed onto the page. (If the telephone receiver was Freud's analog for the "instrument" of the analyst, the author might be located at the other end of the line, telegraphing pulses into publication.) And the laws that govern this process need not be stated or even brought into awareness; they are "incorporated," embodied, in the practice of making literature, the library hush of noncommunication, the quiet respite of *eros* from the noise of the sexual.

Tuned to the key of this short story, to the *Stimmung* of *Gradiva*, Freud declares unequivocally the curative power, the loving creation, produced in the company of the speaking, speechful other (that which, for Laplanche, is all the unconscious ever was in the first place). What would it mean, then, to conceive of the analytic function as this kind of aesthetic responsiveness, to regard the interpretive function of the analyst as a type of story writing, as an act of creation, an improvisational musicality? So the analyst's ability to make sense—that is, to interpret—would rest upon achieving of a state of maximal tunability, as surrendering to a musical vulnerability, as the expression of an ethic of affectedness by the other, by the other's music? Heard in this way, the analyst becomes less an authority on the patient's psychical problematics and more of a model for how to first unwrite and then rewrite oneself into being. Freud's reading of *Gradiva* is psychoanalytic not only because of the metapsychological principles he employs in his analysis but in its record, as in all meaningful psychoanalytic writing, of the author in a state of (non)communicative inspiration (that is, direct communication with oneself). When thinking about psychoanalytic theory becomes, as Laplanche suggested, a psychoanalytic experience—a fascination with enigmatic messages—psychoanalytic writing becomes a kind of case history of its own unfolding. (*The Interpretation of Dreams* is the case history of Freud's transformation into an author through becoming a new kind of doctor to himself, listening to himself as his friends and mentors once had.) The particular short-story form traditionally associated with case histories—from initiation, through phases, toward termination—becomes just one of many arcs this collaborative writing can follow. And possibly not its most exemplary, anxious as these "histories" always are about the scientific status of their genre, overly convinced as to the most effective technology for sharing our work. (Laplanche and his students are champion critics of this assumption.)

Freud may have been a doctor and an author, but the stories he wrote (like the stories we continue to write in his genre) were rarely as freely associative as he imagined an author's, or a dreamer's, to be, constrained as they always were by the standards of their day jobs. But in writing about someone else's short story, Freud notices the parallel between the author's quality of attention to unconscious life, through which one's creativity is expressed, and the doctor's freeing the passions of love, the lifting of resistances through the liberation of repressed associations, the rehabilitation of dream-work. The dawn of dream-work, of Freud's reporting and interpretation of his own dreams, is a reinvention of how to be written by one's own otherness; the analyst, accordingly, leads the way toward the otherness within oneself, establishing poetic communion with the dreamworld of the unconscious, heeding its gravitational pull, its relapses into love, its refinding of the object; once a Copernican other, now a Ptolemaic core. The transferability of this creative form through identification—much more than the reading of any particular story it produces—is central to Freud's model of cure; transference, in this configuration, has less to do with refinding the object of one's love in the person of the analyst and more to do with the relapse itself, the resumption of lapsing, the reopening of the gap where desire comes through, the going-on-being of desire—not the love of *Gradiva* but the *gradiva* of love. In its direct (non)communication of going-along-well, its *Bertgang*, this endless love begets the (pro)creation of new life, fresh tides, new stories. And the reproduction of this love loop, at its best, becomes a form of repetition, a reliably repeated figure, a way of having a type. Psychoanalytic models that lament the persistence of infantile wishes, the entrenched stability of pathological organizations, and the compulsion to repeat as obstacles to overcome, as resistances to work through, often miss the structuring potential of these repetitions for exploding former configurations of psychical life toward new ways of apprehending the world, of conditioning desire. The rhythmic substratum of what the musicologist Robert Fink calls "recombinant teleologies," whose only end is the continued spiraling of their own continuity, becomes the beating heart of creative, erotic life, from the level of culture itself to each of its constituents. "In the culture of Eros," Fink writes,

> repetition is a technique of *desire creation*, a more-or-less elaborately structured repetitive entrainment of human subjects toward culturally adaptive goals and behaviors. . . . Process music's *recombinant teleology* supports a revisionist (and perhaps transgressive) interpretive conclusion: its repetition is not the negation of desire, but a powerful and totalizing metastasis. Minimalism is no more celibate than disco; processed desire turns out to be the biggest thrill of all.[20]

The reference to disco is instructive. By the turn of the most recent century, three distinct disciples of disco had emerged within the dance-music cosmos, each with its own organizing ethos, its own *gradiva*, its own muse: the ecstasy of *trance*, the pulse of *techno*, and the groove of *house*. Each animus accords its own form, an expansion of a particular aspect of disco, an emergent difference from the repeated element that is consistently invariant among them: a "straight," unsyncopated quarter note in the kick drum known as "four-on-the-floor" (or colloquially as "oontz-oontz"). Trance, more dramatically than disco before it, dramatizes the building and layering of instrumental components, building towers of sound only to drop them away, then to bring them back again, each nodal inflection an opportunity to reorganize the psyche-soma through contracting tension and explosive release. Techno, alternatively, emphasizes the more purely rhythmic element, stacking loops of percussion to the point, as in African drumming, of self-shattering vibration, but whereas live drumming induces its participants into communal undifferentiation by enlisting each member as a player, techno comps this demand on its participants through the mechanical provision of metronomic regularity, both a symptom of the digital age and its creative remastering and aesthetizing, as were the distinctly noncelibate pieces of the twentieth-century minimalist composers. But what many would consider the heart and soul of disco—R&B chordal harmonies, triumphant vocal performance, sizzling orchestration—is found currently, when the occasion arises, in house music, which involves an unmistakable (if descriptively challenging) sense of *soulfulness*. (Soul, of course, its own genre of music, is a signifier for a distinctly African cultural tradition of music making; soul music, and therefore house music, like all American music, was originally Black music. It was something of a cultural event when the American soul royal Mary J. Blige traveled to London to record with two pale-white brothers from Surrey, who began producing music, at ages eighteen and twenty-one, under the name Disclosure—a word to which we shall return—to record what would become some of the most popular house music ever produced, crossing over from dance floors to radio waves and back again; the song "Latch," featuring a vocal performance by the British crooner Sam Smith, is the most successfully pop-charting dance song of the last decade.)

Music is transmitted through repetition. And the psychical potential of repetition is what psychoanalysis may be uniquely suited to apprehend, and thus it may possibly help illuminate the phenomena of appropriation and exploitation (not to mention the legal study of sampling and copyright). Following the jagged and arresting serialist music written by Schoenberg and Boulez (and championed by Adorno), which approached a kind of limit in the struggle to find new forms of musical expression, the repetitive music of minimalism and disco was an acute spiraling in dialectical oscillation from difference back toward repetition, and this latter term has only become more dominant since. "What truly characterizes Schoenberg," Adorno writes in "The Dialectical Composer," "is a very exemplary change, both in principle and historically, in the way the composer behaves toward his material. He no longer acts like its creator, nor does he obey its ready-made rules," but rather renders in the music itself its own struggle for originality. Adorno continues:

> In Schoenberg, the contradiction between strictness and freedom is no longer transcended in the miracle of form. It becomes a force of production; the work does not turn the contradiction toward harmony, but conjures up its image, again and again, looking for duration in its cruelly ravaged traits. "Patchwork, like everything else," the Master wrote in a dedication copy.[21]

If Schoenberg's compositional intensities offered fresh allegories of the never-ending crisis of its own music making, the more contemporary practice of recombining existing musical material (through sampling and the endless repetition of beats) into new, elongated forms, by contrast, eschews the originality of an individual voice to prioritize the task of keeping the music going, both by preserving and repurposing recorded music, copy-and-pasted with more sophistication through each generation's technological ingenuity, and by creating pieces of longer length, going all night long.[22] In conditions of attunement, of going-on-playing, human experience is infused by the sustaining capacity of shared forms that transcend the limits of corporeal and temporal selfhood, engaging levels of psychotemporal experience that exceed conscious perception. That music which functions, conversely, like a nineteenth-century short story in its suggestion of beginning, middle, and end—verse, chorus, bridge, chorus, for example—invites the listener to wrangle the entire arc of a piece of music in mind at once, to control the experience rather than surrender to it. (Aaron Copland, in his textbook-treatise *What to Listen for in Music*, argues that listening to a Bartok symphony, for example, in any way other than this traditionally structured, narrative-like unfolding is essentially a waste of time; many case write-ups suggest that psychoanalysis would endorse this position, at least within its own medium.)[23] But music that more or less repeats itself beyond the frontier of conscious graspability does not lend itself to this "anthropic" way of holding the whole of something in mind at once and thus induces a different way of listening. "Recombinant teleologies," Fink writes,

> tend to disregard this anthropic principle. They create musical universes in which tension and release are pursued on a scale that far outstrips the ability of the individual human subject to imagine a congruent bodily response.... Recombinant teleologies abandon the cherished "one piece, one orgasm" model... a complete-tension-release arc might be much smaller than the piece, perhaps as small as the four-bar rhythmic cycle (three bars of groove plus a final "turnaround" bar that leads back to the beginning again) that is the primary building block of disco, house, and techno, or the four-to-six fold repetitions of measure-long modules in a typical minimalist process piece. Hundreds of these might be added together to make a piece that is cyclically teleological at every moment but has no *necessary* long-range goal.[24]

Condensing the arc of tension and release into something like a building block—like a fifty-minute session and the silences that frame it—looped indefinitely creates a particular kind of musical universe, attunes a particular experience of oneself, a particular mood of going-on-being. In their shift toward basking in the undisturbed groove of the here-and-now, both the music and the psychoanalysis of the 1970s implicitly decathected the arcs of long-range plotlines in favor of local completion, reduced to the point of subliminality, the imperceptible energizing of the psyche-soma from moment to moment, an arc so atomized in its density that it is always ending, always dying, structuring conditions of longing into a kind of musical intensive-care unit, a framework for suffering the passion of desire that never has to end.

Each of the progenic subgenres of disco, which collectively comprise a near-total ubiquity in current dance-club culture, amplifies a corresponding element in the field and practice of psychoanalysis. Techno, with its rhythmic primacy, renders aesthetically the beating heart of the frame, steadily marking time in its reliable regularity, literally beating the psyche into time. Trance dramatizes the condensation and sublimation of energy, building to the point of explosion, evaporating to the point of evanescence, arresting in its moment-to-moment texturing of experience, which accrues into a consciousness-altering expansion of the temporal self. But the richness of house music, which retains more elements of popular music than either of its disco-inspired brethren, endows it with a special power. Moving one's body in time with the beat of a trance or techno track feels somewhat optional when compared to the movement induced by the groove of house. It cannot be denied. Sitting still, standing on the wall, while this music plays is a form of torture, electrical insulation, suspended animation, body insomnia. The music wants, through the lived body, to go on being, a form of emergence that the Greeks called *disclosure*, a form of truth. And like Disclosure, the effect produced through the recombination of historical elements toward the proliferation of musical continuity is the ongoing revelation of the self as it unfolds in time, the echoing of bodily presence through the past toward a never-ending future, known in psychoanalysis as *après-coup*.

Laplanche suggested that there were two psychoanalytic mechanisms, two genres, for this translational work. The first, what he called "full" transference, aims to disclose how sexuality, transmitted through enigmatic messages from the other, have been constructed into fantasies, which now present themselves simply as reality, the sexual-as-translat*ed*. Many analyses end here, often with a feeling of relief, even success. But Laplanche was even more interested in what he called the "hollowed out" transference, which aims to disclose the fact of the translational function itself: that the patient is a translator, an agent, an author, a DJ, always recombining samples of sound, potentiating new translations, scouring the bins for fresh records. (Bion, for his part, emphasizes the analyst's role in this process—how to become expert at living in a state where meaning is always collapsing, how to cope as meaning unravels.) "The author," Adorno writes, "approaches the work the way Oedipus approached the Sphinx, as a person who must solve riddles. Where is this harmony heading, he asks, and feels his way into the 'emotional life of sound.'"[25] This feeling-of-one's-way is the sexual-as-translat*ing*, what Winnicott called playing, or, as Freud, having once "lost his way" in a clinical encounter, wrote to Fliess: "I really believed I would have to give up on the spot. I found a way out by renouncing all conscious mental activity so as to grope blindly among my riddles. Since then I am working perhaps more skillfully than ever before, but I do not really know what I am doing."[26]

This inspiring vision of experimental, dialectical, psychoanalytic process places musical continuity, keeping a rhythm going, going on groping, of the astronomy of our bodies in space, finding form, shaping experience— all of this becomes the center of our psychoanalytic cosmology. If it is not the egoic self, the Copernican Other, or even the Ptolemaic unconscious but the very Being woven through musical experience that is most fundamental to the project of being alive, then the capacity of analyst and patient to establish attunement in a psychoanalytic context, not only with each other but to the history, culture, and being of the world, becomes the consummate expression of love. "Side by side with the exigencies of life," Freud writes in "Some Character-Types Met with in Psycho-Analytic Work," "love is the great educator; and it is by the love of those nearest him that the incomplete human being is induced to respect the decrees of necessity and to spare himself the punishment that follows any infringement of them."[27] In the mode of going-on-being, the infringements on long-range continuity itself are more central to suffering, more disruptive of process, than any particular internalized object identified therein. The kind of superego "punishment" that Freud wants to spare his patients, viewed through the paradigm of the musical weave, may be understood less as a conglomerate of encounters with demanding or critical others and more like how it feels to be at the mercy of isolated self-government without the love and inspiration, the respect, of the ego ideal to guide one's movements, to complete one's humanity. (Or, in the key of Winnicott: Privation is an excessively insular version of the otherwise pleasurable experience of being alone together; de-privation is its mirror image, neither together nor alone, no common key to bring the instruments together in tune.) If one's unconscious is neighborly enough to resemble Mister Rogers, animating one's King Friday, the fact of tomorrow's continued labor—"I'll be back / When the day is new / And I'll have more / Ideas for you"—becomes considerably more viable, housed in the neighborhood of the human weave, resident through embeddedness in the music of shared time.

III

Music builds place out of time. A chord is physically constituted by multiple waves, pulsing frequently enough to be heard as pitches, playing simultaneously, which when arranged with other waves evoke and establish a sense of a harmonic world, combining temporalities aesthetically into an ephemeral, aural tapestry. To become attuned at this level of experience is to become rhythmized at more than one degree of temporality, synchronizing amplitudes, congruing patterns among the waves; the more levels, the more *Stimmung*. How might we view this in relation to the passage of time? Heidegger identified distinct temporalities, which he called *Ekstasen* (lit. "ecstasies"), as the conditions of experiencing the present, the same palpable quality on which Wallrup founds his definition of attunement in the lived body. For Heidegger, the meaning of the past in the present is organized by the future, determined above all by the death that awaits us. Laplanche, by contrast, feels the pull of the past to be loosened (or analyzed) so that one can then move into the future—related to what Ogden, from his own angle, has described as the birth of the historical subject, the achievement of not simply what Klein called the "depressive position" but of a *historical* position.[28] Perhaps this also undergirds the ego ideal, an internal guidance system into the future, the sense of how groovy things could be based on how things felt in the past. While the rhythm of the frame (the framing effect of rhythm) attends to keeping things the way they are, the life of the frame, in this sense, anticipates what is to come, a sense of what might be—*futural*, to use the psychoanalyst Mitchell Wilson's recent coinage.[29] The frame of psychoanalytic work provides a way to let go of static frameworks (which can trap one in the past) so that things can move forward in the going-on-being of musicalized living. This involves the development of a metaframing function or capacity, a living frame that allows deadened and deadening frames to fall away. (Laplanche described the frame as a "tub," bound by eros, within which what Freud called the "stereotype plate" [*Klischees*, lit. "clichés"] of the past can be dismantled and freshly assembled.)[30] This future-forming continuity only ever emerges from a concurrent process of having been, which is the work of each present moment; the chord formed by the weave of these temporalities—and, for Laplanche, other temporalities: the temporality of perception, the rhythms of the cosmos—is the music of going-on-being.

The recombinant teleology of psychoanalysis discloses, like minimalism and disco, a veritable genre of music, characterized by the very slow but steady tempo of the frame that blooms eros, both in the macrostructure of the sessions and the microadjustments within them. Certain patients (more and more these days) require the framing function to help them use the analytic hour, orchestrating the timbres and fine-tuning the subtleties of exchange from moment to moment while holding the integrity of the compositional structure of the session in its own right and as a local constant in the wider scope and score of the treatment. Infusing the inanimate world through the prosody of the analyst, conveying cultural forms including style, rhythm, and environmental provision, the frame partially relieves the demand on the person of the analyst to provide the entire framing function. (Psychotherapy conducted under conditions of material limitation such as clinics and schools often rely even more heavily on the component of the frame that is held in the mind of the analyst and the rhythmizing of time.) Once animated in this way, charged at the "glischro-caric" level, imbued by the analyst's aesthetic-spatial and musicotemporal sensibilities, the environment itself becomes available for identification—for better or worse.[31] As Bion commented, "The fact that one turns up in the office so many days a week and expects the patient to do the same, itself suggest [sic] that that is the way to behave. And because I behave or try to behave in a particular way in analysis the patient—like the child who is fascinated by the bad habits of the parent—is most likely to pick our bad habits, not our good ones."[32]

Managing the clinical situation with a vacuum-sealed frame may get picked up like a bad habit and engender that same quality in the internal world, as terrain to be ghettoized and patrolled for fear of leakage. Conversely, a living, breathing frame may facilitate an attitude of open navigation and communicability on which to model the unconscious relation, a way to behave toward it. Framing is like breathing. It goes on unthought and unknown, not-communicated, but if it fails or is impaired, then it cannot sustain psychical life. The quality of going-on-being transmitted through the frame facilitates and ensures the current possibility of one's past becoming meaningful in one's future.

The conditions of musical presence are thus identical to the *Stimmung* of past, present, and future, and vice versa. The generative potential of repetition compulsion is part of this temporal continuity. Formulated from the vantage point of attunement, patients suffer from illnesses of temporality; the repetition compulsion, try as it may, has been unable to simulate sufficiently the kind of continuity from which past, present, and future can emerge. Accordingly, as the Barangers described, the efficacy of psychoanalytic technique is contingent upon the introduction or restoration of temporality. "The specific impact of psychoanalytic interpretation," they wrote, "lies precisely in the repetition, produced at the transference level, that is broken by interpretation. This opens the possibility of temporality, which now breaks out of the vicious cycle of repetition and gives way to the prospective dimension of the future rescued from the repetition compulsion."[33]

Once the frame, by providing its own rhythm (its weekly circle of fifths), has taken on the qualities of repetition so desperately needed for a sense of continuity, the compulsive forms through which repetition were previously maintained are liberated from their narrow function of re-presenting a frozen past, thereby freeing the individual from sensory isolation as the closed loop of compulsion becomes the unfolding spiral of going-on-being. In music, the subtle layering and thickening of the aural palette over repeated figures exemplifies the psychical process through which repetition affords the possibility of becoming a separate self in a sane way, attuning the lived body to a sense of potential, determination, and destiny.

In this sense, repetition is not only the symptom produced by the unconscious in need of psychoanalytic relief but a prerequisite for having an unconscious in the first place. Bion posited that Freud's dream-work (which Bion remixed as a continual "dream-work-alpha" function through waking and sleeping states) manufactures the bricks of the contact-barrier that demarcates conscious from unconscious; Laplanche's own formulation, comparable to the alpha function, which he called meaning making or translation, makes it possible to have *less* accretion and concretion of meaninglessness—in other words, more translation. ("The deriddled Sphinx," Adorno writes, "falls into the abyss of the has-been.")[34] But the alphabetization of unconscious content is subsidiary and subsequent to the beta function of rhythmizing experience, the security of going-on-being, the bed of all dreaming and translational activity. Through the going-on-being of beta function, the psyche uses repetition to generate its own novelty, dissimulating the unfathomable density of psychical life at the undifferentiated level of the frame into the richness of the world.

Therein lies the particular malady of damage at the level of beta function; the message itself, before it ever has a chance of becoming translated, is experienced as a kind of violence to be avoided. The point at which the self contacts the other becomes a no-man's-land, the jungle out there, the bush. And the version of otherness that has already infiltrated the self, now hidden from consciousness, becomes vigilantly managed and regulated not only for what it might mean but for its otherness, its *it*-ness, itself. Psychoanalysis from the get-go has anxiously negotiated its relation to this fraught border of selfhood, this zone of the alien. The frame is a psychoanalytic way of maintaining some form of contact with this barrier; preserving a threshold of shared perception need not be explicitly "processed" or acknowledged and can remain, like the unconscious itself, "unbeknownst" while retaining a vital connection to psychical life.

One's connection to this domain is always cause for hesitation. Things can go wrong at each end of the spectrum, of weaving together and pulling apart. If releasing oneself into the music of shared humanity is essential for a sense of ventilation and vitalizing renewal, there is also a terrifying prospect of being taken over, absorbed. Surrendering one's identity to the rhythms and habits of communal living can involve a loss of freedom and can be experienced in other ways as well: as a coming undone, an invitation to madness, an unending labor. "Oh, busy weaver!" Melville writes in his immortal *Moby-Dick*,

> unseen weaver!—pause!—one word!—whither flows the fabric? what palace may it deck? wherefore all these ceaseless toilings? Speak, weaver!—stay thy hand!—but one single word with thee! Nay—the shuttle flies—the figures float from forth the loom; the freshet-rushing carpet for ever slides away. The weaver-god, he weaves; and by that weaving is he deafened, that he hears no mortal voice; and by that humming, we, too, who look on the loom are deafened; and only when we escape it shall we hear the thousand voices that speak through it.[35]

The weaver Melville places at the floor of his great, syncretic ocean labors ceaselessly, wordlessly, deafened by the humming of his interminable task. Only in the *après-coup* of this rhythm, in the escape of disrupting it, of losing the beat, can the thousand voices comprising it become audible. In sustaining membership in the human race we forfeit a private world, a secret language, a room of one's own; in return, we are held by the rhythmic continuity of weaving—unweaving, of translation—detranslation, of at-one-ment and its disruption, through moments of inevitable loss, in the *fábrica* of mourning. Psychoanalysis, like many communal forms of grieving before it, provides a technology through which this utterly human process can run its course, can course through us—which may take considerable time. The rhythm of the frame, like mourning, is not anthropic. The next beat does not feel inevitable; the pauses, the *fermata*, between hits can tempt doubt, can test faith. If one expects the labor of living to be within the individual's capacity to hold oneself, then whatever threatens one's heroic self-grasp becomes unmanageably threatening. Strategies for severing one's very awareness of these threats and the terrifying feelings they provoke replace the activities of living frame-work, yielding only the anesthetizing relief of wasting time, of getting time over with. Repetition happens one way or another. (Britten: "Grimes will have his exercise.") The hydraulic river of the drive will find its way. Whether the course it takes is through a natural landscape, diverse and rich with nutrients, or mechanical, constricted, and polluted is always in contention.

But even if one has been apprenticed to (that is, induced and conducted into) forms of rhythmic living, it is also crucially important that these forms become adequately enlivened at the psychosexual register, charged by the sensibility of creative living, the seduction of an artist. Through one's very way of being, the analyst demonstrates and discloses the enlivening potential of "suffering" the sexual drive (including, as Bion did, suffering pleasure), while at the same time maintaining an ethical responsibility to protect the patient from sexual overstimulation—a "guardian of the enigma," as Laplanche once put it. (Surely the same principle is operating in Winnicott's notion of *presenting* the objective world in a way that is conducive—in other words, not too seductive—for psychical use.) Surfing the oscillations between the weaving-together of eros and being pulled apart by the sexual (what Adam Phillips has referred to as the "systole and diastole of the soul"),[36] the inevitable transitions from syncretic at-one-ment, of coherence, to what Laplanche called the "countercurrent" of coming apart become vitally disruptive, noncatastrophic life fuel, making life worth living. (It's actually "such a good feeling," as Mister Rogers always emphasized upon parting at the end of each episode, "to know you're alive.")

Accordingly, the analyst's highly personal, idiosyncratic semiotic repertoire, skill, style, and hermeneutic *ethos* are decisive in rhythmizing the conjunction-disjunction patterns, the movement between at-onement and disruption, procession and recession. Merleau-Ponty wrote that the artist doesn't show us what to see but *how to see*, not insight but outsight. This phenomenology of perception, known as *disclosure*, potentiates the unfolding of psychoanalytic experience. The adult is not the child's first object but her first artist. (As Hegel put it: the mother is the genius of the child.) By the time the analyst comes along, one's way of seeing has become a compromise between the inspiration of early artistic experience and the deadening effect of empathic failure, excessive frustration, playing out of tune. To reopen the fundamental anthropological situation is, uncannily, to hear music from one's history for the first time, to reintroduce a brand-new kind of music, familiar enough to catch the ear, strange enough to get stuck in one's head, what Lincoln famously called the mystic chords of memory.

This disclosure process is thus not only a matter of holding or containing (which are of course essential) but also of good-enough seduction. Psychosexuality must be engaged in its human, musical fullness. And because the psychoanalytic seduction must never be physically consummated, which is one among many of its constitutive partialities—patchwork, like everything else—the unconscious always registers the psychoanalytic enterprise as a bait and switch. So the whole thing must be perceived as ultimately worth one's while. Like music to which the body cannot help but move, simply finds itself moving, one must find oneself already induced, already surrendered to the love-relapse, already immersed enough in the human weave that old feelings can take new forms and that new forms can become visible, newly disclosed. In the conditions of attunement engendered by a living frame, it is not insight but sight itself that emerges, not the flash of epiphany but a climate of high-visibility placeness (in which lightning may occasionally strike), the *Stimmung* for dancing and singing oneself into being.

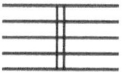

5

THE LIVING FRAME

stereo
eros
ethos

It is because the principle of constancy, of homeostasis, of Bindung *is maintained at the periphery, that analytic unbinding is possible.*
  —JEAN LAPLANCHE, "TRANSFERENCE: ITS PROVOCATION BY THE ANALYST"

Pressure if not excessive means love.
  —DONALD WINNICOTT, "MIND AND ITS RELATION TO PSYCHE-SOMA"

I

In Winnicott's model, the *holding* environment, a live foundation and sanctuary, is the primary precondition for what will eventually become the sense of *potential* space engendered by transitional phenomena and that produces, in turn, in health, a sense of psyche-somatic continuity, of body-dreaming, of *going-on-being*.

holding → potential → going-on-being

The frame of psychoanalytic practice, which conducts the environmental holding function through its pattern of meetings of fixed duration at reliably constant intervals, is essentially a form of repetition—

> WINNICOTT: Only on a basis of monotony can a mother profitably add richness.[1]

—which becomes a living, humanizing rhythm—

> W: It is reliable. But the environmental provision is not mechanically reliable. It is reliable in a way that implies the mother's empathy.[2]

—and which, once repeated and sustained over a sufficient span of time—

> W: *Whole Experiences*: What there is of therapeutics in this work lies, I think, in the fact that the full course of an experience is allowed.... In my observations I artificially give the baby the right to complete an experience which is of particular value to him as an object-lesson. In psycho-analysis proper there is something similar to this. The analyst lets the patient set the pace and he does the next best thing to letting the patient decide when to come and go, in that he fixes the time and length of the session, and sticks to the time that he has fixed.[3]

—comes to constitute and evoke the physical qualities of a setting—

> W: Freud takes for granted the early mothering situation and my contention is that *it turned up in his provision of a setting for his work*, almost without his being aware of what he was doing.[4]

—in which, as Winnicott put it, "the self is reached," and perhaps starts to feel like a self for the first time. Winnicott believed this self-reaching to be a starting place from which all subsequent psychical work could only ever proceed.

Laplanche provides another angle on the basic situation that holds or structures our experience. For Laplanche, the holding situation is actually a zone of communicative exchange, traversed from the start by *messages* that are infused by the (unconscious) sexuality of the parent—

> LAPLANCHE: These zones *focalize parental fantasies* and above all *maternal fantasies*, so that we may say, in what is barely a metaphor, that they are the points through which is introduced into the child that alien internal entity which is, properly speaking, the *sexual excitation*.[5]

—which (again, in health) *seduce* the infant into a life of desire by provoking an urgency, a drive, to *translate* the enigmatic signifiers transmitted through this encounter:

message → seduction → drive(-to-translate)

Accordingly, the activities of infant care become infused with the sexuality of the adult, which Laplanche believed to be itself a rhythm that is constituted not only by negotiating reliability and interruptions in the care-giving relationship but also (following Freud) through the temporality of sexuality itself, initiated by seduction and reworked in *après-coup*, sustained through translation.

> L: Why is it our sexuality alone which is repressed? [Freud offers] several valuable indications concerning specific characteristics of the human sexual drive, notably its "diphasic onset," the fact that it appears in two stages: on the one hand, an infantile phase; on the other, that of puberty and adulthood, the two being separated by a long period called the "latency period." At stake is a characteristic whose import is more important than the simple "maturational" factor which serves as its basis. The process invokes a temporal rhythm: a first, "premature" experience of sexuality; an eclipse through repression; a reassumption of the earlier meanings on the basis of physiological possibilities now adequate to their intention.[6]
>
> ... right at the start, there is something that goes in the direction of the past to the future, from the other to the individual in question, that is in the direction from the adult to the baby, which I call the implantation of the enigmatic message. The message is then retranslated, following a temporal direction which is, in an alternating

fashion, by turns retrogressive and progressive (according to my general model of translation—detranslation—retranslation).[7]

Winnicott, for his part, views this seduction primarily as a form of impingement. Proceeding from a (Kleinian) notion of sexual instinct arising from the infant (as opposed to implanted by the adult), he views "seduction" as provoking reactions that, when excessive, lead to catastrophic disturbances of an otherwise spontaneous, emergent eroticism—

> w: In the extreme there is very little experience of impulses except as *reactions*, and the *Me* is not established. Instead we find a development based on the experience of reaction to impingement, and there comes into existence an individual that we call false because the personal impulsiveness is missing. In this case there is no fusion of the aggressive and erotic components, since the *Me* is not established when erotic experiences occur. The infant does indeed live, because of being seduced into erotic experience; but separately from the erotic life, which never feels real, is a purely aggressive reactive life, dependent on the experience of opposition.[8]

—and threatens to decouple and disintegrate instinctual life from a sense of self.

> w: We now see that it is not instinctual satisfaction that makes a baby begin to be, to feel that life is real, to find life worth living. In fact, instinctual gratifications start off as part-functions and they become seductions unless based on a well-established capacity in the individual person for total experience, and for experience in the area of transitional phenomena. It is the self that must precede the self's use of instinct; the rider must ride the horse, not be run away with.[9]

Laplanche develops our understanding of the role of these impinging traumata in health as well as illness—not just as catastrophes to be avoided at all costs but as the irreducible result of the encounter between infant (or *infans*, lit. "not speaking") and the adult, the unspeakable and the articulate. The byproducts generated by this encounter are largely left untranslated and thus aggregate in their own psychical depository—namely, the unconscious—where there is, by Freud's definition, no time, no re-presentation, no meaning.

> L: The unconscious element is not a representation to be referred to an external thing whose trace it would be ... the passage to the unconscious is correlative with a loss of referentiality. The thing- or word-presentation, in becoming unconscious, loses its status as presentation in order to become a thing which no longer presents anything other than itself.[10]

(Freud's word for this loss of referentiality was *Unbewusste*—as Strachey notes, best translated as "unconscious*ed*," not just unknown but un-*be*knownst; once known, but no longer; what Laplanche (following Lacan) refers to as a *designified* signifier, that which we knew and then un-knew, which makes it known and unknown, or known albeit *meaningless*.)

Combining these two models, the "living frame" (or "body-dream" of psychoanalytic process) could be considered as:

1. the analyst providing a shared, symmetric, inductive *rhythm*, which effects a spatiotemporal structure that
2. clears the way for reopening the original conditions ("fundamental anthropological situation") of being subjected to an asymmetric, seductive, dissonant otherness, effecting a *harmonic* spectrum formed by varying degrees of difference, which in turn
3. generates a potential space, a dance studio, for weaving into choreography the repetitions and differences that emerge in the course of living together into going-on-being *music* together:

    rhythm → harmony → music

In this sense, the frame houses an inspired apprenticeship in conductive living, in *conducting* ourselves, in an aesthetic field grounded in shared apprehension of the world.

This musical conceptualization of the frame implies a technical shift away from valuing "interpretation" as a strategy for meaning making—

L: The German *deuten*, *Deutung*, is here much more eloquent, and much less "hermeneutic" than our word "interpretation": *deuten auf* means to indicate with a finger or with the eyes—"to point" as the Lacanians would say.[11]

—toward understanding interpretation as an invitation to look at something together—

W: If I come over here and read to you a didactic lecture I do not communicate with you, I violate you, except that you can defend yourself by going to sleep or entering into a day-dream. It would be more profitable to think that you and I communicate best when we have something we are both looking at, and this may as well be this paper as anything else.[12]

—an orientation toward the world transmitted through the analyst's attitude toward it—

W: I want to state that the working analyst is in a special state, that is, *his attitude is professional*. The work is done in a professional setting.[13]

—which conveys a fundamental rule, an *ethos*, of how to handle things, how to sense and move through the world grounded in a domain of shared embodiment.

This inductive dimension of interpretation places greater emphasis on psyche-somatic indwelling and the analyst's way of being by "pointing" toward or indicating objects of one's fascination, those notes by which the analyst is musically moved (indeed, seduced). This psychoanalytic project rests on the analyst's own inspired communion with objects in the world, orienting the instinct for meaning making (the sexual drive) toward objects of potentially shared interest, toward establishing and providing a way of conducting oneself, for comporting or behaving oneself in a way that reliably sustains and replenishes interest in the world.

W: The whole thing adds up to the fact that the analyst *behaves* himself or herself, and behaves without too much cost simply because of being a relatively mature person.[14]

Interpretation (or *Deutung*) in this sense functions fundamentally (as in the original situation of seduction) as a form of inspiration, moving the patient to identify with, to *be like*, this creative other. The analyst is always in the position to demonstrate the process of growth or becoming through fresh encounters with the fascinating world, beginning with the material of the session—not what the analyst can say about material but what the analyst can *do* with it with one's whole being. The way the analyst behaves is thus itself an interpretation, the alpha function at work, transmitting a way of being through one's entire comportment in response to the patient. (As the literary critic George Steiner has suggested, the best interpretation of art is art itself; for the psychoanalyst Antonino Ferro, a dream does not *need* interpretation—dreaming *is* interpretation.) In this sense, psychoanalysis, as Winnicott intimates, provides a way to "behave," both to be and to have, to "have" an other simply by being (like) an other, or perhaps to "be↔have"—to oscillate between being and having our objects, to conduct a rhythm between modes of experience. (What else would "behaving" be?) To "behave" in this sense is to hold oneself responsible as what Vivian Chetrit-Vatine has termed a "matricial" analyst who participates ethically by guiding this shared activity[15]—looking *at* objects *with* objects. This entails a symbiotizing rhythm where togetherness is the basis for encountering the world, drawn by the enigmatic pressures that beg translation, resisted by the all-too-human counterpressures, the re-pressions, the unbeknownst. To behave is to live one's life with an allegiance to the music that moves us toward and away from the meaningful world, an *ethos* of musical being-in-the-world, a way of doing something together and finding something together against the off-beat gap of repression, creating a rhythm. The behavior of the analyst, the work of framing, the *frame-work*, which is a fundamental and ongoing aspect of interpretation, supports and sets up the *dream-work* of analysis. Together the frame-work and dream-work of psychoanalytic process form the rhythms and harmonies of going-on-being-music.

As the tessellating pattern of seduction toward the world through perceptual identification with the other expands and consolidates—the parent or analyst replenishing fresh engagements with life sources in the world, the child or patient becoming interested in what interests the parent, in a *way of being interested*—the collective of creative living and human being expands its membership, offering its musicality as the medium through which one develops from inductee to active participant and contributor—

> w: The child is now not only a potential creator of the world, but also the child becomes able to populate the world with samples of his or her own inner life. So gradually the child is able to "cover" almost any external event, and perception is almost synonymous with creation.[16]

—continuing and conducting the intergenerational transmission of creativity that makes life worth living—

> w: Through artistic expression we can hope to keep in touch with our primitive selves whence the most intense feelings and even fearfully acute sensations derive, and we are poor indeed if we are only sane.[17]

—and infusing the frame with the living, animating vibrations, the vitalizing music, of creative living in the world.

II

From an arrangement of Freud's notion of the setting, which Marion Milner named "the frame," into three-part harmony with Winnicott's notion of "holding environment" and Laplanche's "fundamental anthropological situation" emerges a tripartite model of a frame, a *living frame*, that comprises:

1. A physical arrangement in time and space
2. The social contract by which participants are authorized to engage in this activity in this manner
3. The sensory, ethical, and "even-weavened" engagement of the analyst

This living frame, with its beta-elemental rhythmical shapings, which may be described as a living *skin* of the clinical situation—this living frame is nothing other than the shared psychosensorium of patient-analyst, a living *place*. But while Winnicott pointed the way for understanding this holding, framing dimension of psychical life as the precondition for all subsequent play, he did not make as much space as Laplanche for the always confounding, disruptive influence of the sexual on what he would have considered an otherwise ordinary arrangement. (For Laplanche, in a restoration of early Freud, there is actually nothing more ordinary than the trauma of the sexual.) There is no doubt that pleasure in shared sensoriality plays a central part in our clinical work as much as childrearing; it is like the pleasure of musical experience. So one may wonder, listening to Winnicott and Laplanche (in stereo), if framing may have its own erotics. But how to conceptualize this in terms of our categories of sexuality and erotics, which have so much to do with the gap and lack and separation from the object of desire? The frame (or "framing") performs the function of a shared psychosensory conductor, a syncretizer, that brings the experience of the world of objects alive in the clinical situation. By definition, this framing function operates in a presubjective, prereflective, nondifferentiated psychical domain of shared sensoriality. *But what kind of sexuality exists in this domain?*

Perhaps we could begin to answer this question by describing the frame as being bound and animated by *eros* as Freud as others before him defined it, as the essential force that binds all objects in the world, including human beings, together. And switching out Freud's positivist metaphysics for Heidegger's, it becomes conceivable that this world bound by *eros* is, for human beings, always already a shared and *meaningful* world that we are fundamentally attuned to in a relationship of *care* or *concern*. The world matters to us; we can't help it. It draws us into its patterns, textures, shapes, and rhythms. We are bound to it. But this is not realized *naturally*; it takes nurturing, the framing work of culture. In this sense, *eros* is not an innate instinct but rather an effect of a culture of collective induction, an induced state, a love of the world.

This notion of *eros* is virtually indistinguishable from a certain form of *love*, a very specific type of concern and care, which accompanies the activity of framing—something like an intimately attentive chaperoning function, introducing baby or loved one to the world through holding, presenting, handling, squiggling, and transitioning, and the inevitable stimulation and confusion that emerges over the course of these activities. If there is a distinct kind of erotics that operates in the domain of framing, it must emanate from something like the propensity toward shared embodiment in the world, from the musical attunement or harmony that results from these shared rhythms. Thus the animating and binding power of the frame may be nothing other than love itself, not only love of the other but *love of the meaningful world*. (The syncretic function of the ego, when it works, feels really good.) The form first taken by this primordial, ontological love, the love that allows the world to come into being meaningfully, is *musical* for the human being. In this view, "pressure"—as in, the physical or place-like experience of the frame, from the feel of the couch depressed beneath one's body to the light in the room at different times of year, from the sounds of the building to the inflections of tone and prosody of the analyst's voice, the lightest possible physical impression made by the *Stimmung* of the experience[18]—this pressure, when not excessive, doesn't only "mean" love, as Winnicott put it—it *is* love, the way love feels and sounds, the music of the love of the world.

Important modern thinkers, including Freud, have emphasized that this model of the meaningful world also implies that the world is bound and conducted by love. As Mikkel Borch-Jacobsen notes, the concept of love, as it appears in later Freudian works like *Beyond the Pleasure Principle* and *Group Psychology*, "is equivalent to Plato's eros, understood at once as platonic love and as re(as)sembling or (re)unifying power."[19] But already there is a slippage of terms, a qualifying of erotic love as what we colloquially regard as "platonic" (or, in Plato's time, *philia*), by which we typically mean love without sex, the friend zone, the love of friends. Perhaps Winnicott could have accepted this designation. But for Laplanche there is more to it than that, always more of the sexual than one can think about in the moment, always a remainder or enigmatic message to be translated in even the most parental, loving expressions of care. And Laplanche derives this model of message transmission—indeed, he translates it—from Freud; Laplanche provides his own translation of Freud that the latter, having abandoned his seduction theory, could never himself provide. The more Freud tried to explain what he meant about sexuality—and the more of this kind of distraught effort Strachey had to track and himself translate—the more confused its meaning becomes. As Freud wrote, for example, in "'Wild' Psychoanalysis" (a key document in his mounting effort to protect what he considered the discipline of psychoanalysis proper from the "wild" interpretive practices stemming from a widespread misunderstanding of what Freud meant by "sexuality," as if it were nothing beyond or more than explicit, "in the sheets" sex):

> In psychoanalysis, the concept of what is sexual comprises far more; it goes lower and also higher than its popular sense. This extension is justified genetically; we reckon as belonging to "sexual life" all the activities of the tender feelings which have primitive sexual impulses as their source.... For this reason we prefer to speak of *psychosexuality*, thus laying stress on the point that the mental factor in sexual life should not be overlooked or underestimated. We use the word "sexuality" in the same comprehensive sense as that in which the German language uses the word *lieben* ["to love"].[20]

Already, just fifteen years after abandoning the seduction theory—with decades remaining to further complicate the matter in Freud's writing and metapsychology—we have "sexual," "sexual life," "tender feelings," "primitive sexual impulses," "psychosexuality," "sexuality," "*lieben*," "love"—to be followed eventually by narcissism, autoerotism, and sublimation (and all of their pathological correlates). The interlacing and cross-referencing of these words is far from rare in Freud's writing and, perhaps, in any attempt to assign words to these aspects of human experience. Perhaps as Freud became better known, and more widely read, he found himself spending more and more time trying to explain what he meant by these terms, staking much of his claims on a phenomenon that in 125 years of psychoanalysis has never ceased to scandalize its public: the sexual life of very young children. In constructing his sea-change theory of sexuality, Freud ultimately hoped to clarify the nature of amorous, bodily, sexual feelings and their relation to one another by introducing his notion of *infantile* sexuality, which the psychoanalyst Ignacio Matte Blanco, in his own groundbreaking treatise on the unconscious, conceived of primarily with respect to the early era of psychosexual development, in which the psychosensory is still identical to the sexual—at least initially, before their differentiation.[21] The passion, the suffering, of sexual desire, predicated on difference (wanting something other than oneself), is always in tension with the erotics of shared experience at the level of framing, an ongoing counterpoint of binding and unbinding. Or to put it another way: What we colloquially refer to as "sexual," which Freud called "adult sexuality," is rooted in the drive-to-translate the impression, the message (even if nonverbal), left by psychosensory contact with an other that dates to our earliest experiences in the world, before we knew anything about what adults did with one another. "Children, in such circumstances," Freud writes in the Dora case—the circumstances of hearing one's parents in the bedroom next door—"divine something sexual in the uncanny sounds that reach their ears."[22] They know what sexual sounds sound like before they know what sex is, and these sounds (a kind of protomusic) are uncanny, *unheimlich*, un-home-like, the feeling of return to somewhere one has never been.

As to the question of what kind of sexuality operates in the frame, we might then look to the uncanny, which itself could be considered a fundamentally musical experience. Music, when it is good enough, re-sounds in a recapitulation of our early apprehension of the sexual, the confusion of tongues between the nascent sensory capacities of the infant and the fully developed capacity for sexual stimulation in the caregiver that precipitates our efforts at sense making, (re-)living our longing to understand things with our bodies. Music, like love, bridges the erotics of oneness and twoness, stimulating and sustaining this bodily capacity to be unresolved between them, to keep questions open. "Sphinx-like," Adorno writes of music in "The Relationship of Philosophy and Music," "it fools the listener by constantly promising meanings, and even providing them intermittently—meanings that for music, however, are in the truest sense means to the death of meaning. . . . Its relation to the thing that it cannot represent but would like to invoke is therefore endlessly mediated."[23] Music induces and propels this drive to translate not only in its lyrical or symbolic registers, its "love songs," but in all of its vibrational, rhythmic, tensile impact, an awakening at the level of what Anzieu referred to as the bodily ego, a harkening back to the undifferentiation of infantile sexuality, endlessly re-mediating the excesses of mind cognition with the enigma of unfolding and unresolving meaningfulness.

Even a joke, for Freud, a kind of isotope of the uncanny, pivots upon this body memory of the excess and enigma of the youngest recesses of the psyche-somatic reservoir. "For the infantile is the source of the unconscious," Freud writes in his Joke Book, the same year as the Dora case (and the even more famous *Three Essays on Sexuality*),

> and the unconscious thought-processes are none other than those—the one and only ones—produced in early childhood. The thought which, with the intention of constructing a joke, plunges into the unconscious is merely seeking there for the ancient dwelling-place of its former play with words. Thought is put back for a moment to the stage of childhood so as once more to gain possession of the childish source of pleasure. If we did not already know it from research into the psychology of the neuroses, we should be led by jokes to a suspicion that the strange unconscious revision is nothing else than the infantile type of thought-activity.[24]

In this sense, the psychosexual quality of the undifferentiated psycho-sensory domain may in some way be linked to the era of childhood, reverberating in the present through experiences of unison, like getting a joke, the disclosure of seeing something together. But the undifferentiation of shared perception is never a full identity or merger; there remains an irreducible and crucial separation, forming a kind of "binocular" vision, as Bion once put it, or perhaps bin*aural* hearing, like two road-trip companions listening to music on an open highway, an immersive, spacious yet bounded, and deeply musical feeling. (This links to the question of the "double" in the writing of some French theorists—André Green, René Rousillon, the Botellas.) The asymptote of this unison, only achievable through fantasy, would be utter nondifferentiation, looking at the world through the same eyes; actual lived experience, by contrast, always rests upon the irreducible materiality of being in one's own body where there is always a temporomusical difference, a stereo effect.

Thus while it may be a relevant reference for the erotics of framing in important ways, the *après-coup* fantasy of one's childhood known as infantile sexuality approaches an ocean of noise more than the highly evolved pattern-complexity and richness of the weave's musi-language and its accompanying erotics, whatever we may call them. Perhaps it would be more accurate to say that this pairing, sharing dimension of the frame resonates not only in its echoes of infantile sexuality but in the certain psychic position afforded through *homo*erotics,[25] an identificatory process based on sameness that lies in dialectical relation to the *het*erosexual dimension of desire animated by the seduction of encountering otherness. The polarity of homoerotic-heterosexual is a key dimension of Laplanche's thought in which radical, unconscious, enigmatic otherness *is* the essence and motivating force for uniquely human (or infantile) sexuality as he sees it. For Laplanche, the *sexuality* identified by psychoanalysis is, on the deepest level, always "hetero"—not with respect to anatomy but strictly in the sense of an essential, driving otherness of the message. Extending this idea, what Freud referred to as the "oceanic feeling" is only achievable from the shore of shared company. Without the weave, the ocean is nothing more than an uninhabitable abyss in which to drown; only woven into the communal can one, paradoxically, can get back into the ocean, can glimpse a glimmer of God, from the terra firma of dry land, secured by the placeness of human habitation.

The tension between these two poles of erotic identification and sexual otherness constitutes one of the special problems of the sexual in analytic treatment and bears crucially on how we conceptualize our theory and our ethics of sexuality within the living frame, on the experience of being seen, psychically or corporeally, and being spontaneously enjoyed, adored, delighted in, without being co-opted or violated by the other. Always in the mix of the analytic situation is the question of how beauty and enjoyment are secured while also unavoidably and necessarily disrupted by trauma, devolving into the coveted and the tempting. The frame guarantees a mode of discovery based on shared perception and unison of experience, an optimal zone for sustaining conflict and disruption—as Meltzer once put it, for apprehending beauty.[26] The post-traumatic syndrome we know as (hetero)sexual desire, the reverberating aftereffect of the encounter with the irreducibly other, is what adults must teach children how to weave into a comprehensive way of conducting oneself, inspired by the (homo)erotic pleasure of being like a loved one.

If the enigmatic, semiotic message-to-be-translated is always hetero-, then the contact-barrier along which these messages are presented or transmitted could be considered always necessarily homo-, a shared experience approaching sameness that unfurls itself in through musical form. There needs to be some sameness in the life of the weave to substantiate the consistency that enables it to work, to bridge traumatic ruptures by continuously assimilating and capturing that which does not at first fit into its homogenic continuity, generating psychosensory patterns that are always being enriched and elaborated while preserving formal constancy. In this sense,

erotic ↔ sexual

may be a more contemporary way of thinking about the two components or poles of psychosexuality (as opposed to the "erotic → sexual" sequence that is suggested in much of Freud's writing), a clarification of terms that perhaps all philosophers of love have used inconsistently and often squeamishly for precisely the reason that Freud was forced to abandon his most brilliant insight about the lifespan of sexuality: the proximity of adults and children. This erotic ↔ sexual dialectic is exactly how Laplanche reinterprets *eros* and the sexual:

life/binding/*eros* ↔ death/unbinding/sexual

With this polarity in mind, the psychosexual challenge of childhood (historically regarded as the Oedipus complex) is actually to navigate a change at the level of *homo-eros* in which the primacy of the shared, identificatory bond must be renegotiated through seduction toward the otherness of other people, always and only made possible by a sufficiently stable, shared, homoerotic experience and understanding of being that underwrites and organizes the social world. In its own brand of *après-coup*, its tender *après-caresse*, the psyche-soma holds the charge of sociality to fuel our journey through the world, the work of identification its solar panel of conduction and restoration. It is the AC/DC of the weave that animates our participation in all forms of collective membership, the superconductors of social bonds, which secure experiences of the beautiful and the delightful against collapse under the pressure of greed and desperation.

As institutions of social bondedness have become compromised and unwoven, while at the same time expressions of so-called homosexuality have become increasingly unveiled and normalized, clinical psychoanalysis may be one of the places where it is still possible to promote the binding/unbinding process and thus one of the last spaces in which the promise of homoerotic potential can still be fulfilled in safe haven, where the explicit question need not be asked, where the ethics of the frame safeguards what the French historian René Girard called the sacred from the violence of profane exploitation.[27] While care and concern are clearly components of this *ethos*, the main force at play may be the pleasure of sociality, of being like one another, never more so than when we are unified by shared experiences—the sensory surfaces of the contact-dance between patient and analyst, as between infant and parent. And while for Freud an excess of this identificatory bondedness may have posed a threat of self-dissolution, of drowning, so too would a deficiency of pleasure at the level of shared existence result in dis-ease, in what Ferenczi once called, perhaps in reference to his then estranged relation to Freud, "the loss of the love of friends."[28] In this sense, the psychical domain of musicality is not a primitive or atavistic area or an enclave of the sublimated or the artistic, neither something left behind nor a paradise (let alone a lost narcissism). It is right here, right now, at the intersection of the lived body with the world, musicalized through the companionship of shared perception. The rhythm of the frame, like all music, only exists as music insofar as it is experienced through this mutual sensoriality *as music*. As Erkki Huovinen writes in "Understanding Music," "without some connection to the perceptually understood appearances of music, any thoughts concerning heard music would remain empty."[29] Like the sounds of heard music, the structure of the living frame, whatever may happen within it, is facilitated, embodied, engendered, and curated through the reverberating presence of its conductor, the analyst, who understands it not only logistically or technically but *aesthetically* as a foundation of musical experience.

It would be an illusion (or delusion) to think that one can depart from this vitalizing domain of shared selfhood without becoming ill. We live in the domain of musicality and can't live without it. "We are not selves in the way that we are organisms," the Canadian philosopher Charles Taylor writes in *Sources of the Self*. "We are only selves insofar as we move in a certain space of questions, as we seek and find an orientation toward the good. . . . I define who I am by defining where I speak from. . . . There is no way we could be inducted into personhood except by being initiated into a language . . . by being brought into an ongoing conversation by those who brought us up."³⁰ Left out of such a conversation, Taylor posits, the self cannot constitute and reverts to a crisis of identity, unable to even suffer one's isolation, unable to articulate it as such:

> Such a person wouldn't know where he stood on issues of fundamental importance, would have no orientation in these issues whatever, wouldn't be able to answer for himself on them. If one wants to add to the portrait by saying that the person doesn't suffer this absence of frameworks as a lack, isn't in other words in a crisis at all, then one rather has a picture of frightening dissociation.³¹

But while language may be the game (to use Wittgenstein's concept), the common focus of this working group, the implicit activity within this conversation, is neither differentiation nor symbolization but the erotic, binding pleasure of *syncretics*, involving engagement at the level of psychosensory attunement (which is how the frame is set up and maintained), from the establishment of the setting to the conduct of the analyst, including interpretation. One technical instrument of synthesis (as opposed to analysis), as Scarfone has noted, is *elaboration*, which he opposes to the differentiating activity of analytic interpretation.³² The interwoven praxes of elaboration and translation yield the liberated, serial disclosure of new forms, renewing and revitalizing the psyche-soma as it is grounded in the shared being synthesized through the living frame.

III

The meaningful world always rests upon the framing of a shared and meaning*less* world, a bedrock of undreamed experience beneath the communal dream. The human world rests upon the humic earth from whence it came, which is not organized in a meaningful way. And so we rely upon a nonprocess, a beta world, a framed pattern of experience, a repository of percussive empathies, that forms a background, like a painter's canvas that literally at every moment makes the painting possible. We are all always already conductors (and insulators) of the collective and intergenerationally transmitted unconscious to sync up with the unmetabolized sphere, to make living matter of the unmeaningful, beckoning and driving the continued pursuit of felt meaning, feeling that things matter. The collectively repressed unconscious drives the communally preserved weave to provide a way to go-on-being in the world, to surf the ocean of noise with the fluidity and fluency of music. The electrical current of shared being is grounded in the culturally sanctioned and preserved forms of movement that are transmitted from one generation to the next through a network of inductive and seductive processes, identificatory mimesis and enigmatic contact, a *weave* of being human, of human being.

This weave manifests in psychoanalytic work first and foremost in the form of the frame. Both patient and analyst rely on the frame *not* to mean anything, to bind the anxieties that would otherwise arise from keeping the frame at the top of mind, from treating the foundational structure, the medulla oblongata of the treatment, as a required focus of conscious thought, which would be like having to agree at the end of each meeting where to meet next, or finding oneself vigilantly counting down the remaining minutes of every session. There is every reason to take the frame for granted as soon and as often as possible; it keeps us from going crazy. But there is a limit to this relaxation of attention. To rely unconditionally upon the frame, which is exactly what the constancy of the frame induces us to do, is to compromise its vitality for the sake of its predictability. Breaches in the frame—from the habitual interruptions of holidays to the gut-punch of unexpected rupture—may energize the necessary sense of contingency and presence for the frame to respond to the nascency of new life, to sustain the transformational processes that require live drumming, active frame management.

The interruption of the framing function is always consequential, and when it persists, or when the frame falls into disrepair, it approximates the worldlessness of what the French sociologist Émile Durkheim called *anomie*, the normlessness of an isolated, alien existence. Yet the excitement of interruption, against the background of kept time, can make the erotic one's own. (The "love you" of *eros* is always working on the "fuck you" of the sexual, and vice versa.) Thus the work of keeping time, all too easily marginalized or dismissed in our traditional descriptions of psychoanalytic work, is as crucial as receptivity, reverie, and any possible form of meaning making to the psychoanalytic project, the heartbeat along which travel the best practices of listening, interpreting, translating, and, of course, framing itself.

Laplanche, for his part, said very little about how the adult teaches the child to translate. For Laplanche, once seduction has transpired, there is no way back to the prereflective domain of shared experience—even though we are forever driven to return to this fantasied paradise. This might reflect the pessimism and suspicion of collective or oceanic modes of being that marks a lot of French thought after World War II, the period of Laplanche's childhood and intellectual coming of age; the tragic dimension of this sensibility may have something to do with the profoundly sobering loss and grief that marked Laplanche's lifetime in France. What emerges instead, for him, is a dialectic between the binding and unbinding of the source-objects, relics of the adult's messages, which are only ever partially successful, in the now inescapably subjective world.

From the point of view of the weave, the sexual alterity toward which seduction seduces is also a waystation on the route back to the erotics of unison. When the writer George Bataille, for example, emphasized the transgressiveness of sexuality, he highlighted its removal from everyday consciousness (linking it in this way to the sacred); in so doing, he suggested how sexuality is implicated in the search for an undifferentiated state. Viewed this way, sexuality would seem to work ultimately in the service of a syncretic state of unison or primary narcissism,[33] a way of entering the weave of shared psychosexuality, the inflection point back toward the unifying power of *eros*. Along these lines, we might interpret Laplanche's notion of sexuality—as a creation of the mind to compensate for the perceived enigmatic rift with the other—as being, after all, a search for the weave of collective *habitus*, the implicit repertoire of forms and ways of being human. So even the sexual may, in this sense, be understood as a search for a syncretic connection to the weave.

Freud himself toys with this possibility in *Beyond the Pleasure Principle*, reflecting on Aristophanes's myth of original humans, joined back to back, split in two by an angry god, and seeking to reunite through the sexual act:

Shall we follow the hint given us by the poet-philosopher, and venture upon the hypothesis that living substance at the time of its coming to life was torn apart into small particles, which have ever since endeavoured to reunite through the sexual instincts? that these instincts, in which the chemical affinity of inanimate matter persisted, gradually succeeded, as they developed through the kingdom of the protista, in overcoming the difficulties put in the way of that endeavour by an environment charged with dangerous stimuli—stimuli which compelled them to form a protective cortical layer? that these splintered fragments of living substance in this way attained a multicellular condition and finally transferred the instinct for reuniting, in the most highly concentrated form, to the germ-cells?—But here, I think, the moment has come for breaking off.[34]

Freud breaks off just as he approaches what would have been a significant discovery regarding the mutual formation of the erotic and the sexual, the way in which one always inflects the ongoing psychosexual process back toward the other. But while this may have been an insurmountable terminological challenge in the project of theorizing psychosexuality, it was also never Freud's primary focus. Beginning with the "Project" of 1895, Freud was inclined to conceive of all psychical functioning in terms of *energy* conducting itself along neuronal pathways more than he was concerned about differentiating and labeling the varying qualities of that energy in their own right. Accordingly, Freud may have overstated the role of what he called the sexual instinct as restricting the broader category of libido, while referring to a more general life force variously as eros, "sexuality," "psychosexuality," and "love." (It may be no coincidence that he broke ties with Jung, who corrected the error—perhaps, in fact, *because* he corrected it—by staking a claim for the broad universality, and not the strict sexuality, of libido.)

But while the proliferation and application of terms like *eros* and *sexual* may have led some psychoanalytic thinkers since Freud to reduce or diminish the differences between them—Ruth Stein, for example, in her seminal paper "The Poignant, the Excessive, and the Enigmatic," declares on the first page that she will be using them synonymously[35]—it may in fact be useful to preserve the distinction after all, if only to formulate their relation to one another: how the enigmatic excess of adult sexuality in parental care engages the infant's translational capacities, driving the infant toward the psychosexual meaningfulness of being human. And by virtue of that very process, the infant is simultaneously invited back into a community of world-fascination, returned to a kind of audience membership that is already in progress, animated by the erotic (indeed, homoerotic) conduction of energy based on the sameness of shared experience, in contrast to the seduction of the sexual, which draws the psyche-soma toward difference or otherness.

erotic (homo, syncretic) ← [psyche-soma] → **sexual** (hetero, analytic)

If these terms became impossibly convoluted in Freud, as elsewhere, it may have been not only their dialectical continuity but the lack of a common denominator to unify the concepts: a notion of *being*, preserved and exemplified in psychoanalytic practice (via the frame) if not originally in psychoanalytic theory. (It was the painter Milner and not the writer Freud who named the concept as such, borrowing it from her own preferred art form.) As in Heidegger's notion of *Dasein*, the frame operates as the precondition of meaningfulness, the *Durchschnittlichkeit*—often translated as "averageness" but etymologically closer to the *through-line-ness*, which bears a resemblance to what Freud called *Durcharbeitung* (working-through), what Winnicott called *going-on-being*, what Laplanche on several occasions referred to as a *spiral*—that binds the material of the session, the matters being processed within the frame, with the meaningfulness of human being, its spatiotemporal registration engendered by the heritage and habitus of humanized perception.

Contra Freud (and following Laplanche), this primordial, ontological, musical eros and the presubjective, prereflective, nondifferentiated dimension it discloses is *deeper* than the sexuality defined by psychoanalysis; it is the soil from which both sexuality and the individual subject, including the dynamic unconscious, emerges, equiprimordially, through unison, syncopation, and occasional disruption in the music of being. The question for the subject, and often for the analytic patient, is how we get from one to the other, how we go-on, how we be-have, how we conduct the negotiation between infant and adult, speechlessness and speech, alone and together. The greatest source of confusion in Freud's theory of sexuality might have been the hand he tied behind his back when he foreswore his intuitive hunch about the effect of parents on their children, the convolution of which is nowhere starker than in the science fiction of the migration of erotogenic zones over the lifespan, which Freud posited as driven by phylogenesis as expressed in individual development, rather than as something that happens as a creation of human contact in the physical zones of greatest interest to the infant and parent. "This migration is inconceivable," Laplanche writes. "The only way to think of it is that in the self-preservative process there are successive zones or places of the body that take more attention from the parent.... It is through the interrelation of the parents or the carers to the child that sexuality gathers, passes as if through a conductor; it is conducted through the care given to the child."[36]

The reference to conduction here is barely a metaphor; sexuality passes not "as if through a conductor" but is literally conducted as electrical energy, translated into symbolic meaning with only partial success. ("Conductor" here is no more a metaphor than the psyche is a metaphor for the bodily ego, as Freud famously claimed, as opposed to the non-metaphoric simultaneity of what Winnicott simply called the "psyche-soma.") Without a way to move, a way to handle one's body, to de-monstrate being-in-the-world, the infant's body functions not only as a psyche-somatic conductor of this adult energy but as an insulator, a fixator, a site of trauma, a break. And the only way to develop forms of movement—including but hardly limited to verbal thought or speech—is through inspired identification with the adults who seem to know how to do it, a form of being-and-having one's parents that is underwritten by eros itself. The erotic potential of the infant to be moved by the parent, to move with the parent, facilitates and mitigates the ethical seduction into sexuality and does this through the ongoing dance with an *etho-cal* induction into musicality (which carries its own ethics of engagement), what Jean Luc-Nancy describes, in his book of the same name, as *The Creation of the World*—a world being, he tells us, "*a space in which a certain tonality resonates*," a "*totality* of resonances that the elements, the moments, and the places of this world echo, modulate, and modalize." To inhabit such a world is to occupy or "have" it, he continues, "with *a sense of being: it is a manner of being there and of standing in it. A world is an ethos, a habitus and an inhabiting*: it is what holds to itself and in itself, following to its proper mode. It is a network of the self-reference of this stance. In this way it resembles a subject—and in a way, without a doubt, what is called a subject is each time by itself a world."[37]

A good analysis is the creation of a world, a world-syncretics, which is identical with a way of being in a world and which is always, to paraphrase (and pair) Bion and Laplanche, making the best of a fundamentally anthropological situation. Just as for Winnicott there is no model of health without the psychical scar tissue that he called a "false self," there is for Laplanche (and Freud) no model of sexuality, for becoming a human, apart from the intergenerational transmission of sexual trauma. Trauma, in other words, is not just a problem; it is also an inciting action that provokes the translational function that works-through the unavoidable disruptions of going-on-being. To be psyche-somatically alive is to sustain the charge of participation in the communal sensorium, to conduct its electrical energy, to keep this energy moving. And to get this energy going, to optimize this continuousness, psychoanalysis precisely abstains movement, holds back, collects this sexual pressure, and channels it through an erotic vitality, rhythmizing this energy through the world beat of a living frame.

SIDE B

6

RE-MEMBERING, RE-BEATING, AND WORLDING-THROUGH

membership
dissociation
world

Whether I was in my body or out of my body I know not.
—HANDEL, ON COMPOSING *THE MESSIAH*

I

For a drummer, or a conductor—or, we are suggesting, for a psychoanalyst—the first order of business is always to count off, to establish a pattern, synchronizing bodies and rhythmizing experience through the shared beat of a living frame. The beta function of this rhythmized synchrony induces the psyche-soma into the fellowship of musical ensemble, joining up to a collective membership in the community of human being, "keeping time with everyone." Being "membered" in this way, as an individual, is always dependent upon well-tuned embeddedness in this sensorial collective, which provides the necessary percussion and support for its constituents to associate into feelingful grooves and harmonies. Those who stumble or who are unable to join remain *unmembered*, disconnected from the community, and may become *dismembered*, dissociated psychosomatically. We only inhabit our bodies with a full sense of subjective vitality and desire insofar as the psyche-soma realm is incorporated into the body politic, where it can function as a nodal conduit within a human network of sensory aliveness and cultural choreography. When Freud commented that hysterics suffered from their reminiscences—from not being able to *remember*—he was indicating the extent to which the patterned movements of their bodies had become alien to themselves (as had the memories or wishes animating them)—*because* they had become unintelligible to a community of shared meaning. So we can understand an implicit bid in these stereotyped repetitions to return to the scene of a dis-membering crime, an attempt to reconnect through the tuned-in responsiveness of an analyst, to find one's way back to an original membership that makes any communication meaningful, memorable, member-able, at all.

While it is clear that we rely on the meaningfulness generated through this connectivity in order to communicate with one another, the actual current that runs along our weave network, the currency of exchange in the weave, is not exactly "communication" in the typical sense. To induce the wordless, worldless infant into its collective understanding, the environment must enchant the infant at the level of the unspoken, implicit patterning of body position and movement, iterated to the point of reliability and holding function. In this prereflective process, uniting us through the binding power of mimetic identification, each of us is bound to the communal sensibility of being in the world. Through membership in the shared matrix of uses and dispositions of our bodies (what the sociologist Pierre Bourdieu called habitus), a certain existence-anxiety is lifted from us, and we are freed up to cultivate interest in the world. Membered in the collective through the tempos of shared habits and cultural forms, which give us our sense of conscious individuality, we are able to enter the temporality of being a subject. The impressions left by the world on the psyche-soma are no longer felt as imprints on an isolated body-self but as membering us in the world, woven with and among others.

As Laplanche elucidated, relating to oneself always involves an engagement with the other within, an internal otherness that is the residuum of these actual engagements with other human beings. Through even the most ordinary contact resulting from the ongoing activities of world members, we become fascinated with the internal depositories founded in our impressions of that very world, the enigmatic presence of otherness that comes to reside within us, inspiring their translation into what become one's own private thoughts and desires (a circuit that Winnicott once called "cul-de-sac communication"), the elaboration and development of what one likes, of liking some things and not others, of differentiation. The psyche-soma appropriates ways of elaborating oneself, of being true to oneself, from the weave-repository of communal practices, borrowing from the public archive of ways to find the world by moving through it. The weave thus allows us to find ourselves through finding and sensing the world, and vice versa, via cultural objects that conduct the passage between the two. Winnicott believed that before one is ever able to communicate with others (or communicate the otherness within oneself to fellow humans), a transition must occur out of the privacy of subjective phenomena through transitional intermediaries that are imbued with a hybrid quality of insideness and outsideness to bridge the divide. If "the question is," as Winnicott pithily suggests, "how to be isolated without having to be insulated," then the answer, he proposes,

> might come from mothers who do not communicate with their infants except in so far as they are subjective objects. By the time mothers become objectively perceived their infants have become masters of various techniques for indirect communication, the most obvious of which is the use of language. There is this transitional period, however, which has specially interested me, in which transitional objects and phenomena have a place, and begin to establish for the infant the use of symbols.
>
> I suggest that an important basis for ego development lies in this area of the individual's communicating with subjective phenomena, which alone gives the feeling of real.
>
> In the best possible circumstances growth takes place and the child now possesses three lines of communication: communication that is for ever silent, communication that is explicit, indirect and pleasurable, and this third or intermediate form of communication that slides out of playing into cultural experience of every kind.[1]

But in a way that Winnicott may have never needed to explicitly articulate (or perhaps simply undervalued), the infant may first need an *ob*jective sense of the shared world, conducted through the beta function of interwoven unison. The subjective world of the infant is thus not only (or not really) a private carapace into which the mother carefully titrates the reality of frustration; it is actually a return to the communal in the form of a private experience. The paradox is that the internal private world, the "all-me" world, is the domain in which the public, shared world is originally discovered. Here we can refer to the dichotomy of the erotic and the sexual from the previous chapter. For Laplanche, the subjective world is irreducibly other and, thus, irreducibly sexual, a repository of messages that have not been (or can never be) translated, a domain of hermeneutic activity that takes us into ourselves and into the world; Winnicott's model emphasizes and elucidates the "erotic" side of this process, the role of identification, recognition, and incorporation of "subjective objects" into a psyche-somatic continuum that makes us feel creative and alive.

This concept of subjective objects, generally underrepresented in Winnicott scholarship, not only revitalizes the notion of narcissistic objects in the traditional psychoanalytic sense with respect to the potential of transference—the unthinkably historical becoming the palpably livable through the medium of the analyst—but furthermore illuminates one specific function of *musical* objects,[2] the songs or albums that one listens to so many times that nearly every nuance of every moment becomes identifiable, anticipatable, and a veritable part of oneself, in a way that may be partially shared by others but that is ultimately private, even sacred. (For this reason live performances can sometimes be a little depressing—pulling the cultural object too far out of transitional space into the world of others.) Being immersed in this state of musical communion entails being in a particular state of consciousness, here-but-not-here, present but absent, enchanted, entranced. Socrates, as Sloterdijk notes in his magnificent essay "Where Are We When We Hear Music?" seemed to be in another world for hours on end while in deep communion with his thoughts, which, in his own cul-de-sac state, began to bounce, reverberate, and harmonize with one another in a layered and uniquely musical way.

The question of where the thinker is immersed during his absences can hardly be answered without talking about a world of inner voices and tones whose presence may be more powerful than any other sound. If the philosopher is removed to a sphere that seems out of this world to ordinary mortals, his immersion in thought in a situation of deafness to outside noise still has relevance at a deep acoustic level. This is connected with what we call ensoulment and being-in-oneself at such an essential level that we would be unable to specify what the soul is supposed to be if self-referential hearing were not always a part of it.[3]

The conditions of self-reference established in these musical states, so crucial to Socrates's thinking, are always enabled by the tethering function of embeddedness in the shared musicality of the weave. Seen in this way, what Sloterdijk calls "ensoulment and being-in-oneself" is actually the process through which one learns how to be-*with* that which is not (yet) oneself, how to commune with not-me. What might look like a removal of oneself from the communal may in fact be finding one's way into it, a bit of dissociation that actually brings one closer to the world—though the tether can be stretched to the point of snapping, as in the legendary betrayal and demise of Socrates himself. Perhaps it was the failure of communal holding that accentuated the centrality of music for Socrates as he approached his execution, as he wrote in the *Phaedo*:

> In the course of my life I have often had intimations in dreams "that I should make music." The same dream came to me sometimes in one form, and sometimes in another, but always saying the same or nearly the same words: Make and cultivate music, said the dream. And hitherto I had imagined that this was only intended to exhort and encourage me in the study of philosophy, which has always been the pursuit of my life, and is the noblest and best of music. The dream was bidding me to do what I was already doing, in the same way that the competitor in a race is bidden by the spectators to run when he is already running. But I was not certain of this, as the dream might have meant music in the popular sense of the word, and being under sentence of death, and the festival giving me a respite, I thought that I should be safer if I satisfied the scruple, and, in obedience to the dream, composed a few verses before I departed.[4]

Socrates acknowledges in these poignant reflections the through-line of music in his life as a philosopher, the sense in which philosophy was his interpretive expression of musical inspiration, "the noblest and best of music." It is no coincidence that Sloterdijk frames his evocative question about the location of musical experience around the image of an "absent" Socrates, listening for the music, obeying one's dream to make it, encouraged to do what he was already doing, making and cultivating music in the very absenting of himself that constituted being present with something, with the actual living of his life. And as the tragedy of Socrates reminds us, this musical absence is always contingent upon the world's enduring presence through the constancy of fellow humans, upon the weave that cultivates these subjective objects and allows these transient states for the purposes of refinding the world.

Freud had noticed similar absence states ("*absences*") in what he called hysterical patients, sometimes when he least expected it. "What she told me was perfectly coherent," he wrote of Frau Emmy von N.'s normal, social mode of speaking,

> and revealed an unusual degree of education and intelligence. This made it seem all the more strange when every two or three minutes she suddenly broke off, contorted her face into an expression of horror and disgust, stretched out her hand towards me, spreading and crooking her fingers, and exclaimed, in a changed voice, charged with anxiety: "Keep still!—Don't say anything!—Don't touch me!"[5]

While Freud conceived of these *absences* as symptoms of hysteric illness (which contemporary theorists might regard as a state of consciousness or self-state), they may also be regarded (perhaps in a more Winnicottian mode) as a state of affairs, so to speak, a kind of psychomusical key signature, a noncommunicative configuration between bodies in space, a bid for attunement to the state of things, how things are now, a soloist in search of accompaniment, a piece of body music being replayed in case the analyst might pick it up. (It is worth nothing that each of the patient's commands becomes, for better or worse, a cornerstone of psychoanalytic technique.) Insofar as these are transient states, they form potentially usable fragments, which are available for sampling and looping into a more usably musical, "other-worldly" form and as such can be contrasted with more severe dissociation, entire zones of isolation, alterworlds of no musical possibility, in which no therapy can happen and where the transitions that each session replays in miniature cannot be experienced as evolving. It is not an inherently bad thing to enter such a world, to check out of the shared world any time one needs or likes; the question is always whether one can ever return from the Hotel California, whether one can ever leave.

Perhaps we can imagine a spectrum or continuum of sociality, extending from, at one end, the free association of the Freudian enterprise (underwritten by the *as*-sociation of its participants) to the asociality of psychopathology, which is an often highly subtle and skilled way of not tolerating being with people. But to absent oneself from that continuum altogether is to occupy not a self-state so much as a kind of statelessness, *un*membered because of the idiosyncrasy and privacy of its own logic, its own spatiotemporal status outside of shared time. Wherever (and *whenever*) we are when we hear music, we are straddling this threshold of private and public, self and other, alien and familiar. The musicologist Erik Wallrup, who earlier provided us with the concept of *Stimmung* to link musical and psychoanalytic forms of attunement (indeed, to identify them), believes the moment of musical experience is a moment of "new attunement," though this moment happens, he cautions, both "in the flow of time" and somehow "at odds with the flow." And the starting point of this new attunement, he continues, can only be identified after the fact, once the moment is gone.

> Even if, using our reflective powers, we can specify where we begin to become attuned to the new attunement, pointing it out in a score or as an exact second in a recording, it is impossible to say when it became clear. If it starts with a chord, only the next chord shows what the first chord meant, and the musical meaning is evident only when we reflect upon it, leaving the musical flow and therefore the attunemental changes. If it starts with a rhythm, this rhythm is only attainable when the rhythmic gesture has ended, and the musical meaning of this gesture is apparent only through the same kind of reflection.[6]

Where we are when we hear music is at first where we are not, at a moment that is somehow not a moment but presents itself, retrospectively, as having been one. As in quantum physics, we are there and not there, two places at the same time, particle and wave, violating locality. These moments form caesurae in the continuity of consciousness, which we find ourselves going back to, repeating, like residues of the day in dreams of the night. The new attunement of the musical moment is in this sense a *sexual* experience, a reorganizing of time by returning, *après-coup*, to a disruption or break in time, transforming hooks and samples into repetitions and rhythms that in turn erotically charge the ongoing emergence of new musical possibilities, for the music-work to protect us from the intromissive dead zone of Muzak, from music that does no work and allows no psychical work to proceed. (Authoritarianism is always an intromissive perversion of the erotic.) These moments of return, which have been bookmarked for their curiosity, their disruption of previous patterns of continuity, vitalize the psyche-soma with fresh sensation, new notes, to be woven into the fabric of the meaningful world through the workshopping, the groove making, of repetition, the recurrent chance to work-through experiences of enigmatic disruption. The musical moment suspends time in loops of repetition in the service of resuming time, of futurity, of going-on-being.

Music itself exists only in this delayed reaction, in the body-time moments dimensionalized through the afterwardsness of poignant longing. There is ostensibly "music" around us now more than ever, but it only functions as music when we are actually engaged, bodily and soulfully, in the afterwardsness of its erotic and sexual potentials. (No one can be destroyed in effigy, and no one can be enchanted in it either.) The experience of not being in music, of not "getting" it, is hardly rare, and one needs a good reason, an inspiration, to try to find a way in, to move oneself toward the music from the impossible position of disenchantment. To perceive or comport oneself toward a musical object from a position outside the musical *Stimmung*, where we inevitably find ourselves, serves little psyche-somatic purpose beyond a kind of preparation or precontemplation, scanning for a portal, a way into the music. "No hearer can believe that he or she is standing on the edge of the audible," Sloterdijk writes.

> The ear knows no partner; it does not evolve a frontal "view" of objects at a distance, because it knows "world" or "objects" only to the extent

that it is in the middle of the acoustic event—or, we could say, insofar as it floats or dives into the auditory space. It follows that from the beginning a philosophy of hearing would only be possible as a theory of being-inside—as an interpretation of "intimacy" that will become sensitive to the world through human wakefulness.[7]

Wallrup vibes with Sloterdijk, reiterating the centrality of the body in this experience of musically sensitized intimacy:

> Music moves the listener with its movement—and this experience of movement depends on the lived body. The listener does not relate to music as something going on outside him or her, trying to respond to it within; no, the listener is already out there in the music, in that which is a world. Or perhaps even better, just like *Stimmung* is a hybrid, music is placed beyond outside and inside. If the aesthetics of empathy described a relation to music in terms of subjectivity, where the subject identifies itself with the musical movement, the phenomenology of the lived body describes the relation in terms of resonance or of attunement with a world; but in the same stroke it eradicates the difference between subject and object, between inside and outside.[8]

To simply be within range of musical audition, to have one's eardrums vibrated by sound, is not equal to having a musical experience. Having within one's digital reach what the music critic Ben Ratliff has aptly described as "Every Song Ever" may give a false sense of infinity to the universe of one's subjective objects; without the enigmatic fascination of fellow listeners to orient one's attention, the curatorial function is relegated, almost ubiquitously nowadays, to heuristic algorithms, leaving listeners paralyzed, paradoxically, by too much music and not enough humans to help sort through it, leaving us back at square one, stranded in the same old songs. To actually hear music, one must be alive to the movement the music induces, a form of movement that is not inborn but potentiated, as Sloterdijk formulates, through the inductive apprenticeship of bodily aliveness, musical living.

> First, we hear in advance, before individuation, which means that foetal hearing anticipates the world as a totality of noise and sound that is

always in the process of coming; from the darkness the foetus listens ecstatically to the world of sound, usually oriented towards the world, leaning boldly forward to the future. Second, after the formation of the ego we hear backwards—the ear wants to stop the world existing as a totality of noise, it yearns for the archaic euphony of the pre-world interior and activates the memory of a euphoric ecstasy that accompanies us like a night light from paradise. We could say that the individuated or unhappy ear continues irresistibly trying to move away from the real world towards a space of intimate a-cosmic reminiscences.[9]

So there is always a double movement with respect to music. We are beckoned toward a sound-world that is always already there waiting for us, and we long for the ecstasy of harmonies that are always already gone. The unhappy ear, like the hysteric, suffers from these reminiscences and "samples" those signals that may be looped and mined for their musicalizing potential, their promise of resolution, preparing us in turn for new music. Once the nascent psyche-soma, incubated in the rhythms and neurochemical bath of a not-yet-other human being, accumulates experiences of synchronizing anticipation of the world with its ongoing arrival, of found-creation, the developing capacity for musical experience gradually inflects toward a longing for respite from the dissonance of an ever-accelerating noise-surround, a return to a remembered pleasure of musical resolution. As Byung-Chal Han writes, "Beauty is owed to duration, to a contemplative synopsis. It is not a momentous brilliance or attraction, but an afterglow, a phosphorescence of things"[10]—a "nightlight from paradise," as Sloterdijk puts it. Only through this resonant afterglow of this "archaic euphony," through its afterwardsness, does the world become reflectively meaningful to each subject. Unmembered to the world of musical apprenticeship, these mere echoes become perpetually isolated sound-shapes—reminiscences, preserving in amber, in vinyl, an unthinkable curiosity, lying in wait for translation, without which we are always simply on a loop, forever trying to find a way back into the garden.

Wallrup (sampling Sloterdijk) offers a musicalization of Lacan's mirror stage to describe this infinite return, reinterpreting it as what he calls an Odyssean "siren stage," which we enter "when a voice seems to sing about the becoming of the subject: 'By listening closely, the incipient subject opens up and moves towards a particular mood in which it can perceive what is its own with wonderful clarity.' Thus the mood is present before the subject has become a subject; it is part of the becoming of the subject."[11]

It is through resonance in the sounds of the world that we start to become subjects for the first time, recognizing and identifying oneself in the music. But like the mirror stage, the sirens always involve a distortion, a seductive *mis*recognition, that tantalizes the ear with a false sense of coherence, never quite giving us the full picture and stimulating a perpetual search for new music to more fully elaborate and approximate the evolving complexity of being human. The weave welcomes the fetus to a world of sound to sample as a way of recognizing and finding oneself, even as the ambassadors of that same weave, its sirens, seduce the nascent subject off course, distorting the sounds with the all-too-human noise of the sexual, the notes that do not fit, the objects to be endlessly refound. Through this double movement of induction and seduction, an apprenticeship for translating the world can be established, situating us in the world by enchanting us with it. Music, in other words, not only conducts an original fascination with the world, reminding us of an originary response to the sea of noise or the siren's song; it *is the original fascination*, the original state of wonder born of the encounter with music and of lacking the equipment (and in the exemplary case of music, lacking any need for equipment) to translate the experience into representational meaning.

To reenter states of musical immersion is thus also always to be newly disrupted by fresh dissonances, animating desire as it returns us to the familiar, the arousal of longing inseparable from the erotics of belonging. The movement between oneness and twoness states is henceforth always haunted by the trauma of the original journey. The decomposition of the world, however necessary, is not welcomed by the uninitiated, not advised for the unmembered, not to be tried at home (though is precisely where its deadly work begins). The same unbinding that relaxes the individual into the sensory presentationality of the world also inevitably, at the same time, dissolves some previously cherished representations of that world, alarming the ego with the threat of lost meaning. (An infant is never afraid of states of oneness; it is returning to these undifferentiated states, their afterwardsness, that scares the adults into alarming the children.) But only through the sexual disruptions of the ego does the continuity of going-on-being trace its way through the dissolution of subjectivity, just as it eventually inflects back toward psyche-somatic coherence and communal wovenness, where sexuality is dormant, where the mind doesn't have to work on what to do with the drives as their knocks disrupt our sense of control. (In this sense there is no such thing as The Body but only sensorial experience that, through repetition, becomes anticipatable through a kind of body memory that eventually takes on the fixed outline of a coherent "me" with an identity and a social definition. The concretion of the physical body, in this sense, is more of a disintegration product of psychosensory failure than a catalyst or conduit of psyche-somatic embodiment.) And when the safety and resolution of this integrity become excessively palliative or maddening, violent instead of sacred, at the limits of (homo)erotic binding and fortification, the sheer voltage (what Winnicott called the "muscle eroticism") of infantile sexuality thrusts the psyche-soma beyond its existing identifications toward the experimentation of the avant-garde, a little bit like speaking in order to find out what one will say, as an analysand does—to find out what kind of life one is living.

The genius of Freud's technical invention, his discovery of what Bollas has described as our "deep ontological need," was to induce this particular state of absentia (lying down, saying whatever came to mind) in the presence of an attentive other, who weaves the material into what Freud called a *construction*, what Winnicott suggests is a kind of depth (as opposed to a simply chronological designation of "early" experience): "The conception of the environmental has to be added by the analyst . . . the analyst must imaginatively clothe the earliest material presented by the patient with the environment, the environment that is implied but which the patient cannot give in analysis because of never having been aware of it."[12]

The key word here is "conception." Those whose depth has not been imaginatively elaborated by a fellow human have not only never been born ("dead babies," as the psychoanalyst Francisco González has devastatingly named them); they have never even been *conceived*. The labor induced by analysis may of course, as Winnicott explicates, rebirth the patient, through the clothing of transference, into the state, the statu nascendi, of one's early object relations, but in cases in which object relations cannot be assumed as given—in fact, where the network of humanity cannot be found—the musicalizing power of the analytic setup may be necessary to induce the labor of birth for the first time.

This raises the question of the analyst's activity in response to patients with this deficit—a failure of environmental provision that may have been uncommon but today seems ubiquitous. With contemporary patients, engagement at the level of musicality, of shared rhythmic and hypnotic experience, may be crucial in forming an experiential continuity from which all psychical life of greater dimensionality emerges. And the states of optimal induction, the best spatiotemporal point from which to embark, are spontaneous moments of shared interest, of unannounced perceptual intensity, of momentary preoccupation, of musical *absence*. As Ferenczi wrote:

> In all free association there is necessarily an element of self-forgetful abstraction; it is true that, when the patient is called upon to go further and deeper in this direction, it sometimes happens—let me frankly confess, with me very frequently—that a more profound abstraction arises. Where this takes a quasihallucinatory form, people can call it auto-hypnosis if they like; my patients often call it a trance-state. What is important is that one should not abuse this phase, in which the subject is unquestionably much more helpless than usual, by urging upon his unresisting mind one's own theories and phantasies. On the contrary, we ought to use our undeniably great influence here to deepen the patient's capacity for producing his own material. Putting it in a somewhat inelegant way, we might say that in analysis it is not legitimate to suggest or hypnotise things into the patient, but it is not only right but advisable to suggest them out.[13]

Nothing other than the analyst's musical taste, much more than a set of universal criteria or normative values, could help the analytic couple navigate what to encourage and what to suggest out, putting aesthetic capacity at the heart of the analytic process—kind of like every other relationship where one person aims to facilitate the growth of another or others: teaching, coaching, parenting, ministering. The main thing analysts do for their patients, in other words, is select what material they respond to and what to "suggest out." As John Ruskin wrote: "Taste is the only morality. Tell me what you like and I'll tell you what you are."[14] To tell one's patient which material from the session resonates within oneself is to tell the patient how well their analysis is going.

What Ferenczi calls "suggesting out" intervenes in the pathological organization of self-experience, disrupting deadening structures, so that a "more profound abstraction" can arise, which remains free of suggestion, simply encouraged. This binding, supportive function, which for Laplanche falls broadly under the category of psychotherapy (literally "soul-care" or "soul-cure"), is as crucial an element, as powerful an influence, as the unbinding, deconstructive, interpretive dimension of psychoanalytic work. "Therapy" is etymologically linked to the Greek *therapon*: an attendant, one who pays attention—which, in the case of working with dissociation, may feel more like a form of physical activity than a passive directing of one's interest: rhythmizing fascination. But *therapon* can also be translated as "ritual substitute"—the one who, in substituting for what has been a private, repetitive ritual of the patient, "members" (or *re*-members) the dis-membered into the weave through the frame and its shared, socially binding rituals. To be brought back into the weave, re-membered through the clothing of one's repetitions with the imaginative scenography of environment, is thus not only an act of construction but of *composition*. (If, as Scarfone has written, "remembering is recomposing one's whole mind," to immerse oneself in weave-music is to recompose one's whole body-mind, to be recomposed by the music.)[15]

These rituals are expressions of culture, which makes and remakes us anew with every breath we take. So the most crucial activities of human living may be less a cognitive matter of memory or symbolization and more a perceptual and ontological question of membership, of *being* in music. (You don't have to remember how to be a parent; in fact, you *can't* remember how to be a parent. And if one finds oneself trying to remember, something is already going wrong.) A familiar piece of music may literally reset one's perceptual organization, attuning it to the music in a physically synonymous way to all other experiences of listening to it throughout one's life, but so too does music re-*organ*-ize the psyche-soma, make living organ of the otherwise simply material body, organicity out of mere matter. In the *après-coup* of one's archive of subjective (musical) objects, the early of past events can become the depth of historical subjectivity, the deep of having an embodied history.

The induction ceremony into the human race known as psychoanalysis interpellates the excessively alter-worldly movement of the patient as a looping, repeating sample of a traumatic experience. "Thus I was able to trace back, with certainty," Freud (1897) once wrote to Fliess, "a hysteria that developed in the context of a periodic mild depression to a seduction, which occurred for the first time at 11 months and [I could] hear again the words that were exchanged between two adults at that time! It is as though it comes from a phonograph."[16]

When John Fletcher describes Freud as a "scenographer of trauma"—*trauma* being Greek for "a break in the body"—he is making plain the quintessentially psychoanalytic function of helping the music to resume, constructing from the ever-looping symptom a traumatically seductive "scene" in which the sexual broke the body, in which the electricity of enigmatic otherness blew a fuse, the memory of which is relegated to the unconscious, leaving the patient none the wiser, with nothing but a symptom, a decontextualized repetition, a repeating loop, to show for it.[17] ("A person," Freud writes in his discussion of the Emmy von N. case, "who has made up his mind at the dentist's to keep his head and mouth still and not to put his hand in the way, may at least start drumming with his feet.")[18] When the trauma of broken embodiment becomes iterated into the repetition of a sampled loop (sometimes called a symptom), a disruption in the continuity of going-on-being becomes a patterned, anticipatable, musical landscape, a ritual substitute through which to harness otherwise totally chaotic noise. Musical compositions, in this sense, apprehend the enigma of that which fascinates us long enough for it to become beautiful, providing a temporal framework in which to dwell between the predictability of home and the arena of the world. Admitted to the members-only club of the human race, the psyche-soma achieves the quality of what Sloterdijk calls *ensoulment*.[19] Like the Freudian symptom (and like Freud), music is always doing two jobs at once, moving, like a screen memory, in both temporal directions: spiraling out, in what Sloterdijk calls "an incessant gesture of life," toward the world, while reaching back from the world of distinction toward the indistinctness that is not by that virtue devoid of substance and that always precedes refinding the world anew. This alternating movement, which is found at every level of the Freudian psychical topography—from the reaching out and retracting of perception, as he describes in "A Note

Upon the 'Mystic Writing-Pad'" to the bearing of loss and absence explored in "Mourning and Melancholia" and the famous *fort* and *da* of *Beyond the Pleasure Principle*—becomes the to-and-fro of subjectivity itself, being in music at the same time as one is being made by the music.

||

We are learning all too well nowadays what happens when this to-and-fro collapses, when the tether snaps, as the opportunities for personal isolation multiply. At the extremes of not enough membership, or never having been membered, emerge the phenomena of alter-worlding, the often subtle reconfiguring of otherwise shared, material reality, intended precisely to withdraw and distance oneself from the communal, resulting in isolated and alienated isotopes of music, irreducibly dissonant to all but the most attentive and musical DJs. There is always some version (or perversion) of "music" playing in these alter-worlds, but the orienting, unifying potential of musical experience, which normally draws the psyche-soma into the weave of humanity (the work of the Muses themselves), is now mobilized in reverse, as a sound blocker, a hazmat suit, to buffer the dissociated body from the terrifying, threatening voltage of being alive, to sever and cauterize the sensory conductors of human contact, detuning one's instrument from the collective, harmonic homeworld. "Statelessness represents the lack of world," Hannah Arendt wrote. "It is the condition of world emptiness . . . the deprivation of membership to a public life."[20] One need look no further than the daily news to find nightmare visions of this inhuman alter-world, the Upside Down, charting its parallel universe before our very eyes, right under our noses, under the skin, in noise-cancelled chambers of unholy cruelty. "As 'agents cut off Mr. Khashoggi's head and dismembered his body,'" a *New York Times* columnist contemplates, "a Saudi doctor of forensics who had been 'brought along for the dissection and disposal' had some advice for the others, *The Times* reported Wednesday. 'Listen to music, he told them, as he donned headphones himself.'[21] What music? The soundtrack to *Sweeney Todd*?"

The joke here—if one can manage to joke about such horrors, joke-work being no less vital in the face of trauma than dream-work—may in fact be onto something. In the backstory of its libretto, the eponymous antihero of *Sweeney Todd* has been twice expelled from human membership: "un-membered" when he is sent overseas to a penal colony by a corrupt judge on a trumped-up charge and "dismembered" from his sartorial blades, the instruments of his craft, hidden and preserved for him over the decades by the unsavory Mrs. Lovett, who now runs a bakery beneath his old tonsorial parlor. Sweeney sings the first love song in the musical, "My Friends"—among the most gorgeous pieces in the entire work and a contender for the most gorgeous among all of Sondheim's—not to Mrs. Lovett (to her aching chagrin) but to the blades themselves. The musical result is undeniably hypnotic (Sondheim insisted that actors perform this song with a "trance-like quality.... He's falling into a state of self-hypnosis, so it must have that feeling.... This is non-conversation. This is a ritual.").[22] One hears in the mesmerizing poetry of these lyrics about the rhythmic, unison, identificatory love of re-memberment, of being made whole, routed not in this case through other people but through a kind of cultural object, a fetish: *"At last my arm is complete again."* (Mr. Todd falls into this trancelike song with each of his patrons before slitting their throats.) Only through the conduction of these precious metal implements is Sweeney found, claimed, healed, and redeemed through music, haunting and murderous as the song may be. Music here is no less an instrument of revenge than an instrument of reconciliation, delicately balancing tension and resolution, alienation and return, dissonance and harmony.

The question as to which kinds of psychical projects music may be recruited to manage, for better or worse, is often a question of electrical intensity, of how much energy must be screened out by what Freud called the stimulus barrier, the filtering and titration of stimuli that amount to an alternation of sensory search and withdrawal, the periodicity of perception itself. But regardless of how well the perceptual apparatus regulates the influx of sensory input, the psychical impact of other people is always slipping through the gates; we are always letting in more than we bargained for. The well-regulated titration of electrical input is always sabotaged by the excesses of unconscious transmission; there is always more heat being produced than the system predicted. And the only source of relief from the electrocution of unconscious sexuality, transmitted unwittingly (through the provision of help) from caregiver to cared-for, is by harnessing the creative potential of sexuality, the capacity of the sexual drive to propel the body back into musical movement and transmute the seizure of trauma into conducted energy, to ground the current. For those messages that are translatable, where there is good-enough music, the energized elements can be translated and incorporated into one's ever-emerging musicality, can fit into the personal score. (We could also call this *eros*, or binding.) The function of enchantment, of musical "ritual," as Sondheim (echoing Laplanche) puts it, is not only to re-member the dismembered body but also as a complicated (even perverse) attempt to be re-membered by, or into, the collective weave, to embed the otherwise merely humanoid body, Frankenstein's monster (and an increasing number of highly dissociated patients), into a recognizably human life. Embeddedness in this weave is the only position, the only neighborhood, through which to translate (or perhaps trans*duce*) the electricity of becoming sexual into the life drive of being human.

But in the case of what Laplanche called intromission, the weave of musicality is torn, making it impossible to find the erotic conduit that would allow the sexual to be experienced as the engine of psychical life. The translational effort is short-circuited, forbidden; all "it" knows is that it is not fitting in. At the end of the first act, when Sweeney slits his first throat—someone recognizes him from the old days and tries to blackmail him—and then narrowly misses his true target (the judge), he unleashes the horrific "Epiphany," his dissonant soliloquy, perhaps what the pure death drive sounds like in musical form. (*Tod* is German for "death.") The song cannot stay or stabilize in a harmonic key, constantly modulating abruptly across harsh intervals, slipping into other songs, breaking the fourth wall, and landing in a pseudotriumphant F major with a tritonal, B-natural haze seeping out of it like a kind of harmonic nausea. The music rides him; banished from the weave of humanity, he can barely find any form, any movement, through which to conduct it. From the position of this dilemma, the alienating effects of being unmembered, of unfriending the human race, of unplugging from the electrocution of the sexual drive, might seem more than reasonable, the cost of psychosomatic dissociation a preferable alternative to the agony of humiliation. (Recent neuroscience has indicated that the region of the brain responsible for this lobotomizing autoseverance is the "insula.") The unleashing and triumph of the death drive occurs precisely where re-memberment doesn't work. When post-traumatic (re)binding really fails, it unleashes pure, ecstatic, blind repetition, a kind of omnipotent, "joy"-ful, but hopeless freedom in exile. "Epiphany" here is the spiritual revelation of a satanic force.

Which brings us back to Khashoggi's executioners, piping songs through individual pairs of insulating earbuds that, if they did don them, would presumably isolate each butcher (as Sweeney now becomes and remains for the rest of the tragedy) in his own antimusic sound system, a dissociative cocoon. In health, perhaps, music is the primordial medium and force working on the side of binding, membering, remembering, or *eros*, but perverted to the service of an unusually pure form of the sexual (death) drive, music mutates into a deadly *amusia*. It is true that music can be employed in this dissociated, fetishistic, repetitive way, a blunt-force mode—think of a death march—in which no psychical work is being done, in which being is not going-on but just endlessly looping, insulating against feeling, precluding the potential for growth, demanding submission. This stands in contrast to the humanizing function of music, a nonfetishistic, essential process that is so instrumental in promoting feelingful, meaningful membership in the fabric of being human.

One way of reconciling the ambiguity of these ideas, the alternating life-giving and death-driving characters of music, is to consider two varieties of rhythmic repetition. A living rhythm (which the analytic frame facilitates), on the one hand, provides the beat through which the psyche-soma learns what it feels like to be musically continuous in time. But if the form of repetition that is rhythm is to function in service of collective membership, as opposed to becoming a death-driven insulation against it, perhaps this repeated choreography must remain *transitional* in quality or in character, like a provisional scaffolding, an education in living together. This original continuity taps into a communal structure through which one may ultimately spiral out one's own sexuality or idiom of being in the world. Sexuality, as the effect of the drive, could be considered fundamentally as a psyche-somatic impetus for the reinvigoration of being, desire endlessly shopping for new objects for itself in order to conduct the otherwise anarchic drive. From this point of view, procreative sex is more of a byproduct of this self-generating continuousness than some instinctual goal of what Freud called genital sexuality in its own right. The human predicament, from this perspective, was never simply the primordial struggle to gather polymorphous infantile sexuality into an ultimate synergy of procreative intercourse under the regime of the genital drive, as many post-Freudian theorists believed, but was rather a search for habitable forms for conducting sexuality, for a way to allow the life force to chart its own course, to die in its own way, to take the long way toward death. For Laplanche and Winnicott alike, culture provides both the available objects to desire and the available ways of desiring them, both the precondition and the product of the psychofamilial environment, the garden of good-enough parenting, the foundational membership in which to gather oneself for the journey toward the world (to which the same environment is always optimally, unconsciously, seducing us).

Thus the only true antidote to the trauma of dismemberment, the only remedy to the psychical exile of not being membered, would be the inweaving effects of re-membering and being re-membered, of *commemoration*. And effective commemoration, in a psychoanalytic context, first requires effective induction—the commonality of beta function, sensory symbiosis, and shared rhythm—culminating ultimately in the musical moments, the *absences*, in which the patient is newly able to conduct an otherness within oneself, to *improvise*, requiring the analyst, as the psychoanalyst Stephen Purcell has noted (echoing Ferenczi), to let the patient lead while keeping the patient company—though this assumes the patient is already sufficiently inducted, fueled enough to chart a course for us to follow. Only through the unifying, rhythmizing mechanism of the frame can the patient develop sufficient musicality to produce a melody for the analyst to "follow"—otherwise, analyst and patient just chase each other around the loop of repetition. (Where there is only dis-sociation, there can be no as-sociation.) Through the repetition of the frame emerges, as Deleuze writes, a "univocal affirmation" of difference, a melody, which is then available for the deep accompaniment of harmony. While Mrs. Lovett joins contrapuntally against Sweeney's melody in "My Friend," she occasionally stacks a harmony in moments of double entendre between Sweeney's blades and Lovett's Sweeney. We follow her following him, following them.

Perhaps nowhere is the repetitive, hypnotic, re-membering function of music more evident than in the blues, especially in its earliest forms, blending African and Western elements by and for people who, being enslaved, had been violently torn from their place of belonging, dis-membered. Not unlike Greek tragedy, blues music provides a kind of case study for two ways that music can be psychically engaged at the same time, both mournfully and melancholically. The standard twelve-bar blues progression is, harmonically speaking, a guaranteed repetition, practically the opposite of Mister Rogers's circle of fifths, never modulating, always sliding back into itself (V7–IV7–I7). In this sense, the blues are a kind of companion soundtrack for loss and tribulation, an accompaniment or technology (certainly a recombinant teleology) for dwelling in sorrow in a full way. (Certain sessions call for this kind of accompaniment, where the analyst must find and join the repeated phrases of hopelessness in the patient's feeling state and preclude one's own sense of futurity for the sake of unison at the crossroads of no past and no future.)

But the quintessential characteristic of the blues mood, its "blue note," or flat 7th (the lowered or minor-7th scale degree), bends the consonance of the diatonic scale, disrupting its consonance to free up new degrees of harmonic uncertainty and possibility, for responding to the disruption of trauma itself by providing a medium through which its rupture can take on musical form. In Toni Morrison's novel *The Bluest Eye* (which she calls a "blues novel"), the character Cholly, forsaken, banished, humiliated, abused, and traumatized almost beyond belief, is described, following a breakdown, as "dangerously free. Free to feel whatever he felt—fear, guilt, shame, love, grief, pity. . . . Abandoned in a junk heap by his mother, rejected for a crap game by his father, there was nothing more to lose. He was alone with his own perceptions and appetites, and they alone interested him."[23]

He goes on to rape his daughter. Through her novel, Morrison succeeds in restoring (re-membering) even Cholly, primarily through the musicality of her prose, which, like all blues music, allows the psyche-soma to linger in a state of mourning without arresting the movement of the drive, instead conducting it, looping it, through a tolerably dissonant, anticipatable (tolerable because anticipatable) harmonic landscape. Held in the repetition of ritualized indwelling, a state of shared mourning, blues music induces and animates the life of the drive through the amplification of shared music, of choral sympathy, bringing the music almost unbearably close to the trauma of dismemberment from which it is born. (In this regard, the blues scale is the particular harmonic river irrigated by the drive under the sociohistorical conditions under which it became the defining characteristic of the genre.) And perhaps it is no coincidence that blues music feels, however mournful in its historical origin and practice, irreducibly sexy. Trauma, after all, is by definition shot through with sexual potential that is often expressed in violent and terrible ways; the blues walks this line, harnessing the anarchic power of the sexual drive through the potential of a cultural form, a "blues scale," that now runs through not only the blues but almost every genre of popular music, often working as the point of greatest emotional access for musical feeling.

We need tragedies like *Sweeney Todd* and *The Bluest Eye*—which, by rendering conditions of threat, show us the contours and necessity of the struggle against them most clearly—to remind us (as the Greeks' tragedies reminded them) that translation always endangers us as much as it relieves us, plunging us into the woods as it works to get us out of them, making music out of the very traumata that threaten to silence it. "Being there in the world," Sloterdijk writes, "has always meant being exposed in a sphere where non-music is possible for the first time."[24] Translation is a political act, risking the severest of consequences and retaliation. As the late Jamal Khashoggi wrote in his final column, "What the Arab World Needs Most Is Free Expression":

> My publication, *The Post*, has taken the initiative to translate many of my pieces and publish them in Arabic. For that, I am grateful. Arabs need to read in their own language so they can understand and discuss the various aspects and complications of democracy in the United States and the West. If an Egyptian reads an article exposing the actual cost of a construction project in Washington, then he or she would be able to better understand the implications of similar projects in his or her community.[25]

The construction project of human membership is never free of the destructive project of the unbound sexual, the death-driven violence of which forever corrodes our communal-bodily integrity, effecting the statelessness of the unmembered. These are sequelae of sexuality unframed. To frame a part of the world in time, as an analyst or a journalist or a parent does, is to provide a playground for the translational activity of the mind under protection from its own disruptions, securing us through the erotic from the erratic. Come talk to me, Freud was saying; stop doing some things—abstain certain movement—so that something else can happen. Stop the sexual enough to get into the groove; turn down enough noise that you can hear the music.

|||

Where are we, then, when we hear music? The location of the place remains vague—all we can be sure of is that people can never be completely in the world when they are listening to music. Hearing in the musical sense has always meant either going toward the world or fleeing from it.[26]

In music we are never, as Sloterdijk suggests, in one place at one time. Whether going toward or fleeing the world, from the frame-work of musical erotics to the dream-work of musical seduction, joining established forms or varying idiosyncratically upon them, music—as Heidegger might have said, if he had cared about music—*worlds worlds* for the first time. Heidegger's "world" is not the physical world or the universe "out there" but a fully humanized domain (like the family, or baseball, or psychoanalysis) that we create and sustain and inhabit and that inhabits us. To find oneself in a space that isn't somehow "worlded" is to find oneself in a psychotic or dissociated state (which Heidegger called "anxiety" and which Freud called "panic"), like a film without a soundtrack. The music of the world organizes our perception of that world, as Merleau-Ponty might put it, providing the only filter through which to apprehend a world at all. "We could call it a sonorous *cogito*," Sloterdijk continues. "I hear something inside me, therefore I am—at least I have enough reason to claim that I am certain I can 'deduce' my existence from the act of hearing inside myself."[27] It's not that we exist because we think our own thoughts; we hear and feel the music inside and out, which forms the foundation of our existence. (In this Sloterdijk comes very close to Winnicott's idea that the psyche-soma is the imaginative elaboration of bodily experience.) The feeling that one exists is always an aftereffect of musical sensation, deducing our being only once we are induced by the music.

Like perception (and the formalization of perception we call music), sexuality is largely determined by the way it is organized, which language is available for forming what Freud called sexual theories, what kind of thoughts become possible in a particular sexual system. To reprise Freud's own sexual theory: By grounding it in the excesses of childhood trauma, in the sheer unintelligibility of the adult world, Freud might have also made an unwitting contribution to the discourse of phenomenology; that the tendency to want to make sense of the world, our hermeneutic tendency, is fundamentally driven by the not-making-sense from which all sense-making efforts ensue, the traumatogenicity of an original helplessness, a primary wordlessness, that precipitates a search for viable forms of meaningfulness. And as it becomes implicitly imbued with meaningfulness by the way the adults handle it, how they conduct themselves through it, the world also becomes *sexual* through the unworded excesses of unconscious life stowed away in the holding and handling of the child, in the presentation of the world. What Ruskin claims for the art one likes applies equally to one's sexuality: Tell me what comes to mind, Freud said, speak (*only* speak) your sexuality, and I'll tell you what kind of life you're living, what kind of world you're living in—which, in the psychoanalytic telling, always becomes the analyst's world as much as the patient's.

Whatever meaning psychoanalysis makes of sexual life, in other words (and whatever sexuality does with psychoanalytic meaning), is always structured and sustained by the world in which meaning becomes possible, which may *world* itself in the course of psychoanalytic work, deducing a scenography around a decontextualized (or deworlded) symptom, a world-work-beta supporting its dream-work-alpha. If one finds oneself, or one's patient, addicted to dating apps, for example, one might easily infer that sexual life has become impossibly diffuse, cheapened, transactional, interchangeable, and libidinally inert or, alternatively, that one is seeking equally a kind of reassurance that one is a member of some larger community, that there are other single people, or other gay people, or other sexual people less than a hundred feet away, as much as one is seeking a hookup, let alone a relationship. Sexuality requires a sensuous backdrop of membership in a shared world as much as it requires anything else, even an object; without the erotic bond through which to join a community of others, becoming like them, there is no track for sexuality to run on, no life for it to live. Having forfeited the seduction theory, which at least provisionally explained the irreducible asymmetry of human relatedness, Freud was left to construct an inherent struggle, an *inborn* struggle, in the sexual enterprise, a labored journey through the phylogenetic Oedipus to the proverbial mountaintop, but it might have been (and may still be) just as feasible, with the seduction theory in play, to suppose that the primary struggle of sexuality—and even the struggle to gather the component instincts into an integrated personality—is the struggle of a social apprenticeship, of figuring out how to channel one's erotic capacities, of getting the hang of living in a psychosexual body within the weave.

Inevitably culture functions not only as a reservoir of somatic forms through which to channel one's excess and exuberance but also as an articulator of limits and prohibitions, forcing erotic capacities into hiding (mistaking them, perhaps, as "sexual"), limiting demonstrations of how to be fully alive to the point of obscuring the vision entirely. "People are in general not candid over sexual matters," Freud explained on his first trip to the United States. "They do not show their sexuality freely, but to conceal it they wear a heavy overcoat woven of a tissue of lies, as though the weather were bad in the world of sexuality. Nor are they mistaken. It is a fact that sun and wind are not favourable to sexual activity in this civilized world of ours; none of us can reveal his erotism freely to others."[28]

Here the conflation of the sexual and the erotic is especially limiting. If Freud conceived of psychoanalysis as the revelation, the disrobing, of sexuality through what he called free association, he equally relied upon the binding associations (which are precisely erotic) that help us weather the storm, "woven" of the civilized lies, what Winnicott would call the false selves, that facilitate sociability. If, from Laplanche's view, sexuality is initially and fundamentally enigmatic or alien or other—"hetero" in the literal sense—we always need an erotic fellow to weave us into good-enough *homo*erotism, to help us harness and elaborate our blue notes *through* and *with others*, to model how to move in and out of the flow of the music that supports and guides being oneself in the world. (Violating this homoerotic ethic, exploiting it through sexual violation, is the reason Laius was cursed in the first place, sealing Oedipus's fate.) Before fantasy or any other kind of thought, we learn how to catch a wave of the mind—*fluctuat nec mergitur* ("tossed but not sunk"), as Freud often quoted—a way to surf one's thoughts:

> The sonorous *cogito* is the exact opposite of that which Descartes demands of the logical *cogito*; it is not a base, because it doesn't support anything, nor is it something unshakeable, because it cannot be fixed. The most certain thing is, in truth, the most useless. Focusing on inner voices and sounds means being able to be shaken—being open for acoustic presences to come; it does not mean that I obtain a solid base from them but rather that they subject me to their sounds. Anyone who listens to the voice of thinking is immersed in a sphere that other people always cause to quiver. Thinking is in the subject like sound is in the violin, by dint of a relationship of vibration. Insofar as people think, they are, so to speak, musical instruments for performances that mean the world.[29]

This vision of thinking as musical vibration, an openness to presences, acoustic and otherwise, is an account of disclosure in action. And being able to think, to be open in this way, requires *induction* into shared perception, *seduction* into perturbation by the enigmatic message, and *conduction* of the resulting accrual of energy through identificatory movement. These processes constitute what Chetrit-Vatine synthesizes as the "matricial" function, conducted by a sometimes-separate caretaker who is perpetually grappling with the unconscious push and pull of sexual seduction (love, murder, etc.) by staking a lived ethical posture toward the child (and, by extension, toward all others). For Chetrit-Vatine, this posture primes the caretaker for a "reiterated ethical shock," a reciprocal inducement toward responsibility through the power of rhythmized, ethical living.[30] The parent's response to the ethical shock, in other words, is rooted in and informed by the rhythm, the musicality, the perception of the world organized through the weave, perception woven into ethical attention. The weave "tells" the parent how to be a parent and thus how to humanize the child; the message may be enigmatic, but its conduct must be ethical. The lived ethical posture of the analyst, no less than the parent, draws its character from the weave. Absent the deep connectivity, separation becomes the context for estrangement, for the dehumanizing effects of the unethical (literally sexual), the nonethical (perversion, which arrests continuity), and the antiethical (messages that do not seduce but, as Laplanche says, "intromit"—dying in someone else's way).

Ferenczi found this aspect of parenting crucial for how society at large should cultivate its members, for how to treat one another as *Nebenmenschen*, as near one another, as neighbors.

> Here we get light, of some significance for education, on the course which we ought also to follow in the rational upbringing of children. Their suggestibility and their tendency, when they feel themselves helpless, to lean, without any resistance, on a "grown-up" (that is to say, an element of hypnotism in the relation between children and adults) is an undeniable fact, with which we have to reckon. But instead of doing what is commonly done, going on using the great power which grown-ups have over children to stamp upon their plastic minds our own rigid rules as something externally imprinted, we might fashion that power into a means of educating them to greater independence and courage.[31]

If induction is fundamentally ethical—bringing the child into the ontomusical, shared weave—then seduction is its unethical counterpoint, the unavoidably disruptive dimension of human contact, that which does not fit into the weave. (Yet.) The sexual is noise to the weave's music, the noise we can't escape. Finding or making a place for it in the weave is our driven passion (suffering), our life-work of transforming the unethical into the ethical—which might be a description of psychoanalysis; where the noise was, the music shall become, where the unethical was, there the ethical shall be. (Mister Rogers, the ultimate neighbor, always helped his viewers bear the sometimes-separateness of ending each episode by singing to them, bridging what would otherwise be its total dehumanizing estrangement, its going black, with the staying power of shared music.)

What the French sociologist Pierre Bourdieu called *hexis* is the bodily locus and manifestation of a whole ethical world that informs ethical practice. *Hexis* is the ontological dance of everyday life that everyone in a community needs to know, varying in tempo and rhythm and harmony from culture to culture, weave to weave.[32] When there has been ethical parenting (including ordinary interruptions and failures), entering into the *ethos* of analysis may be relatively straightforward, but when one has been un-, non-, or antiethically parented, when the emergence of shared musicality has been suppressed and suffocated by murderous intromission, a miscarriage in being understood, it requires of the analyst a different form of being; some form of *analytic* activity is admittedly required in order to break down pathological organizations, activity authorized by nothing other than the weave itself. Here the analyst uses the weave to set something in motion, a particular kind of activity, in order to recover a living framework that will allow the membership activities to occur—conducting the weave through the work of analysis, inducing the world of analysis in the name of the weave.

Through his fundamental rule, Freud attempted to inscribe a late-nineteenth-century European ethos of confessional self-knowledge (as Foucault has illuminated) into a therapeutics of free-associative catharsis. (When the Rat Man asks if he could skip the gory details of the story that would become his haunting sobriquet, Freud confides, "He might just as well ask me to give him the moon.")[33] In our own era, the psychoanalytic work maintains a vestige of harbor from the mania of modern life, the frenzied ascension toward self-optimization and psychic impenetrability (Sloterdijk's "anthropotechnics"), preserving an ethos of attunement and musical movement in accompanying one's patients through stretches of despair as much as through the occasional clearings of hope.[34] (Despairing over one's patient's inhumanity implicitly communicates to the patient that human is a thing to be in the first place.) In each case, the analyst is always doing something to the patient, carrying an ethical responsibility to conduct this activity within a form of musical living. When we as analysts seek out and cultivate actual musical experiences in our actual lives—when we, to paraphrase Socrates's dream, "practice music," as performers and audience members alike—we train ourselves to relinquish our reliance on habitual patterns of voice, thought, and world apprehension in favor of transiently joining together in evolving modes of shared perception, attunement, and comprehension. Musical living thus allows for the commensurate expression of passion (even as it inhibits the narrow aim of the drive), providing an education in conducting oneself as a human being, an encouraging grown-up for weathering the storm.

If making oneself sensible to other people is always in service of the weave, of binding, then the command to stop making sense, to observe one's free associations, to free fall, to not remember (or desire) but to be dismembered by the death drive, to be analyzed, is to be made by sense, to let sense make you. The music that proves psychically useful for elaborating one's psychical dialect, for enriching and amplifying its world, becomes as dear to us as loved ones. This music presents us with an optimal challenge, good-enough enigma, a hook, that stretches erotic capacities and allows for tolerable contact with music from that other place, the *andere Schauplatz*. Beloved music, in other words, is claimed through considerable psychical labor, and once we are born through it, we never forget it. When the music we remember re-members us, we become indistinguishable from it; it feels, as much as anything, like who we are. Through its framing function, music allows new experiences of not-me, blue notes, to become eligible for reintegration, for sampling and remixing the world, for interpreting one's life like a musician, by figuring out how to play it.

7

STRANGE LOOP

joking
dreaming
sampling

A serious and good philosophical work could be written consisting entirely of jokes.

—LUDWIG WITTGENSTEIN

I

Five years after he started a revolution by transducing his analysis of his own dreams into a new dream he called psychoanalysis, Freud turned his attention (or found his attention turning) from the logic of the dream to the logic of the joke, that other psyche-somatic mystery, and to the question of what the difference between the two might be. If dreams are always fundamentally dreamed alone (even though we dream up links to our unconscious lives only through the cultural supply of symbols made available to us) and only occasionally told to another person, there is something about a joke, with its related play upon the systems of thought, that necessarily requires a listener. We may hold a joke, like we may hold a piece of music, in our minds, but unlike a dream, a joke is only truly activated upon delivery. Freud calls our attention to the collaborative relations of jokes when he asks, in *Jokes and Their Relation to the Unconscious*: "Why is it that I do not laugh at a joke of my own? And what part is played in this by the other person?" To investigate the matter, Freud structures his Joke Book (which is all but forgotten in contemporary psychoanalytic discourse, especially compared to his Dream Book), in three parts—just like a joke, he explains:

> Joking as a play with one's own words and thoughts is to begin with without a person as an object. But already at the preliminary stage of the jest [Strachey's word for "joke"], if it has succeeded in making play and nonsense safe from the protests of reason, it demands another person to whom it can communicate its result. But this second person in the case of jokes does not correspond to the person who is the object, but to the third person, the "other" person in the case of the comic. It seems as though in the case of a jest the other person has the decision passed over to him on whether the joke-work has succeeded in its task—as though the self did not feel certain in its judgment on the point.[1]

Joke-work, for Freud, always involves three participants. The "first person (the self)" tells the "third (the outside person)" a joke about the second, the "object." Like points of a plane, you need three to make one, with three corresponding achievements at stake:

> First, to give me objective certainty that the joke-work has been successful; secondly, to complete my own pleasure by a reaction from the other person upon myself; and thirdly—where it is a question of repeating a joke that one has not produced oneself—to make up for the loss of pleasure owing to the joke's lack of novelty.[2]

By confirming our ability to bring about pleasure in others, which pleases us in turn, all while replenishing the pleasure of previously deadened material, jokes bring us together in a shared experience of all three pleasures. (In jokes Freud discovers the need for another person to experience pleasure, an original picture of sociality.) And it is shared pleasure, Borch-Jacobsen believes, that precedes and precipitates any pleasure we may feel in the privacy of our own company. "To achieve its own pleasure," Borch-Jacobsen writes, "the ego has to take a detour, one that causes its own pleasure to pass through that of another. And this detour is identification (*mimesis*), resemblance (*homoïosis*). One only enjoys, in fantasy, as another; tell me whom you are miming and I'll tell you who you are, what you desire, and how you enjoy."[3]

Contrary to its popular connotation, the ego can never actually take pleasure in itself reflexively; it must always be routed through an other. In Freud's formulation, jokes provide this crucial detour by psychesomatically synchronizing its participants, inducing a shared, embodied experience of laughter, which always involves laughing about not getting the joke. Nothing is funny for the object who doesn't get the joke; the joke is on it. It remains unaffected, a subtly haunting reminder of way back when, a moment ago, that moment before we got the joke, what the joke might have felt like before there was a "we" through which to get it.

The Joke Book is arranged in three parts: "Analytic," "Synthetic," and "Theoretic." The great joke of the Joke Book is theory and analysis laughing at synthesis, 1 and 3 laughing at 2; laughing at the fantasy of keeping everything together, of free-standing cohesion, a laugh about making too much sense (or at least trying to), about being none the wiser as to the disruptions and arrhythmias of being alive. Jokes remind our bodies that someone else's pleasure—and not just, for example, someone else's penetration, but also someone else's reverberation—can reanimate and revitalize our relationship to otherwise inert psychical material. Jokes are thus an excellent example of what Laplanche called *inspiration*. We are enlivened by the other's laughter and pleasure when we share a joke, yet at the same time, we learn to accept that we don't know the full extent of how and why someone finds our joke funny and are moved by the enigmatic ways in which they do.

We might ask, then: What does it mean that psychoanalysis has placed greater value on the interpretation of dreams than on determining jokes' their relation to the unconscious? Both of Freud's early works try to demonstrate and analyze the presence of the unconscious in everyday experiences, but the joke, unlike the dream, is shared, intimate, and explicitly playful and pleasurable. What if Freud's books on those subjects had traded places in terms of their influence on Freud's thought and the thought of his followers? What if psychoanalysis became as good at getting jokes as it is at getting dreams? (One feels a particular kind of transgressive pleasure when a joke erupts or disrupts or trips up the more common rhythms of clinical conversation; there is a particular jealousy when one imagines or overhears the pleasures that other clinicians have with their patients.) If we told and got our jokes like we tell and get our dreams, where would we be now? Would laughter replace tears as the signal of clinical breakthrough?

Surely we wish to hear dreams no less than jokes. Freud invented psychoanalysis by writing *The Interpretation of Dreams* as an exposition of his communication with his own unconscious, seducing us all to listen in. But in his treatise on dream interpretation Freud did not address the dimension of what might be called communal dreaming, the fact that the private activity of dreaming is always dependent on the psychic presence of fellow dreamers lending us their dream equipment. But many dreams are never communicated, are not preserved long enough in consciousness to be recalled. Unlike a joke, we need not remember a dream in order for it to work (quite the opposite: Freud thought we only remembered dreams when they were threatening to fail in their duty to preserve sleep). If dream-work is a creature of primary process that may take on secondary-process qualities as we remember them throughout the day, then jokes work in the opposite direction, cashing out the surplus in a laugh and freeing the psyche up to joke and dream the world anew in one another's company. It may be the requirement for company that destined *Jokes* to be a lesser book than *Dreams*, which does not require an audience, any more than Freud required an analyst, to complete its pleasure; the Dream Book induces its reader to wonder at both Freud's dreams and one's own, while the Joke Book always feels on some level like it is trying, awkwardly, to make us laugh—which it seldom does, especially in translation—its success never confirmed. But *Jokes* is no less profound than *Dreams* in its implications for psyche-somatic life. In *Dreams*, the alpha function of the unconscious mitigates the censorship of consciousness to produce conditions in which the body can sleep; in *Jokes*, the joke-work of the unconscious, which results naturally from the logical mode of the unconscious (condensation, timelessness, non-negation), cooperates with the rationality of consciousness to create conditions in which the body can laugh. Each describes a form of restorative efficiency, a body system in its own right.

As always when it comes to jokes (and music), timing is everything. Perhaps another reason the Joke Book may have gotten lost in the mix is that it was published the same year as the *Three Essays on the Theory of Sexuality* (arguably his most important theoretical statement, especially for future scholars like Laplanche) and the first of Freud's major case histories, the *Fragment of a Case of Hysteria*—though each of these does in fact touch upon the questions of dreams and jokes, the teamwork of unconscious and conscious life, in its own way. Dora, the "object" of Freud's report, did not get the joke, which means she was the joke, a curiosity to amuse and mystify the adults. (Little Hans was a veritable punch line: What's the worst that could happen, Freud seemed to be unwittingly setting up, if parents started analyzing their own children?) But if the gendered trouble of the Dora case is not (and never was) much of a laughing matter, the thesis at the core of the *Three Essays* is about the joke we never stop telling. The great setup of constitutional bisexuality, the true discovery at the heart of the *Three Essays*, is that no one has to be the joke, because everybody is. We are always in on some jokes while not in on others, and we get to laugh either way, whether we're in on it or not. "We can be fobbed off by the satisfactions of getting it," Adam Phillips writes in *Missing Out*, "and oddly enlivened by the perplexity of not getting it"—"not getting it" (for which he names his essay, "On Not Getting It") meaning not getting sexuality, which in-forms the source-objects that animate our jokes and dreams, the very reasons why we do and do not get them.[4] We can see in Laplanche that seduction is always optimally something like a comedy, a kind of joke we don't get at first, a sexual riddle wrapped in an enigmatic excess; for Phillips, the key psychoanalytic discovery about sexuality is that we must not get it, to create conditions in which not getting it is preferred to getting it, "a life in which not getting it is the point and not the problem; in which the project is to learn how not to ride the bicycle, how not to understand the poem." The work of going-on-being, of having a self, is primarily a project of having our satisfactions dismantled, sustaining our desire. We wouldn't have it any other way; the only other way, the only alternative to the comedy of not getting it, is the tragedy of getting it. Tragedies end in the catharsis of shared despair, lamenting the futility of defying one's fate to repeat; comedies end in marriage, signifying new life. Families need humor in order to weave their members together; the tragic life, the tragic picture of human life, is the individual isolated by getting all too well that the joke is on him. In the Oedipal tragedy, a very bad joke about the curse of being in a family becomes the never-ending drama of not getting what you want; in the Oedipal comedy, everyone sings along to a shared anthem: You can't always get what you want.

Getting it, in other words, especially in psychoanalysis, has been drastically overrated. We used to go to record stores (which some of us still do) to find the love songs we use to bear not getting something and to re-fascinate our not-getting when we have gotten too much—and for the clerk to cop an attitude toward our burgeoning proclivities as much as to endorse them. "Did I listen to pop music because I was miserable? Or was I miserable because I listened to pop music?" asks Rob, the record store clerk-hero of Nick Hornby's classic 90s novel-turned-film *High Fidelity*, in a paradoxical formulation that might have pleased Winnicott, another amateur musician. Rob invites us to think about the relationship between music and misery and the uses the one might have for the other. One reason we may use music to deal with being miserable is that it is readily available for use, even more now than in Rob's day. In the absence of whatever or whoever one is being denied, the presumed cause of misery, songs present no such resistance. They are there for the taking, the listening, the laughing, the crying, the sing-along. Music helps us miss things because we never have to miss music; it keeps us company, in vivo, in memory. It is the accompaniment itself, more than the loss it represents, that endows music with its usefulness in bearing states of longing in relation to a former lover or a memorable cultural experience. But music seems to know too much about our desire to leave it at that; it knows, in other words, that one way it can make bearable the misery of missing other people is by missing other music.

||

If one has heard anything at all about the nineteenth-century composer Robert Schumann, it may be that he had a wife named Clara, whose talent rivaled that of her husband (and was never appreciated as such), and that her husband, (this) Rob, spent a lot of time missing her. The tragic story is well documented: For some eleven years of protracted legal struggles and conflicting professional endeavors, which kept them apart, Rob and Clara were prevented from marrying. (Clara's father, who was a teacher and mentor of Schumann's, did not consider him socially or psychologically fit to marry his daughter and took him to court over it.) Schumann biographers are keen to locate fragments of Clara's own compositions (and even the spelling of her name with corresponding musical notes) in pieces that Schumann composed during their estrangement, commemorating the pained solitude of Schumann's legendary longing, his tortured and tragic tale. A compelling bit of evidence for these interpretations is found in the opening movement of the *Phantasie in C Major* (1836), which sounds somehow like it starts in the middle of something. Whereas music preceding Schumann's era almost uniformly states a theme before varying and reinventing it, here Schumann evokes a sense that we are already in progress elaborating a theme that has not been played but that feels, through a kind of musical projective identification, like we have somehow heard it before, like a dream that is just being lost upon waking, what the late American pianist and writer Charles Rosen (echoing Freud) called a "reminiscence."[5] The variations here sound like musical secondary process, attempts to hold onto a memory of something as it slips away. And then fittingly, as if resulting from this near-dream-work, the source material is laid achingly bare: A melodic fragment from Beethoven's song "An die ferne Geliebte" ("To the distant beloved"), written two decades earlier in 1816.

This first movement, Rosen explains, embodies the aesthetic of the fragment, a nineteenth-century musical form that Schumann (along with Liszt and Chopin) helped create. Fragments function much like unsaturated interpretations; they leave something out, something for the listener to fill in. They orbit a musical idea like the navel of a dream, swirling around an elusive absence, an *objet petit a*. The fragment produced by this *Phantasie* (and perhaps by all phantasies) conjures up one such absent origin and works its way back to it. "For hours," Schumann wrote to Clara, "I have been playing over and over again a melody from the last movement of my *Phantasie*.... Are you not the secret tone that runs through the work? I almost think you are."[6] The thought itself feels like an evocative fragment, fragment-thinking; he almost thinks she is; he *almost-thinks*. For Freud, to think is to remember, to replace a feelingful absence with a thoughtful presence; to *almost* think, by contrast, is to repeat in action what remains unthought or unthinkable, as Schumann repeats—or, in contemporary lingo, he "samples"—Beethoven's melody. (It was the almost-thought repetitive movements of his patients that formed the basis for Freud's elaborative "constructions," not simply to unearth their underlying trauma but to stage a scene for psychic experience to proceed, to enable something new, to find and resume an ontological groove.) As Rosen identifies in his fascinating history of Schumann's musical era, *The Romantic Generation*, Schumann alerts his public to the presence of a secret by the epigraph to the *Phantasie* published in the first edition, another sample from a verse by the German poet Friedrich Schlegel:

> Durch alle Töne tönet
> Im bunten Erdentraum
> Ein leiser Ton gezogen
> Für den, der heimlich lauschet.
>
> [Through all the sounds that sound
> In the many-colored dream of earth
> A soft sound comes forth
> For the one who listens in secret.][7]

Schumann asks Clara whether she is the secret tone, the piece of melody that has inscribed itself into his music, because he almost thinks she is. But he does not know that she is, perhaps cannot bear to know; the source of the tone, its latent dream-content, is repressed, secreted, so that the joke is on Schumann, unless he gets it. He needs to not get the joke in order to compose; to get the joke is to end the *Phantasie*. All he knows as he writes to Clara is that he can't get something about her, a sample, a melody, out of his head; he can't stop hearing what's going in what Freud called *der andere Schauplatz*, the other scene, the next room, beyond and within him.

Like perhaps all creative artists, Schumann is here little more (and need be nothing more) than a conduit between the secret tone that haunts him and the distant beloved secreted behind the law of her father. Schumann doesn't get the joke between the haunting tone and its secreted source (Beethoven) any more than he gets the joke between Clara's father and his secreted daughter; Schumann is, in a sense, the butt of both jokes. But it is not getting these jokes that drives Schumann to find and create the music he uses to bear his lovelorn, excluded position. He needs to not get the joke long enough to find the music. Not getting the joke is necessary for inscription into the Oedipal, into the world of meaning, because if we knew everything, there would be no way to be interested in the world (once we find a world in which to be interested). The Oedipus is the one joke we're never meant to get. In what Lacan called the Imaginary, you think you know what's going on, you are beholden to one thing, the object of desire, but in the realm of the Symbolic, the whole notion of a singular meaning explodes. In the triangular space of a joke-world, we can laugh about the monomania of a dream-world. Humor, from its etymological origins, refers to moisture, fluidity, flow, exchanging the solidity of certainty for the surf of possibility. (Narcissus is a frozen statue.) To humor someone is to change their mood, to induce and indulge the possibility of other states. In the psychophysics of the weave, one finds an optimal, aqueous zone of humor, where things can be liquid. Our longing for our objects is necessary to set desire in motion, to rouse the psyche out of narcissistic calcification, even as the same longing threatens to accelerate the psychical tempo into vaporized frenzy; it is only the temporizing sensibility of music that offers a more stable, viable groove and provides the humanizing tempo that allows us to find our objects, which are never just one thing to us but many things.

Schumann longs for his object in the epigraph to his *Phantasie* and the letter he writes to Clara about it, but he *conducts* his longing, musically, through the variations on his "secret tone" theme, each of which evokes and reaches for an original phrase that the listener senses has already been heard (even though it only arrives at the end), as if this musical conduit for his longing makes it possible to bear the separation, to frame beyondness itself, to claim longing, as Rosen does, as inherent to the structure of desire:

> Above all, at the end of Schumann's first movement, the quotation from Beethoven appears not as a reminiscence of another composer, but as at once the source and the solution of everything in the music—up to that final page. The reference becomes self-reference: the phrase from

Beethoven seems as much to derive from what has preceded as to be the source. In fact, one cannot take the full measure of Schumann's accomplishment in this work without observing the quotation from *An die ferne Geliebte* sounds as if Schumann had written it.[8]

What music historians call "quotation," a term originally derived from textual citation (as in how many lines were quoted), may be properly designated a century-and-a-half later, in the age of recombinant music processes, as a sample. The sound that comes forth to Schumann from Beethoven presents itself for psychical use, an example (an *Es-sample*) of something to be creatively modified, translated, and made suitable for culture, for cultivation, for growth. Schumann may have stumbled here upon a new musical possibility for developing one's own idiom, starting with the arrival of a bit of material that is familiar enough ("sounds as if Schumann had written it") that it will engender or stimulate longing if situated at an optimal distance, just out of reach, the finish line of an achingly beautiful obstacle course of uncannily familiar variations. At this distance, an object—the more traditionally psychoanalytic term for "beloved"—gets desire going; at a too-satisfying proximity, desire is preempted, stifled, stoved. (The Schumanns had a fantastically difficult time actually living together once they were finally married.) Rosen understands this aesthetic capture of the sometimes tantalizing quality of that which is not there as the defining quality of the Romantic aesthetic of the fragment; psychoanalysis, through its own aesthetic, capitalizes on experiences of longing—following a weekend, for example, or a usefully unsaturated interpretation—to develop psychical capacities, musical strategies, for tolerating absence, for elaborating nostalgia, for going-on-wishing, for making ourselves less miserable (or, as Freud once put it, more "commonly unhappy," unhappy-in-common)—more able to use music in a meaningful, emotional way.

If music of the Romantic generation began to anticipate the creative possibilities of linking the music of now with the music of then—and even if it could have imagined some futuristic, technological capacity to catalyze this referentiality—it is unlikely that anyone, even of Schumann's genius, could have guessed that popular music would one day find itself permanently revolving around this transgenerational phenomenon. Which is to say that we are now living, undeniably, in the age of hip-hop.

As every musician since Schumann has had to negotiate the relation of current music to the musical generation before it, every developing musician must now contemplate one's musical-historical distance from the cultural epicenter that is hip-hop, which by its very nature builds upon the dynamics of distance from some other musical form. Music is now, in an essential way, the art of referring to other music, or, if this is what, as a form of thought, music has always implicitly and necessarily been (an inweaving of cultural inheritance), then hip-hop perhaps accelerates, globalizes, and reveals it to be so more fully, more explicitly, than any other genre in Western music history.

At this center of this genre, which is now identical to the center of the broader popular culture it has come to dominate, few figures have loomed larger that that of Kanye West, who through some alchemy of business acumen, spontaneity, controversy, and psychical fragmentation we find perennially at the creative, cutting edge of the genre, and thus the modern musical form, and thus modern culture as we know it. Kanye has made his mark in a form that is structured in relation to absence through a kind of insistent omnipresence (punctuated by bouts of institutionalized care). One may find oneself, regardless of personal affinity for his music, full of unbidden thoughts about Kanye. The episodes that have contributed most directly to his household recognizability—his pronouncement after Hurricane Katrina that President Bush "does not care about Black people"; his spontaneous display of outrage that a young, white, female pop star (Taylor Swift) won an award he felt should have gone to a young, Black, female pop star (Beyoncé); his highly publicized transformations through marriage and fatherhood; his cryptic aspirations toward becoming president and baffling coziness with the previous one—make it all too easy to overlook his moments of genuine artistic invention and contribution to his craft. The sound for which Kanye came to be recognized in his early work was precisely a form of sampling, the use of previously recorded music in a new work, an artifact of DJs in the late 1970s using turntables to create long stretches of dance music; his personal spin on the practice—which peaked on his 2004 debut *The College Dropout*, a watermark achievement in sampling—was to speed the sample up and use it as a chorus hook.

Perhaps this signature sped-sampling paralleled the acceleration of genre modification in postwar music, as if music itself was frantically trying to recall its own history, and the proliferation of these popular genres could be read as a kind of cultural illness, a symptom of the failure of the sensory commons that produces and stabilizes our shared history in the form of enduring traditions. But the acceleration can also be read as a form of political urgency, each a new idiomatic possibility of reconciliation with cultural trauma. As the aforementioned headline-samples suggest, thoughts about race are never far from West's mind, and at particular junctures, such as "Blood on the Leaves" from his celebrated 2013 album *Yeezus*, history collides with the samples themselves. The track features a slightly sped sample of Nina Simone's "Strange Fruit," itself a cover of the same song famously sung by Billie Holiday in the 1940s, despite the unbearable image to which its title refers: a lynched Black man, hanging from trees by a rope.

The song is based on a poem, which is based on a photograph that was used to protest the mob-murder of African Americans in the 1940s; each iteration struggles to capture in a new medium the unbearable horror and to sustain it in the popular imagination. One way it achieves this feat is through commemorating loss, by transforming the image sufficiently from its original form—as poem, song, cover, and beat; through the dream-work of Black music—such that it becomes a terrifying compromise, a memorable dream, permitting grievous slumber (rather than a night terror in which, as Ogden notes, no dream-work occurs). Sampling, like other forms of musical repetition, allows the psyche to hold more than it could handle on its first try. Through a community of shared practices, the psyche learns how to convert traumatic disruptions into musical continuity through the technologies of reproduction afforded by the historical era. "Every day the urge grows stronger to get hold of an object at very close range by way of its likeness, its reproduction," Walter Benjamin writes in "The Work of Art in the Age of Mechanical Reproduction," a moment at which sampling was becoming, through new media for recording music and film, something between a kind of surgery and a kind of magic. Benjamin distinguished the "magician" (historically regarded as a "healer"), who "maintains the natural distance between the patient and himself . . . by virtue of his authority" in contrast to the "surgeon," who "abstains from facing the patient man to man; rather, it is through the operation that he penetrates into him." He continues: "Magician and surgeon compare to painter and cameraman. The painter maintains in his work a natural distance from reality, the cameraman penetrates deeply into its web. There is a tremendous difference between the pictures they obtain. That of the painter is a total one, that of the cameraman consists of multiple fragments which are assembled under a new law."[9]

Herein lies an inherent tension of great psychoanalytic interest. Is the analyst a magician or a surgeon, a specular painter or a penetrating cameraman, a healer or an engineer, an accompanist or a beatmaker? Beginning in the days of hypnosis, Freud's therapeutic technique invariably involved removing, to some degree, the participation of his patients, their right to the privacy of their thoughts—*doing* things to them, like a surgeon. But at the same time, Freud was always the magician, inspiring the patient to play along. (If you refuse to play, you can't be hypnotized.) Doing magic to someone is always doing magic with someone. Even when employing the most objectively surgical psychoanalytic technique, which "abstains from facing the patient man to man" and tries to use interpretation as a scalpel to unbind unconscious resistances, the analyst nevertheless retains the aura of a magician, hidden behind the couch, suspending disbelief through what Michael Parsons once described as "negating" everyday reality, decentering familiar experience.[10] A very different picture emerges depending on one's vantage point in this magical-surgical duality: The magician, like a painter, is positioned at a natural distance, but one held in a humanizing relation to the other and where the magic engages a mutual enchantment, an on-the-job training in inspired creativity. Unlike the surgical cameraman, the magician paints a total picture, designating a space in which to induce states at a human level.

There is a point when children realize that the magician is not actually performing magic. But they still enjoy the show. At this point, the magician becomes a performing artist, or even a kind of teacher, doing tricks that audience members might even be able to figure out and perform themselves with practice. (It is hard not to envy anyone who can do practical magic if you can't.) To an audience member, a great musician is beyond magical, a demigod; to become a musician, to become *music*, is to learn the tricks of this trade, to get the hang of it, to enter the weave of fellow players in musical conversation. Sampling imbues music with this sense of conversation, weaving that magical bond between musician and audience, then and now, beholding an object together.

It is unclear whether Benjamin could have imagined social activities that are potentiated by the "new laws" of technorepetition; the heyday of serialist music (predated by Benjamin's writing, but not by much) could be understood as an expression of a deep anxiety about repetition. But repetition always poses the question of what Michel de M'Uzan famously called the *same* and the *identical*, the question of whether repetitive iterations function essentially to neutralize variations or rather function as the basis on which new variations can be generated.[11] "Whether we use [repetition] for good or ill," Fink writes, "for engagement or escape, is up to us. Process music that mirrors advertising's repetition—or for that matter, any aspect of the culture of repetition—needn't only represent capitulation to its effects; the work might take on the burden of repetition as commentary, as critique, even as a kind of callisthenic mental toughening."[12]

Freud attempted to contrast the capitulating and callisthenic properties of repetition in his significant (if convoluted) paper "On Narcissism," in which he defines the ego ideal (later to become the superego) as *progressive*, preserved in the heritage and habitus of shared forms of movement.[13] It shows us how to do the trick, instilling our communal values in our collective bodies, helping us along from wherever we just were to beyond wherever we are now. The ego ideal says, *There's a way to do things*, and then does them. To resemble the ego ideal is to re-assemble the psyche-soma, calling forth the inceptions of childhood pleasures, the bodily self that enjoyed something. Freud calls this the lost narcissism of childhood and describes how it is set up as part of ourselves that unconsciously guides us toward satisfying activities. There is no internal guidance toward such pleasures that has not already benefited from the experience of musical submersion with others, so those who were never woven into the music simply cannot guide themselves toward what can be enjoyed.

The ego ideal is always as vulnerable to trauma as the culture that surrounds it, and an unavailable or damaged ego ideal yields the defensive self-interest that Klein supposed was an original state of human nature, what Freud considered less (though still) problematically to be secondary narcissism. (Primary narcissism, in this context, may be little more than a fantasy of what it might have been like to have an ego ideal to be like.) But a system of humanization in which the ego ideal is presented and available for identification through the weave in favor of something like the magic of psychosexual fascination emphasizes audience participation. The magician's audience is always partially responsible for the illusion; the surgeon's patient, likewise, relinquishes responsibility for survival, consciousness itself, in order to heal. Within the surgeon always remains, "hidden," a magician, a performance artist, who bodies forth a well-practiced composition that is not natural but "super"-natural, not instinctual but a way of handling nature, including one's own nature, that can be learned but that appears to those who haven't learned it yet as magic. Like a magician-healer, Freud laid hands on his patients to help close the distance between ego and ego ideal; like a cameraman, he created a new technology for assembling the fragments of experience under a new law, a new calisthenics, a frame, beginning with what Freud believed to be a revelation of the secret of dreams, his Romantic discovery, a soft sound coming forth, a new way to sample the world.

III

"The achievements of the dream-work," Freud reminds us in *Jokes* (sampling his earlier hit),

> can be described as follows. A tissue of thoughts, usually a very complicated one, which has been built up during the day and has not been completely dealt with—"a day's residue"—continues during the night to retain the quota of energy—the "interest"—claimed by it, and threatens to disturb sleep. This "day's residue" is transformed by the dream-work into a dream and made innocuous to sleep. In order to provide a fulcrum for the dream-work, the "day's residue" must be capable of constructing a wish—which is not a very hard condition to fulfill.[14]

To dream is to day-sample, to quote a disturbingly wishful quota of energy from a tissue, to take a culture from the day, a sample of the stimuli that have produced incomplete longing, which the dream resumes by fulfilling the wish. As a kind of repetition compulsion—the repetition of the day in the dream, the repetition of the day's noise as a sample in the night's music—sampling creates conditions of psychical lingering, allowing work to continue. The work of the sample, like the work of *nachträglichkeit*, is bidirectional; it links the listener, through nostalgia, to old music and to the fresh sounds carried in the uncannily familiar, the new music in what Freud called a refinding of the object. Sexual fantasies are often sample-heavy and never exactly in time; they repeat themselves indefinitely even as they start to temporalize the otherwise anarchic timelessness of the sexual drive through *narrative*, the form (as the French philosopher Paul Ricoeur has formulated) through which human beings constitute time. The weave not only provides material to generate the fantasy; it also provides music for harnessing it, creating a repeating figure over which variation can occur as a continuous dialectic between the erotic and the sexual, the old and the new, tradition and improvisation, history and future.

Jokes and dreams differ clearly not only in their performative aspect but in the way their actions pivot at this juncture of old and new. Dreams revive lifelong fascinations by hooking onto the stimuli offered up by the cultural artifacts of everyday life, which are then reanimated and played out on a private stage in the theater of the mind. Jokes also sample the shared artifacts of cultural life but stage them publicly, relieving longstanding repressions, one laugh at a time, through the novelty of their being stimulated by another person, born anew through the delivery of a joke. A joke entails the embodied enjoyment of laughter and hence a fresh activation of mind-body, conscious-unconscious connectivity. A joke takes us behind ourselves; we laugh despite ourselves, beyond what we really understand, so that we can lose and refind ourselves in the shared experience. Even very young children can tell there's a joke going on before they get a joke (and certainly before they can tell one); they start laughing, whether they get it or not, joining the strange and wonderful rhythms of movement corresponding our bodies and theirs. They learn how to laugh, which may itself be a sample of how one's parents laugh, a little sample of how to be a human. ("A human being," Winnicott once wrote, "is a time-sample of human nature.")[15] This protojoking is a way of learning how to play a role in a trio, which is itself embedded in a weave.

Psychoanalysis yields the pleasure of laughing with and at oneself, the pleasure in which this distinction is no longer material, the relief of having to analyze everything to our satisfaction. We only want to be satisfied until we are satiated, but we never stop wanting to be continuous in time, even if only to disrupt it. When one falls out of time (or has never fallen into time), perhaps the disaster of permanent timelessness can be averted by sampling a bit of shared time, literally for the time being. Like the ego ideal, a good joke can remind us, through laughter, of the ecstasy of rhythmized embodiment, of moving through time together, when time has all but stopped. As Scarfone points out, Freud repeatedly reminded us in the postwar period, sampling doesn't just take time; it *makes* time: "Remember that in more than one place Freud himself proposes as a mechanism to represent time, a device that periodically, repeatedly, deploys its antennae, palates, and tastes samples from the outer world. So there is no radical separation between temporality and atemporality in the apparatus of the soul."[16]

The anticipatory aspect of sampling may be understood as a bid for translation, for forming a way for shared being-in-the-world to express itself; a bit of bafflement waiting for a magician-translator, for the time and space to imbue it with meaning; an Instagram, waiting for likes. This bid, under the right circumstances, converts the confusion of trauma into the seduction of enigma, if only we can rest upon it in a four-dimensional time structure built through life rhythms and not left only at the mercy of death drives. Repetition only becomes rhythm through the musicality of the analyst, through the analyst's way of organizing perception, the analyst here as a cultural agent. Otherwise, it's just reality, repetition of the real. (As patients often say in periods of profound deadness: *It is what it is.*)

Music is the weave in action, sampling the world, constructing its frame-work. Even the purest, death-driven repetition, recorded and played back repeatedly, never making it to the next musical landmark, can start to take musical form, doing the work of music, potentiating musical structure when inspired to work as a living frame. Woven into the habitus of shared living, bits of reality can become the tapestry of musical continuity. Sampling itself brings the clinical exchange closer to music, shifting the modality closer to play, inducing the patient into the weave, which henceforth absorbs impinging reality with both greater resilience and greater sensitivity. Recall from chapter 5 that Winnicott wrote: "Now the infant's growth takes the form of a continuous interchange between inner and outer reality, each being enriched by the other. The child is now not only a potential creator of the world, but also the child becomes able to populate the world with samples of his or her own inner life. So gradually the child is able to 'cover' almost any external event, and perception is almost synonymous with creation."[17]

For Winnicott, the capacity to sample one's inner life, to be in communication with oneself, depends upon the barrier between inside and outside—"more or less bounded by the skin," he says (as opposed to Anzieu's notion of a skin ego, in which the barrier is a richer, more active player)—which makes it possible to perceive-create the outside world, despite its potential for impingement.[18] If you can sample, you can cover. When inner and outer reality begin to enrich each other, the child has become a potential creator of the world but also a potential-creator of the world, a creator of potential space, a dreamer, a musician.

Joking is our dream-training. Can we say that the joke precedes the individual dream? Joking is part of what rhythmizes, musicalizes, and induces us into communal dreaming. If dreaming is a benchmark of becoming a human being, we must nevertheless learn how to dream by being woven in with others. This entails borrowing the dream-function (Bion) from others, but even more fundamentally, it requires being inducted into the cultural ways of seeing and being. Jokes help us learn the ways of the weave. But not all jokes are funny, not all laughter on the side of life. Without the weave, jokes become impossibly private and generate only the laughter of madness, the jokes no one else can get, a perversion of the equipment of the weave, using it the wrong way. (Thought disorder, in this view, might be reclassified as weave disorder.) And while jokes only function as jokes if they can be shared, dreams can only do their dream-work if one can eventually wake up. The question is therefore always whether we can move in and out of states, a capacity that is itself a weave skill, an aspect of weavecraft. The weave may be nothing so much as the communal repertoire of possibilities for moving from one state to another, an aesthetic sensibility for assembling a playlist of communal potentialities into a stylized way of living. By sampling the resonances of the world, the weave delimits degrees of separateness and otherness, constructing a contact-barrier between sound and silence, notes and rests, the absences in which music can be felt, the things that don't happen so that other things can.

While the constructive activity of sampling establishes the spatiotemporal pattern upon which the deconstructive activity of analysis may proceed, so too does sample-work operate as a mechanism for finding one's way into the world, for effecting shifts in psychical functioning that are best detected through what Ogden has recently referred to as the "ontological" perspective of theorists like Winnicott and Bion (which he opposes to the "epistemological" psychoanalysis of Freud and Klein).[19] Seen through the ontological perspective, the transformative potential of psychoanalysis is to facilitate and reconcile elements of the shared, human world into what we might consider the musical wherewithal of each constituent player; as Ogden puts it (sampling Winnicott), "to weave other-than-me-objects into the personal pattern"—in other words, to sample the world. The incorporative activity of weaving samples of the human world into one's personal pattern simultaneously opens a gateway between the subjectivity of individual personality and the intersubjectivity of shared perception and meaningfulness, recalling what has become Ogden's most transformative contribution to the theory and practice of psychoanalysis, the concept of the analytic third. In his seminal paper on that concept, Ogden attends to the mundane things to which his mind is drawn, following this attentional pull toward the sensorial dimension of psychical experience, entering into a shared world in which ordinary objects pop up, little things that get him to see something that maybe the patient can also see, becoming "analytic objects" of shared perception.[20] By permitting himself to become more or less hypnotized by objects in the room, Ogden allows his state of mind to change in order to find a way to be with his patient, entering the "third" of the weave through perceptual activity. The interpretations he ultimately makes, based on what he (sampling Bion) calls "reverie," are not made out of whole cloth, so to speak, but rather out of the extensively shaped, humanized weave patterns in which perception must become embedded, whether or not it is to eventually support the associative work of reverie and meaning making. Following this primary movement of sensorial investment in the presentational dimension of physical objects, Ogden's subsequent interpretations begin to re-present in words the sensory quality of the sessions themselves, which becomes a shared floor of experience to sustain the push of progressive psychical movement toward a dreamworld of immersive accompaniment and inspiration. Through this newly dimensionalized thirdness, interpretation becomes less about understanding the meaning of a symptom or the dynamics of a transference and more like getting the hang of something, less like obsessionally thinking one's way out of a problem, of taking it too seriously (as Adam Phillips has remarked, "Freud showed us—if we needed showing—that it is not more truthful to be serious"),[21] and more like having a dream or getting a joke.

If we were to read *Jokes* as seriously as *Dreams*, we might place greater emphasis on the role of induction into the weave of a shared psychosensory framework from which any other analytic activity could only ever proceed. And the most common technical manifestation of this inductive activity in all of psychoanalysis may be the art of sampling. While the antecedent, late-nineteenth-century genre hypnosis involved the patient not actually being there for it (and therefore never learning how to do the trick on one's own, locking the hypnotized subject into a state of dependence), analysands can eventually get the hang of how to do this work, midwifed by the analyst's handling of one's nature. We can look at Freud's original approach to dream interpretation through this lens: the sampling of material elements back to the patient (as when Winnicott "presented" objects to the infant, as in the game where he produces a spatula for the infant to sample). A patient has a dream that "samples" some bit of day residue (an enigmatic message, a beta element) and brings the analyst a sample, a "culture," of the dream, without yet having found a way to use it. (Laplanche refers to the death drive as "pure culture of otherness.")[22] In Freud's original technique for dream analysis, he "samples" each element back to the patient for associations, as if to say, *We can turn these bits into music, you're already producing the notes that we need, we just need to give them a (cultural) form*—so that it is this sampling, musicalizing activity itself, the induction of humanizing meaning making, sexuality-as-translating, more than any given translation or interpretation, the dream-training itself, that is the mechanism of therapeutic action. As Hamlet said, the play is the thing. (Sampling in this way also "saves energy" the way Freud thinks a joke does—it implicitly says, *Everything we need to know is already here—we just need to loop it and find the groove*.)

Bion showed how the child borrows the dreaming faculty from the parent: *I dream for you before you can dream for yourself*. But the containing mother's dream-work-alpha capacity depends itself on communal dreaming. Winnicott had famously proclaimed that there is no such thing as a baby, no baby living independently of a caregiver, but, equally, "there is no such thing as a human nature independent of culture," writes the American anthropologist Clifford Geertz:

> Men without culture would not be the clever savages of Golding's *Lord of the Flies* thrown back upon the cruel wisdom of their animal instincts; nor would they be the nature's noblemen of Enlightenment primitivism or even, as classical anthropological theory would imply, intrinsically talented apes who had somehow failed to find themselves. They would be unworkable monstrosities with very few useful instincts, fewer recognizable sentiments, and no intellect: mental basket cases.[23]

Translated into the language we are using: It is only possible to have a sense of self when one is already secured in the weave of culture. The weave is the metaphysical dimension of the unconscious, always beneath our physical apperception of the world, which we are always collectively producing. We live unconsciously all the time, in a place that makes us what we are what we are, what makes us human. There is nothing more real to human being than culture, which conducts our conduct, like a conductor, beyond the limits of genetic predisposition into the musical weave of being human. Geertz continues:

> To supply the additional information necessary to be able to act, we were forced, in turn, to rely more and more heavily on cultural sources—the accumulated fund of significant symbols. Such symbols are thus not mere expressions, instrumentalities, or correlates of our biological, psychological, and social existence; they are prerequisites of it. Without men, no culture, certainly; but equally, and more significantly, without culture, no men.[24]

And no men *and* no culture, without the weaving function of music to connect the two, to function as a conductor between culture and men. Before baby can dream, the parent must conduct beats that make the world musically legible—"symbols," in Geertz's sense (which are ontologically prior to symbols in Lacan's sense)—so that the dreaming mind has something to dream about and so that communal dreams become usable. In this sense, singing and moving together would underwrite the potential use of communal dreams.

We are authors by day but DJs by night. The frame of the session, like the screen of the dream, provides conditions under which the psyche speaks through selections, through *decoupage*, reassembly of material it identifies as wish-laden, as rife with longing, with potential. Our secondary process, often unwittingly, samples our primary process, toward the possibility of transience. This is what distinguishes the creative potential of mourning (and joking) from the stasis of melancholia, which is the miscarriage of mourning, an incomplete form of loss, loss interrupted, on repeat. If insanity is doing the same thing over and over and expecting something new to happen, melancholia is a vaudevillian joke about madness, and no one is laughing. "There are certain queer times and occasions in this strange mixed affair we call life," Melville writes in *Moby-Dick*, "when a man takes this whole universe for a vast practical joke, though the wit thereof he but dimly discerns, and more than suspects that the joke is at nobody's expense but his own."[25] Melancholia is an absurd state that one doesn't know is absurd, a practical joke played by the universe at one's expense. The second you realize it, you're on your way out. This is why it is a most promising moment with a melancholic patient when we are able to make a joke, to enter into its shared body-dream. The dreaming psyche samples the day's residues and plays them back to us until we get the joke our dream is telling us. By sampling the wish in the form of day-residue in the slumber of the subsequent night's dreams, the psyche re-presents the object of longing, the *ferne geliebte*, for another round of psychical work, a kind of grief-work, a working toward libidinal freedom to the possibility of moving on to repeat a fresh cycle in the day to come. The structure of this process is reiterated (even sampled, in a way) in the work of dream interpretation, remixing the leftovers of dreaming, the remainders, that are occasionally available upon waking. The remaining dream-samples can be contemplated together, submitted for interpretation, to be sampled back and elaborated.

Perhaps all interpretations, especially when they are constructed into speech (making them "interventions"), apply a similar logic. Preparing the patient for an interpretation, something new, the analyst may sample something that the patient has just said. This kind of interpretive activity conveys a metamessage to the patient: *You're quotable*, sampling says to the patient, *I feel the musical potential of this material*, in the spirit of singing a cover song or looping a drum sample into a beat. Perhaps patients get interested in the music of the analyst when it samples a song that was just playing through them, through free association, whatever record was just spinning. Of course, nothing can sound more alien than what one has just said, as if it were spoken not by but *through* the patient; the same uncanniness can occur for the analyst, who may initially have more training, more apprenticeship, in a kind of curiosity about the otherness transmitted through speaking freely. And if sampling prepares the interpretive act by establishing a consensual analytic object or experience, the therapist's contribution of words is equally likely, in the wake of Ogden's work, to be nothing so much as a sampling one's own reverie. (Perhaps these inspired associations are most useful because they fully recapitulate not only the function of dreaming but the structure of it, the sampling.) When patients sample analysts in return, it can feel like an homage or expression of gratitude, but it is more than that; it is an indicator, evidence, that mutually formative identification has occurred.

Sample-work pervades all activities of psychoanalytic culture—though like all clinical technique, it can always go either way. Excessive identical repetition has the effect of dehumanizing instead of rehumanizing. We are always learning how to better put repetitive functions to the work of sampling. Supervision samples the process notes, curating what is relevant and worthy of attention. Thinking and writing about psychoanalytic theory, which Laplanche believed should be a psychoanalytic experience, renders in writing its own sample-construction, its playlist of source-drives. "The attunement of playfulness," Wallrup writes, appears in different historical guises."[26] Perhaps playfulness, in the form of sampling, is the attunement, the *Stimmung*, of free association, as longing was the *Stimmung* of Schumann's Romanticism. Both Schumann and Nietzsche suffered breakdowns at the age of forty-four from which they never recovered, in an age when the current spectacle made of Kanye's psychical decompensation would have been unimaginable. There is the potential for great art, and devastating suffering, for those with one foot in and one foot out of the weave, enough to long for it but not enough to get in. Nothing makes one sing like knowing what one is missing. (Kanye has in recent years foresworn rapping in favor of recording traditional gospel music at his residence in rural Wyoming.) We are in the weave when we hear music, and we need music to get into the weave, to get back into the groove. And if the groove disruption was not rupturing and did not leave us stranded too long (too "intromissive," in Laplanche's language), then we may find ourselves back on track—which is pretty good, a pretty good human life.

Even poor Rob knew how to tell a joke. Rosen describes Schumann's piano piece *Humoreske*, as exemplary of a "romantic paradox":

> There are three staves: the uppermost for the right hand; the lowest for the left; the middle, which contains the melody, is not to be played. Note that the melody is no more to be imagined as a specific sound than it is to be played: nothing tells us that the melody is to be heard as vocal or instrumental. This melody, however, is embodied in the upper and lower parts as a kind of after-resonance—out of phase, delicate, and shadowy. What one hears is the echo of an unperformed melody, the accompaniment of a song. The middle part is marked *innere Stimme*, and it is both interior and inward, a double sense calculated by the composer: a voice between soprano and bass, it is also an inner voice that is never exteriorized. It has its being within the mind and its existence only through its echo.
>
> At one point the paradox is stretched further still. . . . When the first phrase begins again at bar 17, the "inner voice" is momentarily blank—it reappears only with the second bar of the melody. For one bar a voice which was not present before is *not*, now, *not present* . . . the empty bar is a poetic joke, a reminder of the impossibility of conceiving the nature of the unspecified sonority of which the music we hear is an echo.[27]

The absent melody is the joke Schumann is telling to his player, to himself, teacher to student, inspiration. (The joke is on the audience; we don't even know what we're missing.) In longing, the joke is always on us; to get the joke, once and for all—that the thing we long for was never there—is impossible. (Fortunately.) And in music, the joke is always on longing: Why be gutted by the irreducible distance of one's beloved when you can suffer, as Nietzsche put it, tragedy born out of the spirit of music? (And for Freud, we might say, the joke is on music: He doesn't understand what all the fuss is about.) The art of music, of jokes, of dreams, transposes longing to the cultural realm, transports us back to the weave, where we can move and breathe. Music is a digestive system for experience, transforming wails into requiems, as dreaming turns sensory experience into psychical reality, as play turns impossibility into paradox. "Because we are always shadowed by the possibility of not getting what we want," Phillips writes, "we learn, at best, to ironize our wishes—that is, to call our wants wishes: a wish is only a wish until, as we say, it comes true—and, at worst, to hate our needs."[28] So the *Stimmung* of hating one's needs is envy. There is a fine line, and world of difference, between the analyst's forms of interpretation (or ways of being an analyst), which implicitly communicate an unreachable certainty and authority of the analyst's mind, on the one hand, and the analyst's acting in such a way that supports and inspires one's own meaning-making activity, including through sampling (which instantly communicates that the patient's material is "conducive" to making music together)—an optimal distance between ego and ego ideal.

One of Freud's best magic tricks was to invent a kind of medicine that did not involve touching, an ingenious deconcretizing of the formerly literal light touch (not to mention surgical penetration), replacing physical contact with the bracing, spatiotemporal holding capacity of both the frame and its sample-heavy technique of psychoanalysis, producing not only a metapsychological theory for generating symbols but a practice for inhabiting the habitus of being human. The analytic task is to provide an alternative atmosphere that is assertively, if not aggressively, supportive and appreciative of psychic meaning, thought, freedom, and dignity in the patient. Sampling is remembering in both senses—first, literally remembering the content enough to reproduce it, and second, as the psychoanalytic activity of inducting the patient into the weave, (re-)membering the patient into the weave of human being, as opposed to the reverse—putting it on the patient to make music out of the analyst's reified, isolated music, a broken record—what Bion was getting at about memory and desire, clearing the way for re-membering to happen in live company.

Freud's tripartite model of joke telling constitutes something like what Bion would later call a basic assumption group, though one reserved for groups of three. To be in a trio, in other words, is always to be configured for a joke to be told by one member to a third about the second—and for each member to occupy each position at all times. And the participation of the members in this activity begets an enlivening economy of psychical expenditure that we know as humor. To be made the butt of a joke can be humiliating, but to *surrender* to parental exclusion is also to launch oneself into a world of creative and erotic possibility. Perhaps psychoanalysis is uniquely positioned to generate a particular form of group, of thirdness, the threeness of a musical trio, an improvised freedom supported by the harmonics of attunement and the drumbeat of the frame. And once inspired to identify with this tripartite musicality, its creative potential, the overlapping unconsciousness of the psychoanalytic dyad is free to defuse. We go to analysis because there is a joke we cannot take; we leave when we find ourselves laughing, whether or not we get the joke.

8

THIS IS HOW WE DO IT

habitus
mimesis
identification

|

An *ethos* is not a force of nature but a force of *human* nature—essentially a force of habit, or a system of habits shared by every member of the culture, what the French sociologist Pierre Bourdieu referred to as *habitus*, a shared, meaningful cultural system of physical comportment (which he called *hexis*) that is always already there, before (and enabling) any emergence of an individual experience of having a self or even of having a body.[1] Through habitus, the whole system of meaningfulness lights up before the individual takes his or her place in it. In a way that is difficult for members of our contemporary culture to grasp, Bourdieu believed that the child, before becoming a subject, exists in a shared, social habitus, embodying the music of *hexis* before finding or using words to speak or sing its subjectivity:

> A whole group and a whole symbolically structured environment... exerts an anonymous, pervasive pedagogic action.... The child imitates

not "models" but other people's actions. Body *hexis* speaks directly to the motor function, in the form of a pattern of postures that is both individual and systematic, because linked to a whole system of techniques involving the body and tools, and charged with a host of social meanings and values: in all societies, children are particularly attentive to the gestures and postures which, in their eyes, express everything that goes to make an accomplished adult—a way of walking, a tilt of the head, facial expressions, ways of sitting and of using implements, always associated with a tone of voice, a style of speech, and (how could it be otherwise?) a certain subjective experience.[2]

So it is not simply (as documented through recent developments in infant observation and development research) that each mother-infant dyad (and, subsequently, each analyst-patient dyad) create unique forms of musical communication and embodied attunement but also that they *find* meaningful forms made available in the cultural commons, as it were, the shared fabric of perception that underwrites what Winnicott describes as the transitional area, the area of the "found-created," where usable cultural objects are discovered, paradoxically, as one's own invention. The frame of psychoanalytic work, in this sense, acts as a metonym for the larger habitus by which and through which we conduct ourselves, providing a forum and a form for finding-creating oneself, for "free association"—a literal figure of speech, complete with its own *hexis* of physical posture and interpersonal configuration. The embodied framing matrix *in*-forms, through its faithful constancy, the full spectrum of psychical phenomena without the latter having to be *trans*-formed into symbols by interpretations before weaving them together; the weaving is organically induced by the tending to and sustaining of the macro- and microrhythms of the frame itself.

Which other conductors of habitus are baked into the framing function? Freud reportedly shook hands with all his patients at the start and end of every session. Could this unwittingly have been a way of introducing elements of a consensorial dimension of the practice, a habitus that might underwrite and enable the analytic process? A rhythmic regulated recharging at the bookends of the hour? The handshake, in other words, whatever else it may come to signify (that is, through symbolic transformation and associations), constitutes a fullness of shared contact that language is always a little too late to capture (as Bion wrote in "Evidence"), an experience that language always limps after (to borrow Laplanche's metaphor). This nonspontaneous habitus aspect of the analyst's activity (a way of setting the session in motion) functions primarily not as a conveyor of meanings or symbolic meanings but as a necessary form of mutual induction, activating aspects of the experience that allow patient and analyst to come together. In this way, patient and analyst are embedded in a shared spatiotemporal structure (rhythm, time, climate, handshake). In this sense the weave is akin to Bion's idea of "O," which is real but unknowable, an unknown lived, which is iterated and made flesh in every session. (As Yeats once wrote, "Man can embody truth, but he cannot know it.")

One finds (or creates) a crucial rendering of these aspects of the sensory-somatic framing function in Didier Anzieu's seminal study of what he termed the *skin ego*, among whose functions he listed both a "libidinal recharging of the psychical functioning," which he linked to Freud's notion of contact-barrier in the "Project" of 1895, and what he calls "common sense," which registers the traces of impressions presented to the skin by the environment:

> This Skin Ego function develops upon a dual base, biological and social. Biologically, it is upon the skin that a first picture of reality is registered. Socially, an individual's membership of a social group is shown by incisions, scarifications, skin-painting, tattooing, by his make-up and hairstyle, and by his clothes, which are another aspect of the same thing. The Skin Ego is the original parchment which preserves, like a palimpsest, the erased, scratched-out, written-over first outlines of an "original" pre-verbal writing made up of traces upon the skin.[3]

In the "original" skin-forming contact with the world, the responsiveness of live flesh (as opposed to the deadness of what Searles called the nonhuman environment)[4] forms the surface on which all subsequent forms of contact will be superscribed. A palimpsest of these contacts (what Björk once called a history of touches) condenses multiple registers into a lower dimensionality, approaching nondifferentiation, which makes it difficult for "thinking" in the traditional sense, given the limited range of dimensionality available to thinking. (We can't really think—though we can in fact dream, as Freud discovered—in less than two dimensions or more than four.) If this foundational layer, constituted prior to the differentiation of psyche from soma, is functioning properly, it becomes the contact-barrier that underwrites all subsequent developments of psychical life. But perhaps Anzieu separates the biological and social too cleanly or too much. When he writes "Biologically, it is upon the skin that a first picture of reality is registered," this biological reality is already a humanized, woven world, a whole thing, impressed upon our bodies from the first contacts with the world in a kind of psychosensory Big Bang. That is human "reality," our ontological palimpsest, the foundational layer—composed of culturally shared forms, imposed, ideally, in a loving way—that Heidegger called "being." A whole world impresses itself precisely in the way, in the particular physical form, in which a baby is held, and in a handshake too, and somehow we get it all at once. That's how the weave works. "When we first begin to believe anything," Wittgenstein wrote, "what we believe is not a single proposition, it is a whole system of propositions. (Light dawns gradually over the whole.)"[5] If the whole is not illuminated, we live in the darkness of dissociation (desocialized—*socii*: tribe) as isolates, idiosyncrats ("idiots" in the Greek sense), in an imitative alter world. Freud's manner of shaking hands might have been the most important communication in many of his analyses: *Welcome to the human world.*

This foundational, ongoing inweaving enables any of the more articulated marks to be meaningful and thinkable; every subsequent trace becomes in effect a derivative sign of membership or a scar of its failure. A circumcision, for instance, memorializes an induction into weave membership that has already occurred; otherwise it's a scar that marks a trauma, a violent and meaningless rupture. Without induction and membership in a functioning weave, the space that is normally organized by the dialectic of conscious-unconscious—repression, sexuality, translation, subjectivity—is filled with the unbearably demanding presence of others' enigmatic messages that just keep coming in with every new encounter. Other people become a terrifying, traumatizing mystery; bureaucratic management, homeland security, becomes the only viable option.[6]

The weave *gives us our human body,* allows us to *dwell* in our bodies, by providing the forms of movement that allow us to have a body in the first place; as Phillip Boast, following Merleau-Ponty, writes in "The Musical Body," "the body itself is an expressive form of consciousness."[7]

(In the absence of a weave, disconnected from it, we would be left to fabricate a body from scratch or deny that we need one at all—"a picture of frightening dissociation," to recall Charles Taylor's phrase.) And the primary medium for transmitting and conducting this weave function is the dimension of music intrinsic to all sustainable forms of communal living that have evolved steadily over time and are preserved through tradition and the reliability of their enchanting effects. Music provides the conduit through which we become seated in our bodily selves through primordial enchantment, held in the pocket of a groove, comported in the manner of our ancestors. As the anthropologist and travel writer Bruce Chatwin notes in his study of the "songlines" of aboriginal Australian natives:

> Aboriginal Creation myths tell of the legendary totemic beings who had wandered over the continent in the Dreamtime, singing out the name of everything that crossed their path—birds, animals, plants, rocks, waterholes—and so singing the world into existence... the Ancestors had been poets in the original sense of *poesis*, meaning "creation."... The man who went "Walkabout" was making a ritual journey. He trod in the footprints of his Ancestor. He sang the Ancestor's stanzas without changing a word or note—and so recreated the Creation.... Aboriginals could not believe the country existed until they could see and sing it—just as, in the Dreamtime, the country had not existed until the Ancestors sang it.[8]

The musicophysical dimension of the weave, the repeated words and tunes of the Ancestors' stanzas, layered upon the ground beneath our feet, constitutes us as musical posterity of our poetic progenitors, inducing us, *homo-nizing* us, into weave-heritage, at which point the weave itself begins to conduct our now humanized (or *homo*-nized) perception and meaningful experience of the physical world. In this sense what is originally physical—the primordial musical forms themselves, beta function in the flesh—begins to function *meta*physically as the hidden, transcendent source of the properly human world, running through everything, lighting it up, organizing it, enchanting it and us as we induce new members (also known as children), recreating Creation every time, speaking the whole of existence.

"In theory, at least," Chatwin writes, "the whole of Australia could be read as a musical score."[9] The legendary Ancestors in Chatwin's *Songlines* are musical totem poles, nothing but the generational layering of their own ancestral elements, a palimpsest amplified to the height and depth of nature's physicality, a stacked chord, harmonic heritage.

||

When Borch-Jacobsen uses the term "identification," he means it in its most totemic sense of being the same as one's Ancestors, no-different than those with whom one identifies. We are first claimed as members of our home cultures, interpellated as new members, by the melody of speech that surrounds our infant bodies, the habitus of the way we are held, the very air that we breathe. Like Freud's handshake, these inaugural identifications confer an identity, telling the human in one's care something they did not already know (including that they are human). Once identified *by* these care-giving others, we become eligible to identify *through* others in Borch-Jacobsen's sense, a register of communion with fellow humans that is less about securing a connection between two bodies and more about imaginatively erasing the distance between them, more about being the same thing. (Both of these stages precede the more traditional notion of identification in psychoanalytic developmental theory, a form of introjection or projection taking place between separate individuals who exist and separate, unit selves who choose or decide to identify *with* one another.)[10] "It is as if wish fulfillment did not so much consist in *having* the object as in *being* the one who possesses it," Borch-Jacobsen writes.[11] Wish fulfillment, at its core, he reiterates (paraphrasing Girard), is always about being a wisher, about being *like* other wishers, belonging to a family of wishers, more than it is a property of the object for which one wishes, because "desire has no object, at least not before some mediator—teacher, friend, books, fashion, culture, etc.—intervenes to tell it what is desirable." He continues,

> Thus we must not imagine some essential bond between desire and its object: the desire for an object is a desire-effect; it is induced, or at least

secondary, with respect to the imitation—the mimesis—of the desire of others. In other words, desire is mimetic before it is anything else. It is first mobilized by a "model" to which it conforms (with which it identifies), not so much because there is some sort of desire to imitate, some sort of "imitative instinct" (that would still be conceding a great deal to the idea that desire has aims of its own), but rather because mimesis informs desire, directs it, and, more broadly speaking, incites it.[12]

Identification generates desire through and out of mimetic repetition; it has "no goal (*Ziel*) of its own," Borch-Jacobsen writes, "is indifferent with respect to pleasure and unpleasure," and therefore "lies 'beyond' the pleasure principle, and 'before' unpleasure" (32). But Borch-Jacobsen pushes the point even further. Identification itself is, for Borch-Jacobsen, its own end, rather than a means to an end; desire is not only routed through but fundamentally *toward the pleasure of being like* one another, the pleasure of being in the weave.[13] (Here he echoes Chatwin: "The trade route *is* the Songline. . . . Because songs, not things, are the principal medium of exchange. Trading in 'things' is the secondary consequence of trading in song.")[14] "Identification is not a means for the fulfillment of desire," Borch-Jacobsen continues, "it is that 'fulfillment' itself."[15] By this logic, we buy to be *like* other buyers and only subsequently want what we buy because we are already buying it. (To paraphrase William James, we are afraid of the bear because we are running away from it, and not the other way around.) We become lovers to become *like* other lovers.

But thankfully these identifications with one another, in all their rhythmic repetitions, are never identical copies. They are always being frustrated and syncopated, like music, by life itself, which, in the context of good-enough identifications, stimulates our desire, switching up metronomic regularity with the nuances of ongoing subjectivity. In one of his most important essays about music, "On Jazz," Theodor Adorno—who may have been, along with Theodor Reik, among the first synthesizers of music theory and psychoanalysis—analyzes the role of syncopation in jazz music, which infuses the rhythmic quality of the music with accents and phrasing without disrupting the symmetry of time, which is preserved in "the *continuo* instruments which are subordinate to it," repeating periods of fixed duration, "their authority unchallenged." It is the fruitful tension between regularity and disruption, "the possibility of letting the rigid vibrate, or more generally the opportunity to produce interferences between the rigid and the excessive," that for Adorno defines the "jazz-sound."[16] Might it also define psychoanalytic work? The variations that Adorno describes occur at almost every level of musical experience, from the way melodies are inflected or ornamented to the qualities with which individual notes are produced, provided that sufficient elements are *continuo*-ed, and against which these fluctuations can be perceived bodily, relative to other bodies in space. In its own habitus of musical repetition, the psychoanalytic frame provides the *continuo*, the principle of constancy, against which the syncopations of disruption take on the idiomatic qualities of accent and phrase. Treatments, like musical ensembles, take on their own timbral qualities as their *continuo* elements become shaken, vibrated, jerked, animated as a living frame, and even at times take on the qualities of bodily excess—stiffening, vibration, and release associated with sexual activity.

But in Adorno's psychoanalysis of jazz—which, as he anticipated at the time, has sustained its value as a psychoanalysis of music, including even the most contemporary pop music—pulsing rhythms and orgasmic releases are only, in a sense, the manifest sexual content of the musical dream. The latent content to which Adorno associates is about association: In the couplets of the verse, the voice of the solo instrument "speaks as if in isolation, precisely out of the contingency of his individuality," making a bid for social confirmation by the collective in the chorus. "The intended, unconscious process which the public performs is thus one of establishing identification," he continues. "The individual in the audience experiences himself primarily as a couplet-ego, and then feels himself transformed in the refrain; he identifies himself with the collective of the refrain, merges with it in the dance, and thus finds sexual fulfillment."[17]

Psychoanalysis, at its most musical, recapitulates the movement from fragile contingency, speaking "as if in isolation"—*as if*, as opposed to actual isolation, where no living speech is possible—to social confirmation, transforming an individual, through the (erotic) potential of identification, into communally authorized forms of *continu*-ity, of psychosexual conduction. Tensions and conflicts that inhere in the work of identification are mitigated and sustained through the musical momentum, the having and being, *being-with* (*Mitsein*), of identification. As Borch-Jacobsen claims (with palpable echoes of Adorno): "Identification is thus both the locus of the difficulty and the site of its resolution, or perhaps it is both the way one 'enters into' the Oedipus complex and the way one 'gets out' of it."[18]

Such is the about-face or reversal from which the ego ideal derives—the double-sided, two-faced ideal: one identifies with the father (the rival) so as not to identify with him (so as not to be his rival). Not *out* of love, consequently, but *in order* to be able to love him. The law, the double law that assigns the subject, is thus stated as follows: "Identify without identifying." Or, more simply still: "Identify yourself *as* a subject."[19]

The forms of musical living through which we "identify" with one another, through which not-me objects are woven into one's personal pattern (to paraphrase Ogden's favorite Winnicott sample), through which the infant is found-created, become in turn the means by which the infant is physically guided toward finding-creating the world, how we subject the world to ourselves and ourselves to the world, how we become psychesomatic subjects in and out of natural, material bodies. It is the pulsing ethic, the *ethos*, of shared ways of being that fuels the desire-effect of being oneself, an endless spiraling in and out of identification with one another (and identification of oneself through and among others) that constitutes the *continuo* enchantment of human being. The to-and-fro of this pulse—perhaps originally formulated in Marion Milner's distinction between the "feeling of oneness, of being united with everything, and the feeling of twoness, of self and object"[20]—manifests in treatment as a wave function. In the first phase of this macromovement, the analyst is essentially tasked with catching a case of the patient, becoming "infected," through identification, with what must become a shared ailment, the co-occupation of an impossible position. In his own creative way, Searles imagined that the analyst must ultimately be cured of an actual illness, the particular pathological hook for which each particular patient can be curative or therapeutic. Hooks in this sense are the necessary infection, the vaccination, that provokes the antibodies of inweaving to neutralize the threat of infection by incorporating it into the homeostasis of the larger system. Otherwise one has only allergies, condemned to the isolation of dissociative retreat. This constructive contagiousness is the identificatory level of countertransference, the mimesis by which to take on the illness, to enter this particular scene, fostered by an even attunement between members. The state of attunement is always, in this sense, a state of maximum vulnerability, of sheer infectability. (As new parents will confirm.) To make oneself available for purposes of therapeutic conduction is inevitably to expose oneself to colonization; they are two ends of the same continuum. And the flow to this ebb, the latter phase of this two-phase movement, is when the patient catches a case of the analyst, the power to be moved by another's music. It is the music that catches one's attention, that gets stuck in one's head, that guides the way toward objects of desire, activating the psychosensory apparatus to animate the fulfillment of wishes, a way of becoming a wanter, a wish to wish. To wish is to be vulnerable to what might happen, to inhabit a state of potential (dis)satisfaction, of anticipatory being, in which one will spend much more of one's life than in satisfaction proper (the latter actually being a state of relaxation, of resolution, of death, beyond the pleasure principle).

We enter a state of excitation, of frustration, every time we open ourselves to a new cultural experience (never more so than to a new piece of music), as a kind of training in being open to one another, or perhaps a reminder of the original opening of infancy, a readiness to be musicalized. Music, in this sense, would not only remind us of the pleasure of surrendering to one another; surrendering to one another, listening to one another, reminds us of what it feels like to be taken over by music. "All perception is at bottom listening," wrote the French philosopher Philippe Lacoue-Labarthe, "Or, in other terms that come down to the same thing, listening is the paradigm (not the metaphor) of perception in general. The unconscious *speaks*. And the voice, that is, the *lexis*, is that by which it speaks—which presupposes, in a perfectly classical manner, that language is determined essentially as a language of gesture, a *mimicry*."[21]

If Freud's royal road to the unconscious is the images of dreams, perhaps the *aural* road to the unconscious, "what happens when one goes back from Narcissus to Echo," as Lacoue-Labarthe frames it (what happens, perhaps, when one goes back to Freud through Reik, through Adorno) reveals, in its lossless sound quality, its pure echoes, the mimesis at the heart of unconsciousness, the unrepressed repetitions about which we are mercifully unconflicted. Music is never conflicted about its own repetition, but is always ready-at-hand, available for sampling. Through this repeatable accessibility, music takes on, Lacoue-Labarthe believes, a "homeopathic" quality. "In short," he writes, "music heals." Music provides the mimetic reduplication through which

> the subject can be engulfed in it through emotional discharge, but without losing itself irretrievably—drawing from it, on the contrary, that specifically theatrical form of pleasure that Freud will define as "masochistic." To put this in other terms, music's catharsis is such that it permits the subject to mime the return to the originary One, to the undifferentiated, to chaos (even while preserving itself, thanks to the "protective screen" of the myth or of the example, which, like the representative scission of representation, allows for identification without risk).[22]

Through animation and cultivation at the level of shared experience, of being like one another—"A human being," Adorno wrote in *Minima Moralia* (1951), "only becomes a human at all by imitating other human beings"[23]—music engenders a therapeutics of emotional charge safeguarded by the habitus of frame-rhythms that bind its surplus energy, emerging from the foundations of the music that has always been toward the possibilities of the new music one is becoming.

III

There are simply two kinds of music, good music and the other kind.
—DUKE ELLINGTON, "WHERE IS JAZZ GOING?"

Some music stays with us, while other music remains... other music. Some sound is music; the rest is noise. But sometimes noise draws us backward not toward the familiar, established forms but toward new sonic and expressive possibilities, ways to grow new shoots out of the shared soil of human culture. Much Western music pivots on the ecstatic tension and resolution between the known and unknown, the familiar and unfamiliar (and the uncanny in-between) structured by chordal harmony, which vibrates sonic dramas of harmonic in-betweenness into the stability of key signature. The most memorable musical moments are often those that surf the edge of some harmonic friction, bending blue notes, stretching the ear in just the right way. In the soaring chorus of "Rhythm of the Heat," the opening song on Peter Gabriel's fourth and last eponymous album (and inspired by Carl Jung's meditations on African drumming), a percussive landscape supports a *continuo* of minor tonality that brilliantly cracks open in the final two bars, when it resolves to an unexpected major-key scale degree as Gabriel rounds off the lyric ("The rhythm has my soooooooo-uuul"). From the collective unconscious of shared rhythms opens a window of new harmonic possibility of ecstatic resolution.

But what if the note had not resolved to a chord, major or minor, but remained simply suspended, simply went-on-being? What if the music leaves us unresolved, in a state of longing? If we use identification in order to get the wishing system going, perhaps the way to do this is to turn to certain music, which we collect in the form of samples, in order to form the identificatory tapestries that we call our selves, in order to replenish and vivify our experiences of wanting, of fascinated nonresolution. Perhaps the avant-garde serves this purpose, to provide experiential templates of harmonic possibilities as they push the boundaries of the relatively more constricted formats of familiar musical forms. In such innovative explorations of the unresolved, such as Steve Reich's *Music for Eighteen Musicians*, the potentiality of suspension is given primacy over the comfort of a harmonic resolution that is implicit but never articulated; the music is propelled by the interlocking patterns and textures of the instruments rather than the traditional out-and-back of sonata-form harmony. The modus operandi of what Robert Fink calls process music is to structure a tolerable, vitalizing continuity of tension-release arcs that sustain appetite for life itself by never sounding the chord it makes us long for but offering instead a multitude of locally usable bits—a turn of phrase, a disturbance in the psyche-soma, a disruption of the familiar—to beckon our curiosity and sustain our appetite for the world. (Psychoanalytic process could thus be considered a form of avant-garde composition, as in the consummate musical framing of John Cage.)

The nonresolving music of the late twentieth century provides a model of nonresolution that captures something of the optimal longing that, when it occurs in more traditional song formats, produces the elusive, musical magic known colloquially as a "hook." Hooks always frustrate our expectations even as they stimulate our musical appetites, relying on the predictability and regularity of a known, expectable song structure to produce a moment of unanticipated surprise and curiosity. Getting a hook stuck in one's head occurs as a bit of other-worldly thought inception, the musicohypnosis of everyday life. Hooks graze the edges of the key in which we think we live, rubbing up against where we live musically, the musilanguage we use to navigate the waves of living among one another. They push the boundaries of the habitable zone of psychesomatic intelligibility, evolution in action, beckoning us toward the outer harmonics of the cosmos.

The reverberations of the postwar period drove music toward even fuller liberation from harmonic resolution, beyond the gravity of harmonic keys altogether, toward the pure textures of sounds themselves, what the Hungarian composer Gyorgi Ligeti termed *sonorism*, a field of musical play grounded in the materiality of *timbre* over the relationality of intervals or the regularity of meter. "Impatient with the clichés of musical pointillism, with what he called the pattern of 'event—pause—event,'" Alex Ross writes in his tome of twentieth-century music criticism *The Rest Is Noise*,

> Ligeti resolved to restore spaciousness and long-breathed lines to instrumental writing.... Ligeti's version of the style is called micropolyphony; large structures are assembled from multiple layers of microcosmic contrapuntal activity.... The opening chord [of his 1961 piece *Atmosphérés*] has fifty-nine notes spread over five and a half octaves: the effect is mysterious rather than assaultive, a seductive threshold to an alien world. Later, half-familiar entities, quasi- or crypto-tonal chords, are glimpsed in the sonic haze. The dominant process in Ligeti's music is one of emergence—shapes come out of the shadows, dark cedes to light.[25]

Ligeti's sonorism opens up the beta level of music, its emergent texturalism, renewing the listener's perception of objects in the world. The tonal trajectories of events and pauses plotted by his musical predecessors are now shattered into micropolyphonic effects, the linear narrative of more traditional music now rendered as a microcosm of emergent sound, a world worlding. The entropic potential of this harmonic undifferentiation does not sound or imply an obvious "home" key or tonal center but simply ebbs and flows with nowhere in particular to go. Likewise in the final moments of the second song on Gabriel's album ("San Jacinto"), the harmony modulates to a vamp that feels like it could go on forever, trailing out as Gabriel sings a mantra of musical memory ("Hold the line"). The song's refusal of harmonic resolution underscores the sustained memory of the genocidal destruction of the Native Americans who inhabited the San Jacinto mountain range. Through an unfolding harmonic process that goes on playing without resolution to a tonal "home," "San Jacinto" emerges as a harmonic-lyrical *continuo* that bends ever toward an unknown horizon.

The evidence of music's power to energize and sustain our humanity continues across the spectrum of music production, even in the dimension of musical performance. Beyoncé, for example, is a performative magician in this regard; we behold her, flanked by hundreds of dancers and musicians in lockstep choreography, harnessing the psychosexual, etho-cal power of music to blow our minds, leaving us in a state of awe-struck after-blow. And she does all this, every time, with just the right amount of "knowingness" that we are watching, that optimal balance of release and tension, proximity and distance, ego and ego ideal. She is possibly the last pop star of this caliber we will see for some time, as our collective attention is atomized into so-called personal taste. The performative magician's illusions and misdirections, so elaborate in the heyday of late-twentieth-century pop stardom, have been exploded by the twenty-first-century fascination with the "reality" genre barrage of uninterrupted self-broadcasting, narcissistic surveillance. But if something has been lost from the period of pop superstars, there may be other gains in open-sourcing our collective musical knowhow. The same streaming media that have splintered our cultural attention have also massively proliferated sounds and images of musical inspiration, fascination, and education, the new magic of how one can produce one's own music, how to extract a beautiful sound from a guitar, or how to stack a harmony on a melodic line, how to play with music, how to be an artist. Music hides its magic in plain sight, presenting itself to be learned to those who are so inspired. And the most inspiring interpretations, in music and psychoanalysis alike, are the ones that inspire others to try their own hand at playing, to play along. Little Hans once asked his father: "Does the professor talk to God?"[26] Freud is still a "real" magician at this point, a guardian of the tricks of the trade, as he remained for other patients and even more so for his followers. But to those he regarded as his students (or "physicians practicing psycho-analysis"), showing us how to do the trick, once the magic has inspired us to learn, secured the future of his newfound praxis, its eligibility to be woven into the habitus of modern living as one of the great discoveries of the twentieth century. He showed us, in other words, how to do it, or, in Winnicott's terms (and in Winnicott's work), how to behave ourselves.

Freud, for his part, ascribes the practical-magical quality of human conduct to an infantile wish to be able to do things like the grownups, like humans do. At one point in his study of Leonardo, contemplating the childhood dream of being able to fly—and Leonardo's fascination with being able to fly, which would have been (and would eventually become) a hell of a magic trick—Freud, true to form, interprets the wish to fly as

> nothing else than a longing to be capable of sexual performance. This is an early infantile wish ... to get big and do what grown-ups do. This wish is the motive of all their games. Whenever children feel in the course of their sexual researches that in the province which is so mysterious but nevertheless so important there is something wonderful of which adults are capable but which *they* are forbidden to know of and do, they are filled with a violent wish to be able to do it, and they dream of it in the form of flying.[27]

As Laplanche later elaborated, what Freud calls the "early infantile wish" is not inborn or innate but provoked ("goaded on") by the need to translate the sexuality that infuses the parent's handling of one's nature (including keeping the child alive) so that the child can eventually start to get the hang of it and pull off a trick of one's own. What Laplanche calls the fundamental anthropological situation is, in other words, a sort of magic school where, if all goes well, you learn how to turn helplessness (*Hilflosigkeit*) into human being—or, if the teachers are subpar, you flunk out and are left hating everyone who finished learning how to do magic, "filled with a violent wish to be able to do it." But perhaps sexuality is only one kind of "something wonderful of which adults are capable," a complicated kind, because it is forbidden from being known; it provokes a most necessary flight in children, so that it must be approached anew. One must be apprenticed in the endless possibilities of the weave in order to transform the enigma of sexuality into the everyday magic of musical being.

The properly human world really is enchanted in both senses, the magical and the musical. The only way to join it is to learn how to play, to learn it *as* play, despite the way music playing is often taught. What if music was taught with the sensibility of a holding environment, a psychoanalytic understanding of potential space, an ethic of psychosexual responsibility? As the British editor and writer Nicholas Spice writes in his remarkable essay "Winnicott and Music" (quoted here at length for its relevance and ingenuity),

> The Winnicottian music lesson would work against and seek to dismantle the structures of compliance which hold the traditional music lesson in place. The first and most subversive step in this direction would be to depose performance as the governing principle of the music lesson and enthrone play in its stead. Music lessons conducted under the principle of play would promise no results. With no promise of return, the ownership of the music lesson by the parental and music cultural constituencies would cease to be worth anything very definite. The music lesson would be handed back to the child.
>
> In this radical and insurgent manoeuvre, the music teacher would necessarily play a vital role. For now, inverting the order of things, the music teacher would be there, not to deliver results to the parent or to the music business, but to protect the child from the demands of both these authorities. As such, the Winnicottian music teacher would recognise with an acute sensitivity the nature of what was at stake for the child. As things currently stand, it often seems as though parents think of music lessons much as they might think of tennis lessons: there's a technique to be learnt and a professional to impart it, and that's that. But music lessons are much closer to sessions of psychotherapy than to a course of tennis coaching.
>
> In most cases, taking music lessons is the only chance the child gets of a regular one-to-one meeting in private with an adult professional, usually for between half an hour and an hour, at least once a week, and sometimes over an extended period of time, even several years. The

purpose of this encounter is not psychotherapy, but it is to teach the child how to make individual use of an expressive medium with a rich if elusive relationship to emotional, psychological and somatic states of being. Music is highly charged stuff. In Winnicottian terminology, music is a world of transitional objects, and the music lesson is a transitional space of a sort, a holding environment in which the child can take time to find music in herself and to find herself in music.[28]

This poignant form of meeting in private with an adult includes at least three functions: (1) a provision of care, "holding" in Winnicott's sense; (2) the seduction conveyed through that care, the enigma of sexuality (which Winnicott did not mention); and (3) the identificatory potential, the homonics, for managing sexual disruption, the groove with which to register and accommodate syncopation, to play the piece like your teacher can. Some of this environmental education involves learning how to get used to something, how to tolerate being novice or new; one prerequisite for movement into seduction, toward the world, is learning how to have a tough skin, how to keep trying. Music, above all, as the philosopher Susanne Langer emphasized, "suspends ordinary time," giving us enough chances, over time, to work something out.[29] And what we have to work out is sexuality, which is not only a matter of the psychosexual drives or only of making meaning but always of physical translation of a prior moment through a new point in time, connecting the two.

The playing of music, sex, a game of sports, a session of psychoanalysis (at its best); each provides a highly ordinary time-frame, allowing the psyche-soma to work these translational muscles, hopefully without pulling them. The pain of overwhelming sensation, the burn of psyche-somatic electrocution, convulses the body into retreat from the shared, spatiotemporal sensorium into an isolated subjectivity that is in fact completely out of time, frozen in an anticipatory "looking forward" to some fantasy of perfect reconnection or dread of disaster. (If anything actually starts to happen, the alarms go off.) A good-enough suspension of ordinary time, by contrast, is precisely a relief from the confines and demands of subjectivity, permitting a novel discovery of the world against a backdrop of being together in shared time that goes on ticking even when we stop paying attention to it. To genuinely look forward to something is always to look forward to the useful suspension of time.

A reactive, defensive, dissociative retreat forfeits an essential wovenness within the fabric of humanity, foreclosing the world in which the enigmatic message can be translated, in which the musical work can vibrate the soul. The world disappears, which in turn changes the sound of music. "When the world belonging to the work is gone," Wallrup writes, "the world worlding in the work is radically changed or even abolished. The attunement is therefore changed, too, and a phenomenon appears that can be called 'distunement.' We have lost our entrance to that world; it has become foreign to us."[30]

Music only works, only *exists*, in a world, at least the way it was meant to work in the world belonging to it. Transplanted from its home world, once it has been lost, the insurgent music, like sexuality, worlds the world anew, bringing new life surging into culture (or in Bion's terms: the contained disrupting and demanding a new container). In this sense, Wallrup continues, "Distunement can be a beginning and how a gradual attunement may follow. Described in other terms, it is a process starting in alienness and leading to acceptance or recognition. This change can be described as a 'foreign world' becoming part of the 'home world.'"[31]

Distunement, in other words, is not disenchantment; being out of tune retains some potential, some longing, to get back to the music. (Perhaps this is why Winnicott was way more concerned about depersonalization and depression than about misbehavior.) Disenchantment loses the world by losing the music; distunement pulls for the even pitch, hooks us into longing for the home key, making the home world home, showing us the way. Disenchantment is like an autoimmune disorder, a reaction to being dropped out of the weave; distunement is more like a vaccination, titrating disease, or unease, in such a way that the body can use it to grow.

The psychoanalytic situation must create the conditions in which this unease can be transmitted, and the creation of these *sostenuto* conditions is what Laplanche called "psychotherapy"; the psychotherapist takes care of the patient—musical care, "of a strictly 'homeopathic' nature," to use Lacoue-Labarthe's phrase—while the psychoanalyst, the same person, both carefully and unwittingly, repeats the trauma.[32] Cure in this sense could only ever occur after the disruptive effect of this blow, in the after-blow, before it happens again; only within what Winnicott called the patient's omnipotence could the trauma ever be transformed. It is only when one's traumatic forms of being have been sufficiently repeated to be brought into a world that a new difference, a singular voice, could ever affirm itself. The music of the analysis is composed of the myriad ways that the analyst, and soon the patient, actively deploy, tweak, amplify, sample physical elements of the weave in the service of induction, conduction, and, eventually, improvisation. Therein lies a musical or playful or psychoanalytic (obviously not a carnal) version of consummation, when things go very well, when things seem less like a surgical procedure and more like a magic trick, more like a music lesson.

8

9

THE ART TEACHER

inspiration
spiral
education

|

The wait was short, but seemed to him an eternity. No one called him, but a man entered the room. A very old man, it seemed to him at first, not very tall, white-haired, with a fine, clear face and penetrating, light-blue eyes. The gaze of those eyes might have been frightening, but they were serenely cheerful as well as penetrating, neither laughing nor smiling, but filled with a calm, quietly radiant cheerfulness. He shook hands with the boy, nodded, and sat down with deliberation on the stool in front of the old practice piano. "You are Joseph Knecht?" he said. "Your teacher seems content with you. I think he is fond of you. Come, let's make a little music together."

Knecht had already taken out his violin. The old man struck the A, and the boy tuned. Then he looked inquiringly, anxiously, at the Music Master.

"What would you like to play?" the Master asked.

The boy could not say a word. He was filled to the brim with awe of the old man. Never had he seen a person like this. Hesitantly, he picked up his exercise book and held it out to the Master.

"No," the Master said, "I want you to play from memory, and not an exercise but something easy that you know by heart. Perhaps a song you like."

Knecht was confused, and so enchanted by this face and those eyes that he could not answer. He was deeply ashamed of his confusion, but unable to speak. The Master did not insist. With one finger, he struck the first notes of a melody, and looked questioningly at the boy. Joseph nodded and at once played the melody with pleasure. It was one of the old songs which were often sung in school.

"Once more," the Master said.

Knecht repeated the melody, and the old man now played a second voice to go with it. Now the old song rang through the small practice room in two parts.

"Once more."

Knecht played, and the Master played the second part, and a third part also. Now the beautiful old song rang through the room in three parts.

"Once more." And the Master played three voices along with the melody.

"A lovely song," the Master said softly. "Play it again, in the alto this time."

The Master gave him the first note, and Knecht played, the Master accompanying with the other three voices. Again and again the Master said, "Once more," and each time he sounded merrier. Knecht played the melody in the tenor, each time accompanied by two or three parts. They played the song many times, and with every repetition the song was involuntarily enriched with embellishments and variations. The bare little room resounded festively in the cheerful light of the forenoon.

After a while the old man stopped. "Is that enough?" he asked. Knecht shook his head and began again. The Master chimed in gaily with his three voices, and the four parts drew their thin, lucid lines, spoke to one another, mutually supported, crossed, and wove around one another in delightful windings and figurations. The boy and the old man ceased to think of anything else; they surrendered themselves to the lovely, congenial lines and figurations they formed as their parts crisscrossed. Caught in the network their music was creating, they swayed gently along with it, obeying an unseen conductor. Finally, when the melody had come to an end once more, the Master turned his head and asked: "Did you like that, Joseph?"[1]

Liking music—and perhaps liking anything—always involves two periods in time. There is the moment when something hits us, and there is the "afterblow" in which we cannot forget what we were not fully there enough, for the moment, to now remember. Before the young student hears the first notes of the Master's melody in Hermann Hesse's deeply musical novel *The Glass Bead Game (Magister Ludi)*, he feels only shame and confusion, an eternity of waiting. We are born out of this eternity, into this expectant readiness that the Heidegger scholar Thomas Sheehan has translated as our "thrown-openness," our anticipatory being-in-the-world.[2] We have no idea *what* we would like to play, let alone how to play it. And once we are induced to learn how to play, enchanted by the music of our art teachers, we treasure these vital conductors and never forget them.

We might envision the trajectory of what Winnicott termed going-on-being, of *human* being, as taking the form of a spiral, beginning with our primary not-yet-ness, the rock-bottom reality of human existence, our originary waiting room, before moving us into synchrony with the habitus of our caregivers, our ambassadors to the human race. Out of this original coordination, as we have traced in these essays, evolve the variations of creative difference and dissonance, which come to constitute their own signature style of being—though this relative wholeness is not a calcified, final product but rather a stabilizing provision that enables one to be periodically remade by the senses, shaken up by fresh experiences, resulting in a kind of refound lostness, an embedded unintegration. The stations along this spiraling figure could be conceptualized as follows:

- The infant organism (1) is induced into shared, primary patterns that underwrite the most foundational, sensory level of being alive in an ongoing, shared way through a syncretizing of perceptual experience (2).

(Whatever else a person is capable of doing, if they are excluded from this shared domain, they are essentially performing a facsimile of being human but cannot feel anything.)

- These formative, synchronizing experiences simultaneously open a channel for seduction (3), the stowaway of the sexual, leading the psyche-soma astray of the reliable orbits and rhythms of the weave, precipitating the need to return, to reach back toward the homonics (4) of the weave (Hendrix: *Just ask the axis*) and to draw upon it for more elaborate identifications and choreography of movement in order to conduct the surplus charge.
- Renewed by this enhanced viability, we are more equipped to interpenetrate, to achieve greater harmonic complexity through (pro)creative translation (5), which we will examine in more detail in this chapter.
- As this interactive movement in and with the world of others synthesizes into its own reliable, *continuo* themes, more unforeseen (or "improvised") variations (6) start to lift off, opening new vertices and angles (*theta function*) against the axial background of accompaniment, which eventually synthesize into their own style (7), a particular quality of embodied

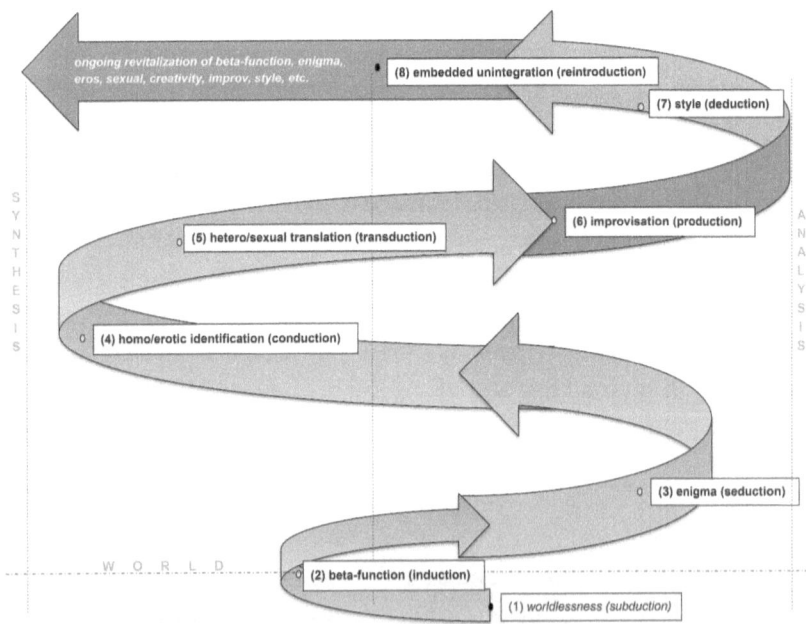

being in the world that can be recurrently revitalized and remade through the inspiration of fresh sensation and experience (8).

The first point (1) on the spiraling scale of humanization is always a position of being not (yet) membered. From this position, the speechless infant is brought into the human world through the shared embodiment of parental care, an original version of what Hannah Arendt called *natality*, the "initiation of new beginnings through human action."[3] In psychoanalysis, this natality is understood in its most foundational form: the child comes into the world looking for something ("an expectation of the breast," as Bion put it),[4] hungry and searching for perhaps nothing so much as the reestablishing of intrauterine music (Sloterdijk's "sonorous *cogito*"), the sounds that nourished the fetus with the first elements of sensation, the first sense of the movements of the human world, the habitus of human being—assuming this corresponding activity on the part of the caregivers, a *living* environment. Perhaps Freud's handshakes at the beginning of each hour—not unlike the natal grab of care giving, pulling the infant out of the *amusia* of helplessness into the weave of culture—presented and expressed anew this living environment, this *ethos* of care, at the outset of each psychoanalytic session. And just like in utero, the only sense not active in Freud's couch-frame is sight. Birth, as Freud commented in his introductory lecture on anxiety, brings with it the first moment of inspiration, of breathing on one's own, which is simultaneously an original trauma (the beginnings of going from oneness to twoness), from which we never recover; it is here (Bion's "caesura") that the work of induction into human patterns begins.[5]

In this sense, a psychoanalyst literally induces labor, facilitating psychic birth or rebirth when necessary, through a provision of rhythmic living and live framing. And the contact at this level, which is the terrain of existential phenomenology, is not, strictly speaking, sexual—that is, not a joining together of two distinctly separate bodies for purposes of reproduction or relief; it is, rather, *erotic*, binding energy through an experience of synchrony or sameness. Rhythmic induction (2) is one half of the one-two movement of *après-coup*, the humanizing power source that charges the psyche-soma and, in turn, generates the sexual. While the premature, not-yet-human infant already has the potentiating hardware to become musicalized—the physical network, like the clanging repetition of a train running along its tracks—our genetic inheritance cannot musicalize this pattern into the groove of rhythmized consciousness without help; only the meaningfulness of shared habitus can rhythmize the mechanics of nature into the music of human nature. As the scholar Robert Harrison has remarked, "Life is the self-ecstasy of matter," the way matter transcends itself; in this sense, the life-transfusion of beta function draws the infant matter out into a second nature through the erotics of human being.

In the erotics of shared embodiment invariably occurs the trauma of seduction (3). To find the beat is always to find oneself losing it again, going astray. Being induced into rhythms of human living does not entail a simple bulk download of the plentitudes of adult harmonies and histories. The world of human rhythms and patterns, just as it is ordered and regularized, is also marked (paraphrasing Laplanche) by untranslatable dissonances, unmanageable arrhythmias. The barely speaking postinfant is now in a more urgent phase of anticipation, a wantingness to make ever-more sense of this enigmatic, vitalizing, and overwhelming contact. The rhythms alone, the beating pulses of humanity, are not sufficiently dimensional upon arrival to contain the multitudes of vibrational varieties that emanate from them. They provide skeletal drumbeats for organizing time and space, but they do not show us how to conduct ourselves through them. For this we require the "homeopathy" of mimetic *identification* (4) to soothe our surplus exuberance, to show us how to move through the world of fellow humans in ways that sustain one's own instrument (*Stimme*) while playing in concert (*Stimmung*) with others.

The animating erotics of being (like) one another through mimetic identification make it not only tolerable but pleasurable for the child to become energized by the otherwise disturbing seduction by the adult—the seduction that becomes sexuality itself, an enduring, embodied fascination with an acquired, idiosyncratic mystery at the heart of one's own being. Identification with a good-enough parent is thus always an apprenticeship in how to be *interested*, identifying with how the parent patiently tracks the stories or dream reports or fantasies that the child, in health, is always wanting to tell them. This immersive, interested, parental engagement supports and cultivates the child's capacity to develop and make use of what Winnicott called transitional objects; the prior experience of psychosensory symbiosis becomes, at this level, something that begins to channel one's own creative potential, a way of borrowing objects (like "pieces" of music) from the collective domain in order to help mediate the tension between the demands of the world for communication and the need to remain incommunicado, to use communal objects for subjective purposes (the need to not be fucked with). Without this "perceptual apprenticeship" (to borrow Leo Bersani's phrase), there would be no way to find those cultural objects that make us feel alive in the world; one could only resort to either the psychotic isolation of a purely subjective world or the zombie normopathy of a purely public self.[6] Trained in this perceptual, attentional orientation, by contrast, we can find ways to actually live together.

There is barely any leap to the clinical version of this process. Freud's original clinical activity, the interpretation of dreams—*Die Traumdeutung* (which could also be translated as "pointing things out about dreams," like pointing out features of a landscape while looking out the window of a train carriage together)—could at its best have this kind of supportive, accompanying, humanizing, inweaving function, an apprenticeship in how to relate to cultural objects, how to play with ideas, how to dream; the way a piece of music operates, "pointing" locally from one moment to the next, subtly building textures or resolving tensions, in order to cohere the sensory experience without use of symbolic referentiality; the indicative dimension of *Deutung* with minimal or zero recourse to the interpretive, conducting people into dreaming. (*Deut* is etymologically connected to "two" or "second"—a second look, another person; the German word for German is *Deutsch*—from the Proto-Germanic *þeudō* meaning people or tribe.) Conversely, the parent who does not provide the child with this model literally makes no sense, no way to *make* sense of sensory stimulation, to experience oneself as a subject as opposed to an object. (The parent is always, for better or much worse, the child's first art teacher.) And the patient interest of the good-enough parent is necessarily informed by the *ethos* of the weave, the ethical posture that allows oneself to be informed in turn by the child's early experiments in narrative, music, and mood.

Collectively there are cultures that sanction, model, and value this listening ethic, and there are those that don't. (Ours, for instance.) As Alfred Gell explores in *The Art of Anthropology*, his ethnography of the forest-dwelling Umeda tribe, cultures that form within landscapes of limited visibility (the Umeda lived entirely under dense forest) develop greater aural capacity for perceiving the musicality of language, a virtual proof of what the French philosopher and a pioneer of phenomenology, Maurice Merleau-Ponty, posited in his seminal 1962 text *Phenomenology of Perception*, a copy of which Gell literally (and perhaps redundantly) brought with him into the field in 1969: "The spoken word is a gesture, its meaning, a world ... words, vowels and phonemes are so many ways of 'singing' the world, not ... by reason of an objective resemblance, but because they extract, and literally express, their emotional essence."[7]

Through the invention of the couch aspect of the frame, Freud inadvertently created a therapeutic technology that shifted the use of language toward its emotional essence, toward what can be heard in speech that is mute in the written word, thus privileging the phonological music of speech over its explicit communication value. (As in the fundamental rule, which might be reinterpreted: Don't worry about making sense—just sing. The psychoanalytic method is a voice lesson.) And through the rhythmicity of the frame's spatiotemporal aspect, Freud instilled his therapeutic practice with a structure of periodic recess from everyday life, what Sloterdijk has termed "co-immunity," the human need to take leave of the world regularly and move into a protected space in order to reflect upon that same world and, paradoxically, to enter more fully into it.[8]

It is these recessional spaces and times appropriated for quiet, patient listening that potentiate creative, musical states that make life worth living. Only at this point on our trajectory could we sufficiently transition to boredom (in Adam Phillips's interpretation of that term) with our identifications, opening us up to fresh sources of inspiration. Being bored, Phillips suggests, is hardly "boring" in the colloquial sense; it is the state in which our desire can truly "crystallize," where we are nourished enough by the past to get hungry for the future, for new music, eager to make it with other people. This generative repetition has very little to do with knowing or learning in the typical senses of those words and much more to do with what one finds oneself doing, the way one's body dreams, the messages that one finds occurring and recurring to oneself in the recess and boredom of what Sloterdijk has termed a "practising life," becoming what he calls our "convictions." On an episode of Robert Harrison's endlessly generative podcast *Entitled Opinions*, Sloterdijk explained that "a contemporary author [can] be a messenger without really knowing by himself what his message could be." He continued: "[The messages are] the effect of, the labor of, experimenting with truth, and finally they condensate into an established corpus of convictions. And *convictions are things you can repeat without being bored by what you say by yourself.* The apostle discovers at the same time that kind of speech that is not afraid of repetition."[9]

Following this formulation, if the labor induced by analysis could be considered "the labor of experimenting with truth," an analysand could be considered the apostle of one's own unconscious. The rhythm of the frame transforms a deathly boredom of pure repetition into the lively realm of musical play, the generative bearings of collective conviction (habitus); the postal route through which messages can be addressed and delivered can become authored (as opposed to authoritarian) into a corpus of repeated figures, of riffs, of convictions. (As Phillips writes: "Who we are is what we can't be talked out of."[10] We are precisely the selves that we can't help repeating.) Through greater fluency in those forms of living that foster and enliven creative union with others emerges a found-created form of practical wisdom, a kind of *improvisation*-in-the-world, speaking without being able to "see" what one is about to say, free associating, live sampling. In the durable singing-out of these newly disclosed convictions lies the potential for counterpoint with other players, a new form of accompaniment that layers rich harmony and counterpoint upon the shared vibrations of a common world.

II

Gratefully, his face glowing, Knecht looked at him. He was radiant, but still speechless.

"Do you happen to know what a fugue is?" the Master now asked.

Knecht looked dubious. He had already heard fugues, but had not yet studied them in class.

"Very well," the Master said, "then I'll show you. You'll grasp it quicker if we make a fugue ourselves. Now then, the first thing we need for a fugue is a theme, and we don't have to look far for the theme. We'll take it from our song."

He played a brief phrase, a fragment of the song's melody. It sounded strange, cut out in that way, without head or tail. He played the theme once more, and this time he went on to the first entrance; the second entrance changed the interval of a fifth to a fourth; the third repeated the first an octave higher, as did the fourth with the second. The exposition concluded with a cadence in the key of the dominant. The second working-out modulated more freely to other keys; the third, tending toward the subdominant, ended with a cadence on the tonic.

The boy looked at the player's clever white fingers, saw the course of development faintly mirrored in his concentrated expression, while his eyes remained quiet under half-closed lids. Joseph's heart swelled with veneration, with love for the Master. His ear drank in the fugue; it seemed to him that he was hearing music for the first time in his life.[11]

Inspiration turns living matter into human being. Language, Harrison tells us, retains the "ecstasies" of temporality—past, present, and future, as Heidegger formulated them—by connecting, through layers of meaning, the words of our ancestors with the creative possibilities of our progeny. The word *inspire* retains one such ecstatic ambiguity that seems to link two things: (1) the Latin *inspirare* (to "breathe" or "blow into")—which can mean to fill someone with the urge or ability to do or feel something, especially something creative, which is the fundamental effect of an *ethos*; and (2) a *spira*, or coil, which may have its roots in the Greek *sparton*, meaning "rope." Unlike a simple, one-dimensional line, the image of a three-dimensional rope conveys not only a sense of wovenness that is crucial to its integrity and flexibility but also a spiraling oscillation between two tensions: coming together and coming apart. And the things one finds oneself saying during this weave-work, the songs and samples one finds oneself singing along the way, become the score of one's life. Sloterdijk suggests that if, as Nietzsche believed, "man is a rope between the animal and the superman"—if one's life is a through line between the expression of natural instinct and the creativity of culture—then the point of a life is to remain, as the French novelist Jean Genet put it, "a messenger of the rope," a singer or player of the emotional truth that is disclosed as each tensile life-rope braids and harnesses these poles at the limits of human nature.

The rope metaphor provides a sense of the wovenness and robustness of this spiral-life as well as its potential precariousness, its sudden tight-ropeness around a sharp curve. In Bion's seminal formulation of container/contained, the temporary intelligibility of our sensory experiences is always heading toward explosion, toward catastrophic change, through which our thinking capacities are remade by our beta elements. (In Bion's words, "thinking has to be called into existence to cope with thoughts."[12]) As the South African psychoanalyst Duncan Cartwright indicates in his book-length study of Bion, *Containing States of Mind*, a reductive and idealized notion of a container found commonly in some contemporary clinical discussions (in which the analyst simply endures the onslaught of beta elements in perpetuity in an interminable effort to "contain" them) fixes and freezes what is otherwise a unending process of increasing complexity, the work that is always going on (*Unterwegssein*, as Heidegger put it, "undergoingbeing," what Bion once called a "loosely-knit reticulum," every container always in search of another container) as we are perpetually thrown into the next space-time unit of world formation.[13]

The continuity of our going-on-spiraling relies therefore on an ongoing container/contained discourse. What Sheehan calls our "thrown-openness," he suggests, has a "bivalent kinetic structure" in which we "run back and forth"—a literal translation of the Latin root of "discourse," an endless rhythm—between "what-one-already-is" and "rendering oneself and things meaningfully present." Sheehan defines discourse (*logos*) itself, as Bion might have, as the back-and-forth movement between first, second, third . . . *n* looks. Once we are inducted into the meaningful world, that world is henceforth *there*, and we are *of* it (being-in-the-world), and we *dis-cover* it, others and ourselves, through the back-and-forth movement of discourse. But what Heidegger and his contemporaries might not have acknowledged is that this back-and-forth originates not only in time but in *space*, the space formed by the shared looks of the parent and child. What is missing from Heidegger's analysis is the active involvement of *another person* in the initiation and facilitation of the humanization process, in *helping* disclose what one always already is and in rendering things meaningfully present.

Freud's model also frequently neglected this other person—though he did, like Heidegger, offer a perception-based model of reaching out to sample things from the world of other people. Freud lucidly identified the perceptual rhythmicity of our being-in-the-world in his theory of "cathectic innervations [that] are sent out and withdrawn in rapid periodic impulses from within," as he wrote in "A Note Upon the 'Mystic Writing-Pad.'" "It is as though the unconscious stretches out feelers, through the medium of the system *Pcpt.-Cs.*, towards the external world and hastily withdraws them as soon as they have sampled the excitations coming from it."[14] Through these rapid, repeated impulses, the "feelers" of perception ("pseudopodia," as he calls them elsewhere) periodically sample the world, foraging for ingredients and creating a rhythm of perception, a rhythmized perception. (Laplanche will add, notably, that these impulses originate in the world, not in the individual, adding a valence to Freud's model while preserving the rhythmic quality of exploring and receding from the world as a model of both perception and psychical life more broadly.)

This rhythmic structure is the perceptual grid that underwrites the meaningfulness of *logos* in Sheehan's bivalent kinetic thrown-openness, a rhythm that the Italian psychoanalyst Giuseppe Civitarese also discovers elsewhere in Freud. In his paper "Masochism and Its Rhythm," Civitarese evocatively contemplates an "invaluable link back to aesthetic experience" from which Freud could have formulated rhythm as an alternative to the death drive: "May we not postulate pleasure of a different kind in the pure repetition of a rhythm? A pleasure linked to the genesis and stabilizing of the ego rather than to the satisfaction of the impulses of the id? A pleasure that is the fruit of the urge-to-be and that derives from confirmation of the feeling that one exists?"[15]

For Civitarese, the train-track repetition of perceptual feelers becomes rhythmized into what we could call a musical continuity, a pleasurable stability (what Winnicott called an "ego-orgasm," the pleasure of being alive in the world as oneself), that supports existential meaningfulness. (In this sense, Civitarese perceives a fundamental shift in Freud's model of pleasure after the First World War, from the unbinding of the sexual to the *eros* of syncretics.) And on top of these two levels of thrown-openness—the perceptual and the rhythmic—Civitarese finds the dimension of love, citing Roland Barthes's *A Lover's Discourse*, locating the pleasures of romantic feeling in the reverberations of rhythm itself, rhythmizing the coming and going of beloved others, their presence and absence, as a way of keeping them alive in one's mind (Barthes himself samples "Beyond the Pleasure Principle" and annotated the following excerpt with a single word: "Winnicott"):

> Absence persists—I must endure it. Hence I will manipulate it: transform the distortion of time into oscillation, produce rhythm, make an entrance onto the stage of language (language is born of absence: the child has made himself a doll out of a spool, throws it away and picks it up again, miming the mother's departure and return: a paradigm is created).... [A] very short interval, we are told, separates the time during which the child still believes his mother to be absent and the time during which he believes her to be already dead. To manipulate absence is to extend this interval, to delay as long as possible the moment when the other might topple sharply from absence into death.[16]

The rhythmic back-and-forth between ourselves and other people, like radar or echolocation, uses sound waves to identify and position oneself in relation to other bodies, claiming more life, richer harmonies, with every oscillation between unison (oneness) and separation (twoness). (Meltzer once described countertransference as the "harmonic response" of the analyst.)[17] And this kinetic back-and-forth—or "buzz," as Sheehan calls it—is precisely the *Stimmung* between two beings, resonating like tuning forks, which constitutes the physical dimension of the weave. If self and other are thus always the source and terminus of a bivalent movement—and are always psychically, paradoxically, swapping positions—then the space between them form the intervals or thresholds of, as Byung-Chul Han puts it, "the topology of *passion*."[18] So the metaphysical spiral of going-on-being, which is always being transformed by forces of binding and unbinding, organization and entropy, retraces the rhythmic course from one pole of experience to the other, just as it vibrates the resonance between physical bodies in space, oscillating between union and separation, syncretics and analysis, identification (4) and interpenetration (5).

The integrity of this continuous line relies upon the improvisational function (6) to keep playing even in moments when resolution is not foreseeable, when the home tones are temporarily (if no less harrowingly) lost. Like Freud's fundamental rule, musical momentum carries an implicit *ethos* to keep going, to say or play what comes to mind, the psyche-soma acting as a conduit for a musical experience unfolding in real time. The onward propulsion of a steady tempo motivates the player, as Freud did his patients, to sustain what the virtuoso pianist Jeremy Denk has described (speaking of Ligeti) as "the infinitely carried-out consequence of the idea," wherever it may lead.[19] This ethic to keep the music going, to keep playing, is essential to what it means for a musician to "interpret" a piece, to infuse the work with the vitality of the not-already-known. This improvisatory quality is likewise essential to Cartwright's understanding of Bionian containment; it is in these uncertain intervals that the knowhow of the weave, or having the weave-music in one's bones, is once again essential to sustain play in the face of hesitations or haltedness, neurotic freezes. (What Freud would have interpreted categorically as "resistances" may in some instances have been, and nowadays may be, closer to simply not knowing how to play; as the scholar Arnold Davidson has suggested, Freud himself frequently "resisted" his own discoveries, absent a collective mentality that might have enabled him to maintain them more consistently.)[20] But ungrounded or unrhythmized by the tempo and *Stimmung* of the ensemble, any aspiring player's effort to persist associatively through the uncertainty of novel experiences or tenuous moments becomes an insurmountable effort to reinvent the wheel—to reinvent the *weave*—producing in most cases little more than self-conscious or defensive fragments that contribute little if anything to the project of psychical transformation.

Not all improvisation, in other words, is psychically usable. (As the choreographer Merce Cunningham is said to have repeated: "The trouble with improvisation is, you repeat yourself.")[21] It may be most accurate to say that improvising, *not-fore-seeing*, can only channel a "true" expression of the self (or an expression of the "true self," in Winnicott's sense) if it is first grounded in the *pro*-vised, the fore-seen—grounded in the *ethos* that is conducted through good-enough musicality. Securely embedded in the weave of humanity, the "true self" may eventually say or sing or do something that is neither a repetitive iteration nor a shriek of unmusical noise but rather something new, something different, something unforeseen, something improvised. And eventually these improvisatory gestures may begin to loop and coalesce into their own repeatability, their own "chops," the sleeve for the next container. We might call this phenomenon something like "style" (7), a developed way of doing things, a particular competence for moving continuously between the rhythms of discourse and breakaway of variation. To achieve a style is to become an artist in a way that retains a binding connection to the world of fellow humans. Harrison refers to this capacity as *suavitas*, or suavity, "a mode of comportment and quality of the voice that rendered one pleasing and attractive to others."[22] Harrison's definition attends to the ways that the *suavitas* of style is always already in negotiation with other people—what we might call, after Freud, a form of sexuality. "Sexuality" here is not to be confused with the disruptive "sexual" of primary seduction; sexuality, by contrast, is a consolidation, a synthesis, an identity, a way of being, a *suavitas* for incorporating unruly blue notes within the weave of key signature and in concert with fellow players.

Sexuality as a style of human being may be seen as the set of experimental improvisations that one develops through (a) good-enough induction and seduction and (b) through good-enough homo-erotic identification and hetero-sexual interactivity, developing into a personal pattern that constitutes a style (sexuality) that stabilizes throughout adult life (one knows what one likes, has a "type," etc.). (The relevant musical concept here would be *timbre*, what each instrument uniquely sounds like.) And from this composition, one can then *de*-duce (à la Bion's "scientific deductive system"),[23] from the general principle of one's sexuality or sexual identity, which varieties of sexual experience will be enlivening and satisfying, largely by pruning and foreclosing which expressions of sexuality will not be viable. This model does not suggest a fluid notion of sexuality (which, like timbre, is stable; a tuba will always sound like a tuba) but rather that subsequent returns to states of unintegration function not to reorganize sexuality altogether but to replenish the sensory undercurrent that animates the higher-order sexual system (and without which the system becomes increasingly narrowed, fetishistic, and deadened). Sexuality is fundamentally a sexual *style*, a unique iteration of a collective expertise in how to handle the world desirously. To develop a sexual style is to become an artist.

Through this expertise, an artist masters the translation of weave material both into personal idiom and then back into the weave, conducting the train of going-on-being in its journey from life to death. In the discourse of music theory, the songline traced by a melody as it crosses the interval from one note to another is known as a *Zug* (or "linear progression"), adding pitches at each station as it charts its melodic course, filling out a harmonic world. The German word *Zug*, (which also means "train") is a key term for Heidegger, as in his description of an expression of "longing for home" (*Zug zur Heimat*), which he also called "boredom." Like Phillips's definition of boredom (that psychical zone in which "desire crystallizes"), Heidegger's "boredom" suggests a withdrawal from the weave, which reopens the channels of longing and desire, a state of *unintegration* (as in Winnicott's "doldrums") that potentiates the conditions for fresh sensation, for new life.[24] In contrast to the statelessness of *dis*-integration (which is a defense organization meant to cope with the anxiety of annihilation), the unintegrated "boredom" of longing for home is a maximal form of freedom. It may be no coincidence that in his early years Freud aspired to become a translator and took John Stuart Mill's 1859 treatise "On Liberty," the cornerstone of liberal democracy, as one of his first projects. (Mills's view of life in a liberal democracy as a series of "experiments in living" became, in turn, a cornerstone of Adam Phillips's thinking.) We could understand this form of freedom as a negotiation between the liberation of recess and the deliberation of sustained interest in the world. Here is one view of the *ethos* of clinical psychoanalysis: how to naturalize and humanize patients into citizens of unintegrated longing (8), the music that never ends. We can view psychoanalysis as a model of how to live in the spiraling habitus of being alive, of going-on-being through catastrophic change, of resuming and sustaining mourning following traumatic disruption, a way to keep playing the transient music of everyday life.

The field of psychoanalysis may currently be in such a state of unintegration, challenged to listen to its own riddles for news of its fate. Which is to say (paraphrasing the psychoanalyst Richard Almond) that the field may be in what the American philosopher Thomas Kuhn might have called a state of crisis, a point at which the extant paradigms have hit their point of exhaustion, have started to fray, their containers exploding.[25] At these junctures, lines of philosophical inquiry (including psychoanalysis) have to expand, dismantle, and remix their models to accommodate both the greater scope of new data and the phenomena accounted for by previous constructs. If it is to rise to the occasion, psychoanalysis must use its greatest asset, its deep humanity, to refind its voice, its music, to keep its long-standing habitus, its groove, going. As Sloterdijk writes: "Rediscovered music is music that links up with the continuum after its catastrophe."[26] It is, after all, the railway carriage of *ein Zug* that Freud used as the central symbol for his fundamental rule, for the psychoanalytic work of becoming rhythmized, of free associating. The destination of this journey is not only death but also the beginning refound, a new world having emerged along the way, an uncanny refinding of the home key in the outer harmonics, that spiraling line that returns us back to where we started, but never the same.

|||

The old man slowly raised himself from the piano stool, fixed those cheerful blue eyes piercingly and at the same time with unimaginable friendliness upon him, and said: "Making music together is the best way for two people to become friends. There is none easier. That is a fine thing. I hope you and I shall remain friends. Perhaps you too will learn how to make fugues, Joseph."

He shook hands with Joseph and took his leave. But in the doorway he turned once more and gave Joseph a parting greeting, with a look and a ceremonious little inclination of his head.

Many years later Knecht told his pupil that when he stepped out of the building, he found the town and the world far more transformed and enchanted than if there had been flags, garlands, and streamers, or a display of fireworks. He had experienced his vocation, which may surely be spoken of as a sacrament. The ideal world, which hitherto his young soul had known only by hearsay and in wild dreams, had suddenly taken on visible lineaments for him. Its gates had opened invitingly. This world, he now saw, did not exist only in some vague, remote past or future; it was here and was active; it glowed, sent messengers, apostles, ambassadors . . . [27]

Induction into the weave of shared practice and experience (Hesse's "unimaginable friendliness") provides entry into an entire domain where dimensions of experience that were unavailable beforehand become possible, a clinical apprenticeship in experience itself—for learning not only from experience, as Bion formulated, but learning *to* experience. In his book *Gardens: An Essay on the Human Condition*, in a chapter titled "Academos," Robert Harrison describes the Greek model of learning as a kind of discourse, an amorous inspiration, as a kind of love—something close to the effect of *Stimmung*. This learning, as humanizing action, is surely what lies at the heart of every great lesson. (And, as any conductor will attest, of every great performance of music.) This kind of learning is rarely dogmatic or declarative in tone and at times exceeds language altogether. In Plato's words (which Harrison calls "among the most beautiful words in the history of philosophy"):[28]

> No treatise by me concerning [knowledge of the matters with which I concern myself] exists or ever will exist. It is not something that can be put into words like other branches of knowledge; only after long partnership [*sunousia*] and in a common life devoted to this very thing does the truth ash upon the soul, like a flame kindled by a leaping spark, and once it is born there it nourishes itself hereafter.[29]

Certain lessons sear themselves into our memory, burning with the luminous power of inspired interest in the history and nature of the shared world. To return to psychoanalysis: What lessons, from which subjects, can inspire a revitalized psychoanalytic theory? What other pitches and timbres, what other stops has our *Zug* picked up along the way from beginning to end, to refinding the beginning?

Some of the lessons or instructive anecdotes we remember best may be those that allegorize the very process of learning, lessons that reflect in their content the dynamic by which they are transmitted. The history of chemistry, for example, includes the story of "phlogiston," which was historically believed to be the source of fire embedded within the environment, eventually replaced by the realization that the air around the burning material is what actually burns, not something inside it. Applying a similar principle to psychoanalysis, we might update our models to reflect the ways that the air we breathe—namely, culture—is the oxygen of human being, rather than some essential substance within a supposedly monadic subject. The weave of culture, from this perspective, is not the object of perception; it is the very modality of perception.

Borrowing an insight from the field of contemporary neurochemistry, there is a growing consensus that what we call "perception" is basically just our hallucinating all the time. We live in a hallucination checked by reality, and some hallucinations are better than others. We require a shared communal dream in order to conduct the dream-work of subjectivity, what we might call—paraphrasing Winnicott and the revolutionary psychiatrist Frantz Fanon—a good-enough hallucination. The politics of how we participate in the communal dream therefore become paramount. The weave giveth and the weave taketh away. Enriching experiences of sameness and difference compete in the modern world with forces of greed and solipsism, which retract our energies back toward exclusive self-interest. Inevitably psychoanalysis has done its share to contribute to both sides of this battle, building conditions of privacy, relatedness, and community at one turn while asserting certainty and imposing models of interior life at another.

There is much that psychoanalysis stands to gain from the neighboring discipline of philosophy, especially thinkers of the century that is contemporaneous with psychoanalysis. "Do a psychoanalysis of Nature," Merleau-Ponty wrote. "It is the flesh, the mother."[30] Merleau-Ponty's inspired idea surely directs us toward the same horizon that Freud contemplated as the "dark continent" of the maternal or the female, or when he sampled the phrase "oceanic feeling" from his friend, Romain Rolland, referring to that dimension of experience ("that primordial being which is not yet the subject-being nor the object-being and which in every respect baffles reflection," as Merleau-Ponty puts it)[31] that is precisely captured in the very laws of the unconscious that Freud discovered, the law of undifferentiation, however unable he claimed he was to find this feeling in himself. (Perhaps this was precisely the problem; having traded metaphysics for metapsychology, Freud was looking *in himself* for a feeling that can only be found *out there* in the world.) But Merleau-Ponty's enigmatic and resonant injunction to "do a psychoanalysis of nature" potentiates not only a more fully humanized communion with the natural world but also an expanded aim for psychoanalysis, a reorientation from the inner world, the phlogiston, of the patient toward the oxygen of the world. These ideas resonate with an important lesson from the German philosopher Hans-Georg Gadamer, whose work is considered crucial to aesthetics and art history. For Gadamer, the experience of art remains an experience of being. Subjectivity is secondary, not the master, in this configuration. We are taken up by a game; our "capacity for capture," Jean Grodin writes in *The Philosophy of Gadamer*, "is not truly our own, but that of the world."[32] Truth in art is thrown at us, without our initiative; truth is the song one can't get out of one's head.

The musicality of truth extends far beyond recent philosophical contributions and back toward the birth of philosophy. In a book he titled (sampling Rilke) *You Must Change Your Life*, Sloterdijk suggests that "the most far-reaching innovation of the ancient world [was] the turn toward the art of education, *paideía*, which initially means something like 'the art of the child.'"[33] Sloterdijk believes this form of education is not only good for the child but constitutive of children in the first place. "Children could, in fact, only come into view methodically as children after the emergence of habits: as those not yet possessed by habits, they attract the attention of the meanwhile lively instructors." And nothing attracts this attention like the liveliness of musicality, beckoning the young psychesoma to play along. As Mary Schoen-Nazarro writes in "Plato and Aristotle and the Ends of Music":

> For Plato man's first education is aimed at forming the whole person, with gymnastics directed primarily towards a child's body, and music directed principally toward his soul. Working together, they help establish and maintain the proper order in man's nature. Not only does education begin by forming the fundamental parts of man, the body and the soul, but it also begins with movements which are natural to man. Plato explicitly indicates this with respect to choric training, which is identical with a child's education through gymnastics and music:
>
> *All young creatures are naturally full of fire, and can keep neither their limbs nor their voices quiet. They are perpetually breaking into disorderly cries and jumps, but whereas no other animal develops a sense of order of either kind, mankind forms a solitary exception. Order in movement is called rhythm, order in articulation—the blending of acute with grave— pitch, and the name for the combination of the two is choric art.*[34]

Freud's "Project" of 1895 was basically about being "full of fire," though he may have at times neglected the choric dimension of the art he invented to deal with it. That "Project," in fact, may be the best place, the very beginning, from which to reclaim certain foundations from the history of psychoanalysis, its original lessons. If Laplanche corrected what he called Freud's "going astray" (or *dis-aster*, a star gone off course) with what he called new foundations, can we begin to rediscover the *old* foundations, the *humus*, in which Freud's genius was grounded?

Freud often focused on taboos and discontents—the discontents stemming from our taboos—at the expense of developing a metapsychology of totems, of *Bildung*, of teaching, of identification, of the weave at the heart of civilization. In the decades preceding the First World War, the fundamental provisions of the social fabric from which Freud emerged may have been less obvious, less in need of language to describe them; as these provisions both figuratively and literally disintegrated and burst into flames, the need for ways to conduct oneself, for teachers with whom to identify, surely became a more pressing concern. The horrors of social trauma (as is true also in excessive personal trauma) become thinkable only in the aftermath of their violence and only through identification with those who have found embodied ways of conducting its otherwise overwhelming voltage, for relieving the demand upon the mind for work. The method of psychoanalysis, in other words, as a form of *conduct*, both facilitates and liberates from the impulsion to think (and in the process, redefines "thinking," what Winnicott later refers to as the intellectual false self, which substitutes a form of perception with a different kind of mental activity). As Phillips writes in one of his many inspiring collections:

> Psychoanalysis is, in fact, the treatment that weans people from their compulsion to understand and be understood; it is an after-education in not getting it. Through understanding to the limits of understanding—this is Freud's new version of an old project. Freud's work is best read as a long elegy for the intelligibility of our lives. We make sense of our lives in order to be free, not to have to make sense.[35]

Freud himself anticipated this idea of a "conductive" principle in that first (unfinished) psychoanalytic "Project," where he first suggested "contact-barriers." We could think about contact-barriers this way, as passing through a protoplasmic level of undifferentiation (as in the repetitive beta function), developing a capacity for differentiation (as in the angular liftoff of theta function), and providing, precisely, an "improved conductive capacity for subsequent conduction." This conduction is supported by the dual capacity of "contact" and "barrier" (destruction and survival, as Winnicott might say), becoming permeable enough to accommodate increased stimulation and, once dis-charged, resuming its limiting function. The contact-barrier's job is to keep that interplay in motion as something like what Winnicott called a "going concern," such that the psyche (ψ) (like the parent or analyst) never has to become a nonporous barrier (what Bion called a "beta screen," a no-contact barrier) and can thus be replenished by new sensory experience (Q) in an ongoing way, sustaining contact with the animating waves of experience through the security of a barrier, like a surfboard.[36] It is the augmentation in conductive capacity provided by the contact-barrier that accommodates the excesses of experience that make us human. And if the psyche is having trouble, the contact-barrier is the natural site for intervention, for recess and rehabilitation, an opportunity for a caregiving analyst to act as a good-enough conductor. And this ultimately provides a function with which the patient can *identify* (it can become one's own), endowing the patient's psyche with "an improved conductive capacity for subsequent conduction" (which produces the effect of being free).

The "Project" of 1895 represents a remarkable (though abandoned) attempt on Freud's part to ground a theory of mind in the electrical energy of embodied experience, a project that can be elaborated through the lens of Laplanche. We are becoming increasingly accustomed to considering the body along multiple dimensions:

- There is what we might call the *real* body with which we are born, the *infans* body, a collection of biological processes, which depends on care giving for survival.
- The activities of care giving, in turn, produce the *sexual* body, which is socially interpellated by others (through unconscious messages), becoming the site of humanizing disruptions. The sexual in this formulation is the counterpart of the recognition of the *social*—one's

sexuality being an idiomatic response to being called upon not just by the unconscious desire of the other/seducer but by the social demand to organize one's unruly real body along the lines of social identity. The sexual body is thus always already transformed through the discourse between the poles of other and of "the Other," what Laplanche calls the "mytho-symbolic," which provides the normative identities (like gender) and "narrative schemas" (like fairy tales or space operas) that children use to begin translating the enigma of sexuality. The whole of the sexual psyche-soma would thus encompass, on the one hand, the pole of unknowable enigmas (which constitute the deepest, most urgent "question" for their children) and, on the other, the pole of social identity and discursive translation (which the child, as an adult, will use to come up with "answers" to the eternal questions of his sexuality).

- We might now consider a third dimension of embodied experience, the *woven* body, which borrows from the commons of somatosensory music (as in Bourdieu's habitus and *hexis*) to induce the body into ways of partaking in shared sensation, to conduct itself through the disruptions and convulsions of the sexual drive, and to sustain the continuity of going-on-being throughout the course of a human life. This body necessarily exists in the communal psycho-sensory arena and has an *actuality* that is neither reducible to the biological body (which is observable and measurable as a property of the individual) nor defined by social discourses. This is not to say that the *woven* body is necessarily lacking and thereby stunted and in need of transformation into thought; it is rather a somatic-sensory domain of actual living that is always itself and nothing else: the somatic, sensory, weave-ready dimension of being embodied.

To the extent that membership has been impaired, barring sensory-somatic participation in the weave, the body becomes isolated in its biological housing, and access to the shared *ethos* is lost. This leaves the self prey to biological events and social determination for its identity; the inability to be rewoven dooms one to the uncanny, suspended animation of the alter world, where life cannot take place. Experience there is limited to the quality of the *actual* in the sense of concrete, atemporal, and immediate (*Aktuell*). Using Scarfone's model, the alter world is a kind of deadly repetition of the actual, characterized by the dominance of *action* over elaboration or dreaming, but so too does this level retain the potential for "affecting, as it were, our being." He continues: "When a well-differentiated psychic structure is already in place, such *presentation* of the inarticulate phrase of affect has two possible results: either what is presented is rejected, denied, repressed, or, to the contrary, its impact is acknowledged, somehow shaking the psychic structure and provoking anxiety."[37]

Here he sounds like Bion: the actual is capable of shaking up the container-contained status quo, though it might have to be denied or dissociated for precisely this reason. Scarfone ultimately feels that the actual is a kind of inarticulate "now" that needs transformation into the "present tense" and that the actual is something that "needs to be worked through toward *representations*," but he emphasizes that while words are often found to name affect, "at other times it is affect that reaches some already-present but as yet 'unaffected' representation." In other words, "actual" affects bring life to the mind. In this sense, the clinical question is always: What is the state of the *actual* body? Is there a tripartite structure in place, such that presentational affect can vivify the music of being-in-the-world?

$$\text{real} + \text{sexual} + \text{woven} = \textit{musical}$$

Or is the actual body completely tyrannized by the (real) instincts and the (sexual) drives, with no way to conduct the voltage, leading to dissociative strategies?

$$\text{real} + \text{sexual} - \text{woven} = \textit{amusia}$$

We can therefore use the term "actual" to describe an aspect of being-in-the-world that escapes representation but affects (and inspires) us; we can also use it as a way to understand pathological disintegration products when there is not enough induction into the weave. In the case of good-enough wovenness, the actual is like nuclear fission, fueling the reactor and erotically powering the psyche-somatic neighborhood through direct induction, without need for explicit or symbolic representation. (Perhaps friendship is most "unimaginable" because it need not be imagined.) Without the weave, the actual is the site of meltdown and permanent emergency that must remain quarantined behind Bion's beta screen.

Like Freud's attempt to construct a scientific model of psychological life, Bion borrowed concepts from the field of mathematics in an attempt to structure a psychoanalytic system known (infamously) as the Grid. The ideas that have been evolving in these pages can be compared with Bion's Grid in a fruitful way.

The first degree in this fixed overtone series, the octave (another C), is identical to the original struck key except that it is higher; when they are actually played together, the ear is often unable to tell whether one or two pitches are being struck. (Think of a "mirroring" interpretation.) The next tone in the series, the perfect fifth, barely introduces a sense of

TABLE 9.1

Humanization	Bion
	algebraic calculus
embedded unintegration	
	scientific deductive system
style	
	concept
improvisation	
	conception
hetero/sexual translation	
	pre-conception
homo/erotic identification	
	dreaming
seduction	
	alpha
induction (world-beating)	
	beta
worldlessness/un-memberment	

difference, the closest to a "perfect" match to the original note without being identical to it. Next comes another C, another identity, a return home (think of the first three notes of Strauss's *Also Sprach Zarathustra* at the dawn of Kubrick's *2001: A Space Odyssey*). Then things start to get really interesting. The next tone is the third, which gives any basic chord in which it appears the definitive quality of being either major or minor (in this case major); we depend on the third to discern this quality. Then, continuing on the series, another fifth, and then a bluesy flat-seventh, major with a minor inflection, creating a delicious tension that leaves the ear begging for resolution to a new key—a resolution that does not occur. We could think of this as a recurrence of the original home tone, which somehow doesn't quite feel like home anymore.

In these initial harmonics of the overtone series, one finds nature's template not only for the relationships of musical intervals but for human being itself, which is observable in the trajectory from the unwoven helplessness of infancy through the cycles of identification and differentiation that are potentiated through embeddedness in the weave of fellow humans, while each degree simultaneously operates autonomously as the modalities and channels through which bodies commune.

It is certainly viable to read this scale as a developmental model, as each degree on the scale emanates out of the preceding one and generates the variety of experience that follows it, providing a topography of a

TABLE 9.2

Humanization	Overtone series (in c)	Theme
worldlessness/un-memberment	fundamental (C)	isolation
induction (world-beating)	octave (C)	doubling
seduction	perfect fifth (G)	otherness
homo/erotic identification	octave (C)	reunion
hetero/sexual creativity	major third (E)	configuration
improvisation	perfect fifth (G)	accompaniment
sexuality	minor seventh (B♭)	style
embedded unintegration	octave (C)	home (*unheimlich*)

human life. But the scale's congruence with the overtone series alerts us to the fact that its trajectory is more than a model of development. It is something like a model of the weave's own overtones, the degrees of human experience that result and resound through the habitus of our shared practices, their ripple effects. It is the human-natural overtones which rest upon physical-natural overtones, the sound waves we hear as music constituted by constant and stable effects of sine waves—the waves of the weave. Melville conveys this effect through his image of the loom: Through the repetitive, discursive to-and-fro of weaving "as the shuttle flies," rhythmized by its pedal pulse, "figures float forth from the loom," each unique tapestry a derivative of a constant, communal habitus and *hexis*. Every iteration of weave activity is inevitably influenced and bent by contingencies in the environment, producing a Darwin-like evolution through microvariations, irregularities in the fabric, funky syncopations, recombinations. It is as if the repercussions of this rhythmized practice culminate in the patterned material and psychosensory impression of every tapestry, an effect known to the Greeks as *phronesis*, resonances of practical wisdom that amplify the harmonics of the world into the music of human experience.

These harmonics illuminate not only our diachronic, linear development as individuals but also our synchronic harmonies, the intervals through which we resonate together in dynamic proportions. While each overtone in the series does represent a psychological achievement, a landmark on a progressive journey of developmental growth, it importantly *presents* a particular effect that is lit up by the course of a human life as one lives in and through the practices of cultural heritage.[38] And these moments of percussive resonance between the particularities of individuality and the universality of human being are reinforced by the pleasure of their union (Bion modeled this using Hume's concept of "constant conjunctions").[39] To the extent that such contact produces the friction of frustration, Bion suggested, the result is a coping mechanism he called "thinking." What psychoanalysis adds to the bioanthropological picture is an understanding that what precipitates the infant's induction into the weave of culture, the reason the infant "takes to" it, is the visceral need for forms of movement to conduct the body as it sustains the need to be in the world, despite the disruptions of the pleasure of undifferentiated being that result in the sexual drive, the drive to search for a way back into the psychosensory weave. The sexual syncopations of the *eros* groove demand that we up our game to keep the music going, to form a sexuality container to contain the sexual elements, to weave them into a personal, idiomatic pattern of movement. In this sense "sexuality" would be the psyche-soma's response, its anti-bodies, to the foreign invasion of seduction. And our resulting sexuality, in turn, samples the weave for sexual fantasies, assembling a viable, idiomatic way of sustaining continuity while moving through the human world.

The degrees of life-giving inspiration charted in this humanization scale designate the points at which the music of the weave can be expressed through the human instrument (each one of us being an instrument). It turns out that every single one of these "overtones" (and many more, further into the series) vibrates to varying degrees in every musical sound; it is precisely how much energy resonates at every overtonal station that gives each instrument its distinct quality, or *timbre*, why a B-flat sounds totally different on a piano from the way it sounds on a French horn. Or, perhaps, in the human instrument: Through the cultural resonance (or lack thereof) at every point on this series in the course of a life, each individual accumulates energy (or deficit) at every degree of this overtone series, in every musical zone of psychical life, which gives each human a unique quality (or, as in Freud's "economic" model, a unique *quantity*, a unique sexuality). These resonances operate not according to genetic predisposition or destiny but rather according to the induction and reinforcement of choral unison (as in the concept that "cells that fire together wire together"). We must first be *humans doing* in shared ways in order to become *human beings* in unique ways. As the image of the spiral suggests,[40] the trajectory of a human life is recurrently shaped by the physical overtones of music, conducted through the binding beauty that forms the weave. (As the art critic Dave Hickey writes in *The Invisible Dragon*: "The utility of beauty as a legitimate recourse resides in its ability to locate us as physical creatures in a live, ethical relationship with other human beings in the physical world.")[41] Our sense of meaningfulness, therefore, may emanate not only from resonating at increasingly complex degrees on the overtone scale but rather, as Adorno said of the "meaning" of a musical composition, in the coherence of a dynamic set of interrelationships as perceived in a shared way—indeed, Adorno emphasizes, through musical *analysis*, reinvigorating and remusicalizing our psychoanalytic understanding of our own masthead.[42] *If the weave is the DNA of human existence, the double helix that oscillates between binding and unbinding, carrying the blueprint of human nature through self-replication, then the spiral is the RNA of human nature, the individual messenger that carries these building instructions and expresses their genetic code in order to synthesize life-giving proteins*, messengers of the rope. (Psychoanalysis would be the enzyme that repairs and heals damaged RNA.)

Of these psychoharmonic overtones, psychoanalysis has said the most—when it has said anything about music—about the level of accompanied improvisation, the second iteration of the perfect fifth. This dueting (as the psychoanalyst Steve Purcell has referred to it) is an evolved unison relative to the primary preoccupation of the original octave; it concerns itself not with what already is but with what might be, an anticipatory mode of being-in-the-world, as in Mitchell Wilson's model of the proleptic unconscious.[43] In an elaboration of this original function, this form of accompaniment now works as the established harmonic ground, the "left hand" (the frame), from which the "right hand" can improvise melodically toward the development of one's own sexual style of being-in-the-world. These moments occur at points on the spiral of humanization, repeatedly as one works up to increasingly authentic ("creative" in Winnicott's sense) being and living, and the second perfect fifth fits very well as a second moment of, as Heidegger puts it, "rendering oneself and things meaningfully present," sounding one's instrument in a full way.[44]

But Heidegger did not have the body in mind (he acknowledges it as an "important problem" in *Being and Time*, one he doesn't have time for); it took Merleau-Ponty's phenomenology to restore the primacy of embodiment to the ontological model. The good-enough parent needs to be first and foremost (like the listening, pointing clinician) a phenomenologist—and decidedly, crucially, *not* an analyst. It is bad news when parents analyze their children because it can so readily constitute an abandonment of the principle of joining, a particular way in which the task of weaving can be perverted or betrayed in the name of understanding (telling the child *what* they mean when they need help with *how* to mean). Similarly, a principle of weaving (psychosyncretism) before interpreting (psychoanalysis) may be most helpful for training analytic therapists. For one thing, it leavens the notion that practicing analysis depends on being a purely analytic state first and foremost, rather than being an ordinary person-living-in-a-body drawing sustenance from the earth moving in space and time along songlines. When the phenomenologist-parent and the child perceive and point at something together, even when it seems to be maximally private and "pure," it's always already determined by the weave, which is being transmitted by the parent, induction in action, and this is true in analysis, too (classical claims of neutrality notwithstanding). We (as analysts) are not only seeing and pointing together; we are also *teaching* both how to perceive and what is worth pointing out—and, implicitly, why. The simultaneity of perceiving and implicit teaching or *paideía*, the *Bildung* of perception itself—it is (ideally) an asymmetrical seeing-together, the parent/analyst using the weave to orient perception itself, inducing the child/patient into unreflective, sensorial engagement in the now-shared world through mimetic and inspired identification. "When I begin to reflect," Merleau-Ponty writes in the introduction to *Phenomenology of Perception*,

> my reflection bears upon an unreflective experience; moreover my reflection cannot be unaware of itself as an event, and so it appears to itself in the light of a truly creative act, of a changed structure of consciousness, and yet it has to recognize, as having priority over its own operations, the world which is given to the subject because the subject is given to himself. The real has to be described, not constructed or formed. Which means that I cannot put perception into the same category as the syntheses represented by judgements, acts or predications. My field of perception is constantly filled with a play of colors, noises and fleeting tactile sensations which I cannot relate precisely to the context of my clearly perceived world, yet which I nevertheless immediately "place" in the world, without ever confusing them with my daydreams. Equally constantly I weave dreams round things. I imagine people and things whose presence is not incompatible with the context, yet who are not in fact involved in it: they are ahead of reality, in the realm of the imaginary. If the reality of my perception were based solely on the intrinsic coherence of "representations," it ought to be forever hesitant and, being wrapped up in my conjectures on probabilities. I ought to be ceaselessly taking apart misleading syntheses, and reinstating in reality stray phenomena which I had excluded in the first place. But this seems not to

happen. The real is a closely woven fabric. It does not await our judgement before incorporating the most surprising phenomena, or before rejecting the most plausible figments of our imagination. Perception is not a science of the world, it is not even an act, a deliberate taking up of a position; it is the background from which all acts stand out, and is presupposed by them.[45]

Following Merleau-Ponty, we can understand that in the matter of perception, the analyst can never be "neutral," not simply because the analyst is irreducibly subjective in the matter of "judgments, acts, or predications" (the traditional stuff of psychoanalysis) but because perception itself, which is always *woven* perception (if it functions *as* perception, making a fabric out of the real) can only exist on a spectrum from lucid to obscure. The analyst's job, in this sense, is to conduct the session in a way that promotes and secures perception, not *what* to perceive but, as Merleau-Ponty suggested, *how* to perceive. So psychoanalysis, like the music lesson, is equally positioned to destroy this potentiality as it is to cultivate it, to *ab*-duct the patient. The patient thereafter lives not as oneself but as a colonized body, a character inside the analyst's head, encysted by the analyst's interminable refusal to be harmonically induced by the patient, trapped in the same old song instead of living in a world of music.

For this reason we must bear in mind that induction is always mutual. There is broad consensus regarding the analyst's responsibility to "get" the patient, a notion often linked exclusively in psychoanalytic theory with the question of symbolic understanding, but this "getting" also happens (or doesn't) in two directions. This mutuality is especially evident at the level of beta function, where mimetic identification between patient and analyst acts as a conduit to the weave. (And where, for example, the broken record of the repetition compulsion can become a sampled loop, resuming the music.) When re-membering one's patients through these identificatory repetitions—picking up on idiosyncratic irregularities of movement and speech, which show up first in the analyst's own bodily comportment (and thus perception), incorporating aspects of the patient into one's thoughts and dreams—one allows oneself to be induced into whatever ways of being the patient has managed to construct out of whatever patch of the weave has been afforded them.

Accordingly, any "understanding" or attunement depends upon the psychosensory union, the "inside out" of resonant identification, as a portal into the patient's idiosyncratic mode of being. For this reason, the analyst must always be alive to the ways that one's own aesthetic position might lead one to miss genuinely musical aspects of the patient's idiom, the very elements through which patient and analyst could begin to find their way together.[46] The analyst has to *be there*, in the mode and at the place of *da-sein* (*being-there*, in the "pre-understanding of being"), at the beta level of pre-confusion, before there are two things, in order to conduct the music of *being-with* (*mit-sein*), where there is only oneness. Induced into the patient's *dasein* (or way of being in the world), inhabit-ed by some of the patient's habitus, the analyst forms the necessary, identificatory bond to induce the patient, in turn, using one's own style and skills to provide a conduit to the larger cultural weave into which the patient can be more fully and freely woven.

And if induction is mutual, so too is seduction. There's no way to avoid either one, just as there's no way to avoid it from parent to child in Laplanche's fundamental anthropological situation, because of the essential, radical sociality and suggestibility of the human being. When Laplanche said the analyst must be the "guardian of the enigma," he meant that the analyst has an ethical responsibility to never forget the effects of seduction in the functioning and communicative activity of both parties, to never forget that we can never fully understand what is going on in any human activity, relationship, or subjective experience. As Wilson has elaborated, to accept this inherent decenteredness, doubt, and disorientation and to open oneself to a ceaseless labor of figuring out how to *use* it as an aspect of one's practice and style is to become free enough to do analytic work in an ethical way.[47] On the other hand, to disavow or to attempt to master the enigma is to enact a perverse seduction or abduction—in Laplanche's terms, *intromission* (lit. "mental penetration," mind-fucking)—rigor mortis of the soul. In its musical *ethos*, the ethical practice of psychoanalysis guards the enigma by protecting the patient from overstimulation, acting both as a conduit of energy, powering the psyche-somatic dimension like a solar battery, and as a barrier against excess, a good-enough surge protector. And the only way to function properly in this regard, to perceive the insufficiency or excess of energy at any given moment with any given patient, to measure the voltage, is to be plugged in at the beta level, grounded through mutual induction, moved like a needle by the groove of the force, the *ethos* of shared music.

Good-enough conduction, in other words, is always the harmonic effect of good-enough seduction, the right degree of enigma. (Hyperconduction would be the analyst frying the patient with excessive stimulation; hypoconduction, a dead frame, leaves the patient at the mercy of one's own voltage, forced to short-circuit, typically showing up as somatic illness.) Guarding the enigma involves having to conduct with varying degrees of embodied feeling, alternatively generating and insulating the charge. Good-enough conduction is the process by which analysis becomes and remains a "going concern," in Winnicott's term—care in action, in motion, on the move (and in the groove)—the actual background therapeutic action of psychoanalysis, the bodily activity on the part of the analyst that makes the whole thing salutary.

There is no conduction without the structural and electrical engineering of hardware and network. Nothing works without a frame. Being able to study, to learn, to be-with requires a designated space, sustained in time, a recess (a *going back*—that most popular hour of the schoolday, making the work of being in school possible for the child), a *reduction*, a *leading-back*. Sheehan remarks, in an episode of *Entitled Opinions*, that this reductive mode is "a matter of just staring at things as if through a window so that your involvement with those things is not operative, it's not noticed, it's not brought to the fore."[48] These windows, or clearings, are traditionally structured by the weave, which in each of its cultural ecosystems preserves time and space for this form of suspension, for stepping outside the flow and temporality of everyday life that allows repair and promotes co-immunity. To refer to one's "patient" as such is an inductive gesture in its own right, gesturing toward the frame of slowness, recess, sabbath, hospital—a *patient induction* into the contemplative practice and convalescence of looking at something together.

Conceiving of the frame of psychoanalysis as a recessional activity provides an opportunity to rethink our idea of psychoanalytic abstinence. Abstinence prevents sexual intercourse, not only to frustrate the patient into growing up, as Freud proposed, but to cultivate a space for the domain of the weave, for grounding perception in the woven body. Abstinence is thus a form of engagement, not (only) a prohibition, a way to start something, not (just) to prevent. It allows for the discovery of a consensual space for uninterrupted perception (the analyst provides a space in which the patient does not have to deal with the analyst). The inductive function of the living, musical frame, legislated by the abstention of physical intercourse, makes possible the emergence of a different kind of space, underwrites a negative capability (which Bion called "O") that makes possible and invites the patient toward a *human* domain of a newly and endlessly fascinating, meaningful world and to create their own meanings, grounded in the sensoriality of the *natural* world—bringing the two together. Laplanche thought the analyst must make two refusals: We don't tell patients what to do with their lives, and we don't say what is in the patient's unconscious. We don't mind-fuck them, and we don't colonize them. Instead, the analyst offers a way to be fascinated, an attitude toward that which no one else can ever translate and that nobody should ever tell you they could.

An *ethos* of slowness, of patience, of co-immunity, portends far more than the sublimation of psyche-somatic energy into the clouds, the photosynthesis of sunlight into ever-changing states of growth—though this is hardly even a metaphor for one thing analysis can actually do. But so too in cooler temperatures, in lower states of energy—when, as the psychoanalyst Francisco Gonzalez has remarked, condensations of abstraction dismantle into material components, when the clouds rain—psychoanalysis returns us to the undifferentiation of liquid,[49] the potential of oceanic waves to recombine and penetrate the solid states, the silent earth, from which we came, and to which, like our ancestors before us, we shall return.

10

OLD FOUNDATIONS IN PSYCHOANALYSIS

silence
garden
rest

I have nothing to say, and I am saying it.
—JOHN CAGE, *LECTURE ON NOTHING*

|

An episode of the cultural miracle that is "Carpool Karaoke" (from the *Late Late Show with James Corden*) presents a moment that to a psychoanalytic sensibility can be described as a piece of work, mourning-in-action.[1] Corden and his guest, Sir Paul McCartney, drive around the latter's hometown of Liverpool. An atmosphere of comfort and friendliness one would associate with old friends (which they are not) fosters the tempo of relaxed and humorous exchange, buffering their car-bound, duet renditions of (naturally) "Drive My Car" and (upon arrival) "Penny Lane." Gazing out the window at the neighborhood of his youth, Sir Paul reflects on the unlikeliness of his transcendent stardom, including moments when his longevity and creative continuity felt perilously uncertain. "I had a dream," he reports, "in the [19]60s, where my mom, who died, came to me in the dream, and was reassuring me, saying, 'It's gonna be OK. Just let it be.'" The song begins. Just before the chorus, Paul drops an unexpected harmony, not present in the original recording, a sumptuous major third below the melody. Corden's voice cracks on the next line. "Oh man. It got me emotional there, Paul," he reflects afterward. "I didn't feel it coming. It's too much for me. I was, uh—"

Paul gently lets out a mezzo *portamento*, a downward sliding octave. "*Whooo*."

"—I couldn't feel—I didn't see that one comin' round the corner." Corden laughs as his eyes well up with tears.

"That's great, man," McCartney responds. "I tell you, that's the power of music. It's weird, isn't it? How that can do that to you."

"Well, I can remember—I can remember my granddad, who's a musician, and my dad, sitting me down and saying, 'We're gonna play you the best song you've ever heard.' [*Pause*.] And I remember them playing me that."

"Really."

The two men, side by side, gaze together toward the road ahead. "If my granddad was here right now he'd get an absolute kick out of that."

"He is."

Silence. Corden wipes tears from his face. "*Whooo*," McCartney repeats, as they pull up to his childhood home.

He is, Paul says. Not, "He is *here*" (or "He *is* here") but *He is*. Two words, two beats. Not one more. Clearly this is an entirely musical impulse, unfolding in real time, a virtuoso sensibility from a master of the popular musical form, which like only the fewest of peers (Elvis, Michael Jackson) engenders the power to induce fainting with a passing glance. If, as André Green once wrote, art is a form of revenge against the real, then pop stars, like all gods, are revenge against loss. To bear loss through the communion of musical mourning is to achieve the authenticity of what James Baldwin once called saying yes to life. Like all of our so-called "interventions," McCartney's response has as much to do with what he doesn't say, with keeping silent, as it does with choosing the words to speak. The right absence of words, the felt presence of their abeyance, is crucial to the psychoacoustic dimension of therapeutic action, what Lacan once called "keeping silent," a provision of aural space for something to resound, to reverberate meaningfully—a pause in which to hear and feel the weave resonating with us. (Perhaps Winnicott had this phenomenon in mind when he wished, reflecting upon his career, that he had interpreted less, or in his observation that when he spoke a lot in sessions, he was probably tired.) It is from this silence, Merleau-Ponty once wrote, that language was made, that the music on which meaning is modeled can emerge.

"Silence is the poetics of space," writes the acoustic ecologist Gordon Hempton, "the presence of time, undisturbed."[2] For Hempton, who pursues rare degrees of natural silence in order to record and archive otherwise unheard "sounds" (of snow melting, of the sun rising), and for whom being in nature is a kind of divine communion, silence is the absence of *human* sound, the ambience of "undisturbed" nature in which the physical substrate of the weave can be actually heard, akin to hearing one's own heartbeat, a sensory experience of the fundamental rhythm that subtends resonance. This kind of silence (which is the way the weave regards the sound of nature) is hard to come by these days, though one may discover outdoors a few inch-minutes of naturally "silent" space-time, evoking the very aesthetic of reduction and time-presence that the frame is designed to provide and protect. But there is never total silence. Our physical materiality does not permit it. Natural silence is everywhere penetrated by human sounds—a plane overhead in the middle of the woods, the flapping of sails in the middle of the ocean. Whether any given disturbance of space-time by sound is experienced as generative or deadening, usable or intrusive, cultivating an intimate body-feel or jarring one out of one's embodied experience, depends upon whether it is framed and mediated by a fellow weave-member, an acoustic ecologist, whether an ethic of interest is expressed and conducted through a provision of kept silence, through a practice of actual listening.

Like a seashell, silent spaces are acoustic chambers for the music of what Freud called the oceanic feeling—"a sensation of 'eternity,' a feeling as of something limitless, unbounded."[3] To call it an oceanic "feeling" (at least in English) may fail to capture the sensory quality of this silent sensation, its particular *Stimmung* or attunement. (As Strachey translates him, Freud alternately refers to the oceanic "feeling" as "sensation," "purely subjective fact," "faith," "thought," "feeling tone," and "primary nature" in the first chapter of *Civilization and Its Discontents*—and never writes about it again.) As Matte-Blanco once formulated, every "feeling" is an infinity in its own right, which we can only feel absolutely, and only when we are feeling it; any sense of attenuation or degree results only from the co-incidence, the harmonics, of other simultaneous feelings, multiple infinities, infinite sets.[4] (Listening to music is thus essentially a feeling activity, a state where sense and feeling come together.) In his psychomathematical formulation, each feeling is thus "equal" to the entire Ucs., each feeling an oceanic feeling, a silent eternity. It is only from this quality of undifferentiation, the floor of being itself, that the asymmetry of distinct thoughts becomes differentiable. The psychoanalytic frame, which enables silence, acts as the ground for the counterpoint of "free association," for which it clears the way.

Invaluable silences are threatened by the overstimulating demands of the sound environment, alienating us from the silent background that is required to make any sense of the sounds we hear. (As Laplanche suggested of the individual unconscious, noise is sound unbound by the weave, "driving" us crazy.) And when this colonizing noise vacates the premises, moving on to fill the next available weave-vacuum, it leaves a deafening death-silence in its wake, a no-thing, a persecutory experience that demands relief posthaste. These are not the sabbath silences of restoration but the ruptures left by what Han calls the "whizzing" of time.[5] This silence is *nowhere*, the outer space of the weave, and only a remusicalized mode of listening can provide the way back in. If, as Heidegger once indicated, there really is a mood in the room, then we really have to attune ourselves to it, to weave our perceptual and attentional senses into it, in order to feel it, to "make and cultivate music," as Socrates dreamed. Perhaps John Cage's famous "silent" piece for piano, 4'33", is actually a frame for listening to the weave, for hearing the mood in the room as music.

Embedded in the weave of shared experience, silence can help frame and pattern and punctuate an aesthetic experience—the "intervalic consonants which give shape to our primal wail," as Harrison puts it—just as silence can even become a musical experience in its own right, such as the bars of silence the conductor continues to beat at the end of Ligeti's choral work *Lux Aeterna*. But unembedded in this weave, silences can only be terrifying, uncanny, dreadful, claustral. The noise cancellation of digital spaces are decapitated sine waves; little if any music can survive.

Digitally compressed music can have the same squelching effect on the ears as cancelled noise, a vacuum of inner-outer space. Music plays all around but remains useless, even mocking. "*Music do I hear?*" asks Shakespeare's *Richard II*, cancelled and dethroned, un- and dis-membered, waiting for death (like Socrates) in his prison cell:

> Ha, ha! keep time: how sour sweet music is,
> When time is broke and no proportion kept!
> So is it in the music of men's lives.
> And here have I the daintiness of ear
> To cheque time broke in a disorder'd string;
> But for the concord of my state and time
> Had not an ear to hear my true time broke.
> I wasted time, and now doth time waste me.[6]

What makes "sweet music sour" is when its relationship to time is disordered, "when time is broke," when time can do no work. The king knows that time is broken when it ceases to do its job, when it leaves him in a state of disarray with "no proportion kept." Laid low by his tragic circumstances, Richard has become preoccupied with this fundamental order of things, to their brokenness, their sweetness gone sour. Music is fundamentally an ordering and patterning of time, waves of energy grouped in relation to frequency (rhythm) and one another (harmony). Psychoanalysis as both a theory and a practice of psychotherapy is designed in some sense to rhythmize the noise. What we hear from our patients (and in our theories) is the music of time in a state of collapse, the "actual" gone sour: "So it is in the music of men's lives"—or, as one hears often (and painfully) at the beginning of treatment, "It is what it is," no longer what it might be (or even what it might have been). These empty, disenchanted, nihilistic silences, the silences of nowhere, are one of the surest tells of nonmembership in the weave: silence where one needs to speak, empty noise where one needs generative rest.

Every piece of music, like every analytic session, begins and ends in silences, which also recur throughout the duration of the piece—at times, as Freud interpreted, as a form of "resistance" or "stoppage," of arrests in the conductive flow of creative speech, but also frequently as intervals of rest and, at times, great noncommunicative potential. The restorative, erotic use of silence is crucial to the rhythm of going-on-being, to the co-immunity of the weave. The mutual requirements of discourse (including psychoanalytic work) inherently require moments of silence in which one can finish speaking before the other begins; these in turn become a reciprocal "keeping" silent—*fermata*, in musical terms (a type of *caesura*), when the music is suspended by the instrumentalist for an undetermined amount of time, *kept* in tension by a presiding conductor of musical energy. The distance between performer and audience, not to mention audience members, vanishes in these moments, as if all the surrounding music were meant to frame this "quiet union" (to use Winnicott's evocative phrase). Even a single word, a single note, would simply be, in these moments, in the way. "Silence becomes a medium through which to experience the analytic holding environment," Bollas writes in *The Shadow of the Object*. "It is something like the silence of a small child some ten to twenty minutes before falling asleep. During this very special transition from wakeful life lived in relation to important objects, to unconsciousness and the dream, children lie tranquilly in their beds, eyes open, *imagining* their life."[7]

These silences, kept for us by other people, make us human, clearing a space in which something new can happen, for something to present itself, as Freud emphasized, in the rests formed by the sudden inability to speak, when the *fermata* of parapraxis suspends or syncopates an established discursive rhythm, particularly when that rhythm has lost the vitality of sensing the world on the edge of time. What Lacan (1960) called "the paradox of analytic discourse" is that "it becomes worthwhile only insofar as it stumbles or even interrupts itself—were not the session itself instituted as a break in false discourse, that is, in what discourse realizes when it becomes empty as speech."[8] Lacan's interest in the negative of speech, the spaces in between, informs his ethical refusal to suggest, a position consistent with the original psychoanalytic departure from its ancestral practice of hypnosis. The negative capability of this refusal forms a silent sphere of deep communion in which analysis actually takes place, the resonant silence of the time-space when-where we actually live. The noncommunication of the analyst's kept silence in response to even the most common stoppages in clinical work ("What should I talk about?" "Where did we leave off?") can induce the patient into the experiential dimension of living, a moment of silence in which to jointly attune to the fundamental ground of human being. "*Dasein* in the stillness of the world is a string of an instrument quivering with its own tension," Sloterdijk writes. "Perhaps everyone who has meditated through the ages has sought silence and stillness because existence hearing itself as the noise dies down helps to tauten the string. For this reason, music not only celebrates our linking into the continuum again but also, if it is more than a sedative or an anesthetic, it perpetually reminds us of the cosmic stillness of existence."[9]

The analyst doses these cosmic reminders, this strong stuff, judiciously. What we call psychoanalysis, what Laplanche considered the psychoanalytic "act," is supremely dependent upon the work of disassembly, of analysis, is just as dependent upon what we don't say, the material we frame with silence. The analyst's silence may function like the tightening and slackening of tension between knowing and not knowing (Bion's ♂ and ♀), helping existence to hear itself, to find the requisite pressure that allows the string to sing. The "evenly weavened" tuning of the analyst, like that of an instrument (or that of Sir Paul), determines the acoustics of clinical resonance, the suitability of conditions for the otherwise unbearable process of suffering loss. "We can only wait until the patient himself finds the courage to make the almost impossible possible," Reik wrote in *Listening with the Third Ear*. "The rest is silence."[10]

||

The rest is silence, and the silence is rest. Silence is the sound of the frame's recessional respite, the acoustics of Bleger's "non-process," the deep frequency of the weave. In defining pleasure as relief from instinctual need, Freud may have missed a quieter pleasure of membership in shared human living (all the more pleasurable for its provision and availability, its unprocessed organicity, its merciful respite from the overprocessed world, never needing to be planned, only to be played). It is pleasurable to be in the weave, in the *groove* of it. (Freud did in fact consider in "The Economic Problem of Masochism" that pleasure might be a *temporal modification* of instinctual life, a rhythmizing of the instincts.)[11] And it is only through the ordinary continuity of this woven pleasure that we grasp (and are grasped by) the way the human world is made. There is *no* process without the *non*-process of the weave.

The weave dimension of human being—not unlike the ecological dimension of natural being—increasingly demands our clinical focus, imperiled as it has become by more dominant forms of (in)attention. To attend to the earth is to ponder our materiality and mortality, which may be partly why, as Searles once formulated, we treat it so badly ("to ensure that we shall have essentially nothing to lose in our eventual dying.")[12] We periodically tolerate an awareness of our inevitable return to stardust through rituals of mourning, which are nearly always musical and absolutely always shared. Could Freud possibly *not* have thought, when writing "Mourning and Melancholia," about the Kaddish or the many other rhythmic, communal laments that are devoted only to the purpose of containing loss? The intimate connection between music and loss, which Freud formulated most pointedly in the rhythmic concept of *fort-da*, remains nevertheless underrepresented in psychoanalytic theory: the need of the bereaved to be held by forms of repetition that are patterned and preserved through culture (not to mention the need to be relieved of having to do or say something original in the wake of significant loss).

In Western culture we often and increasingly forget that we cannot mourn by ourselves. Musical mourning rituals are how the collective "contains" loss, in Bion's sense of that term, though primarily through physical embodiment; how culture transforms the shock or trauma of death into the communal, meaningful, ritual choreography of lament; grounded in our connection to the earth, but meaningfully connected only through ritual, through "rehearsed and highly formal gestures of externalization, as Harrison writes in his 2013 book *The Dominion of the Dead*, "whose purpose is first and foremost to depersonalize the condition of grief by submitting it to a set of public, traditionally transmitted codes." The kindest thing we can do for the bereaved is to relieve them of the privacy of personalized subjectivity, to weave them into the habitus of collective movement, swaddling the wounded subject in the recess of the weave. Harrison continues: "By dictating the rules for 'how one mourns,' ritual lament helps assure that the psychic crisis engendered by loss, especially in its initial stages, will not plunge the mourner into sheer delirium or catalepsy. . . . Ritualization thus serves to contain the crisis of grief in the very act of objectifying its content through scripted gestures and precise codes of enactment."[13] Through its prescribed repetitions, which reverberate throughout the movements of all its members, the cultural practice of lamentation "submits the emotive spontaneity of grief to impersonal forms of externalization, it *creates a chorus* or community of voices sharing in the lament of the bereaved." Perhaps this chorus recapitulates what the French philosopher and psychoanalyst Julia Kristeva has termed the "semiotic chora" of early infancy, that undifferentiated sensorial chaos out of which humans are formed;[14] returning the dead to their humic dominion, musical lamentation releases us back into a state of unintegration, embedded in the chorus of mourners, from which we can be born again in the wake of loss.

The psychoanalytic frame, an expression of the weave, provides a conduit and instantiation of a culture's mode of address, of ritual lament. Analysts are, in this sense, professional mourners. It is precisely at points of traumatic blow to one's sense of the world that the chorus of the weave is most needed; for the individual patient suffering a private perdition, the analyst serves this purpose as ambassador from the weave, providing a form of repetition and interruption, and hence a rhythm of mourning, that conducts an enduring sense of the living world, the pulse of culture. "The depressed person," Kristeva writes, "is a radical, sullen atheist."[15] Without a metaphysical pulse through which to sustain (to "repress," in Laplanche's sense) the *pulsión* (drive) of traumatic disruption, without a weave to hold the psyche-soma through its reactivity, the de-pressed person is left radically unaccompanied, the tautness of the weave gone slack, the psyche-soma left floating faithless in the deathly silence of inner outer space.

Only in the live company of keepers of the subliminal weave-pulse can the ongoing demands for work on the psyche be sustained, which is to say, the ongoing work of mourning, clearing the way for new life to grow. It is worth noting that at virtually the same time he wrote "Mourning and Melancholia," in which he foregrounds the "lost object," Freud also wrote "On Transience," in which it is the *new* object, the new thing, which is most important—the object toward which we are always moving, for which we are always working-through.[16] When Freud famously wrote, "In mourning it is the world which has become poor and empty; in melancholia it is the I itself," he assumed that melancholia was an individual, narcissistic problem, that the worst thing that could happen was to lose one-*self* when one loses the object of one's love.¹⁷ But perhaps a more profound contrast implicit in his formulation of mourning and melancholia is not the status of the self but the state of the world, the status of the weave function. The crucial question is not whether the world or the self has been lost, because to lose one's object is always to lose both the world and the self as one knew them. The crucial question is *whether one loses the weave*, whether one is dismembered by a violent disruption in one's sense of reliable world-continuity and consequently left at the mercy of melancholic repetition and the whizzing frenzy of an alter world or whether one is held, through ritual lament and communal copresence, and humanized as an injured weave-member sufficiently to sustain the movements of impoverishment and replenishment of the world in the wake of loss. Good-enough mourning is thus only ever an aftereffect of the weave's provision of a grief habitus in which to dwell, a coordinated choreography of the rhythms and rituals we use to contain and sustain our all-too-human mortality.

The woven individual is recurrently and recursively nourished by these practices and many others like them which "under-stand" each member by providing common denominators to infinite variations. Paradoxically, change comes from repetition. Like Darwin's theory of evolution, it is pure replication that inevitably provides the ground for novelty and variation, like the trunk of a tree provides the fundament for branching arborescence or like the slight imperfections that make each tapestry its own "wave" of the weave function, a syncopation of the drumbeat. In the key of human beings, this might take the form of the practicing actor one day asking: Why am I doing this? The taking-off of this curiosity, this tiny shoot of organic matter, achieving a slight angle (theta function) out of loops of repetition (beta function) is like the gardening of one's life, enriching the soil of communal living with the ethical practice of care. "Given that Cura formed *homo* out of *humus*," Harrison writes, "it is only natural that her creature should direct his care primarily toward the earth from which his living substance derives ... human beings experience time as the working out of one care after another."¹⁸ For Harrison, "care, in its self-transcending character, is an expansive projection of the intrinsic ecstasy of life"; we feel alive when we are able to care, "where giving exceeds taking."¹⁹ Perhaps the therapeutic aspect of becoming a patient in psychoanalysis is related to the opportunity to begin to transcend oneself through the ecstasy of care; to be "cured" is to become a curator (from the Latin *curare*, "to take care") of one's embodied experiences through mimetic identification with a caring other, to internalize a practice that will gestate into a form of conduct, a form of navigation. (It is one thing to visit a museum or have access to an infinity of songs, another to find a path through, a songline, to care about the objects embedded therein.) The weave sponsors our curated navigation of the world, lighting things up along the way, making songs out of sounds, dreams out of day residue. We rely upon the weave, as Harrison puts it, "to re-enchant the present."[20] The weave is our musical immunity that protects us against the tonelessness of narcissism, dissociation, and insincerity. It protects our humanity; it makes us human by making us care about the world. (As the philosopher John Haugeland noted: "The trouble with computers is that they just don't give a damn.")[21] The weave cares about us, which shows us how to care about the world (our "selves" included).

As Harrison suggests, to care is to experience time, to temporalize experience; the enchantment of the cared-for world musicalizes experience into soulful patterns. Writing about his favorite garden near his office at Stanford, a place he cares about very deeply, Harrison reflects:

> Aristotle once wondered: "How is it that rhythms and melodies, although only sound, resemble states of the soul?" (*Problemata*, c. 19). In the same vein one could ask: how can a garden made of plants, water, and stone resemble a state of the soul? I would not even use the word *resemble*. Kingscote Garden [at Stanford] does not resemble my *ataraxia* [peace of mind, lit. "without perturbance"], nor do I bring that state of mind with me into the garden; rather, I find it there. If Kingscote were to disappear one day, so would the special inner tranquility it provides access to. There are no states of the soul that do not have their proper place in the world; and if there were no places in the world, there would be no soul in it either.[22]

When Bion cautioned not to get taken up with cure—Be without memory and desire, he said—he may have been urging practicing analysts to get taken up with *care*, with curation, with gardening. This orientation toward the *activity* of clinical work guides care itself, an *ethos* of caring *for* our patients (as opposed to, as Ferenczi once put it, the "professional hypocrisy" of purporting to care *about* the patient). Freud approached this ethic in his own way when he wrote, "A surgeon of earlier times took as his motto the words: *'Je le pansai, Dieu le guérit.'* ['I dressed his wounds, God cured him.'] The analyst should be content with something similar."[23] Harrison's meditations on gardens can orient the working clinician toward the habitable zone of human care: It is in the hydrated soil between our aqueous and humic natures, between the ocean of silence from which we all emerge and the terra firma of dry land to which we all return that garden music conducts our safe passage from our oceanic ancestry through our *homo* practices toward our *humic* rest.

III

Habitus forms the gardens in which humans grow, where we "practice" being human. ("Humans live in habits," Sloterdijk writes, "not territories.")[24] These gardens are always in turn dependent on the surrounding territory, never independent from the environment surrounding them. The Italian psychoanalyst Antonino Ferro once posited what he thought of as two impacts of culture on the mind: a *"relational microculture"* of the family (the traditional purview of psychoanalysis), which is "microenvironmental" and "represents the mind's [alpha] function and oedipal function, on which the development of the capacity for thought of every human child within his or her environment depends," and a "social macroculture (within which the relational microcultures live in a kind of osmosis)" and toward which psychoanalysis "cannot claim to be indifferent." Ferro emphasizes the dynamic between the macro- and microculture: "A central issue is the extent to which the social macroculture acknowledges the mental and emotional, the vital importance of relationship to the development of the mind, as well as the space and time that culture allows for making available the functions of reverie, fantasy and dreaming."[25]

The psychoanalytic frame reiterates this dynamic; the "framing" of one's individual history, the historicizing of one's experience, relies entirely on the culture of the living frame, the extent to which the frame provides a time-space where a version of culture can be lived in a personal way. This constitutes what Pontalis once called "*a no man's land that protects the two*"—patient and analyst—"*though none is certain from what.*" Pontalis sees this interplay in the psychoanalytic activity par excellence, the presentation of a dream:

> The introduction of a dream in a session is often experienced as a calm excitement, if one may put it that way; a truce, a lull, *an enraptured complicity*. The complicity arises in part from the fact that one has something in common to analyse, in a sensorial exchange of the visual with hearing. But the lull arises from the fact that something absent becomes sentient on the horizon from our dual stare and listening—becomes present by staying absent.[26]

The analytic session functions, in this sense, as a framed recessional, a walled garden, in which nature (mind's activity during sleep), under conditions of calm care, becomes the excitement of human nature. The living framework within which psychocultivation can proceed, like the walled garden of horticulture, provides the space-time to become enraptured and enchanted, to refind the wide world through the framed world and vice versa. So the analyst must conduct and frame things to facilitate access to the macro through the micro and to bring the micro alive through the macro, keeping alive the micro and the macro alike. The microculture of the frame conducts the macroculture of the world in miniature through the musicality of the analyst, to repurpose Wallace Stegner's phrase, through the analyst's "angle of repose." ("Repose is a state of mind made possible by the structuring of one's relation to one's environment," Harrison writes, "a kind of orientation.")[27] "The dream," Pontalis continues, "can only achieve its 'binding' function after a kind of 'prebinding' has been established. The dream process cannot function according to its own logic unless the dream-space—the 'psychic system'—has been constituted as such."[28]

The binding of the dream only ever follows the (pre)binding of the dream-screen—the "dream catcher" of the weave, the calm excitement of kept silence. To a musician, silences (called *rests*) are just as big a deal as sound. Sonic events like speech or singing form the amorphousness of silence into the force fields and angles and punctuations of expression.

These musical shapes constitute the sensuality of language, as well as its reliability. Words can be reassuring, silences awkward. Depending on its shape, silence may be either constructive or destructive in relation to rhythm, the potential space for music to occupy or the vacuum of creative collapse. Silences can get (or keep) things going or stop them in their tracks. "How is it that these sub-symbolic processes generate a sense of 'moving along' or 'flow'?" Cartwright poses in *Containing States of Mind*. "My view is that proto-containing qualities emerge because the concept of negation does not exist at this level of experience. At this level of mind the non-conscious perception of 'sameness' and 'difference' does not undergo a categorical analysis. One object cannot be separated from the other, rather they are experienced as different points in a field of sensory intensities."[29] At the subsymbolic level of sensory intensities, it matters less what we are saying to one another and more the way we are saying it, the extent to which word and pause, presence and absence, are generating conditions in which it may become tolerable (not to mention pleasurable) to be psyche-somatically intact and present. Silence literally *does* nothing—which we desperately need it to do.

But through the paradigm of what Heidegger considers the "technological understanding of being" that characterizes our current epoch, empty silence is signified as a no-thing, a threat, a loser. Our present-day politics threaten to readily and seamlessly deform the great institutions of woven silence. (You won't feel a thing until it's too late.) Future generations will see (as previous contractions of humanity reveal to us) how tyrannical, authoritarian structures exercise their unholy work by attacking our recessional spaces, our portals to the weave. The to-and-fro of feeling things together becomes impoverished of its musicality. We know now more than ever how despotism can set up this pattern: convulsed by the death drive, making sense only momentarily before jumping spastically from one unrelated point to the next, relying on shock and awe to subdue his victims into a whizzing, traumatized oblivion. This *amusia* constitutes a perversion of the weave, an abuse of it.

The painstaking work of repairing the weave: this is what despots and autocrats fail to do. Autocracy means not having to hold two things in mind at once or sustain paradoxes or behave oneself. Whereas music by its very nature does the work of the weave; it always has more than one thing going on. By calling it a "rest," music theory renders silence a musical object—or, rather, an absence that renders presence, imbuing silence with musicality—as can be ecstatically dramatized when the beat drops out and then drops back in again. It is in these resonant pauses that the mimetic power of beta function can truly be appreciated, recognized (in its breach) as constitutive of human being itself, and, at the same time, subtly alarming us in its resemblance to its alter ego, the death-silence of the alter world, the zero gravity of the uncanny. "The absence of rhythm," Lacoue-Labarthe writes, "is equivalent to the infinitely paradoxical appearance of *the mimetic itself*"[30]—the mimesis of rhythm being nowhere so evident as in its absence, in the breach, in the exception to the pulse's rule. But this "kept" silence is haunted (and sexualized) by its evocation of a world in which rhythm is not just temporarily absent (and thereby present in negative form, like when the beat drops) but fundamentally devoid of rhythm, never-been-rhythmized. In this case, the patterns of life-movement cannot be woven into shared ways of being human. As Lacoue-Labarthe writes, "*Nothing* occurs: in effect, the *Unheimliche*.... In which case, rhythm would also be the condition of possibility for the subject."[31] The *Unheimliche*, the "uncanny" (lit. "un-home-like") gives the senses a fleeting impression of our original, prehuman undifferentiation, the unwoven statelessness of nonexistence, a chilling glimpse of what we have come to know as "home" would feel like denuded of its vital soundtrack, what perception itself feels like unrhythmized, how things feel when there are no conditions *for* possibility. What freaks us out about the uncanny is that it teases us, perhaps, or needles us with a "memory" of what Freud called "the phenomenon of the double" (and later generalized to the repetition compulsion):

> This [double] relation is accentuated by... what we should call telepathy—, so that the one possesses knowledge, feelings and experience in common with the other. Or it is marked by the fact that the subject identifies himself with someone else, so that he is in doubt as to which his self is, or substitutes the extraneous self for his own. In other words, there is a doubling, dividing and interchanging of the self. And finally there is the constant recurrence of the same thing—the repetition of the same features or character-traits or vicissitudes, of the same crimes, or even the same names through several consecutive generations.[32]

The uncanny reminds us not simply of our erotic union or connection to one another through identification (a "phenomenon of the double") but furthermore reminds us of the void of isolation from which we are rescued by the weave, the "nothing" we would be without it. For Freud, the uncanny feeling—which, like the oceanic feeling, he claimed he could not find in himself—gets triggered (and immediately repressed) by any reminder of our fundamental transcendentalism. As adults (like Freud) secure a sovereign distance from this immersive state, these uncanny reminders—indeed, *reminiscences*—threaten to drown us with a sense of the infinity, our mortal return to the ocean of stardust. ("From having been an assurance of immortality, [the double] becomes the uncanny harbinger of death.")[33] Over the course of a human life, that brief interval between birth and death, the endlessness of the oceanic feeling becomes rhythmized on land. The uncanny is always the poignant resonance through every other overtone of the human series, everywhere we have ever lived, now seen (or heard) from the current position. It is both the music of our loss and the music of our salvation.

Perhaps this is why the same piece of music can sound both identical and utterly different at different times in one's life: a reminder of the first time we heard it, as well as a reminder of a world before it existed for us, when we had never heard it before and when we might never have heard it at all (if not for, usually, a fellow human, henceforth forever associated with the song). There is a world of difference between the never-found and not-yet-found, between a state of preconfusion and being confused, between being enchanted and being bemused, lost again and lost forever. When Nietzsche remarked that "without music life would be a mistake," he might have meant something like this: that without induction into the weave, a life misses its take; it doesn't begin, it isn't a human life.[34] (In his native tongue, Nietzsche would have said that without music life would be an *irrtum*, an error, from the word *irren*, which means "to wander"—so without music life would be "wander-dom," lost-ness.) To be lost is to fall out of the weave, to need someone to induce us back into it. Like Anne Alvarez's crucial notion of "reclamation" in her work with autistic children, Nietzsche's comment suggests the need incumbent upon the analyst to reach into the outer-inner space of the not-yet-humanized organism, the ethical responsibility to inweave new members into the centrifugal force of weave-gravity, to encourage them along a continuous spiral that traces a path through nodes of integrity and loss, through thick and thin, ups and downs, sickness and health, coming together and coming apart, the genres of experience that a human life traverses.[35] The analyst, in the words of Socrates, must make and cultivate music. If the analytic frame becomes a dead institution and loses its porous, conductive capacities, its resonance, then it fails in its weaving task, which is the potential for connecting clinical experience and the human world. Under these conditions of frame mortification, any repetition compelled by the transference is doomed to be little more than a dead end, an echo, a reliving of the trouble that psychoanalysis attempts to cure—a dead garden.

There may be no more fundamental issue to our human being than this question of musical induction, enshrined in the rituals of weave membership, commitments (like psychoanalysis) that aim to embody the weave in action. The primary human psychical entity is neither the individual nor the family but the *tribe*, where the weave lives and evolves. As the philosopher and psychoanalyst Jonathan Lear notes in the opening pages of *Radical Hope*, the Native American Crow chief Plenty-Coups offers tragic testimony on this point: "When the buffalo went away the hearts of my people fell to the ground, and they could not lift them up again. *After this nothing happened. There was little singing anywhere.*"[36] The deep link between communal membership and musicality is further echoed in James Joyce's famous short story "The Dead," a devastating (and devastatingly beautiful) account of the difference between a lost and found soul and the moment the former transitions to the latter. Here are the final two paragraphs, where a soul is membered and the universe becomes the human world:

> Generous tears filled Gabriel's eyes. He had never felt like that himself towards any woman, but he knew that such a feeling must be love. The tears gathered more thickly in his eyes and in the partial darkness he imagined he saw the form of a young man standing under a dripping tree. Other forms were near. His soul had approached that region where dwell the vast hosts of the dead. He was conscious of, but could not apprehend, their wayward and flickering existence. His own identity was fading out into a grey impalpable world: the solid world itself, which these dead had one time reared and lived in, was dissolving and dwindling.

> A few light taps upon the pane made him turn to the window. It had begun to snow again. He watched sleepily the flakes, silver and dark, falling obliquely against the lamplight. The time had come for him to set out on his journey westward. Yes, the newspapers were right: snow was general all over Ireland. It was falling on every part of the dark central plain, on the treeless hills, falling softly upon the Bog of Allen and, farther westward, softly falling into the dark mutinous Shannon waves. It was falling, too, upon every part of the lonely churchyard on the hill where Michael Furey lay buried. It lay thickly drifted on the crooked crosses and headstones, on the spears of the little gate, on the barren thorns. His soul swooned slowly as he heard the snow falling faintly through the universe and faintly falling, like the descent of their last end, upon all the living and the dead.[37]

Here the snowflakes—an undifferentiated blanket of highly differentiated members, instantiated at the threshold between liquid and solid—enchant the physical world surrounding Gabriel into a living frame of human ancestry, "conditions of possibility for the subject," in the wake of inductive and seductive contact with a fellow human, of falling in love. In this highly musicalized state, erotic life and sexual death interweave in the transcendental paradox of culture, without which life would be a mistake.

Music helps us with life because it is itself always dying. As a tenor voice sings in Benjamin Britten's own meditation on death, a setting of a poem by Tennyson:

> Blow, bugle, blow
> Set the wild echoes flying,
> Bugle blow; answer, echoes
> Dying, dying, dying . . .[38]

Musical sound is ephemeral, which is to say that it is in a state of constant decay; we are always losing it. Each sonic event is always already bound to its disappearance. If "pieces" of music effect an ongoing experience of psychosensory fluctuation, they simultaneously structure an ever-replenishing experience of loss, framing the loss of each musical moment in the inevitable return to silence, mourning this loss through the after-blow (*après-coup*) of musical resonance, resonating through the weave. Like the best psychoanalysis, music reminds us, as Freud intimated in his late paper "Finite and Infinite Analysis," that we have to stop, so that we can go on.[39] It never ends, Winnicott added, because we're never gonna get it, as Phillips put it. But, as Bion believed, we *feel more* because we *know less* at the end than we did at the beginning. We are able to enter different frames that are not fantasies. Because they are actually here.

ACKNOWLEDGMENTS

This book might never have been woven together without guidance and encouragement from Sarah Goldberg, Deborah Melman, Chip Scarborough, Joyce Lindenbaum, Adam Phillips, Ania Wertz, and Hannah Zeavin; our deeply musical editor, Wendy Lochner, who took a chance giving our demo a spin; and the rhythmic support and even-weavened resonance of our friends and loved ones.

NOTES

PREFACE: LINER NOTES

1. Jean Laplanche, *Freud and the Sexual* (New York: International Psychoanalytic Books, 2011), 202.

1. THE BODY'S WAY OF DREAMING

1. Thomas Ogden, "'The Music of What Happens' in Poetry and Psychoanalysis," *International Journal of Psychoanalysis* 80 (1999): 979–94.
2. See, for example, Steven Knoblauch, *The Musical Edge of Therapeutic Dialogue* (New York: Taylor & Francis, 2000); Henry Markman, "Listening to Music, Listening to Patients: Aesthetic Experience in Analytic Practice," *Fort Da* 12 (2006): 18–29; Riccardo Lombardi, "Time, Music, and Reverie," *Journal of the American Psychoanalytic Association* 56 (2008): 1191–211; Dianne Elise, "Moving from Within the Maternal: The Choreography of Analytic Eroticism," *Journal of the American Psychoanalytic Association* 65 (2017): 33–60; and Stephen Purcell, "Psychic Song and Dance: Dissociation and Duets in the Analysis of Trauma," *Psychoanalytic Quarterly* 88 (2019): 315–47.
3. We use the idiomatic "psyche-somatic" throughout the text to retain the connection to Winnicott's notion of "psyche-soma" as a form of experiential continuity (as opposed to "psychosomatic," which is generally used to describe a symptom).
4. See José Bleger, "Psycho-Analysis of the Psycho-Analytic Frame," *International Journal of Psychoanalysis* 48 (1967): 514.
5. See Walter Benjamin, "The Work of Art in the Age of Mechanical Reproduction" (1936), in *Illuminations: Essays and Reflections* (Boston: Mariner, 172).

6. Theodor Adorno, "On the Fetish-Character in Music and the Regression of Listening" (1938), in *Essays on Music* (Berkeley: University of California Press, 2002), 306–7.
7. Jacques Lacan, *The Four Fundamental Concepts of Psycho-Analysis* (New York: Norton, 1981), 176; Friedrich Nietzsche, *Daybreak* (Cambridge: Cambridge University Press, 1997), 143.
8. Henry Markman, "Accompaniment in Jazz and Psychoanalysis," *Psychoanalytic Dialogues* 30 (2020): 432–47.
9. See André Green, "The Construction of Heterochrony," in *Time and Memory*, ed. R. J. Perelberg (London: Karnac, 2007), 1–21.

2. THE RHYTHM OF THE HEAT

1. Sigmund Freud, "On Beginning the Treatment (Further Recommendations on the Technique of Psycho-Analysis I)" (1913), in *The Standard Edition of the Complete Psychological Works of Sigmund Freud*, ed. James Strachey et al. (London: Hogarth, 1955), 12:135. Hereafter *SE*.
2. Adam Phillips, *Side Effects* (New York: HarperCollins, 2009).
3. Jacques Derrida, "Introduction: Desistance" (1989), in *Typography: Mimesis, Philosophy, Politics* (Stanford, CA: Stanford University Press, 1998), 3.
4. Nicolas Abraham, *Rhythms: On the Work, Translation, and Psychoanalysis* (Stanford, CA: Stanford University Press, 1995), 21.
5. Sigmund Freud, *Three Essays on the Theory of Sexuality* (1905), *SE* 7:123–246; Sigmund Freud, "Obsessive Actions and Religious Practices" (1907), *SE* 9:115–28; Sigmund Freud, *Beyond the Pleasure Principle* (1920), *SE* 18:1–6; Sigmund Freud, "The Economic Problem of Masochism" (1924), *SE* 19:155–70.
6. Abraham, *Rhythms*, 22.
7. Abraham, *Rhythms*, 70–71.
8. Theodor Adorno, "On the Fetish-Character in Music and the Regression of Listening" (1938), in *Essays on Music* (Berkeley: University of California Press, 2002), 288.
9. Abraham, *Rhythms*, 22.
10. In *The Letters of Virginia Woolf: 1923–1928* (London: Harcourt Brace Jovanovich, 1977), 247.
11. Donald Winnicott, "The Theory of the Parent-Infant Relationship," *International Journal of Psychoanalysis* 41 (1960): 586.
12. César Botella and Sára Botella, *The Work of Psychic Figurability: Mental States Without Representation* (London: Brunner-Routledge, 2005).
13. Michel de M'Uzan, "Slaves of Quantity," *Psychoanalytic Quarterly* 72 (2003): 711–25; For "disintegration products," see Heinz Kohut, "Introspection, Empathy, and the Semi-Circle of Mental Health," *International Journal of Psychoanalysis* 63 (1982): 403.
14. For pairs and couples, see Harold Boris, *Envy* (London: Aronson, 1994).
15. Didier Anzieu, ed., *Psychic Envelopes* (London: Karnac, 1990), 226.
16. Anzieu, ed., *Psychic Envelopes*, 227.
17. Freud, "The Economic Problem of Masochism," 231.

18. Freud, *Three Essays on the Theory of Sexuality*, 201–2.
19. "And so the marriage between this patient and himself has never really been consummated." Wilfred Bion, *Clinical Seminars and Other Works* (London: Routledge, 1987), 163.
20. Harold N. Boris, *Passions of the Mind: Unheard Melodies, the Third Principle of Mental Functioning* (New York: New York University Press, 1993), 18.
21. Frances Tustin, *Autistic Barriers in Neurotic Patients* (New Haven, CT: Yale University Press, 1997), chap. 15.
22. Abraham, *Rhythms*, 71.
23. Abraham, *Rhythms*, 71–72.
24. Abraham, *Rhythms*, 72.
25. Winnicott, "Mind and Its Relation to Psyche-Soma" (1949), in *Through Paediatrics to Psycho-analysis* (London: Hogarth, 1975), 246.
26. Abraham, *Rhythms*, 22–3.
27. Sigmund Freud, "Psychical (or Mental) Treatment" (1890), *SE* 7:298.
28. Maurice Merleau-Ponty, *The Visible and the Invisible: Followed by Working Notes* (Evanston, IL: Northwestern University Press, 1968), 115.
29. Jessica Wiskus, *The Rhythm of Thought: Art, Literature, and Music After Merleau-Ponty* (Chicago: University of Chicago Press, 2013), 37.
30. Abraham, *Rhythms*, 22–23.
31. Abraham, *Rhythms*, 75.
32. Mikkel Borch-Jacobsen, *The Freudian Subject*, trans. Catherine Porter (Stanford, CA: Stanford University Press, 1988), 230.
33. Freud, "Obsessive Actions and Religious Practices," 118.
34. Byung-Chul Han, *The Scent of Time: A Philosophical Essay on the Art of Lingering* (London: Wiley, 2017), 32.
35. Sigmund Freud, "'Civilized' Sexual Morality and Modern Nervous Illness" (1908), *SE* 9:187.
36. Freud, "'Civilized' Sexual Morality and Modern Nervous Illness," 188.
37. Freud, "'Civilized' Sexual Morality and Modern Nervous Illness," 198. Italics in original.
38. As cited in Willy Baranger, "Spiral Process and the Dynamic Field" (1979), in Madeline Baranger and Willy Baranger, *The Work of Confluence: Listening and Interpreting in the Psychoanalytic Field* (London: Taylor & Francis, 2019), 45–62.
39. Richard Sterba, "Psychoanalysis and Music," *American Imago* 22 (1965): 104.
40. Sterba, "Psychoanalysis and Music," 104.
41. Jacques Lacan, "On a Question Prior to Any Possible Treatment of Psychosis" (1956), in *Écrits: The First Complete Edition in English*, trans. Bruce Fink (New York: Norton, 2006), 25; Michel de M'Uzan, "The Same and the Identical," *Psychoanalytic Quarterly* 76:1205–20.

3. MIND WAVES

1. Mikkel Borch-Jacobsen, *The Freudian Subject*, trans. Catherine Porter (Stanford, CA: Stanford University Press, 1988), 137.

2. Borch-Jacobsen, *The Freudian Subject*, 295.
3. Borch-Jacobsen, *The Freudian Subject*, 140.
4. Sigmund Freud, "New Introductory Lectures on Psycho-Analysis" (1933), in *The Standard Edition of the Complete Psychological Works of Sigmund Freud*, ed. James Strachey et al. (London: Hogarth, 1955), 22:140. Hereafter *SE*.
5. Peter Fonagy et al., "Epistemic Petrification and the Restoration of Epistemic Trust: A New Conceptualization of Borderline Personality Disorder and Its Psychosocial Treatment," *Journal of Personality Disorders* 29, no. 5: 575–609.
6. Sigmund Freud, "An Autobiographical Study" (1925), *SE* 20:41. As cited in Mikkel Borch-Jacobsen, "Simulating the Unconscious," *Psychoanalysis and History* 7 (2005): 13.
7. Borch-Jacobsen, *The Freudian Subject*, 149.
8. Borch-Jacobsen, *The Freudian Subject*, 149–51.
9. Borch-Jacobsen, *The Freudian Subject*, 159.
10. Michael Balint, *The Basic Fault* (Evanston, IL: Northwestern University Press, 1979), 75.
11. Thomas Ogden, "On Holding and Containing, Being and Dreaming," *International Journal of Psychoanalysis* 85 (2004): 1350.
12. Mikkel Borch-Jacobsen, "Hypnosis in Psychoanalysis," *Representations* 27 (1989): 101.
13. George Makari, "Soul Machine and the Invention of the Modern Mind," San Francisco Center for Psychoanalysis, Scientific Meeting, April 9, 2018.
14. Jean Laplanche, *Freud and the Sexual* (New York: International Psychoanalytic Books, 2011), 256.
15. Borch-Jacobsen, "Simulating the Unconscious," 13. Italics in original.
16. Gilles Deleuze, *Difference and Repetition* (New York: Columbia University Press, 1994), 1.
17. Robert Fink, *Repeating Ourselves: American Minimal Music as Cultural Practice* (Berkeley: University of California Press, 2005), chap. 1.
18. Erik Wallrup, *Being Musically Attuned* (Burlington, VT: Ashgate, 2016), 1.
19. Mikkel Borch-Jacobsen, "Ecce Ego" (1982), in *The Freudian Subject*, 121.
20. Hans-Georg Gadamer, *Truth and Method* (London: Bloomsbury, 2013).
21. Janine Chasseguet-Smirgel, *The Ego Ideal* (London: Free Association Books, 1985), 77.
22. Donald W. Winnicott, *Playing and Reality* (London: Taylor & Francis, 1971), 142.
23. Byung-Chul Han, *The Scent of Time: A Philosophical Essay on the Art of Lingering* (London: Wiley, 2017), 17.
24. Borch-Jacobsen, "Simulating the Unconscious," 10.
25. Emmanuel Levinas, *Totality and Infinity* (Dordrecht: Kluwer Academic, 1961).
26. Deleuze, *Difference and Repetition*, 57.
27. Deleuze, *Difference and Repetition*, 10.
28. Deleuze's concept of a "dark precursor"—like the trail of a bolt of lightning that darkens before the strike—could be conceived as a version of après-coup; what looks like a precursor is in fact a retroactive construction, a resonance, as opposed to an origin, a virtual positing after the fact.

29. Deleuze, *Difference and Repetition*, 23.
30. Mikkel Borch-Jacobsen, "The Primal Band" (1982), in *The Freudian Subject*, 231.
31. Sigmund Freud, "Totem and Taboo" (1913), SE 13:1–162.
33. Borch-Jacobsen, "Hypnosis in Psychoanalysis," 97.
34. Sigmund Freud, "The Moses of Michelangelo" (1914), SE 13:211.
35. Marion Milner, "The Concentration of the Body" (1960), in *The Suppressed Madness of Sane Men: Forty-Four Years of Exploring Psychoanalysis* (London: Taylor & Francis, 2005).
36. Sigmund Freud, "Some General Remarks on Hysterical Attacks" (1909), SE 9:233.
37. In the key of Laplanche: Hypnosis exploits the channels of passivity to install a command, an intromission, demanding compliance with someone else's idea of how to be; induction suggests, in the mode of implantation, how interesting it might be to listen to and translate one's thoughts, less as commands to obey and more as music to tune into, to liberate more feeling through one another's company, to free association.
38. Philippe Lacoue-Labarthe, "The Echo of the Subject" (1979), in *Typography: Mimesis, Philosophy, Politics* (Stanford, CA: Stanford University Press, 1998), 162.
39. Madeline Baranger and Willy Baranger, *The Work of Confluence: Listening and Interpreting in the Psychoanalytic Field* (London: Taylor & Francis, 2019), 191.
40. For Freud's original formulation, see "Mourning and Melancholia" (1917), SE 14:246. Combining Freud's original formulation with this inversion gives us a way of conceptually linking multiple, overlapping forms of loss: the loss of a world, the loss of a self, the loss of an other upon whom one is dependent (in Winnicott's sense), the loss of another whom one loves, and the loss of another whom we expect to someday tell us, or translate, what they really meant to convey to us (as in Laplanche's model). The question of mourning always rests on the integrity of the wider "weave" to sustain the injury of loss. Embedded in the weave, the bereaved can grieve; the music can continue.
41. For a comprehensive treatise on resonance, see Harmut Rosa, *Resonance* (Cambridge: Polity, 2019).
42. Josef Breuer and Sigmund Freud, *Studies on Hysteria* (1893), SE 2:160.
43. Mikkel Borch-Jacobsen, "Mimetic Efficacy" (1989), in *The Emotional Tie: Psychoanalysis, Mimesis, and Affect* (Stanford, CA: Stanford University Press, 1993), 109.

4. LEARNING TO LIVE TOGETHER

1. Donald W. Winnicott, "Ego Distortion in Terms of True and False Self" (1960), in *The Maturational Processes and the Facilitating Environment: Studies in the Theory of Emotional Development* (New York: International Universities Press, 1965), 141.
2. Erik Wallrup, *Being Musically Attuned* (Burlington, VT: Ashgate, 2016), 16.
3. As cited in Donald W. Winnicott, "Communicating and Not Communicating Leading to a Study of Certain Opposites" (1963), in *The Maturational Processes and the Facilitating Environment*, 179.

4. José Bleger, "Psycho-Analysis of the Psycho-Analytic Frame," *International Journal of Psychoanalysis* 48 (1967): 511.
5. Wallrup, *Being Musically Attuned*, 35.
6. Wallrup, *Being Musically Attuned*, 40.
7. Wallrup, *Being Musically Attuned*, 94.
8. Wallrup, *Being Musically Attuned*, 96.
9. Dominique Scarfone, "Laplanche and Winnicott Meet . . . and Survive," in *Sex and Sexuality: Winnicottian Perspectives* (London: Karnac, 2005), 42.
10. Winnicott, "Communicating and Not Communicating," 183.
11. Winnicott, "Communicating and Not Communicating," 188.
12. Clare Winnicott, "D.W.W.: A Reflection," in Donald W. Winnicott, *Psycho-Analytic Explorations* (Cambridge, MA: Harvard University Press, 1989), 16.
13. Jean Laplanche, *Freud and the Sexual* (New York: International Psychoanalytic Books, 2011), 233.
14. Morgan Neville, dir., "Won't You Be My Neighbor?," Focus Features, 2018.
15. Wallrup, *Being Musically Attuned*, 220.
16. Wallrup, *Being Musically Attuned*, 238.
17. Wallrup, *Being Musically Attuned*, 218.
18. Sigmund Freud, "Delusions and Dreams in Jensen's *Gradiva*" (1907), in *The Standard Edition of the Complete Psychological Works of Sigmund Freud*, ed. James Strachey et al. (London: Hogarth, 1955), 9:90. Hereafter *SE*.
19. Freud, "Delusions and Dreams in Jensen's *Gradiva*," 9:92.
20. Robert Fink, *Repeating Ourselves: American Minimal Music as Cultural Practice* (Berkeley: University of California Press, 2005), 8–9.
21. Theodor Adorno, "The Dialectical Composer" (1934), in *Essays on Music* (Berkeley: University of California Press, 2002), 205.
22. It may be no coincidence that psychoanalysis, which often acts as a barometer for such cultural phenomena, underwent a radical shift toward intersubjectivity, relationality, and its own process attributes, the so-called here-and-now, in the same era that music became more invested in simply sustaining its own continuity.
23. Aaron Copland, *What to Listen for in Music* (New York: New American Library, 2011).
24. Fink, *Repeating Ourselves*, 44–46.
25. Adorno, "The Dialectical Composer," 205.
26. Letter from Freud to Fliess, March 11, 1900, in *The Complete Letters of Sigmund Freud to Wilhelm Fliess, 1887–1904*, trans. Jeffrey Masson (Cambridge, MA: Harvard University Press, 1985), 404.
27. Sigmund Freud, "Some Character-Types Met with in Psycho-Analytic Work" (1916), *SE* 14:312.
28. Thomas Ogden, *The Matrix of the Mind: Object Relations and the Psychoanalytic Dialogue* (Northvale, NJ: Jason Aronson, 1993).
29. Mitchell Wilson, "The Proleptic Unconscious and the Exemplary Moment in Psychoanalysis," *International Journal of Psychoanalysis* 100 (2019): 1084–1101.

30. Jean Laplanche, *Essays on Otherness* (New York: Taylor & Francis, 1999), 109; Sigmund Freud, "The Dynamics of Transference" (1912), *SE* 12:100.
31. The term "glischro-caric" is taken from José Bleger, *Symbiosis and Ambiguity: A Psychoanalytic Study* (New York, Routledge, 2013), 37.
32. Wilfred Bion, "Evidence" (1976), in *Clinical Seminars and Other Works*, ed. Francesca Bion (London: Karnac, 2018), 246.
33. Madeline Baranger and Willy Baranger, *The Work of Confluence: Listening and Interpreting in the Psychoanalytic Field* (London: Taylor & Francis, 2019), 49.
34. Adorno, "The Dialectical Composer," 206.
35. Herman Melville, *Moby-Dick; or, The Whale* (Boston: Harvard University Press, 1892), 422.
36. Adam Phillips, *Promises, Promises: Essays on Literature and Psychoanalysis* (London: Faber, 2000), 205.

5. THE LIVING FRAME

1. Donald W. Winnicott, "Primitive Emotional Development" (1945), in *Through Paediatrics to Psycho-analysis* (London: Hogarth, 1975), 153.
2. Donald Winnicott, "The Theory of the Parent-Infant Relationship," *International Journal of Psychoanalysis* 41 (1960): 592.
3. Donald W. Winnicott, "The Observation of Infants in a Set Situation" (1941), in *Through Paediatrics to Psycho-analysis*, 67.
4. Donald W. Winnicott, "Metapsychological and Clinical Aspects of Regression Within the Psycho-Analytical Set-Up" (1954), in *Through Paediatrics to Psycho-analysis*, 284.
5. Jean Laplanche, *Life and Death in Psychoanalysis* (Baltimore, MD: Johns Hopkins University Press, 1985), 24.
6. Laplanche, *Life and Death in Psychoanalysis*, 30.
7. Jean Laplanche, "Notes on Afterwardsness" (1991), in *Essays on Otherness* (New York: Taylor & Francis, 1999), 265.
8. Donald W. Winnicott, "Aggression in Relation to Emotional Development" (1955), in *Through Paediatrics to Psycho-analysis*, 217.
9. Donald W. Winnicott, "The Location of Cultural Experience" (1967), in *Playing and Reality* (London: Routledge, 2005), 133.
10. Jean Laplanche, "A Short Treatise on the Unconscious" (1991), in *Essays on Otherness*, 92.
11. Jean Laplanche, "Interpretation Between Determinism and Hermeneutics: A Restatement of the Problem" (1991), in *Essays on Otherness*, 164.
12. Donald W. Winnicott, "Communicating and Not Communicating Leading to a Study of Certain Opposites," presented to the San Francisco Psychoanalytic Institute, October 1962.
13. Donald W. Winnicott, "Counter-Transference" (1960), in *The Maturational Processes and the Facilitating Environment: Studies in the Theory of Emotional Development* (New York: International Universities Press, 1965), 161.

14. Winnicott, "Metapsychological and Clinical Aspects," 286. As the psychoanalyst Dominique Scarfone, a former student of Laplanche, writes: "In a given analysis, if the re-opening of the fundamental anthropological situation places the analysand before the analyst's enigma, thus prompting transference, the analyst, according to Laplanche, still offers a 'hollow' for this transference, a holding capacity (*contenance*). . . . In this sense, one could argue that the opening carried out by the instatement and the reinstatement of the analytic situation"—in other words, a rhythm—"presents itself as a philosophy in action, or rather, as the methodically performed actualization of an ethical stance that would be termed psychoanalysis." Dominique Scarfone, *The Unpast* (New York: Unconscious in Translation, 2015), 61.
15. Vivian Chetrit-Vatine, "Primal Seduction, Matricial Space, and Asymmetry in the Psychoanalytic Encounter," *International Journal of Psychoanalysis* 85 (2004): 841–56.
16. Donald W. Winnicott, "From Dependence Towards Independence in the Development of the Individual" (1963), in *The Maturational Processes and the Facilitating Environment*, 91.
17. Donald W. Winnicott, "Primitive Emotional Development" (1945), in *Through Paediatrics to Psycho-analysis*, 150.
18. For *Stimmung*, see Hans Gumbrecht, *Atmosphere, Mood, Stimmung* (Stanford, CA: Stanford University Press, 2012).
19. Mikkel Borch-Jacobsen, "The Primal Band" (1982), in *The Freudian Subject*, trans. Catherine Porter (Stanford, CA: Stanford University Press, 1988), 154.
20. Sigmund Freud, "'Wild' Psycho-Analysis" (1910), in *The Standard Edition of the Complete Psychological Works of Sigmund Freud*, ed. James Strachey et al. (London: Hogarth, 1955), 11:222. Hereafter *SE*.
21. Ignacio Matte Blanco, *The Unconscious as Infinite Sets: An Essay in Bi-logic* (London: Karnac, 1998), chap. 21.
22. Sigmund Freud, "Fragment of an Analysis of a Case of Hysteria" (1905), *SE* 7:80.
23. Theodor Adorno, "The Relationship of Philosophy and Music" (1953), in *Essays on Music* (Berkeley: University of California Press, 2002), 140.
24. Sigmund Freud, *Jokes and Their Relation to the Unconscious* (1905), *SE* 8:170.
25. Freud, *Three Essays on the Theory of Sexuality* (1905), *SE* 7:144, credited Ferenczi for associating homo- and Eros with the term "homo-erotism."
26. Donald Meltzer and Meg Williams, *The Apprehension of Beauty: The Role of Aesthetic Conflict in Development, Art, and Violence* (Manila: Phoenix, 2018).
27. René Girard, *Violence and the Sacred* (Oxford: Athlone, 1995).
28. Sandor Ferenczi, "The Nosology of Male Homosexuality" (1911), in *Sex in Psychoanalysis* (New York: Basic Books, 1916), 315.
29. Huovinen continues: "[Though] the formal content may in some ways be ambiguous or open . . . aesthetic understanding has an objectivity that is grounded in the correspondence between the formal content of the music and what the listener understands. . . . Such correspondence implies that musical understanding, on this perceptual level, is not merely subjective but intersubjective." Erkki Huovinen, "Understanding Music," in *The Routledge Companion to Philosophy and Music* (London: Taylor & Francis, 2011).

30. Charles Taylor, *Sources of the Self* (Cambridge: Cambridge University Press, 1989), 34.
31. Taylor, *Sources of the Self*, 31.
32. Dominique Scarfone, "The Time Before Us," *Psychoanalytic Dialogues* 26 (2016): 519.
33. As Marcuse conceived it in *Eros and Civilization* (Boston: Beacon, 1968), 168–69, primary narcissism "operates at a scope well beyond autoeroticism; it engulfs the 'environment,' integrating the narcissistic ego with the objective world. . . . In other words, narcissism may contain the germ of a different reality principle: the libidinal cathexis of the ego (one's own body) may become the source and reservoir for a new libidinal cathexis of the objective world—transforming this world into a new mode of being."
34. Sigmund Freud, *Beyond the Pleasure Principle* (1920), *SE* 18:58.
35. Ruth Stein, "The Poignant, the Excessive, and the Enigmatic in Sexuality," *International Journal of Psychoanalysis* 79 (1990): 253.
36. Jean Laplanche, "Kent Seminar," in *Seduction, Translation, Drives: A Dossier*, ed. John Fletcher (London: Institute of Contemporary Arts, 1992), 24.
37. Jean-Luc Nancy, "The Creation of the World" (2002), in *The Creation of the World or Globalization*, SUNY Series in Contemporary French Thought (New York: SUNY Press, 2007), 42–43.

6. RE-MEMBERING, RE-BEATING, AND WORLDING-THROUGH

1. Donald W. Winnicott, "Communicating and Not Communicating Leading to a Study of Certain Opposites" (1963), in *The Maturational Processes and the Facilitating Environment: Studies in the Theory of Emotional Development* (New York: International Universities Press, 1965), 187–88.
2. These may be closer to what Freud originally called "auto-erotic" objects in the *Three Essays*, where he repeatedly made note of the "rhythmic" quality of autoerotic and infantile sexual behavior.
3. Peter Sloterdijk, "Where Are We When We Hear Music?" (2014), in *The Aesthetic Imperative: Writings on Art* (London: Polity, 2018), 29.
4. Plato, "Phaedo," in *The Final Days of Socrates: Euthyphro, Apology, Crito, and Phaedo*, trans. Benjamin Jowett (New York: Cosimo, 2011), 72.
5. Josef Breuer and Sigmund Freud, *Studies on Hysteria* (1893), in *The Standard Edition of the Complete Psychological Works of Sigmund Freud*, ed. James Strachey et al. (London: Hogarth, 1955), 2:49. Hereafter *SE*.
6. Erik Wallrup, *Being Musically Attuned* (Burlington, VT: Ashgate, 2016), 203–4.
7. Sloterdijk, "Where Are We When We Hear Music?," 28.
8. Wallrup, *Being Musically Attuned*, 103.
9. Sloterdijk, "Where Are We When We Hear Music?," 31.
10. Byung-Chul Han, *The Scent of Time: A Philosophical Essay on the Art of Lingering* (London: Wiley, 2017), 48.
11. Wallrup, *Being Musically Attuned*, 105.

12. Donald W. Winnicott, "On the Contribution of Direct Child Observation to Psycho-Analysis" (1957), in *The Maturational Processes and the Facilitating Environment*, 113.
13. Sandor Ferenczi, "Child-Analysis in the Analysis of Adults," *International Journal of Psychoanalysis* 12 (1931): 475.
14. John Ruskin, "The Crown of Wild Olive, Lecture 2" (1866), in *The Crown of Wild Olive* (New York: H. M. Caldwell, 1894), 45.
15. Dominique Scarfone, *The Unpast* (New York: Unconscious in Translation, 2015), 34.
16. Letter from Freud to Fliess, January 24, 1897, in *The Complete Letters of Sigmund Freud to Wilhelm Fliess, 1887–1904*, trans. Jeffrey Masson (Cambridge, MA: Harvard University Press, 1985), 226.
17. John Fletcher, *Freud and the Scene of Trauma* (New York: Fordham, 2013), 240.
18. Freud and Breuer, *Studies on Hysteria*, 2:91.
19. Sloterdijk, "Where Are We When We Hear Music?," 29.
20. Hannah Arendt, *The Origins of Totalitarianism* (San Diego: Harcourt Brace, 1951), 150–51.
21. Bret Stephens, "Khashoggi's Killing Isn't a Blunder. It's a Crime," *New York Times*, October 18, 2018.
22. "Sondheim Teaches 'My Friends' from *Sweeney Todd*," YouTube video, https://www.youtube.com/watch?v=DBCVaFqGJwg.
23. Toni Morrison, *The Bluest Eye* (New York: Knopf, 1970), 159.
24. Sloterdijk, "Where Are We When We Hear Music?," 44.
25. Jamal Khashoggi, "What the Arab World Needs Most Is Free Expression," *Washington Post*, October 17, 2018.
26. Sloterdijk, "Where Are We When We Hear Music?," 34.
27. Sloterdijk, "Where Are We When We Hear Music?," 37.
28. Sigmund Freud, "Five Lectures on Psycho-analysis" (1910), *SE* 11:41.
29. Sloterdijk, "Where Are We When We Hear Music?," 38.
30. Vivian Chetrit-Vatine, "Questioning the Paternal Function in Light of Contemporary Parenthood: The Feminine-Maternal Origin of Ethics," San Francisco Center for Psychoanalysis, October 22, 2018.
31. Ferenczi, "Child Analysis in the Analysis of Adults," 475.
32. In the original encounter between infant and parent, in the pure emergence of the infant's impact, that which Chetrit-Vatine calls the "enormity" of the infant's existence is shocking (as in, traumatizing) to the parent; it breaks the ordinary continuity of thinking and demands a realignment. (Winnicott called this "primary maternal preoccupation.") The adult's ways of living in time, for conducting one's sexual drive, are disrupted and diminished at precisely the moment of greatest need, of maximal physical contact and dependence with the most forbidden of sexual others, one's own child. But the reiteration, the repetition, of this shocking encounter makes it eligible for a kind of rhythmizing, calling forth (or interpellating) the musical capacities of the parent to integrate these disruptive shocks into the rhythms of time and *hexis* in a principled music, in a sane way. As the infant's meaning-making inclination is hyperactivated by the sexual unconscious of the parent, the parent's ethical, music-making

inclinations are correspondingly what feel like the cacophony of the as-yet-unwoven infant. They induce each other, just as the analyst imagines the patient as a human being—the human that the patient was insufficiently humanized into being—and treats the patient accordingly, interpellating the patient into becoming the person that they never knew they never were (to riff on Christopher Bollas's term, an unthought, unknown, human being). If, for Chetrit-Vatine, psychopathology is the result of not having been ethically parented, psychoanalytic work hinges upon the musicality of the analyst to provide this animating ethos, to ethicize (or ethos-ize) sexuality itself. The good-enough parent has to be creative enough in their use of the weave to respond to the infant not only as a caregiver but as an artist.

33. Sigmund Freud, "Notes Upon a Case of Obsessional Neurosis" (1909), *SE* 10:166.
34. For anthropotechnics, see Peter Sloterdijk, introduction to *You Must Change Your Life*, trans. Wieland Hoban (Cambridge: Polity, 2019), 1–18.

7. STRANGE LOOP

1. Sigmund Freud, *Jokes and Their Relation to the Unconscious* (1905), in *The Standard Edition of the Complete Psychological Works of Sigmund Freud*, ed. James Strachey et al. (London: Hogarth, 1955), 5:143–44. Hereafter *SE*.
2. Freud, *Jokes and Their Relation to the Unconscious*, 156.
3. Mikkel Borch-Jacobsen, *The Emotional Tie: Psychoanalysis, Mimesis, and Affect* (Stanford, CA: Stanford University Press, 1993), 21.
4. Adam Phillips, *Missing Out: In Praise of the Unlived Life* (New York: Farrar, Straus and Giroux, 2012), 58.
5. Charles Rosen, *The Romantic Generation* (Cambridge, MA: Harvard University Press), 103.
6. As cited in Rosen, *The Romantic Generation*, 101.
7. Rosen, *The Romantic Generation*, 101.
8. Rosen, *The Romantic Generation*, 103.
9. Walter Benjamin, "The Work of Art in the Age of Mechanical Reproduction" (1936), in *Illuminations: Essays and Reflections* (Boston: Mariner, 2019), 185.
10. Michael Parsons, "Psychic Reality, Negation, and the Analytic Setting," in *The Dove That Returns, The Dove That Vanishes: Paradox and Creativity in Psychoanalysis* (London: Routledge, 2000), chap. 10.
11. Michel de M'Uzan, "The Same and the Identical," *Psychoanalytic Quarterly* 76:1205–20.
12. Robert Fink, *Repeating Ourselves: American Minimal Music as Cultural Practice* (Berkeley and Los Angeles: University of California Press, 2005), 66–67.
13. Sigmund Freud, "On Narcissism: An Introduction" (1914), *SE* 14:67–102.
14. Freud, *Jokes and Their Relation to the Unconscious*, 160–61.
15. Donald W. Winnicott, "The Psyche-Soma and the Mind" (1954), in *Human Nature* (London: Free Association Books, 1988), 11.

16. Dominique Scarfone, *The Unpast* (New York: Unconscious in Translation, 2015), 140. Freud addresses this point most explicitly in most explicitly in *Beyond the Pleasure Principle* (1920), *SE* 18:1–64; "A Note Upon the 'Mystic Writing-Pad'" (1925), *SE* 19:225–32; and "Negation" (1925), *SE* 19:233–40.
17. Donald W. Winnicott, "From Dependence Towards Independence in the Development of the Individual" (1963), in *The Maturational Processes and the Facilitating Environment: Studies in the Theory of Emotional Development* (New York: International Universities Press, 1965), 91.
18. Winnicott, "From Dependence Towards Independence, 91.
19. Thomas Ogden, "Ontological Psychoanalysis or 'What Do You Want to Be When You Grow Up?,'" *Psychoanalytic Quarterly* 88 (2019): 661–84.
20. Thomas Ogden, "The Analytic Third: Working with Intersubjective Clinical Facts," *International Journal of Psychoanalysis* 75 (1994): 3–19.
21. Adam Phillips, *On Flirtation* (Cambridge, MA: Harvard University Press, 1994), xi.
22. Jean Laplanche, *Essays on Otherness* (New York: Taylor & Francis, 1999), 107.
23. Clifford Geertz, *The Interpretation of Cultures* (New York: Basic Books, 1973), 49.
24. Geertz, *The Interpretation of Cultures*, 49.
25. Herman Melville, *Moby-Dick; or, The Whale* (Boston: Harvard University Press, 1892), 216.
26. Erik Wallrup, *Being Musically Attuned* (Burlington, VT: Ashgate, 2016), 195.
27. Rosen, *The Romantic Generation*, 8–9.
28. Phillips, *Missing Out*, xi.

8. THIS IS HOW WE DO IT

1. Pierre Bourdieu, *Outline of a Theory of Practice* (Cambridge: Cambridge University Press, 1977).
2. Bourdieu, *Outline of a Theory of Practice*, 87.
3. Didier Anzieu, *The Skin Ego* (New Haven, CT: Yale University Press, 1989), 105.
4. Harold Searles, "Concerning the Development of an Identity," *Psychoanalytic Review* 53 (1966): 7–30.
5. Ludwig Wittgenstein, *On Certainty* (Oxford: Blackwell, 1969), 21.
6. Bourdieu's notion of habitus as the substratum of all subsequent habits makes it easy to see why Bion was always associating "O" with God and mysticism, as those are the traditional ways that humans have tried to think and talk about this dimension. Our concept of a common, unifying force coursing throughout the communal body was severely injured by the "death of god" and rise of scientism and the subsequent "disenchantment of the world" that Weber spoke of and Freud enthusiastically pursued; Bion, a genius of the unwoven (having been blitzed out of the weave during the First World War), fully grasped the loss and danger and was reaching for a way to retrieve its essence.
7. Phillip Boast, "The Musical Body: Instrumental Performance and Bodily Intentionality," academia.edu, 2016, 1.

8. Bruce Chatwin, *The Songlines* (New York: Viking, 1987), 14.
9. Chatwin, *The Songlines*, 13.
10. As Laplanche and Pontalis wrote, identification can be understood as a "constitution of the subject on the model of the other person—a mode not dependent upon any prior establishment of a relationship in which the object can at first lay claim to an autonomous existence. Primary identification is closely bound up with the relation known as oral incorporation." We could conceive of musical identification as a kind of "aural" incorporation, inviting the individual into a shared domain. Jean Laplanche and J.-B. Pontalis, *The Language of Psycho-Analysis*, trans. Donald Nicholson-Smith (New York: Norton, 1973), 336.
11. Mikkel Borch-Jacobsen, *The Emotional Tie: Psychoanalysis, Mimesis, and Affect* (Stanford, CA: Stanford University Press, 1993), 18.
12. Borch-Jacobsen, *The Emotional Tie*, 26.
13. In the later part of his career, Winnicott used the term "cross-identifications" to indicate the ability for people to identify without projecting, a being-in-the-world-together kind of mode. He wrote that "much of our lives is spent interrelating in terms of cross-identification." Donald W. Winnicott, "Interrelating Apart from Instinctual Drive and in Terms of Cross-Identifications," in *Playing and Reality* (London: Routledge, 2005), 185.
14. Chatwin, *The Songlines*, 57.
15. Borch-Jacobsen, *The Emotional Tie*, 45.
16. Theodor Adorno, "On Jazz" (1936), in *Essays on Music* (Berkeley: University of California Press, 2002), 471.
17. Adorno, "On Jazz," 487.
18. Borch-Jacobsen, *The Emotional Tie*, 202.
19. Borch-Jacobsen, *The Emotional Tie*, 218.
20. Marion Milner, "Aspects of Symbolism in Comprehension of the Not-Self," *International Journal of Psychoanalysis* 33 (1952): 101.
21. Philippe Lacoue-Labarthe, "The Echo of the Subject" (1979), in *Typography: Mimesis, Philosophy, Politics* (Stanford, CA: Stanford University Press, 1998), 162.
22. Lacoue-Labarthe, "The Echo of the Subject," 187–88.
23. Theodor Adorno, "§99 Gold assay" (1951), in *Minima Moralia: Reflections from Damaged Life* (London: Verso, 2005), 154.
25. Alex Ross, *The Rest Is Noise* (New York: Farrar, Straus, and Giroux, 2007), 467.
26. Sigmund Freud, "Analysis of a Phobia in a Five-Year-Old Boy" (1909), in *The Standard Edition of the Complete Psychological Works of Sigmund Freud*, ed. James Strachey et al. (London: Hogarth, 1955), 10:42. Hereafter *SE*.
27. Sigmund Freud, "Leonardo da Vinci and a Memory of His Childhood" (1910), *SE* 11:126.
28. Nicholas Spice, "Winnicott and Music" (2001), in *The Elusive Child*, ed. Lesley Caldwell (London: Karnac, 2002), 200–1.
29. Susanne Langer, *Feeling and Form* (London: Routledge, 1953), 110.
30. Erik Wallrup, *Being Musically Attuned* (Burlington, VT: Ashgate, 2016), 217.

31. Wallrup, *Being Musically Attuned*, 218.
32. For Laplanche's distinction between psychotherapy and psychoanalysis, see Jean Laplanche, *Freud and the Sexual* (New York: International Psychoanalytic Books, 2011), chap. 17.

9. THE ART TEACHER

1. Herman Hesse, *The Glass Bead Game (Magister Ludi)* (1943; New York: Picador, 1990), 52–54.
2. Thomas Sheehan, *Making Sense of Heidegger* (London: Rowman & Littlefield, 2015), 21.
3. As cited in Robert Harrison, *Gardens: An Essay on the Human Condition* (Chicago: University of Chicago Press, 2018), 14.
4. Wilfred Bion, *Elements of Psycho-Analysis* (Bath: Pitman, 1963), 23.
5. For Strachey's review of Freud on birth and anxiety, see Sigmund Freud, "Introductory Lectures on Psycho-Analysis" (1916), in *The Standard Edition of the Complete Psychological Works of Sigmund Freud*, ed. James Strachey et al. (London: Hogarth, 1955), 15:397n2. Hereafter *SE*. For Bion's discussion, see Wilfred Bion, "Caesura," in *Two Papers: The Grid and Caesura* (London: Karnac, 1989).
6. Leo Bersani, *Is the Rectum a Grave? and Other Essays* (Chicago: University of Chicago, 2010), 44.
7. Alfred Gell, *The Art of Anthropology* (London: Routledge, 1999), 243.
8. For co-immunity, see Peter Sloterdijk, *You Must Change Your Life*, trans. Wieland Hoban (Cambridge: Polity, 2019), 450–52.
9. "'I Am Not A Man, I Am Dynamite': Peter Sloterdijk on Friedrich Nietzsche," *Entitled Opinions* (podcast), with Robert Harrison, Stanford University, December 15, 2016.
10. Adam Phillips, *Promises, Promises: Essays on Literature and Psychoanalysis* (London: Faber, 2000), 176.
11. Hesse, *The Glass Bead Game*, 54–55.
12. Wilfred Bion, "The Psycho-Analytic Study of Thinking," *International Journal of Psychoanalysis* 43 (1962): 306.
13. Duncan Cartwright, *Containing States of Mind: Exploring Bion's "Container Model" in Psychoanalytic Psychotherapy* (London: Routledge, 2010), chap. 8; Bion, *Elements of Psycho-Analysis*, 40.
14. Sigmund Freud, "A Note Upon the 'Mystic Writing-Pad,'" *SE* 19:231.
15. Giuseppe Civitarese, "Masochism and Its Rhythm," *Journal of the American Psychoanalytic Association* 64 (2016): 896.
16. Roland Barthes, *A Lover's Discourse: Fragments*, trans. Richard Howard (New York: Farrar, Straus & Giroux, 1977), 16.
17. Donald Meltzer, *Dream Life: A Re-Examination of the Psychoanalytical Theory and Technique* (Manila: Phoenix, 1984), 165.
18. Byung-Chul Han, *The Scent of Time: A Philosophical Essay on the Art of Lingering* (London: Wiley, 2017), 36.

19. NPR, "Jeremy Denk: György Ligeti's Piano Etudes," *In Practice*, YouTube video, https://www.youtube.com/watch?v=MThqIWwzL78.
20. Arnold Davidson, *The Emergence of Sexuality: Historical Epistemology and the Formation of Concepts* (Cambridge, MA: Harvard University Press, 2001), 91.
21. Douglas Dunn, "Winging It," *New Yorker*, December 10, 2018.
22. Harrison, *Gardens*, 77.
23. See Wilfred Bion, "The Grid," in *Two Papers: The Grid and Caesura* (London: Karnac, 1989), 2.
24. Adam Phillips, "On Being Bored," in *On Kissing, Tickling, and Being Bored* (Cambridge, MA: Harvard University Press, 1993), 69; Donald W. Winnicott, "Communicating and Not Communicating Leading to a Study of Certain Opposites" (1963), in *The Maturational Processes and the Facilitating Environment: Studies in the Theory of Emotional Development* (New York: International Universities Press, 1965), 186.
25. Richard Almond, "On Background Assumptions in Psychoanalysis: The Continuing Pursuit for Common Ground," San Francisco Center for Psychoanalysis, Scientific Meeting, January 14, 2019; Thomas Kuhn, *The Structure of Scientific Revolutions* (Chicago: University of Chicago Press, 2012), 62.
26. Peter Sloterdijk, "Where Are We When We Hear Music?" (2014), in *The Aesthetic Imperative: Writings on Art* (London: Polity, 2018), 44.
27. Hesse, *The Glass Bead Game*, 55–56.
28. Harrison, *Gardens*, 65.
29. Cited in Harrison, *Gardens*, 65.
30. Maurice Merleau-Ponty, *The Visible and the Invisible: Followed by Working Notes* (Evanston, IL: Northwestern University Press, 1968), 267.
31. Maurice Merleau-Ponty, "The Concept of Nature," in *Themes from the Lectures at the Collège de France, 1952–1960* (Evanston, IL: Northwestern University Press, 1970), 65–66.
32. Jean Grondin, *The Philosophy of Gadamer* (Ithaca, NY: McGill-Queen's University Press, 2003), 39.
33. Sloterdijk, *You Must Change Your Life*, 198.
34. Mary Schoen-Nazzaro, "Plato and Aristotle and the Ends of Music," *Laval Théologique et Philosophique* 34, no. 3 (1978): 261.
35. Adam Phillips, *Missing Out: In Praise of the Unlived Life* (New York: Farrar, Straus and Giroux, 2012), 63.
36. Sigmund Freud, "Project for a Scientific Psychology" (1895), *SE* 1:298–302; Donald W. Winnicott, "The Baby as a Going Concern" (1949), in *The Child, the Family, and the Outside World* (Harmondsworth: Penguin, 1964); Bion, *Learning From Experience*, 23–25.
37. Dominique Scarfone, "A Matter of Time: Actual Time and the Production of the Past," *Psychoanalytic Quarterly* 75 (2006): 827.
38. Freud may have unwittingly acknowledged this process in reverse when, on only a handful of occasions, he referred to a "complemental series" through which development oscillates between the forces of "sexual constitution" and the limits of culture, forming compromises or "symptoms"—as opposed to resonating between points of

shared contact with the weave of humanity and the traumatic enigmas that constitute the sexual.

39. Bion, *Elements of Psycho-Analysis*, 85.
40. At the end of his book *New Foundations for Psychoanalysis* (New York: Unconscious in Translation, 2017), Laplanche acknowledged that the psychoanalytic process itself has a spiral form; Scarfone picks this image up and applies it to Laplanche himself, whom he once described as "an astronomer of Freudian psychoanalysis—an astronomer rather than a Freudologist, an historian or archaeologist of Freudianism." He explains: "Laplanche's telescope is therefore pointed at Freud's texts with a view to refract them—if I may extend the metaphor—through the prism of the very method developed by Freud. Such refraction disperses the whole of Freud's theorizations, which are then re-clustered around sketched nodal points, only to be dispersed once again. Returning again and again to the same theorization, each time in a different context, at a different level, this approach takes the form of a spiral—or rather a helix—to borrow the image often used by Laplanche to account for the modality of his exploration of psychoanalytic theory." Dominique Scarfone, *Laplanche: An Introduction* (New York: Unconscious in Translation, 2015), 3–4.
41. Dave Hickey, *The Invisible Dragon: Essays on Beauty* (Chicago: University of Chicago, 1993), 118.
42. Theodor Adorno, "On the Problem of Music Analysis" (1969), in *Essays on Music* (Berkeley: University of California Press, 2002), 162–80.
43. Mitchell Wilson, "The Proleptic Unconscious and the Exemplary Moment in Psychoanalysis," *International Journal of Psychoanalysis* 100 (2019): 1084–1101.
44. As cited in Sheehan, *Making Sense of Heidegger*, 170.
45. Maurice Merleau-Ponty, *Phenomenology of Perception* (London: Routledge, 1962), x.
46. See Francis Grier, "Musicality in the Consulting Room," *International Journal of Psychoanalysis* 100:827–51.
47. Wilson, "The Proleptic Unconscious and the Exemplary Moment in Psychoanalysis."
48. "'Heidegger's Being and Time—Thomas Sheehan," *Entitled Opinions* (podcast), with Robert Harrison, Stanford University, May 18, 2010.
49. "[The] personal influence is our most powerful dynamic weapon. It is the new element which we introduce into the situation and by means of which we make it fluid." Sigmund Freud, "The Question of Lay Analysis" (1926), *SE* 20:224.

10. OLD FOUNDATIONS IN PSYCHOANALYSIS

1. *The Late Late Show with James Corden*, "Paul McCartney Carpool Karaoke," YouTube video, https://www.youtube.com/watch?v=QjvzCTqkBDQ.
2. As cited in Adam Loften and Emmanuel Vaughan-Lee, "Sanctuaries of Silence," *New York Times*, March 27, 2018.
3. Sigmund Freud, "Civilization and Its Discontents" (1930), in *The Standard Edition of the Complete Psychological Works of Sigmund Freud*, ed. James Strachey et al. (London: Hogarth, 1955), 21:64. Hereafter *SE*.

4. Ignacio Matte Blanco, *The Unconscious as Infinite Sets: An Essay in Bi-logic* (London: Karnac, 1998).
5. Byung-Chul Han, *The Scent of Time: A Philosophical Essay on the Art of Lingering* (London: Wiley, 2017), chap. 4.
6. William Shakespeare, *Richard II* (1595), in *The Oxford Shakespeare: Richard II* (Oxford: Oxford University Press, 2011), 277.
7. Christopher Bollas, *The Shadow of the Object* (New York: Columbia University Press, 1987), 263.
8. Jacques Lacan, "The Subversion of the Subject and the Dialectic of Desire in the Freudian Unconscious" (1960), in *Écrits: The First Complete Edition in English*, trans. Bruce Fink (New York: Norton, 2006), 678.
9. Peter Sloterdijk, "Where Are We When We Hear Music?" (2014), in *The Aesthetic Imperative: Writings on Art* (London: Polity, 2018), 45.
10. Theodor Reik, "In the Beginning Is Silence" (1948), in *Listening with the Third Ear: The Inner Experience of a Psychoanalyst* (New York: Farrar, Straus and Giroux, 1983), 122.
11. Sigmund Freud, "The Economic Problem of Masochism" (1924), *SE* 19:160.
12. Harold Searles, "Unconscious Processes in Relation to the Environmental Crisis" (1972), in *Countertransference and Related Subjects* (New York: International Universities Press, 1979), 366.
13. Robert Harrison, *The Dominion of the Dead* (Chicago: University of Chicago Press, 2010), 57.
14. Julia Kristeva, *Revolution in Poetic Language* (New York: Columbia University Press, 1974), chap. 2.
15. Julia Kristeva, *Black Sun: Depression and Melancholia* (New York: Columbia University Press, 1989), 5.
16. Sigmund Freud, "Mourning and Melancholia" (1917), *SE* 14:237–58; Sigmund Freud "On Transience" (1916), *SE* 14:303–7.
17. Freud, "Mourning and Melancholia," 246.
18. Robert Harrison, *Gardens: An Essay on the Human Condition* (Chicago: University of Chicago Press, 2018), 6–7.
19. Harrison, *Gardens*, 33.
20. Harrison, *Gardens*, 39.
21. As seen in Tao Ruspoli, *Being in the World* [documentary] (Mangusta Films, 2010). Original quote in John Haugeland, "Understanding Natural Language," *Journal of Philosophy* 76, no. 11 (1979): 619.
22. Harrison, *Gardens*, 125.
23. Sigmund Freud, "Recommendations to Physicians Practising Psycho-Analysis" (1912), *SE* 12:115.
24. Peter Sloterdijk, "Exercises and Misexercises" (2009), in *You Must Change Your Life*, trans. Wieland Hoban (Cambridge: Polity, 2019), 407.
25. Antonino Ferro, *Seeds of Illness, Seeds of Recovery: The Genesis of Suffering and the Role of Psychoanalysis* (London: Brunner-Routledge, 2005), 16–17.
26. J.-B. Pontalis, "Dream as an Object," *International Review of Psychoanalysis* 1 (1974): 127. We can see that the very dimension of shared experience that is more or less

absent (though possibly implicit) in Laplanche's writing (not to mention Heidegger's) appears emphatically—"something in common to analyse, in a sensorial exchange"—loud and clear from his most well-known collaborator.

27. Harrison, *Gardens*, 43.
28. Pontalis, "Dream as an Object," 129.
29. Duncan Cartwright, *Containing States of Mind: Exploring Bion's "Container Model" in Psychoanalytic Psychotherapy* (London: Routledge, 2010), 120.
30. Philippe Lacoue-Labarthe, *Typography: Mimesis, Philosophy, Politics* (Stanford, CA: Stanford University Press, 1998), 194.
31. Lacoue-Labarthe, *Typography*, 195.
32. Sigmund Freud, "The Uncanny" (1919), *SE* 17:234.
33. Freud, "The Uncanny," 235.
34. Friedrich Nietzsche, *Twilight of the Idols*, trans. Duncan Large (Oxford: Oxford University Press, 2008), 9.
35. See Anne Alvarez, *Live Company: Psychoanalytic Psychotherapy with Autistic, Borderline, Deprived, and Abused Children* (London: Routledge, 1992), chap. 5.
36. Jonathan Lear, *Radical Hope: Ethics in the Face of Cultural Devastation* (Cambridge, MA: Harvard University Press, 2009), 3.
37. James Joyce, "The Dead" (1914), in *Dubliners* (New York: Penguin, 2014), 193–94.
38. Alfred Tennyson, "Blow Bugle Blow," in *Poems* (Boston: Fields, Osgood & Company, 1842), 222.
39. Here we are retranslating the title of Sigmund Freud, "Analysis Terminable and Interminable" (1937), *SE* 23:239–54.

INDEX

aboriginal Australians, 202
Abraham, Nicolas, 42, 64; on rhythm, 29–31, 44–46, 47
absence, 155, 162, 229; Freud on, 81–82, 148–149
abstinence, 249
accompaniment, 91
actuality, 239
Adams, John, 35
Adorno, Theodor, 14–15, 31, 106, 109, 113, 244–245; on jazz, 204; on music, 128
advertising, 185
aesthetics, xiii
African Americans. *See* Black music
Ahnlehnung, 38
aliveness, 9, 12, 14, 48, 52, 60, 151–152. *See also* psyche-soma; continuity of, 86; embeddedness and, 97
Almond, Richard, 232
alpha-elements, Bion on, 4–5
alpha function, 25, 35, 113, 123
Also Sprach Zarathustra (Strauss), 242
altered states, 23–25, 87. *See also* dissociation
alter world, 239–240
Alvarez, Anne, 266

analytic third: interpretation and, 190–191; Ogden describing, 190–191
ancient Greeks: education, 234; ethos and, xiii–xiv; on music, xiii–xiv
anomie, 134
anthropotechnics, 170
Anzieu, Didier, 15, 128; on repetition, 34; skin ego described by, 200–201
après-coup, 109, 114, 119, 129, 150, 221; rhythm of, 52–53; temporal and spatial dimensions transcended by, 100
Arendt, Hannah, 158, 221
art, Freud on, 80–81
Art of Anthropology, The (Gell), 223
associational effects, 7–8
attachment, 60
attunement. *See also* distunement; *Stimmung*: conditions for, 100–101; embodiment linked to, 10, 92; membership via, 96–97; psychoanalytic theory on, 69; *Stimmung* as requirement for, 100; via music, 68–69, 110–111; Wallrup on, 68, 90, 100, 111, 149
authoritarianism, 150
Autobiographical Study, An (Freud), 80

autocracy, 264
auto-eroticism, 281n2
auto-hypnosis, 65
avant-garde music, 16

Bach, Johann Sebastian, 91, 92, 96
Bacon, Francis, xiv
bad faith, 74; repetition in, 75–76
Baldwin, James, 252
Balint, Michael, 63
Baranger, Madeline, 112–113
Baranger, Willy, 112–113
Barthes, Roland, 228–229
Bataille, George, 135
beat-function, of infants, 29–30
beats: of beta function, 26; monotony of, 44–45
beauty, 244
Beethoven, Ludwig van, 178, 181
behaving, 47, 123
Being and Time (Heidegger), 245
being-in-oneself, 147
being-in-the-world, 8, 12, 17; rhythm of, 227–228; sampling for forming, 188
Being Musically Attuned (Wallrup), 68
Benjamin, Walter, 13; on magician and surgeon, 183–184
Bersani, Leo, 223
Bertgang, 105
Besetzung, 85. *See also* cathexis
beta-elements: Bion on, 4–5; of music, 210–211
beta function, 4–5, 21, 25, 260; beats of, 26; development of, 34; of frame, 53–54; going-on-being of, 113; mimesis and, 247; world-building through, 31
beta screen, 238, 241
Beyoncé, 182, 211
Beyond the Pleasure Principle (Freud), 126, 135–136, 158, 229
Bildung, 71, 246
binaural hearing, 129

Bion, Wilfred, 7, 39, 61, 64, 139, 200, 221, 269; on beta-elements and alpha-elements, 4–5; on catastrophic change, 82, 84; container/contained theory of, 75, 227; on dreaming, 191–192; on dream-work, 29, 113; on dream-work-alpha, 29; on the Grid, 30, 241; on identification, 112; ontological perspective of, 190; on thinking, 243–244
birth, 221
bisexuality, 176
Björk, 200
Black music, 106, 183
Blanco, Ignacio Matte, 127
Bleger, Jose, 9, 39, 90–91, 257
Blige, Mary J., 106
"Blood on the Leaves" (West), 183
blue note, 163, 167, 171, 231
blues music, 163
Bluest Eye, The (Morrison), 163
Boast, Phillip, 201–202
body, the: actual, 239–240; the mind and, 8–9, 22–23; musicality of, 8; music and, 5; in ontological perspective, 245; rhythm related to, 30; speaking, 4; the unconscious incorporated by, 73–74; Wallrup on centrality of, 151–152
body language, 12–13
body time, 25–26
Boethius, xi
Bollas, Christopher, 154, 256
Borch-Jacobsen, Mikkel, 47, 59, 74, 80, 126; on hypnosis, 61–64, 66–67; on identification, 203–206; on mimesis, 204; on pleasure, 173–174; on primordial crowd, 57; on subject formation, 77–78; on wish fulfillment, 203–204
boredom, 224; Heidegger on, 232
Boris, Harold, 33, 40–41
Botella, César, 32, 52, 129
Botella, Sára, 32, 52, 129
Boulez, Pierre, 106

Bourdieu, Pierre, xvi, 144, 169–170, 284n6; on subjectivity, 198–199
Bowlby, John, 60
breakdown, 32
Breuer, Josef, 69, 80, 86
Britten, Benjamin, 268
Bush, George W., 182
buzz, 229

caesura, 150, 221, 256
Cage, John, 209, 251
care and care giving, 89, 93, 132; ethos of, 221; temporality of, 261–262; Winnicott on, 191–192
Cartwright, Duncan, 227, 264
catastrophic change, 82, 84
catharsis, 80, 176–177
cathexis, 85
Chasseguet-Smirgel, Janine, 71
Chatwin, Bruce, 202–203, 204
Chetrit-Vatine, Vivian, 123, 168; on infancy, 282n32
circumcision, 201
Civilization and Its Discontents (Freud), 253–254
Civitarese, Giuseppe, 228
clinical psychoanalysis, 131–132; ethos of, 232; hypnosis in, 64; induction in, 70; interaction patterns in, 20; music in, 17–20; as rhythmic, 49
co-immunity, 224
College Dropout, The (West), 182
colonization, conduction and, 207
comedy. *See also* jokes: seduction as, 176
commemoration, 162
common ground, 94
communal dreaming, 175, 235
communication, 144; cul-de-sac, 145; subjects merging in, 59; Winnicott on, 93–95, 145–146
communion, 203
community, 59

conduction and conductors, 36, 39, 54, 74, 81, 121, 168; analysts as, 20; colonization and, 207; the frame as, 125; Freud on, 237–238; good-enough, 249; of habitus, 199–200; Laplanche on, 138; rhythms of, 51–52; of sexuality, 138
consciousness, rhythmizing, 31, 33, 42, 45–46, 50
constructions, 154; of Freud, 179
contact-barrier, 31–32, 41, 114, 237–238; the weave establishing, 189
container/contained theory, 75, 227
Containing States of Mind (Cartwright), 227, 264
continuo, 205, 206, 209
convictions, 225
Copland, Aaron, 107
Corden, James, 251
couch, as frame, 221, 224
countertransference, 18, 42, 206–207; Meltzer on, 229
counting off, 143
couple, 40–41
Creation of the World, The (Nancy), 138
creativity, 124; the unconscious and, 104
cross-identifications, 285n13
cul-de-sac communication, 145
culture, 156, 207, 234–235; Ferro on, 262; Geertz on, 192; humanity lost by devolution of, 72–73; human nature and, 192; of living frame, 262–263; macroculture vs. microculture, 262; sampling in popular, 182; in the weave, 192–193, 234–235
Cunningham, Merce, 230
cure, 215–216, 261; Freud on process of, 102–104

dark precursor, 276n28
Darstellung, 21
Dasein, 248; Heidegger on, 137; Sloterdijk on, 257

Davidson, Arnold, 230
"Dead, The" (Joyce), 267
death drive, 54, 160–161, 171, 188, 228
dedifferentiation, 23
deferred action, 25
Deleuze, Gilles, 67, 75, 77, 162, 276n28
"Delusion and Dream in Jensen's *Gradiva*" (Freud), 101–105
democracy, 232
Denk, Jeremy, 230
Derrida, Jacques, on rhythm, 28
Descartes, Rene, xiv, xv
desire, 180–181; mimesis generating, 204
deuten, Deutung, 121, 223
"Dialectical Composer, The" (Adorno), 106–107
difference, 75–76
Difference and Repetition (Deleuze), 75
differentiation, 57
digital compression, 255
disclosure, 116, 168
Disclosure (musical act), 106, 109
disco, 68, 105–106, 108
disenchantment, 69; distunement distinguished from, 215–216
dismembering, 69, 144, 159, 171; antidotes to, 162
dissociation, xvii, 16, 20–21, 69, 147, 160–161, 215; mechanism of, 22; mind and body in, 22; trauma and, 22–23
dissociative detachment, 22
distunement, 100–101; disenchantment distinguished from, 215–216; Wallrup on, 215
Dominion of the Dead, The (Harrison), 258
double, the, 129; Freud on, 265–266
dreams: Bion on, 191–192; communal, 175, 235; dream states, 8; jokes contrasted with, 174–175, 187, 189, 191; presentation of, 263; as sampling, 186–187
dream-work, 24, 76, 123; Bion on, 29, 113; Freud on, 78–79, 104–105, 186; jokes work compared with, 174–175

dream-work-alpha, 113, 166; Bion on, 29; parents in, 191–192
drive. *See* sexual drive
"Drive My Car" (The Beatles), 251
drumming, 43–44, 143
-duction, 79. *See also* conduction and conductors; induction; reduction; seduction
duetting, 52, 245
Durkheim, Émile, 134
dwelling, 163

"Ecce Ego" (Borch-Jacobsen), 71
echolocation, 229
education, ancient Greek, 234
ego, 39–40, 71–72, 174
ego ideal, 54, 71–72; defining, 185; identification in, 206; vulnerability to trauma, 185–186
Ego Ideal, The (Chasseguet-Smirgel), 71
Eigen, Michael, 60
Einstimmigkeit, 100–101
elaboration, 133
Ellington, Duke, 208
embeddedness: aliveness and, 97; patterning of, 97; in the weave, 97, 160
embodiment, xvi, 4–5, 157; attunement linked to, 10, 92; dimensions of experience of, 238–239; erotics of shared, 222; language of, 8–9; live embodied interaction, 16–17; music and, 13–14; rhythm and, 30–31; via the weave, 201–202
emotional storms, 100
emotions, musicality and, 10–11
enchantment, 68, 70, 85. *See also* disenchantment; human nature as, 213; remembering and, 160
enigma, 98, 103–104, 115, 130–131, 188, 239; guarding, 249; Laplanche on, 248
Enlightenment, the: ethos in, xiii–xiv; human nature conceptions in, xiv–xv; psychoanalytic theory influenced by, xvi

Enlightenment Now (Pinker), xv
ensoulment, 147, 157
Entitled Opinions, 224–225
envy, 196
"Epiphany" (Sondheim), 160
epistemic trust, 60, 72–73
epistemological perspective, 190
eros, 125, 135; of syncretics, 228
Eros and Civilization (Marcuse), 281n33
eroticism, 167, 221; auto-eroticism, 281n2; of shared embodiment, 222
ethics: of analyst, 169; of the frame, 130, 132; of listening, 223–224; of parenting, 169–170
ethos, 70, 94, 226; ancient Greeks and, xiii–xiv; of care, 221; in the Enlightenment, xiii–xiv; as force of human nature, 198; of rhythm, 47; of slowness, 250; of the weave, xviii–xix
ethos, of clinical psychoanalysis, 232
evenly-suspended attention: Laplanche on, 96; even-weavened (gleichschwebende), 96, 124
experiential time, 25, 26

false self, 139
Fanon, Frantz, 235
Ferenczi, Sandor, 56, 132, 155, 169, 262
fermata, 256
ferne geliebte, 193
Ferro, Antonino, 123; on culture, 262
Fink, Robert, 27, 67, 105–107, 209; on repetition, 185
flamenco music, 32
Fletcher, John, 157
Fonagy, Peter, 60, 72–73
fort-da, 30, 43, 158, 258
4'33" (Cage), 254
Fragment of a Case of Hysteria (Freud), 176
fragments, 178–179
frame, the, 90–91, 95–96, 114. *See also* living frame; beta function of, 53–54; breaches in, 134; as conductor, 125; couch as, 221;

224; death of, 267; ethics of, 130, 132; going-on-being transmitted through, 112; as holding environment, 196; as love, 125–126; metaframing, 111; as metonym for habitus, 199–200; musicality of, 25; as recessional activity, 249–250, 263; rhythm of, 40–42, 115, 224–225; sexuality and, 39–40, 125; shared psychosensoriality of, 39–40; temporality of, 24–25, 55–56
Frankenstein (Shelley), xvii
free association, 24, 56, 62, 66–67, 149, 254; difficulties of, 27–28; Freud on, 27, 95–96, 167
frequency, 35–36
Freud, Sigmund, xvii–xviii, 28–29, 64, 69, 157; on absence, 81–82, 148–149; on art, 80–81; on conduction and conductors, 237–238; constructions of, 179; on cure process, 102–104; on the double, 265–266; on dream-work, 78–79, 104–105, 186; fears of, 27–28; on free association, 27, 95–96, 167; fundamental rule of, 27–28, 39–40, 61, 170, 230; handshakes of, 199, 203, 221; on helplessness, 82, 88–89; on hypnosis, 45, 56–57, 58–61; on interpretation, 191; on jokes, 128–129, 172–176, 196–197; on libido, 136; on loss, 277n40; on love, 101–102, 110, 125–126; on mourning, 259–260; on music, 6, 80–81; on narcissism, 185–186; on oceanic feeling, 253–254; on perception, 228; on pleasure, 257–258; on rapport, 61; on remembering, 178–179; on repetition, 48; on resistances, 35–36; on rhythm, 29–30; on seduction, 83; on sexuality, 36–38, 51, 101–102, 127, 135–138, 166, 167; taboos focused on, 237; on trance, 65; transference theorized by, 65–66; on the unconscious, 79–80, 121; in United States, 167
Freud and the Sexual (Laplanche), 66
Freudian Subject, The (Borch-Jacobsen), 47, 57
friendship, 240–241
fugue, 60

fundamental anthropological situation, 38–39, 116, 121, 124, 212; Laplanche describing, 62–63
fundamental rule, 27–28, 39–40, 61, 170, 230
futural, 111

Gabriel, Peter, 209, 210
Gadamer, Hans-Georg, 71, 236
Galileo, xiv, xv
gardens, habitus forming, 261–263
Geertz, Clifford, xvi; on culture and human nature, 192
gefügig, 60
Gell, Alfred, 223–224
Genet, Jean, 226–227
Ghent, Emmanuel, 58–59
Girard, René, 132, 203
Glass Bead Game, The (Hesse), 217–219, 233–234
going-on-being, xix, 105, 117–118, 176; of beta function, 113; disruption of, 157; the frame transmitting, 112; human nature and, 219; Winnicott on, 30
González, Francisco, 154, 250
Green, André, 25, 129, 252
Grid, the (Bion), 30, 241
grief, 115, 193, 258–259. *See also* mourning
Grodin, Jean, 236
groove, xix, 43, 150; disruption of, 195; as hypnotic, 67; the weave and, 195
Group Psychology (Freud), 126
Gumbrecht, Hans Ulrich, 90

habitus, xvi, 54, 135, 144, 198, 243; conduction of, 199–200; the frame as metonym for, 199–200; gardens formed by, 262
hallucinations, 235
Han, Byung-Chul, xvi, 50–51, 55, 72, 152, 229, 254
handshakes, 199, 203, 221
harmonics. *See* overtone series

Harrison, Robert, xvi, 222, 224–225, 231, 254–255, 260–262
Haugeland, John, 261
hearing, 15–16
Heidegger, Martin, xvi, 52, 125, 219, 226, 227, 245, 264; on boredom, 232; on *Dasein*, 137; temporalities defined by, 111; Wallrup on, 91; on worlds, 165
helplessness, 62–63; Freud on, 82, 88–89; transformation of, 212
Hempton, Gordon, 253
Hendrix, Jimi, 10, 220
Hesse, Hermann, 217–219, 233–234
heterochrony, 25, 53
heterosexuality, 129–130, 231
hexis, 31, 169–170, 198–199, 243
Hickey, Dave, 244
High Fidelity (Hornby), 177
Hilflosigkeit, 50, 88, 92. *See also* helplessness
hip-hop, 35, 182
holding environment, 42–43, 144; the frame as, 196; of Winnicott, 117–118, 124–125
Holiday, Billie, 183
homoeroticism, 129–130, 167–168, 231
hooks, defining, 209–210
Hornby, Nick, 177
house (music), 105–106
humanization, 219–221; scale, 241–244
human nature and human being: culture and, 192; development of, 219–220; as enchantment, 213; the Enlightenment and notions of, xiv–xv; ethos as force of, 198; Geertz on, 192; going-on-being and, 219; humans as subjects, xiv; metaphysics of, xvi; as palimpsest, 201
Hume, David, 88
humor, 180. *See also* jokes
Humoreske (Schumann), 195
Huovinen, Erkki, 132, 280n29
Hurricane Katrina, 182
hypnosis, xvi; Borch-Jacobsen on, 61–64, 66–67; in clinical psychoanalysis, 64; Freud on, 45, 56–57, 58–61; induction in,

56–57; as magic, 184; psychoanalysis breaking from, 57–58, 61–62, 64, 67; transference of, 66
"Hypnosis in Psychoanalysis" (Borch-Jacobsen), 64
hysteria, xvii, 48

identical, the, the same and, 185
identification, 30, 50; asymptote of, 54; Bion on, 112; Borch-Jacobsen on, 203–206; cross-identifications, 285n13; in ego ideal, 206; erotics of, 222; as homeopathy, 222; Laplanche on, 285n10; Oedipus complex and, 206; with parents, 222–223; Pontalis on, 285n10; primary, 285n10
idiom, 239
improvisation, 18–19, 162, 225; the weave and, 230
induction, 20–21, 39, 87, 162, 168, 267; in clinical psychoanalysis, 70; in hypnosis, 56–57; in interpretation, 122; mutuality of, 247–248; into psyche-soma, 89–90; seduction and, 153; into the weave, 233–234
infants, 33; beat-function of, 29–30; Chetrit-Vatine on, 282n32; development of, 219–221; sexuality of, 83, 99, 127–128, 129–130, 138; Winnicott on development of, 188–189
information, digitization of, 72
innovation, 16
inspiration, 174, 226, 243
Instagram, 188
institutions, 131–132
interpretation, 18, 66; analytic third and, 190–191; Freud on, 191; induction in, 122; as inspiration, 123; as interventions, 193–194
Interpretation of Dreams, The (Freud), 86, 104; *Jokes and Their Relation to the Unconscious* compared with, 174–175
interventions, 193–194
intromission, 160, 248
Invisible Dragon, The (Hickey), 244

jazz, 18–19; Adorno on, 204; syncopation in, 204
jokes, 159, 179; dreams contrasted with, 174–175, 187, 189, 191; Freud on, 128–129, 172–176, 196–197; longing and, 195; Oedipus complex as, 180; Phillips on, 176; the unconscious and, 174–175; in the weave, 189
Jokes and Their Relation to the Unconscious (Freud), 173; *Interpretation of Dreams* compared with, 174–175
jokes work, dream-work compared with, 174–175
Joyce, James, 267
Jung, Carl, 58, 209; on libido, 136

Kaddish, 258
Keats, John, 90
Khashoggi, Jamal, 158, 161, 164
Kleinians, 19, 63, 69, 99, 120
knowledge, 234
Kristeva, Julia, 259
Kubrick, Stanley, 242
Kuhn, Thomas, 232
Kundera, Milan, 55

Lacan, Jacques, 15, 19, 50, 152, 252–253, 256
Lacoue-Labarthe, Philippe, 83–84, 265; on music, 207–208
Langer, Susanne, 214
language, temporality and, 226
Laplanche, Jean, xvi, xviii, 77–78, 85, 115, 228, 238, 239; on conduction, 138; on enigma, 248; evenly-suspended attention, 96; fundamental anthropological situation described by, 62–63; on identification, 285n10; on psychotherapy, 215–216; on refusals of analyst, 250; Scarfone and, 288n40; on seduction, 135, 176; on sexuality, 37–38, 49–50, 78, 83, 119, 125, 130, 135, 139, 167; on state of nature, 65–66; on subjectivity, 77–78; on time, 52; on transference, 109, 280n14; on

Laplanche, Jean (*continued*)
    translation, 109, 113; on unintelligibility of unconscious, 98–99; Winnicott contrasted with, 92–94
"Latch" (Disclosure), 106
laughter, 187–188
leading-back, 249
legato, 78
lessons, 234
Levinas, Emmanuel, 75
liberal democracy, 232
libido, Freud and Jung on, 136
Ligeti, Gyorgi, 210, 254–255
light rock, 14
listening, 7–8, 12–13; ethic of, 223–224; perception as, 207
Listening with the Third Ear (Reik), 257
living frame, xvii, 46, 116; culture of, 262–263; defining, 121; sexuality in, 130
Locke, John, xiv
logos, 227
longing: jokes and, 195; in music, 209
loss, Freud on, 277n40
lost objects, 259
love, 105; the frame as, 125–126; Freud on, 101–102, 110, 125–126; rhythm of, 228–229
Lover's Discourse (Barthes), 228–229
"Love to Love You" (Summer), 68
Lux Aeterna (Ligeti), 254
lynching, 183

madness, Winnicott defining, 82
magicians, 183–184
Makari, George, 65
Marcuse, Herbert, 281n33
Markman, Henry, 18–19
"Masochism and Its Rhythm" (Civitarese), 228
mass bond, 59–60, 66
matricial function, 168
Matte-Blanco, Ignacio, 254
McCartney, Paul, 251–252
melancholia, 193

Meltzer, Donald, 130; on countertransference, 229
Melville, Herman, 114, 193, 243
membership, 143, 239; scars of, 201; sexuality linked to, 167; via attunement, 96–97
memory. *See also* remembering: music and, 177
Merleau-Ponty, Maurice, xvi, 45–46, 50, 116, 165, 201–202, 224, 253; on perception, 246–247; on psychoanalysis of nature, 235–236
metaphor, 20
metaphysics, of human nature, xvi
Mill, John Stuart, 83, 232
Milner, Marion, xvi, 11, 81, 124, 206
mimesis, 30; beta function and, 247; Borch-Jacobsen on, 204; desire generated via, 204; perception and, 33
mind, the: the body and, 8–9, 22–23; Winnicott on, 77
mind, theory of, 238–239
mind objects, Winnicott on, 44
minimalism, 67, 105
Minima Moralia (Adorno), 208
mirror stage, Wallrup on, 152–153
Moby-Dick (Melville), 114, 193
momentum, 229–230
Morrison, Toni, 90, 163
"Moses of Michelangelo, The" (Freud), 80–81
mourning, 86, 258; Freud on, 259–260; melancholia contrasted from, 193
"Mourning and Melancholia" (Freud), 158, 258, 259
music. *See specific topics*: Adorno on, 128; ancient Greeks on, xiii–xiv; attunement via, 68–69, 110–111; beta-elements of, 210–211; Black music, 106, 183; the body and, 5; at center of human existence, xii; in clinical psychoanalysis, 17–20; colloquial definitions of, 6; commoditization of, 15; defining, xi; development of subjectivity and, 153; embodiment and, 13–14; formative role of,

4–6; Freud on, 6, 80–81; Lacoue-Labarthe on, 207–208; longing in, 209; memory and, 177; presentational dimension of, 6; psyche-soma accessed via, 11–12, 150; psychic function of, 7–8; psychoanalytic description of, 9–10; quotation in, 181; referentiality in, 181–182; repetition transmitting, 106–107; as shared language, 11–13; shared perception as, 132; Sloterdijk on, 150–152; Socrates on, 146–147; soul linked to, xiii; subjective objects and, 151; symbolic function of, 9–10; temporality of, 26; unresolved states in, 208–209; Wallrup on, 149–151; as the weave, 188–189; Winnicott and, 213–214
"Musical Body, The" (Boast), 201–202
musicality: of the body, 8; defining, 6–7; emotions and, 10–11; of the frame, 25; individual and shared, 11–13
musicalization, xi–xii
Music for Eighteen Musicians (Reich), 209
Muzak, 14, 150
M'Uzan, Michel de, 54, 185
"My Friends" (Sondheim), 159, 162

Nancy, Jean-Luc, 138
narcissism, 281n33; Freud on, 185–186; primary vs. secondary, 185–186
narrative, 187, 239
natality, 221
nature, psychoanalysis of, 235
Nebenmenschen, 169
neurochemistry, 235
neurosis, 48
New Introductory Lectures (Freud), 59
Newton, Isaac, xiv
Nietzsche, Friedrich, xi, 15, 68, 81, 91–92, 194, 195, 266
noise, rhythmizing, 255
non-communication, 94–95
non-process, 39, 90–91, 257
"Note Upon the 'Mystic Writing-Pad,' A" (Freud), 228

object-relating, 93–94
"Observations on Transference-Love" (Freud), 65
obsession, 48
"Obsessive Actions and Religious Practices" (Freud), 48
oceanic feeling, Freud on, 253–254
Oedipus complex, 86, 177; identification and, 206; as joke, 180
Ogden, Thomas, xvi, 64, 69–70, 100, 111; analytic third described by, 190–191
oneiric function, 24
"On Jazz" (Adorno), 204
"On Liberty" (Mill), 232
"On Narcissism" (Freud), 185
"On Psychical (or Mental) Treatment" (Freud), 58
ontological perspective, 190; the body in, 245
"On Transience" (Freud), 259
ordinary unhappiness, 65–66, 181
Orr, Gregory, 88
overstimulation, 23, 36–37, 48, 115; as trauma, 15–16
overtone series, 245; as developmental model, 241–242

pair, 40–41
parents and parenting. *See also* infants: in dream-work-alpha, 191–192; ethics of, 169–170; identification with, 222–223; sexuality of, 119
Parsons, Michael, 184
pathological organization, 19
Pcpt.-Cs., 228
"Penny Lane" (Beatles), 251–252
perception, xiii, 24. *See also* shared perception; Freud on, 228; as hallucination, 235; as listening, 207; Merleau-Ponty on, 246–247; mimetic core of, 33; phenomenology of, 116; of rhythm, 30–34, 47–48, 228; sampling and, 35
perceptual apprenticeship, 223

Phaedo (Plato), 147
Phantasie in C Major (Schumann), 178–179
phenomenology, 166, 224, 245; of perception, 116
Phenomenology of Perception (Merleau-Ponty), 224, 246–247
Phillips, Adam, xvi, xviii, 82–83, 115, 191, 224, 225, 269; on jokes, 176; on patient-analyst relationship, 40; on side effects of psychoanalysis, 28; on wish fulfillment, 196
Philosophy of Gadamer, The, 236
phronesis, 243
Pichon-Rivière, Enrique, 53, 60
Pinker, Steven, xv
Plato, 234
"Plato and Aristotle and the Ends of Music" (Schoen-Nazarro), 236
playfulness: attunement and, 194; Wallrup on, 194
pleasure: Borch-Jacobsen on, 173–174; defining, 257; Freud on, 257–258
Plenty-Coups, 267
Pontalis, 263; on identification, 285n10
popular culture, sampling in, 182
popular music, 16
post-traumatic syndrome, 130
presentational dimension: of music, 6; representational dimension and, 3–4, 8, 17
primary narcissism, 185–186
primordial crowd, 57, 78
privation, 110
process music, 209
"Project" (Freud), 237–238
Prometheanism, xvii
psyche-soma, xviii, 7, 17, 108, 152, 214, 239, 259. *See also* embodiment; defining, 273n3; induction into, 89–90; music as portal to, 11–12, 150; rhythmizing, 138; sexuality as response to seduction, 243–244; Winnicott on, 8
Psychic Envelopes (Anzieu), 34
psychoanalysis. *See also* clinical psychoanalysis; *specific topics*: break from hypnosis, 57–58, 61–62, 64, 67; of nature, 235; as rebirth, 221; relational turn in, 278n22; in unintegrated state, 232–233
psychoanalytic theory: on attunement, 69; Enlightenment influence on, xvi
psychosensory communication, 18–19
psychosexuality, 127, 131, 135
psychosyncretics, 21, 25
psychotherapy, 156, 255; Laplanche on, 215–216
Purcell, Stephen, 52, 162, 245

Queen, 92
quotation, in music, 181

radar, 229
Radiohead, 92
rapport, 58–60, 79; Freud on, 61
Ratliff, Ben, 151
reality TV, 211
rebirth, psychoanalysis as, 221
recessional spaces, 224
recombinant teleologies, 105–107
recording devices, 4
record stores, 177
reduction, 249
Reich, Steve, 35, 73, 209
Reik, Theodor, 204, 207, 257
relationality, 17
"Relationship of Philosophy and Music, The" (Adorno), 128
reliability, 94
religion, 43
remembering, 144, 162–163, 247–248; enchantment and, 160; Freud on, 178–179; sampling as, 196
reminiscence, 178, 266
Repeating Ourselves (Fink), 67
repetition, 29; Anzier on, 34–35; in bad faith, 75–76; callisthenic properties of, 185; compulsion, 105, 112, 113, 247; Fink on, 185; Freud on, 48; music transmitted through, 106–107; psyche-soma attached to, 30–31;

rhythm and, 38–39, 54, 161, 188; of trauma, 215–216; the unconscious relationship to, 113
representational dimension, 49, 50; presentational dimension and, 3–4, 8, 17
repressed, return of, 24
repression, 38, 74; of unconscious, 99–100
reservedness, 100, 101
resistances, Freud on, 35–36
resonance, 100, 153; of the weave, 85
Rest Is Noise, The (Ross), 210
reverie, 190
rhythm: Abraham on, 29–31, 44–46, 47; of *après-coup*, 52–53; of being-in-the-world, 227–228; the body and, 30; of clinical psychoanalysis, 49; of conduction, 51–52; Derrida on, 28; in development of sexuality, 38–39; embodiment and, 30–31; ethos of, 47; of the frame, 40–42, 115, 224–225; Freud on, 29–30; of noise, 255; perception of, 30–33, 47–48, 228; repetition and, 38–39, 54, 161, 188; rhythmizing of consciousness, 31, 33, 42, 45–46, 50; of sexuality, 37–38, 50–53; subjectivity developed via, 36; suspension of, 43, 45–46
"Rhythm of the Heat" (Gabriel), 209
Rhythms (Abraham), 29
Ricoeur, Paul, 187
ritardando, 56
rituals, 23, 28–29, 156, 258–259
Rodgers, Nile, 73
Rogers, Fred, 97, 110, 163
Rolland, Romain, 235
Romantic Generation, The (Rosen), 179
Romantic movement, xvi, xvii, 181–182
romantic paradox, 195
rope, 226–227
Rosen, Charles, 178–179, 180, 181; on Schumann, R., 195
Ross, Alex, 210
Rousillon, René, 129
Rousseau, Jean-Jacques, 65
Ruskin, John, 155–156, 166

same, the, the identical and, 185
sample-work, 194
sampling, 152; being-in-the-world formed through, 188; dreams as, 186–187; as magic, 184; perception and, 35; in popular culture, 182; as remembering, 196; in shared perception, 191; as translation, 188; West use of, 182–183
"San Jacinto" (Gabriel), 211
Sartre, Jean Paul, 76
satisfaction, 36–37
scansion, 28
Scarfone, Dominique, 93, 133, 188, 239–240; Laplanche and, 288n40; on transference, 280n14
Schlegel, Friedrich, 179
Schoenberg, Arnold, 106–107
Schoen-Nazaro, Mary, 236
Schubert, Franz, 91, 92
Schumann, Clara, 177–179
Schumann, Robert, 91, 177–179; breakdown of, 194; Rosen on, 195
Scientific Revolution, xiv
Searles, Harold, 206, 258
secondary narcissism, 185–186
seduction, 38–39, 79, 119, 168, 220; as comedy, 176; Freud on, 83; good-enough, 249; induction and, 153; Laplanche on, 135, 176; mutuality of, 248; sexuality as psyche-soma response to, 243–244; Winnicott on, 120
self-holding, 49
self-knowledge, 170
sensory commons. *See* shared perception
sensory envelopes, 15
serialism, 106, 185
sexual drive, 160, 243, 282n32; "blues scale" and, 164; diphasic onset" of, 119; embodied experience and, 239; Laplanche and, 37, 85; *narrative*, 187; *pulsión* and, 51; reservedness and, 101; "suffering" the, 115

sexuality. *See also specific topics*: bisexuality, 176; conduction of, 138; as flight, 212–213; the frame and, 39–40, 125; Freud on, 36–38, 51, 101–102, 127, 135–138, 166, 167; of infants, 83, 99, 127–128, 129–130, 138; Laplanche on, 37–38, 49–50, 78, 83, 119, 125, 130, 135, 139, 167; in living frame, 130; membership linked to, 167; organization of, 166; of parent, 119; as psyche-soma response to seduction, 243–244; rhythm in development of, 38–39; rhythm of, 37–38, 50–53; as style, 231–232; temporalization of, 50; as translating, 109, 191; trauma inherent to, 139, 164; the weave in, 129–130
sexual theories, 166
Shadow of the Object, The (Bollas), 256
Shakespeare, William, 255
shared perception, 12–14, 32–33; frame as embodiment of, 39–40; as music, 132; sampling in, 191
Sheehan, Thomas, 219, 227, 228, 249
Shelley, Mary, xvii
silence, 253, 263–265; of the weave, 254–256
Simone, Nina, 183
singing, 5
siren stage, 152–153
skin ego, 15; Anzieu describing, 200–201
Sloterdijk, Peter, xvi, 76, 146–147, 157, 164–166, 170, 224; on *dasein*, 257; on music, 150–152
slowness, 55
Smith, Sam, 106
sociality, 149
social trauma, 237
Socrates, 170, 255; on music, 146–147
solipsism, 235
"Some Character-Types Met with in Psycho-Analytic Work" (Freud), 110
Sondheim, Stephen, 160
sonorism, 210
sonorous *cogito*, 221
sostenuto, 215

the soul, music linked to, xiii
Sources of the Self (Taylor), 132
Spice, Nicholas, 213
spirals, 53, 137, 226, 288n40
statelessness, 158, 232
Stegner, Wallace, 263
Stein, Ruth, 136–137
Steiner, George, 123
Steiner, John, 65
Sterba, Richard, 53
Stimmung, 90, 92, 96, 111–112, 116, 126, 149, 196; as requirement for attunement, 100
stimulus barrier, 159–160
Strachey, James, 60, 121, 126, 173, 253
"Strange Fruit" (Holiday), 183
Strauss, Richard, 242
streaming media, 211
Studies on Hysteria (Freud), 86–87
suavitas, 231
subjective objects, 146; music and, 151
subjectivity, 82, 93, 146; Borch-Jacobsen on development of subject, 77–78; Bourdieu on, 198–199; Laplanche on, 77–78; music and development of, 153; rhythm and development of, 36; as secondary to being, 236; suspension of time and, 214–215
sublimation, 48
suggestion, 45
Summer, Donna, 68
superego, 71–72, 110, 185
surgeons, 183–184
surveillance, 211
Sweeney Todd (Sondheim), 159
Swift, Taylor, 182
symbiosis, 9
symbolic functions, of music, 9–10
symptoms, 157
syncopation, 43; in jazz, 204
syncretism, 9, 133; *eros* of, 228

taboos, Freud focusing on, 237
Taylor, Charles, xvi, 132–133, 202
techno (music), 105–106

telepathy, 59
temporality, 23, 249; of care, 261–262; of frame, 24–25, 55–56; Heidegger identifying categories of, 111; language and, 226; of music, 26; of sexuality, 50
Tennyson, 268
theory of mind, 238–239
therapon, 156
theta function, 260
thinking, Bion on, 243–244
Three Essays on the Theory of Sexuality (Freud), 29–30, 36–37, 129, 176, 281n2
thrown-openness, 219, 227
timbre, 210, 231
time. *See also* temporality: body time, 25–26; Laplanche on, 52; subjectivity and suspension of, 214–215
Totem and Taboo (Freud), 78
totems, 237
tragedy, 81, 164, 176–177
trains, 27–29
trance (music), 43, 105, 108–109
trance (state), Freud on, 65
transference, 17–18, 24, 51, 63; Freud theorizing, 65–66; full, 109; hollowed-out, 109; of hypnosis, 66; Laplanche on, 109, 280n14; Scarfone on, 280n14
transference-love, 40, 63
transitional objects, 222–223
translation, 19, 37, 49, 54; failure of, 99; Laplanche on, 109, 113; as political act, 164; sampling as, 188; sexuality and, 109, 191; of the weave, 231–232
trauma, xvii, 69, 130; defining, 157, 164; from dissociative responses, 22–23; ego ideal vulnerability to, 185–186; intergenerational, 78; overstimulation as, 15–16; repetition of, 215–216; sexuality and inherence of, 139, 164; social, 237; Winnicott on, 32, 33–34
Trevarthen, Colwyn, 68–69, 74
Trump, Donald, 62
truth, 236

Truth and Method (Gadamer), 71
Tustin, Frances, 42
2001 (Kubrick), 242

Umeda tribe, 223–224
unbinding, 82
uncanny, the, 128–129, 265–266
unconscious, the, 18, 24–25, 57–58; the body incorporating, 73–74; creativity and, 104; Freud on, 79–80, 121; jokes and, 174–175; Laplanche on unintelligibility of, 98–99; repetition relationship to, 113; repression of, 99–100; speaking, 207
"Understanding Music" (Huovinen), 132
undifferentiation, 91, 238
unintegration, 232
unmembering, 143–144, 149, 152
unrepresented states, 3
unwovenness, 82

vínculo, 60, 63
Vuong, Ocean, 79

waking-dreaming, 24
Wallrup, Erik, 91; on attunement, 68, 90, 100, 111, 149; on centrality of the body, 151–152; on distunement, 215; on Heidegger, 91; on mirror stage, 152–153; on music, 149–151; on playfulness, 194
weave, the, xii, xvi, 39, 114–115, 240–241; beauty of, 244; contact-barrier established by, 189; culture in, 192–193, 234–235; embeddedness in, 97, 160; embodiment via, 201–202; enchantment via, 261; ethos of, xviii–xix; groove and, 195; improvisation and, 230; induction into, 233–234; jokes in, 189; manifestation of, 134; music as, 188–189; resonance of, 85; in sexuality, 129–130; silence of, 254–256; tearing of, 160–161; translation of, 231–232
Weber, Max, 69

West, Kanye, 193–194; sampling used by, 182–183
What to Listen for in Music (Copland), 107
"Where Are We When We Hear Music?" (Sloterdijk), 146
"'Wild' Psychoanalysis" (Freud), 126–127
Wilson, Mitchell, 111, 245, 248
Winnicott, Donald, xvi, xviii, xix, 5, 21, 42, 61, 139, 177, 190, 212; on care giving, 191–192; on communication, 93–95, 145–146; creative living described by, 23–24; on cross-identifications, 285n13; on going concerns, 238; on going-on-being, 30; holding environment of, 117–118, 124–125; on id, 85–86; on infant development, 188–189; Laplanche contrasted with, 92–94; madness defined by, 82; on mechanical coup, 72; on mind objects, 44; music and, 213–214; on psyche-soma, 8; on seduction, 120; on trauma, 32, 33–34
"Winnicott and Music" (Spice), 213
wish fulfillment: Borch-Jacobsen, 203–204; Phillips on, 196
Wiskus, Jessica, 45
Wittgenstein, Ludwig, 5, 133, 172
Woolf, Virginia, 32, 33–34, 77
working-through, 35–36
"Work of Art in the Age of Mechanical Reproduction, The" (Benjamin), 183
world-work-beta, 166

Yeats, William Butler, 200
Yeezus (West), 183
You Must Change Your Life (Sloterdijk), 236

Zug, 232, 233
Zwang, 61

GPSR Authorized Representative: Easy Access System Europe, Mustamäe tee
50, 10621 Tallinn, Estonia, gpsr.requests@easproject.com

www.ingramcontent.com/pod-product-compliance
Lightning Source LLC
Chambersburg PA
CBHW032335300426
44109CB00041B/849